THE SIKH RELIGION, ITS GURUS, SACRED WRITINGS AND AUTHORS (VOLUME 1)

THE SIKH RELIGION, ITS GURUS, SACRED WRITINGS AND AUTHORS (VOLUME 1)

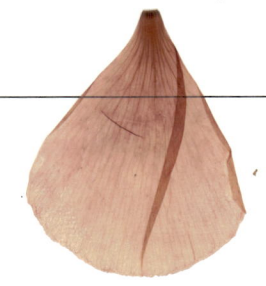

Max Arthur Macauliffe

www.General-Books.net

Publication Data:

Title: The Sikh Religion, Its Gurus, Sacred Writings and Authors
Volume: 1
Author: Macauliffe, Max Arthur, 1842-1913
Publisher: Oxford Clarendon Press
Publication date: 1909
Subjects: Sikhism
India – Religion

How We Made This Book for You
We made this book exclusively for you using patented Print on Demand technology.
First we scanned the original rare book using a robot which automatically flipped and photographed each page.
We automated the typing, proof reading and design of this book using Optical Character Recognition (OCR) software on the scanned copy. That let us keep your cost as low as possible.
If a book is very old, worn and the type is faded, this can result in typos or missing text. This is also why our books don't have illustrations; the OCR software can't distinguish between an illustration and a smudge.
We understand how annoying typos, missing text or illustrations or an index that doesn't work, can be. That's why we provide a free digital copy of most books exactly as they were originally published. Simply go to our website (www.general-books.net) to check availability. And we provide a free trial membership in our book club so you can get free copies of other editions or related books.
OCR is not a perfect solution but we feel it's more important to make books available for a low price than not at all. So we warn readers on our website and in the descriptions we provide to book sellers that our books don't have illustrations and may have typos or missing text. We also provide excerpts from each book to book sellers and on our website so you can preview the quality of the book before buying it.
If you would prefer that we manually type, proof read and design your book so that it's perfect, we are happy to do that. Simply contact us for the cost.

Limit of Liability/Disclaimer of Warranty:
The publisher and author make no representations or warranties with respect to the accuracy or completeness of the book. The advice and strategies in the book may not be suitable for your situation. You should consult with a professional where appropriate. The publisher is not liable for any damages resulting from the book.
Please keep in mind that the book was written long ago; the information is not current. Furthermore, there may be typos, missing text or illustration and explained above.

1

THE SIKH RELIGION, ITS GURUS, SACRED WRITINGS AND AUTHORS (VOLUME 1)

PRINTED AT THE CLARENDON PRESS
   BY HORACE HART, M. A. PRINTER TO THE UNIVERSITY
   PREFACE
   I BRING from the East what is practically an unknown religion. The Sikhs are distinguished throughout the world as a great military people, but there is little known even to professional scholars regarding their religion. I have often been asked by educated persons in countries which I have visited, and even in India itself, what the Sikh religion was, and whether the Sikhs were Hindus, idolaters or Muhammadans. This ignorance is the result of the difficulty of the Indian dialects in which their sacred writings are contained.

   Judaism has its Old Testament; Islam its Quran; Hinduism its Veds, Purans, and Shastars; Bud-hism its Tripitaka; the Parsi religion its Zend-avesta; and Confucianism its Analects, its Spring and Autumn, its Ancient Poems and its Book of Changes. The languages in which the holy writings of these religions are enshrined, though all difficult, are for the most part homogeneous, and after preliminary study with tutors can generally be mastered by the aid of grammars and dictionaries; but not so the mediaeval Indian dialects in which the sacred writings of the Sikh Gurus and Saints were composed. Hymns are found in Persian, mediaeval Prakrit, Hindi, Marathi, old

Panjabi, Multani, and several local dialects. In several hymns the Sanskrit and Arabic vocabularies are freely drawn upon.

There were no dictionaries of the Granth Sahib, 1 or sacred book of the Sikhs, when the author commenced his labours. Some have been since published, but each lexicographer has adopted a system of his own which makes it difficult to find the word required, and even when found the interpretation is not always satisfactory. For these reasons it is necessary for the translator of the Sikh sacred writings to reside for long years in India, and work with the assistance of the few gyanis, or professional interpreters of the Sikh canonical writings, who now survive. It would probably be an exaggeration to say that there are ten such men in the world. Of these few or none is capable of giving an English interpretation. They generally construe in tedious paraphrases in their own local dialects. But more than this, there is hardly any one Sikh who is capable of making a correct translation of his sacred writings. A man who is a good Sanskrit scholar will not know Persian and Arabic, and he who knows Persian and Arabic will not know words of Sanskrit derivation. A man who knows Hindi will not know Marathi; a man who knows Marathi will not know Panjabi and Multani, and so on. Moreover, there are words in the Sikh sacred writings which are peculiar to them, and cannot be traced to any known language. As to these one must accept the traditional inter pretations. The Granth Sahib thus becomes pro bably the most difficult work, sacred or profane, 1 Sahib is an Arabic word meaning lord or master. It is applied by Indians to Europeans and natives of position, but it is particularly used by the Sikhs to denote a thing revered or holy, as 'Darbar Sahib', the holy Sikh Darbar or temple at Amritsar, the Granth Sahib, the sacred book of the Sikhs, c.

that exists, and hence the general ignorance of its contents.

A portion of the Granth Sahib was translated some years since by a German missionary at the expense and under the auspices of the India Office, but his work was highly inaccurate and unidiomatic, and furthermore gave mortal offence to the Sikhs by the odium theologicum introduced into it. When ever he saw an opportunity of defaming the Gurus, the sacred book, and the religion of the Sikhs, he eagerly availed himself of it.

One of the main objects of the present work is to endeavour to make some reparation to the Sikhs for the insults which he offered to their Gurus and their religion. There are, however, many other advantages which I am hoping for, and which will probably be understood by the reader.

All persons of discrimination acquainted with the Sikhs set a high value on them, but it appears that a knowledge throughout the world of the excellence of their religion would enhance even the present regard with which they are entertained, and that thus my work would be at least of political ad vantage to them. In the second place, there is now a large number of Sikhs who understand the English language, but who have no time for the study of the compositions of the Gurus, and I thought it would be useful to them, if only from a linguistic point of view, to read a translation in the very simple English in which I have endeavoured to write it. In the third place, the old gyanis or pro fessional interpreters of the Granth Sahib are dying out, and probably in another generation or two their sacred books will, owing to their enormous difficulty, be practically unintelligible even to other wise educated Sikhs. In the fourth place, the vernacular itself is rapidly altering and diverging more and more from the general language of the Granth Sahib. Words which men still in the prime of life were accustomed to use in their boyhood have now become obsolete, and new vocables have taken their place. It appears, therefore, that it would on every account be well to fix the translation of the many exceedingly difficult passages scattered broad cast through the Sikh sacred writings. In the fifth place there are local legends now rife which we have been able to gather, but which would otherwise pass into oblivion in a comparatively short period of time. Time was when it was not allowed to print the sacred book of the Sikhs. As ancient prejudice gave way, it was printed in parts which it was forbidden to unite in one volume lest it, as the embodiment not only of the wisdom of the Gurus, but of the Gurus themselves, might be treated with disrespect This prejudice has also vanished, and now the book is openly exposed for sale. There was also a prejudice on the part of Sikhs of the old school against trans lating the sacred volume, but those who held it forgot the injunction of Guru Arjan to translate it into Indian and foreign languages so that it might spread over the whole world as oil spreads over water.

Suraj Parkash, Ras III.

There can be no doubt that, were the Gurus and Bha-gats now alive, they would be pleased to see their com positions translated into a language like the English spoken by many peoples throughout the continents and islands which extend far and wide over the earth.

Until the year 1893 I was engaged in judicial duties in India. In that year representative Sikh societies, knowing that I appreciated their litera ture, requested me to resign my appointment and undertake a translation of their sacred works. I acceded to their requests. My first intention was to make only a translation. This occupied my time for several years. It was prepared on what, I believe, is entirely a novel plan. Most translators, when they have completed their ren derings, proceed to publish without subjecting their work to native criticism. On this account there are few, if any, translations of Oriental works made in Europe, even by the most eminent scholars, which are accepted by the learned natives of the East. I resolved that mine should be an exception, and accordingly submitted every line of my work to the most searching criticism of learned Sikhs. This was done either by rough printed proofs or typed copies. I also published invitations in Sikh newspapers to all whom it might concern to visit me, inspect, and if necessary correct my translation. This entailed a voluminous correspondence which occupied a great amount of time, and inconveniently protracted my residence in India.

On the conclusion of the examination of my translation, Bhai Sardul Singh, the Gyani 1 of the 1 The word gyani in Panjabi means a professional interpreter of the Granth Sahib.

Golden Temple, the late Bhai Sant Singh, a very learned Sikh of Kapurthala, and Bhai Prem Singh of Amritsar favoured me with the following:â

We, through the agency of learned Sikhs acquainted with English, have carefully perused the translation of the hymns of the Granth Sahib by Mr. Macauliffe. The perusal cost us a month and a half of continuous labour. Wherever any of us found what seemed to be an error, we all met, discussed the passages, and either corrected it or allowed Mr. Macauliffe's translation to stand. Wherefore we now state that Mr. Macauliffe's translation has been fully revised by us, and is thoroughly correct. The greatest care has been taken in making the translation conformable to the religious tenets of the Sikhs. The translation is quite literal, and done according to all grammatical and rhetorical rules.

We now request the Rajas, Maharajas, Sardars, and the learned and accomplished of the Sikh faith to specially read or listen to this translation, if only for once. They will thus become acquainted with Mr. Macauliffe's labours, and reap the advantage of the true instruction of their Gurus. They should also render all necessary aid to the translator, because he has resigned a high post under Government and spent untold wealth on this undertaking.

I have received piles of somewhat similar docu ments from learned and intelligent Sikhs, and seen numerous critical articles in Sikh, English, and foreign newspapers, which give expression to the strong desire felt for the production of a work such as that now offered. Among them I may be allowed to give the following from The Khalsa, a Sikh publication:â

There can be no denying the fact that the publication of Mr. Macauliffe's work will be the introduction of a new era in our history. Our Scriptures, though written in our own language, have been so much neglected by our people, that it will be no exaggeration if we say that ninety per cent, of our co-religionists do not understand them. The Com munity receiving English education are without any idea of the sublime truths contained in the Granth Sahib. From infancy upwards their minds are moulded in such a way, that it becomes almost impossible for them to talk and write in any other language than English; and we shall not be exaggerating if we say that a great many of them find it difficult even to think in their own mother tongue. This being the case, an English translation of our Scriptures will at once appeal to the ever increasing community of educated men who will be the leaders of thought from the very nature of things. Already prepared by western culture to think and act independently, they will be constitutionally fitted to understand the catholicity of Sikh principles, and will feel a pleasure in spreading Sikh ideas far and wide. Apart from this, a great deal of the misunderstanding that now obtains about the work of our Gurus and Martyrs will be removed, and the thinking public will see with their own eyes the drift of Sikh teachings. The trade of traitors among us who to please our wealthier and more influential neighbours, compromise our beliefs by ascribing to our great men thoughts that they never conceived and deeds that they never did, will languish, the promiscuousness in Sikh ideas will vanish, and Tat (pure) Khalsa will begin to start on a new career.

Not less important will be the result of Sikh teachings on the minds of religious Europe and America. Already the Khalsa has achieved a world-wide renown in the matter of bravery. In the matter of religion, too, the name of the Khalsa will shine resplendently when the glorious deeds of our illustrious ancestors in the moral and religious world are made known far and wide. The translations of Hindu Scriptures by Professors Max Miiller, Wilson, Monier Williams, and a host of other eminent writers on Oriental religions have drawn the attention of the whole civilized world to the Hindus and their literature. These transla- tions have secured for the Hindus the sympathy of hundreds of savants and inquirers after religious truth. What will not the translations of our Scriptures achieve? Unlike the Scriptures of other creeds, they do not contain love stories or accounts of wars waged for selfish considerations. They contain sublimest truths, the study of which cannot but elevate the reader spiritually, morally, and socially. There is not the least tinge of sectarianism in them. They teach the highest and purest principles that serve to bind man to man and inspire the believer with an ambition to serve his fellow men, to sacrifice all and die for their sake.

The late Sir Baba Khem Singh, K. C. I. E., Member of the Legislative Council, who held a most pro minent position among the Sikhs, wrote to me:â

It is fortunate for the Sikh nation to have such a kind of friend as you, whose ideas are naturally inclined to their benefit, and they should ever bear you thankfulness and gratitude. I am glad to express my appreciation of your work, and the labour and trouble you have taken upon yourself to accomplish such a voluminous task.

The late Baba Sumer Singh, the Mahant or Sikh Bishop of Patna, where Guru Gobind Singh was born, wrote to me as follows:â

I fully appreciate your attempt to keep especial eye on the sense rather than on word-for-word rendering, and wherever the sense has been in danger of being absorbed in the language, suitable foot-notes have been interspersed throughout.

The late Bhai Hazara Singh Gyani, who has pub lished a Dictionary of the Granth Sahib, wrote to me as follows, after seeing specimens of this work:â

I have read through the English translation of Japji prepared by Mr. Macauliffe. The translator seems to have taken great care in keeping the rendering in accordance with the Sampardai arths (traditional interpretations). I wish the undertaking a thorough success, and nothing will give me more pleasure than to see the work brought out of press.

The following is a translation of an address presented to me by the Singh Sabha of Amritsar:â

We are informed by very trustworthy gyanis, that you have been studying our sacred books for over twenty years, and that, resigning a good appointment, you have now laboured continually for some years at making an accurate translation of them; that you have revised it seven times; and have now made it as complete as can be done by human effort; and in doing this you have not only spent your valuable time, but also a very large amount of money. Dr. Trumpp's translation is not only generally incorrect, but injurious to our religion; and there was a great want felt for an accurate version when Akal Purukh (the Im mortal God) induced you to undertake it and fulfil our desires. It would have been well, had we executed the translation ourselves; but Akal Purukh granted you the credit of the performance. As the holy Guru Teg Bahadur foretold that men would come from beyond the seas to assist the Sikhs, so you have been rendering us mental and bodily assistance; and we now earnestly recommend the members of our faith, who can afford it, to render you all possible aid in publishing your work, and we trust our wishes will be fulfilled. We desire, now that you have become thoroughly acquainted with our customs, our sacred books, and the tenets of our religion, that you fulfil the promise made in your Circular letter to the Sikhs, in which you stated that you would write nothing prejudicial to their religion. In the lives of the Gurus which you are going to write, we desire you to consult the Gur Bilas, the Suraj Parkash, and such other works as have been compiled from ancient writings not corrupted by the Handalis, the followers of Kabir, and the poets who infused foreign elements into our religion. The Khalsa and the whole Sikh race will be thankful to you for attending to this request. In conclusion we pray Akal Purukh to protect you in every way on your ocean journey, and fulfil your wishes and desires; and that you may be ever a well-wisher and supporter of our sect and our faith. We earnestly hope that your translation of our sacred books will soon be in the library of every true Sikh. 1

Notwithstanding these tributes to the accuracy of my work, to its utility and to my desire to do justice to the sacred writings of the Sikhs, some may possibly be found among them who will differ from the versions I have given. I have met so-called gyanis who could perform tours de force with their sacred work, and give different interpretations of almost every line of it. My Sikh readers may rest assured that in this work all rational interpretations have been considered, and only those selected which seemed most suitable to the context and most in harmony with Sikh doctrines. When second and third interpretations seemed possible, they have been appended in the notes.

When my translation was thus completed and approved of by the most learned Sikh priests and scholars, I found that an account of the Sikh Gurus, saints, and authors was absolutely necessary, and indeed of equal, if not greater importance than even a correct interpretation of their writings. The late illustrious scholar, Professor Max Miiller, who had Indian literature so greatly at heart, expressed in his latest work, Auld Lang Syne, his 1 I did not intend, at first, to publish these extracts, and I regret having to do so now, but some Sikh friends have put pressure on me to adopt this course.

regret that the world knew so little of the Sikh reformers. He wrote:â

It is a pity that we possess so little information about the original Sikh reformers. Their sacred book the Granth Sahib exists, nay it has even been translated into English by the late Dr. Trumpp. But it turns out now that Dr. Trumpp was by no means a trustworthy translator. The language of the Granth is generally called old Panjabi; and it was supposed that a scholar who knew modern Panjabi, might easily learn to understand the language as it was four hundred years ago. But this is not the case. The language of the Granth Sahib is full of local dialectic varieties and forgotten idioms, so much so that it has been said to be without any grammar at all. Mr. Macauliffe, who has spent many years among the Sikhs, and has with the help of their priests paid much attention to their Granth Sahib, has given us some most interesting and beautiful specimens of their poetry which form part of their sacred book.

On perusing the current lives and accounts of the Gurus I found them overladen with puerile, heterodox, or repulsive details; and it required further years of study and consultation with learned Sikhs to complete biographies of the founders of their religion, which were not inconsistent with their sacred writings' The orthodox Sikhs who have read the lives of their Gurus in the voluminous Hindi work entitled Suraj Parkash, and in the current Panjabi works called 'anamsakhis, will understand, and, perhaps, be grateful to me for the manner in which I have presented their religion according to the desires and teachings of their Gurus.

To prevent misconception it ought, perhaps, to be here stated that this work is intended to be an exact presentation of the teaching of the Sikh

Gurus and orthodox writers as contained in their sacred books, and is by no means put forth as a portrayal of the debased superstitions and hetero dox social customs of Sikhs who have been led astray from their faith by external influences.

It must also be stated that the intention of the author has been, in fulfilment of his promise to the Sikhs, to write this work from an orthodox Sikh point of view, without any criticism or expres sion of opinion of his own. Accordingly, miracles which are accepted by many Sikhs will be found reverently described in this work.

A very important question has arisen among the Sikhs as to how my translation of their sacred writings should be presented. The Granth Sahib, as already stated, is to them the embodiment of their Gurus, who are regarded as only one person, the light of the first Guru's soul having been transmitted to each of his successors in turn.

Oi 5' avtt aijL-fyav KOL irapriyyti av irp6cra.

The line of the Gurus closed with the tenth, Guru Gobind Singh. He ordered that the Granth should be to his Sikhs as the living Gurus. Accord ingly the Granth Sahib is kept in silken coverlets, and when it is removed from place to place is taken on a small couch by Sikhs of good repute. Many of my old orthodox Sikh friends feared that if my translation were printed in the order of the original, it would not receive the same respect and attention in foreign countries as in India, and they accordingly desired that it should be published in some other form. This desire of the most holy and respected Sikhs is a great relief to me, for it makes it competent to intersperse many of the sacred hymns in the lives of the Gurus, and thus present my work as much as possible in narrative form, which it is hoped will be more acceptable not only to European, but even to Sikh readers themselves.

Competent Sikhs have also advised me that when the Guru's instruction on various occasions is on the same subject and of the same tenor, it needs be given only once. For instance, in the Granth Sahib there are four hymns beginning with the words, ' In the first watch of night, my merchant friend Two of these hymns are by Guru Nanak, the third by Guru Ram Das, and the fourth by Guru Arjan. The hymns begin in the same manner, are of the same purport, and are only very slightly varied in diction, so the publication of the whole four appears unnecessary.

It is intelligible that repetitions should be found in the sacred books of several religions, for the teachings of their prophets were orally addressed to crowds who clustered round them, and repetitions served to impress on the listeners the instruction accorded; but in a printed work, which the reader may peruse and reperuse at pleasure, repetition does not appear so necessary. Moreover, this work is intended for the European as well as for the Sikh student. It is apprehended that repetition would prove tedious, and deter several even con scientious readers from its perusal.

I find, however, that it is impossible for me to meet the wishes of all parties. Europeans will probably think my work too long, and Sikhs may possibly think it too short. As to the latter objec- tion, I may state that I have followed the advice of the most learned Sikh scholars. They have decided that there is no omission of anything necessary to faith or morals, but that the whole substance of the Sikh sacred writings is here pre sented, and that if any Sikh shapes his conduct accordingly, he will be in no danger of failing to secure absorption in the Creator or a dwelling in the Creator's heaven.

A few of the advantages of the Sikh religion to the State may be here enumerated. One day, as Guru Teg Bahadur was in the top story of his prison, the Emperor Aurangzeb thought he saw him looking towards the south in the direction of the Imperial zenana. He was sent for the next day, and charged with this grave breach of Oriental etiquette and propriety. The Guru replied, ' Emperor Aurangzeb, I was on the top story of my prison but I was not looking at thy private apartments or at thy queens. I was looking in the direction of the Europeans who are coming from beyond the seas to tear down thy pardas and destroy thine empire Sikh writers state that these words became the battle-cry of the Sikhs in the assault on the mutineers in Dihli (Delhi) in 1857, under General John Nicholson, and that thus the prophecy of the ninth Guru was gloriously fulfilled.

When it was represented to Guru Gobind Singh that a Muhammadan army would eventually come to overpower his Sikhs, he replied, ' What God willeth shall take place. When the army of the Muhammadans cometh, my Sikhs shall strike steel on steel. The Khalsa shall then awake, and know the play of battle. Amid the clash of arms the Khalsa shall be partners in present and future bliss, tranquillity, meditation, and divine knowledge. Then shall the English come, and, joined by the Khalsa, rule as well in the East as in the West. The holy Baba Nanak will bestow all wealth on them. The English shall possess great power and by force of arms take possession of many principalities. The combined armies of the English and the Sikhs shall be very powerful, as long as they rule with united councils. The empire of the British shall vastly increase, and they shall in every way obtain prosperity. Wherever they take their armies they shall conquer and bestow thrones on their vassals. Then in every house shall be wealth, in every house religion, in every house learning, and in every house happiness."

It is such prophecies as these, combined with the monotheism, the absence of superstition and restraint in the matter of food, which have made the Sikhs among the bravest, the most loyal and devoted subjects of the British Crown. As to their bravery and loyalty, the following, written by one of them, is by no means an exaggeration: ' As for the bravery and warlike spirit of the Sikhs, no Cossack, no Turk, no Russian, can measure swords with them. There is one trait very peculiar in them such as must make the enemies of the British fear them. The true blood of loyalty and devotion to their master surges in their veins. A true Sikh will let his body be cut to pieces when fighting for his master. The Sikh considers dying in battle a means of salvation. No superiority of the enemies in number, no shot, no shell, can make his heart quail, since his Amrit (baptism) binds him to fight single-handed against millions. Some people may say that a soldier sells his head for the small wage paid him every month. But the Sikh does not do so: he devotes his head, body, and every thing dear to him to preserving the influence of him whom he once makes his master. A Sikh who shows the least sign of reluctance to go, or goes with an expectation of remuneration, when called upon by his benefactor the King-Emperor to fight His Majesty's enemies, no matter how strong they may be, will be condemned by the Gurus."

If there is one superstition more strongly repro bated than another in the Sikh sacred writings, it is pilgrimages to the places deemed sacred by the Hindus. Some of the Sikh States, in ignorance of the teachings of the Gurus, have maintained temples and spiritual arenas at Hardwar and Rikhikesh for the reception of pilgrims. At Hardwar there are held great religious fairs every twelve years at the time when the sun enters the lunar mansion of Aquarius (Kumbh). It is calculated that at least one hundred thousand Sikhs were present at the last great fair at Hardwar. All these pilgrims bathe in the Ganges; while bathing many recklessly yield to the necessities of nature; others drink their excreta with the Ganges water as sacred nourish ment, and die of cholera either at the fair or on their homeward journey. The corpses of Sikhs, as well as Hindus, were pulled out of railway carriages after the last twelfth-year fair and poisoned the country. The pest then extended east and west in all directions. Kabul, of course, on the western boundary of India, was soon affected, and the further progress of the disease towards Europe was thus described by the Paris correspondent of the Morning Post:-

Professor Chantemesse, Director-General of the Public Health Department, made a somewhat disquieting state ment at to-day's meeting of the Academy of Medicine. He pointed out that the cholera epidemic, which originated in India and spread east and west, had established itself last autumn in four European centres, namely Transcaspia, Transcaucasia, Anatolia, and the banks of the Volga between Astrakhan, Saratoff, and Samara. As the winter cold had merely checked the disease, instead of stamping it out, there was every reason to fear it would continue its progress westward, by way of the Baltic ports, the Black Sea, the Danube, or Constantinople." According to another account, seven thousand deaths from cholera occurred in the Punjab since the second week of April. The disease was originally disseminated by the returning pilgrims from Hardwar."

Of course there were also many Hindu pilgrims at the Hardwar fair, but let any one consider what a gain it would be to the world if the one hundred thousand Sikhs l who attended it possessed such a very elementary knowledge of their religion as to know that their action was reprobated by all their holy Gurus.

It is known to every Sikh that tobacco is forbidden by his religion, but it is not generally known that wine is equally forbidden. After I had quoted the Sikh tenets on this subject in public lectures at Simla, it was taken up by the enlightened Singh Sabha of Patiala; and a resolution in favour of total abstinence was signed by several of the best educated and most influential Sardars of the State.

1 At my request the Panjab Government ascertained from the Government of the United Provinces the approximate population of the Sikh pilgrims.

The freedom of women and their emancipation from the tyranny of the parda may be inferred from the manner in which Bhai Budha received Mata 1 Ganga the wife of Guru Arjan, from Guru Amar Das's refusal to receive a rani who had visited him when she was closely veiled, and from Kabir's address to his daughter-in-law.

The high moral and enlightened teachings of the Gurus, their prohibition of the heinous crime of infanticide, and other injunctions for the public advantage will be found or understood from the composition of the Gurus and the Bhagats which we give in these volumes.

The Hindu practice of the concremation of widows was forbidden by the Gurus; though this was not generally known at the time of Lord William Bentinck, who had sufficient courage to issue an ordinance against it.

The Gurus most powerfully and successfully at tacked the caste system and the Hindu belief in impurity and defilement in many necessary and harmless acts of domestic life.

It is admitted that a knowledge of the religions of the people of India is a desideratum for the British Officials who administer its affairs and indirectly for the people who are governed by them so that mutual sympathy may be produced. It seems, at any rate, politic to place before the Sikh soldiery their Guru's prophecies in favour of the English and the texts of their sacred writings which foster their loyalty.

An advantage of a literary or historical nature is 1 The Sikhs give the title Mata or mother to the wives of the Gurus, in the same way as they give the title Baba or father to Guru Nanak.

also anticipated from this work. It is hoped that it will throw some light on the state of society in the Middle Ages and that it will also be useful for the student of comparative theology. Professor Geheimer Hofrath Merx, of the Heidelberg University, a very distinguished German savant, has recently written to me: ' The publication of your work is certainly very desirable. You save in this way materials for the history of religions which, without your help, would probably disappear."

To sum up some of the moral and political merits of the Sikh religion: Â t prohibits ido try, hypo crisy, caste exclusiveness, the concremation of widows, the immurement of women, the use of wine and other intoxicants, tobacco-smoking, infanti cide, slander, pilgrimages to the sacred rivers and tanks of the Hindus; and it inculcates loyalty, gratitude for all favours received, philanthropy, justice, impartiality, truth, honesty, and all the moral and domestic virtues known to the holiest citizens of any country.")

A movement to declare the Sikhs Hindus, in direct opposition to the teaching of the Gurus, is widespread and of long duration. I have only quite recently met in Lahore young men claiming to be descendants of the Gurus, who told me that they were Hindus, and that they could not read the characters in which the sacred books of the Sikhs were written. Whether the object of their tutors and advisers was or was not to make them disloyal, such youths are ignorant of the Sikh religion, and of its prophecies in favour of the English, and con tract exclusive social customs and prejudices to the extent of calling us Malechhas, or persons of impure desires, and inspiring disgust for the customs and habits of Christians.

And here let me remark that the recognition of Panjabi as an official or optional official language in the Panjab, instead of the alien Urdu, would be a most powerful means of preserving the Sikh religion. Panjabi is the mother tongue of all natives of the Panjab, be they Sikhs, Hindus, or Muhammadans. If it were recognized as an official or optional official 'anguage, Sikhs would not have to resort to books written in foreign languages for religious instruction and consolation, and the exalted ethical instruction of the Granth Sahib would be open to all classes of His Majesty's subjects in the Panjab.

After the English occupation of the Panjab the officers sent to administer it were transferred from what were then known as the North-Western Provinces. They took with them Urdu, or what was much the sameâ a bastard Persian with Urdu inflec tionsâ the only Asiatic language they knew, and they found it more convenient to continue to use it than to learn a foreign language which had at the time no status and no literature. The vernacular writers and the officers who brought them were equally igno rant of Panjabi, and so Urdu became the official lan guage of that province. That the officials did not understand the natives, nor the natives the officials, made no difference. The court officials gradually picked up a smattering of Panjabi, and were able to interpret for the Europeans. This state of things was allowed to continue. If the Panjabis remonstrated against neglect of their language their remonstrances were unheeded. Now the Pan jab has become more enlightened, the remonstrances have grown louder, and it remains to be seen whether any Lieutenant-Governor will take the trouble or have the courage to make Panjabi an alternative language for the Panjab, and thus confer a lasting favour not only on the Sikhs, but on all the natives of the Land of the Five Rivers, whose medium of communication it is from their birth. At any rate, there appears nothing to hinder the native states of the Panjab from making Panjabi their official language.

In our time one of the principal agencies for the preservation of the Sikh religion has been the practice of military officers commanding Sikh regi ments to send Sikh recruits to receive baptism according to the rites prescribed by Guru Gobind Singh, and endeavour to preserve them in their subsequent career from the contagion of idolatry. The military thus ignoring or despising the restraints imposed by the civil policy of what is called ' religious neutrality', have practically become the main hiero-phants and guardians of the Sikh religion.

I have been at great pains and expense to obtain details of the lives of the Bhagats, or Indian saints, who preceded the Gurus, and whose writings are incorporated in the Granth Sahib, but I have not been completely successful. I shall be very grate ful to any one who can add to my information regarding them.

The hymns of the Bhagats will in some cases be found different from those preserved in the Hindi and Marathi collections of the saints' com positions in other parts of India. They were taken down by Guru Arjan from the lips of wandering minstrels or followers of the saints.

Parallel ideas and expressions to those of the Gurus and the Bhagats may be found in ancient and modern literature, sacred and profane, and could be largely quoted. Only a few such com parisons, which occurred to the author at the time of writing, have been given in the notes to this work. They are intended to show the catholicity of the Gurus' teachings, and they may also occa sionally relieve the tedium of perusal.

The writers of the Janamsakhis had no maps to guide them, and accordingly in some cases assigned to the Gurus, notably Guru Nanak, impossible itineraries. Accordingly efforts have been made in this work to revise the Gurus' travels and render them consistent with scientific Indian geography. Should learned Sikhs, after full consideration at a general council, prepare maps of the Gurus' travels, they will be inserted in any future edition of this work. So also should learned Sikhs con sider their own accounts of the Gurus, their own order of the Gurus' hymns, or their own versions of words or phrases in the Gurus' compositions superior to the gyanis' and mine, we shall be pleased to receive their suggestions.

H. H. Sir Hira Singh, Malvendar Bahadur, the Raja of Nabha, has at considerable expense caused the thirty-one Indian rags, or musical measures, to which the hymns of the Gurus were composed, to be written out in European musical notation by a professional musician whom he employed for the purpose. The rags were merging into oblivion, and have been collected with much difficulty by Mahant Gaja Singh, the greatest minstrel of the Sikhs. They will be found at the end of the fifth volume of this work. Though they may sound bizarre to European ears, they will be appreciated by the Sikhs and by many European lovers of art who regret the loss of the music to which the Odes of Pindar and Sappho and the choral exercises of the Greek tragedians were sung.

There are also added pictures of the Gurus as far as ascertainable, of famous Sikh temples, and of some scenes memorable in Sikh history. These pictures have been prepared by Bhai Lai Singh under the auspices of the Honourable Tikka Ripu-daman Singh, the young heir to the Nabha gadi.

The expense attendant on the production of this work, which has been the labour of many years, and has been completed with the assistance for long periods of a large staff of Sikh scholars and of English and vernacular copyists, has been very con siderable, and I am indebted to His Highness the Raja of Nabha, His Highness Sir Rajindar Singh, the late much lamented Maharaja of Patiala, His Highness Raja Ranbir Singh, Raja of Jind, the Tikka Sahib of Nabha, and the late Sardar Ranjit Singh of Chich-rauli for defraying a portion of it. His Highness the Gaekwar of Baroda has promised his patronage after the publication of the work.

Several persons have recommended this work to the patronage of the Indian Government and the Secretary of State for India. The distinguished scholar, Count Angelo de Gubernatis, president of the Roman Congress of Orientalists, thus addressed the Secretary of State for India in a letter dated October 19, 1899:â

Dans rinte"ret de la science, je prends la liberte" de vous signaler fort particulierement a votre attention la pro- position de M. Macauliffe, accueillee avec tant d'interet et si chaleureusement recommandee par PAssemblee Generale du XII me Congres des Orientalistes, dans sa seance du 8 octobre, pour edition et illustration critique des textes de la religion des Sikhs. Tout ce quep India Office decider a en faveur de cette noble entreprise ne pourra etre que tres meritoire. Et a ce titre, j'ose vivement recommander a la protection de 1'India Office les interessantes recherches de M. Macauliffe sur les textes canoniques des Sikhs du Panjab.

Count de Gubernatis's letter covered the following proceedings of the Roman Congress:â

A propos de la conference de M. Macauliffe, M. le Prof. L. von Schroeder, Professeur de Sanskrit a PUniversite de Vienne, estime qu'il serait tres desirable de posseder une traduction des livres sacres des Sikhs, telle que M. Macauliffe en a con9u le plan et prepare P execution, tra duction dans laquelle se trouverait incorporee et utilisee la tradition orale des Sikhs eux-memes qui menace de dis-paraitre rapidement. II recommande instamment Pentre-prise de M. Macauliffe a Pappui materiel tant du Gou-vernement de PInde que des chefs Sikhs. Get appui a ete autrefois genereusement accorde a la tentative meritoire mais insuffisante de Dr. Trumpp; il peut seul assurer le succes d'une ceuvre aussi considerable et aussi couteuse.

M. 6mile Senart, Membre de ITnstitut de France, et Vice-President de la Societe Asiatique a Paris, a son tour, de-mande a appuyer la proposition faite par M. von Schroeder, et prie la reunion de recommander instamment a l'appui, soit du Gouvernement de l'Inde, soit des chefs Sikhs, l'en-treprise de M. Macauliffe. II insiste sur l'interet special que presente dans l'histoire religieuse de PInde le develop-pement de la religion des Sikhs, la seule qui y ait pris P allure militante et guerriere que ne semblaient pas faire prevoir ses debuts. Le plus essentiel de la traduction pro-jet ee sera dans cette circonstance, qu'elle preservera d'une perte menagante la tradition orale et Pinterpretation orthodoxe. Nulle part la tradition n'a plus d'importance

PREFACE xxix que dans une doctrine comme celle-ci, qui est voilee d'un syncretisme complique, et dont Toriginalite speculative n'a pu se degager que peu a peu.

Lord Reay, the President of the Royal Asiatic Society, a nobleman who is never wanting to any benevolent or philanthropic enterprise, strongly recommended my work to the favourable con sideration of the Lieutenant-Governor of the Panjab.

Mr. L. W. Dane (now Sir Louis W. Dane, Lieu tenant-Go vernor of the Panjab) has always adopted a sympathetic attitude towards my labours, and, as far as in him lay, assisted in bringing them to a successful conclusion.

And Lord Kitchener of Khartoum, after presiding at my public lecture on ' How the Sikhs became a Militant People ', thus expressed himself:â

It must be a matter of great satisfaction to Mr. Macauliffe that the Amritsar Singh Sabha have accepted his trans lations as being thoroughly accurate. We may say with confidence that in putting the study of the Sikh sacred writings within our reach Mr. Macauliffe has earned the approbation of all who know the great value of the Sikh soldier; the cordial recognition of the rulers of the country, and the gratitude of the chiefs, sardars, and people of the Sikh communityâ a feeling of gratitude which I feel sure will be much increased when Mr. Macauliffe has translated the sacred writings into the ordinary Panjabi of the day, a labour which, I understand, he is about to commence, and which I hope will result in their general dissemination through every Sikh household in the country.

For literary assistance I must acknowledge my indebtedness to Sardar Kahn Singh of Nabha, one of the greatest scholars and most distinguished authors among the Sikhs, who by order of the Raja of Nabha accompanied me to Europe to assist in the publication of this work and in reading the proofs thereof; to Diwan Lila Ram Watan Mai, a subordinate judge in Sind; to the late Bhai Shankar Dayal of Faizabad; to Bhai Hazara Singh and Bhai Sardul Singh of Amritsar, to the late Bhai Dit Singh of Lahore, to the late Bhai Bhagwan Singh of Patiala, and to many other Sikh scholars for the intelligent assistance they have rendered me.

In my translation from the Sikh sacred writings I freely use the subjunctive mood which is fast disappearing from the English language. The solemn form of the third person singular of the present tense I have employed for obvious reasons. My Sikh readers may easily learn that this form is not now used in conversation or ordinary prose. I have avoided the arbitrary nomenclature invented by European scholars, such as Brahmanism, a word which is not used in India; self for soul or con science, c.

The Sikh Gurus were simple men who generally chose colloquial language for the expression of their ideas, and avoided learned words and meta physical subtleties. Hence in my translation I have endeavoured to use such simple language as I believe was intended by them and the reformers who pre ceded them. My aim has been to interpret the sacred books of the Sikhs, subject to what I deem a necessary solemnity of form, in the current language of the day, and without any effort to produce new or startling expressions. In my efforts to use simple language, however, I cannot claim complete success. The ideas of the Gurus and particularly their epithets of the Creator cannot always be translated without

PREFACE xxxi unwieldy periphrasis into any Anglo-Saxon words in ordinary use. Somewhat analogous words and ex pressions may often be found, but they do not con vey precisely the meanings intended by the Sikh sacred writers.

Archaisms, though deemed necessary by poets, and though they often contribute to ornateness of style, I have done my utmost to avoid. In this way I hope my book will be more useful to the Sikhs, and assist them in forming an acquaintance with the English tongue.

Indian proper names I have spelled as they are written and pronounced in India at the present time, and not as they were written and pronounced in the Sanskrit age. In this I am but following the practice of all modern languages. Nobody would now call London Londinium, or Marseilles Massilia, or Naples Neapolis. Nor can I adopt the spelling of Oriental words which has been adopted in this country ostensibly for the use of continental scholars, which causes sh to be printed, f, or s j, g; ch, k, c. Such spelling is repulsive to many persons, and it can hardly be necessary for the Oriental scholars of any country. The different n's, Â 's, r's, and s's of Indian languages I have found it hopeless to represent, nor would it be useful for my work, for they are often confounded in Sikh literature. The spelling of English words is that accepted by the Clarendon Press.

In the languages and dialects with which we have been dealing there is no short e corresponding to the e in bed and no short o corresponding to the o in not. Whenever, therefore, the vowels e and o are found in Indian names in this work, they xxxii THE SIKH RELIGION are always long. E is always pronounced as it is in eh or as the French 4. 0 is always pronounced as in note. The vowel i may be long or short. It is always long at the end of an Indian word, and is then pronounced like the English double e (ee). When it is long in the body of Indian words found in the notes it is marked with a makron, thus l. The vowel a may also be either short or long. When long in Indian words in the notes, it is crowned with a makron, thus a. The final a in Indian words may be generally considered short, like the a in sofa. In the text, in order not to distract the reader's attention, diacritical marks are rarely employed.

This being essentially a work on the Sikh religion we have commenced with Guru Nanak; but if the reader desires to follow the historical development of the Sikh reformation, he had better begin with the sixth volume. This was probably the intention of Guru Arjan himself, for otherwise he could not have included in his compilation hymns quite opposed to the principles and tenets of his predecessors.

The author feels that his work suffers from a special disadvantage, because the scholars of Europe and America are hardly in a position to criticize on its merits the translation of hymns composed in dialects which can only be learned in India from the lips of the few exponents of the Sikh faith who now survive. Nor have European and American scholars had an opportunity of perusing the Indian works which form the basis of our lives of the Gurus and of the saints who preceded them. The diffi culty and extent of the author's labours cannot therefore be understood.

PREFACE xxxiii

It is believed that a work of this nature cannot be accomplished again. In any age it could not be done out of India for want of expert assistance. In India, even under the most favourable con ditions, and when a student had acquired a knowledge of some Indian languages and dialects, the translation of the sacred books of the Sikhs, and the compilation of the lives of their Gurus and holy men, would be the work of years. No one while in the service of the Indian Government could find leisure to accomplish it; and few Euro peans after their retirement from Indian service would care to spend long years and lonely lives in India wrestling with mediaeval Indian dialects and submitting to the caprices of gyanis; but even should such martyrs to the cause of science be found, they would not be able to obtain the requisite assistance, because the principal inter preters of the sacred books of the Sikhs will have passed away with this generation, and, owing to want of patronage, there will be none to supply their place. This fact, too, would soon render a Sikh, even if thoroughly acquainted with the English tongue, and possessed of sufficient resource and in dustry, incapable of producing an authoritative and exhaustive work in our language on his religion.

The preacher of old said that 'of making many books there is no end'. For the last century their publication has increased in geometrical ratio, and prodigious must be the number which find their way into the streets and shops which sell quicquid chartis amicitur ineptis. The author fondly hopes that this work, which contains an account of the last great religion of the world t SIKH. I C xxxiv THE SIKH RELIGION which remains to be exploited, may escape the general fate. At the same time a glance at the shelves of any large library must convince a writer of the vanity of most literary labour, if haply the love of fame is dearer to him than the love of his sub-ject. The blurred and hoary volumes, elaborately illuminated and bound, which no one now ever peruses, were often produced at the expense of years of toilâ nay, of health and even life itselfâ and now remain sad monuments of the transitoriness of fame and the frequent futility of human effort. But there is even a worse fate than this, namely, the obloquy so often meted out to authors instead of the legiti mate recompense of lives of strenuous toil devoted to literary or scientific investigation. Even under favourable circumstances the author of an elaborate work of this description, the production of which has occupied several years of his life, cannot always hope even for temporary reward in the approba tion of those dear to him, those whom he would wish to please; for either their measure of years has grown full, or separation and varied interests have dulled the feelings of mutual pleasure which would result from his success.

MAX ARTHUR MACAULIFFE.
ROYAL SOCIETIES CLUB, LONDON.
VOLUME I PAGE

THE AUTHOR AND SOME OF HIS SIKH ASSISTANTS Frontispiece
GURU NANAK, THE FOUNDER OF THE SIKH RELIGION. i
VOLUME II
GURU ANGAD AND A PUPIL i
GURU AMAR DAS. 58
GURU RAM DAS RECEIVING HIS DISCIPLES. 253
VOLUME III
GURU ARJAN READING THE GRANTH SAHIB. i THE TANK AND TEMPLE OF AMRITSAR.13
GENERAL VIEW OF AMRITSAR. 20
GURU ARJAN'S SHRINE. 101
VOLUME IV
GURU HAR GOBIND.Â,. i
THE AKAL BUNGA. 4
BABA ATAL'S SHRINE 132
GURU HAR RAI BLESSING YOUNG PHUL. 275
GURU HAR KRISHAN. 315
GURU TEG BAHADUR 331
VOLUME V
GURU GOBIND SINGH. i
FATAHGARH 199
AN AKALI. 210
MUKTSAR. 214
THE SIKH TEMPLE (HAZUR SAHIB) AT NANDER. 246
VOLUME VI
NAMDEV'S SHRINE AT GHUMAN. 39 FOLLOWERS OF RAMANUJ AND RAMANAND.105

INTRODUCTION

CHAPTER I

THE fifteenth century of the Christian era was a period of singular mental and political activity. Both in Europe and India men shook off the torpor of ages, and their minds awoke to the consciousness of intellectual responsibility. For this result, it is true, important preparations had been made in the fourteenth century, when the Christian reformers, Walter Lollard and John Huss, preached and suffered death for their opinions; l when the poetical literature of England assumed a tangible form from the genius of Chaucer and Gower; when the Musalmans in Europe penetrated into Thrace and Hungary; and when, after the overthrow and expulsion of Budhism from India by the astute and powerful Brahmans, there flourished the great exponents of Indian monotheism, the saint Kabir, and the enlightened Ramanand.

But it was reserved for the fifteenth century to bear the full fruits of the mental awakening of the fourteenth. In England the ancient language of Greece began to be studied; a further impulse was given to the reformation of the Christian religion; and villenage disappeared as a political institution. In France the Government was consolidated by the union of the great fiefs to the crown; and the daring monarch Charles VII made his successful expedition against the picturesque capital of Southern Italy. In

Germany occurred the birth of Luther, and the revival and development of the invaluable art of printing in movable types. 2 In Italy there was a marvellous resuscitation of the fine arts, and 1 Lollard and Huss were burned for heresy. Wickliffe would have suffered the same fate, had not a paralytic attack anticipated the executioner.

xl THE SIKH RELIGION then were born the renowned navigators Columbus and Amerigo Vespucci, the great masters Michael Angelo, Raphael, and Leonardo da Vinci, and the illustrious patron of letters Lorenzo di Medici.

In Spain Ferdinand and Isabella, though they organized the inquisition in their intemperate religious zeal against the Saracens and Jews, were yet conspicuous for a worldly liberality which deserves the acknowledgement of posterity. In Portugal was born Vasco da Gama, who under the enter prising King Emanuel discovered the maritime route by the Cape of Storms to India. The Musalmans in Europe conquered Turkey and Greece, and seized on the ancient Italian city of Otranto. And in Asia, Taimur extended his victorious arms from Siberia on the north to the Arabian Sea on the south, and from the Ganges on the east to the Hellespont on the west.

There is a wonderful analogy between the spiritual con dition of Europe and India during the dark ages. In Europe most religious works were written in Latin, in India they were in Sanskrit. In both continents all learning was in the hands of the priesthood, and this admittedly led to serious abuses. A great cyclic wave of reformation then overspread both continents. During the very period that Luther and Calvin in Europe were warning men of the errors that had crept into Christianity, several Indian saints were denouncing priestcraft, hypocrisy, and idolatry, and with very considerable success. Several of those great men who led the crusade against superstition, founded sects which still survive; but the most numerous and powerful of all is the great Sikh sect founded by Guru Nanak, which already forms a considerable section of the population of the Panjab, and which is scattered in greater or less numbers not only throughout the whole of India but Kabul, Kandahar, China, and Southern Asia.

A cognate cause is frequently assigned for the establish ment of new religions, namely, that they appear at periods of great political or social depression, when it becomes necessary for men to have recourse to the superhuman for

INTRODUCTION xli guidance and consolation. Then when the hour is darkest some prophet is born, perhaps in a lowly hamlet, to solace the heavy-laden and lift their thoughts to a brighter and happier world. A signal instance has been remarked by historians. Judaea was smarting from the tyranny and cruelty of Herod when he whom the most advanced races of the world call the Messiah was born.

The Gurus too appear to have been of the opinion that God sends a divine guide whenever required by the con dition of the age and country. Guru Amar Das, the third Guru, wrote:â

When the world is in distress, it heartily prayeth.

The True One attentively listeneth and with His kind disposition granteth consolation.

He giveth orders to the Cloud and the rain falleth in torrents.

That is, the Guru comes by God's order and gives abundant instruction to all who may be prepared to receive it.

Indeed several events occurred during the Muhammadan conquests of India in the Middle Ages to force the Hindus to consider life in a serious aspect. Though many of the followers of Vishnu, Shiv, and the other gods of the Hindu dispensation adopted during that period the faith of the Arabian prophet, as the result of force or with a view to worldly advantages, yet others whose minds were powerfully directed to religious speculation sought safety from perse cution and death in the loneliness of the desert or the retirement of the forest, and lived single-minded investigators of religious truth as in the primitive golden age of their country.

We shall here give, from the written accounts of Muham madan historians, some examples of the treatment of Hindus by Muhammadan conquerors of India.

Shahab-up-Din, King of Ghazni, the virtual founder of the Muhammadan Empire in India (1170-1206), put Prithwi Raja, King of Ajmer and Dihli, to death in cold blood.

xlii THE SIKH RELIGION

He massacred thousands of the inhabitants of Ajmer who had opposed him, reserving the remainder for slavery. After his victory over the King of Banaras the slaughter of the Hindus is described as immense. None were spared except women and children, and the carnage of the men was carried on until, as it has been said, the earth grew weary of the monotony. 1

In the Taj-ul-Mcfasir by Hasan Nizam-i-Naishapuri it is stated that when Qutb-ul-Din Aibak (A. D. 1194-1210) conquered Merath he demolished all the Hindu temples of the city and erected mosques on their sites. In the city of Koil, now called Aligarh, he converted Hindu inhabitants to Islam by the sword and beheaded all who adhered to their religion. In the city of Kalinjar he destroyed one hundred and thirteen Hindu temples, built mosques on their sites, massacred over one hundred thousand Hindus, and made slaves of about fifty thousand more. It is said the place became black as pitch with the decomposing bodies of the Hindus. And in the Tabaqat-i-Nasiri by Minhaj-ul-Siraj it is stated that when Muhammad Bakhtyar Khilji conquered Bihar he put to the sword about one hundred thousand Brahmans, and burnt a valuable library of ancient Sanskrit works.

Abdulla Wassaf writes in his Tazjiyat-ul-Amsar wa Tajriyat ul Asar that when Ala-ul-Din Khilji (1295-1316) captured the city of Kambayat at the head of the gulf of Cambay, he killed the adult male Hindu inhabitants for the glory of Islam, set flowing rivers of blood, sent the women of the country, with all their gold, silver, and jewels, to his own home, and made about twenty thousand maidens his private slaves.

Ala-ul-Din once asked his qazi what was the Muhammadan law prescribed for Hindus. The qazi replied, ' Hindus are like the earth; if silver is demanded from them, they ought with the greatest humility to offer gold. And if a Muham madan desire to spit into a Hindu's mouth, the Hindu should 1 The Kamilu-t Tawarikh by ibn Aslr. See also Elphinstone's History of India.

INTRODUCTION xliii open it wide for the purpose. God created Hindus to be slaves of the Muhammadans. The Prophet hath ordained that, if the Hindus do not accept Islam, they should be imprisoned, tortured, and finally put to death, and their property confiscated." At this the monarch smiled and said he had not been waiting for an interpretation of the sacred law. He had already issued an order that Hindus should only possess corn and coarse clothes sufficient to last them for six months.

During the reign of the same monarch men formerly in easy circumstances were reduced to beggary, and their wives obliged to resort to menial labour for their main tenance. In front of the palace were generally seen the corpses of forty or fifty Hindus. Hindus were punished with merciless severity for the most trifling offences. The monarch had his own brother and nephew flayed alive on the mere suspicion of disloyalty. He then had their flesh cooked and forced their children to eat it. What remained after the repast was thrown to the elephants to trample on.

The historian, Ibn Batuta, who visited India in the time of the Emperor Muhammad Bin Tughlak, wrote of him: ' Such was his inexorable and impetuous character that on one occasion when the inhabitants of Dihli revolted against his oppression and wrote him a letter of remon strance, he ordered them to quit the place for Daulatabad, a city in the Dakhan (Deccan), at a distance of forty days' journey. The order was so literally obeyed that when the Emperor's servants searched the city after the removal, and found a blind man in one of the houses and a bedridden one in another, the bedridden man was projected from a catapult and the blind one dragged by his feet to Daulatabad. But the latter's limbs dropped off on the way, and at the end of the journey only one leg was left, which was duly thrown into the new city, "for the order had been that all should go to this place." We shall subsequently see how Muhammad bin Tughlak persecuted the Maratha saint Namdev, an account of whose life and writings will be given in this work.

xliv THE SIKH RELIGION

Amir Khusrau writes in his Tawarikh Alai or Khazain-ul-Futuh that when the Emperor Firoz Shah Tughlak (A. D. 1351-88) took the city of Bhilsa in Bhopal, he destroyed all its Hindu temples, took away their idols, placed them in front of his fort, and had them daily bathed with the blood of a thousand Hindus. Firoz Shah twice plundered the country of Malwa, and took away everything he could find except earthen pots.

Farishta relates that a Brahman called Budhan, who dwelt in a place called Kayathan or Kataen near Lakhnau (Lucknow), was put to death by Sikandar Khan Lodi for stating that as Islam was true, so also was the Hindu religion. The saint Kabir lived under Sikandar Khan Lodi, and was tortured by him. 1

The Emperor Babar's cruelty to the inhabitants of Saiyid-pur we shall find described by Guru Nanak, who was an eye-witness. Both he and his attendant were taken prisoners and obliged to work as slaves.

The Guru thus describes the Muhammadan rulers and the state of India in his time:â

This age is a knife, kings are butchers; justice hath taken wings and fled.

In this completely dark night of falsehood the moon of truth is never seen to rise.

I have become perplexed in my search;

In the darkness I find no way.

Devoted to pride, I weep in sorrow;

How shall deliverance be obtained? 2

There is a glamour of romance cast round the person of the Emperor Jahangir, partly owing to the poetry of Moore and partly owing to his possession of Nur Jahan, the most beautiful and gifted woman of the East; but Jahangir's memory is entitled to no historical commiseration. His 1 Farishta elsewhere describes Sikandar Khan Lodi as just, God fearing, and religious. He prayed five times a day, bestowed large sums of money on indigent and religious persons, and was, according to the historian, a model of a Musalman prince.

father Akbar was disposed to free thought in religion, and it was believed that in this he was encouraged by Abul Fazal, the famous Persian historian. Jahangir caused Abul Fazal to be cruelly assassinated. After his accession he compassed the death of Nur Jahan's husband in order to possess her. He tells in his Memoirs how he disposed of robbers. I accomplished about this period the suppression of a tribe of robbers, who had long infested the roads about Agra; and whom, getting into my power, I caused to be trampled to death by elephants."

Sir Thomas Roe, the British Ambassador at his Court, gives the following further information regarding Jahangir's method of dispensing justice: A band of one hundred robbers were brought in chains before the Great Mogul. Without any ceremony of trial, he ordered them to be carried away for execution, their chief being ordered to be torn in pieces by dogs. The prisoners were sent for execution to several quarters of the city, and executed in the streets. Close by my house the chief was torn in pieces by twelve dogs; and thirteen of his fellows, having their hands and feet tied together, had their necks cut by a sword, yet not quite through, and their naked and bloody bodies were left to corrupt in the streets."

The trials are conducted quickly, and the sentences speedily executed; culprits being hanged, beheaded, im paled, torn by dogs, destroyed by elephants, bitten by serpents, or other devices, according to the nature of the crimes; the executions being generally in the market-place. The governors of provinces and cities administer justice in a similar manner."

The following gives Jahangir's treatment of harmless lovers: ' Happening to catch a eunuch kissing one of his women whom he had relinquished, he sentenced the lady to be put into the earth, with only her head left above the ground, exposed to the burning rays of the sun, and the eunuch to be cut in pieces before her face."

Sir Thomas Roe describes how Jahangir vented his dis pleasure on some of his nobles: ' Some nobles who were near his person he caused for some offence to be whipped in his presence, receiving 130 stripes with a most terrible instrument of torture, having, at the ends of four cords irons like spur-rowels, so that every stroke made four wounds. When they lay for dead, he commanded the standers-by to spurn them with their feet, and the door keepers to break their staves upon them. Thus, cruelly mangled and bruised, they were carried away, one of them dying on the spot."

Jahangir's son Khusrau rose in rebellion against him, and it is not a matter for surprise that he found many adherents. After Khusrau's arrest he was brought before his father, with a chain fastened from his left hand to his left foot, according to the laws of Changhez Khan. On the right hand of the Prince stood Hasan Beg, and on his left, Abdulrahim. Khusrau trembled and wept. He was ordered into confinement; but the companions of his rebel lion were put to death with cruel torments. Hasan Beg was sewed up in a raw hide of an ox, and Abdulrahim in that of an ass, and both were led about the town on asses, with their faces towards the tail. The ox's hide became so dry and contracted, that before the evening Hasan Beg was suffocated; but the ass's hide being continually moistened with water by the friends of Abdulrahim, he survived the punishment. From the garden of Kamran to the city of Lahore two rows of stakes were fixed in the ground, upon which the other rebels were impaled alive; and the unhappy Khusrau, mounted on an elephant, was conducted between the ranks of these miserable sufferers."

Further on we shall see that Jahangir caused Guru Arjan, the fifth Sikh Guru, to be tortured to death, partly on account of his religion and partly because he had extended to Prince Khusrau a friendly reception and hospitality.

Jahangir's grandson the Emperor Aurangzeb was brought up a very strict Muhammadan. The following, according to the Mirat-i-Alam of the historian Bakhtawar Khan, shows how he treated Hindus and their temples for the honour and glory of God and the success of what he considered

INTRODUCTION xlvii the only true religion: Hindu writers have been entirely excluded from holding public offices; and all the wor shipping places of the infidels, and the great temples of these infamous people have been thrown down and de stroyed in a manner which excites astonishment at the successful completion of so arduous an undertaking."

The following is from the Maasir-i-Alamgiri: ' It reached the ears of His Majesty, the Protector of the Faith, that in the provinces of Thatha, Multan, and Banaras, but especially in the latter, foolish Brahmans were in the habit of expounding frivolous books in their schools, and that students, learned Mussalmans as well as Hindus, went there even from long distances, led by a desire to become acquainted with the wicked sciences there taught. The Director of the Faith consequently issued orders to all the governors of provinces to destroy with willing hands the temples and schools of the infidels, and to put an entire stop to the teaching and practice of idolatrous forms of worship. It was subsequently reported to his religious Majesty, leader of the Unitarians, that in obedience to his orders, the Government officers had destroyed the temple of Vishwanath at Banaras. In the thirteenth year of Aurang-zeb's reign this justice-loving monarch, the constant enemy of tyrants, commanded the destruction of the Hindu temple of Mathura, and soon that stronghold of falsehood and den of iniquity was levelled with the ground. On its site was laid at great expense the foundation of a vast mosque."

There arose a sect called Satnamis founded by Jagjivan Das, a native of Awadh (Oude). They appear to have taken many of their doctrines from the Sikhs. Their moral code is thus described: It is something like that of all Hindu quietists, and enjoins indifference to the world, its pleasures or its pains, implicit devotion to the spiritual guide, clemency and gentleness, rigid adherence to truth, the discharge of all ordinary, social, or religious obligations, and the hope of final absorption into the one spirit which pervades all things." l xlviii THE SIKH RELIGION

The Muhammadan historian thus describes this pious sect and their treatment by the Emperor Aurangzeb: ' A body of bloody miserable rebels, goldsmiths, carpenters, sweepers, tanners, and other ignoble beings, braggarts and fools of all descriptions became so puffed up with vain glory as to cast themselves headlong into the pit of de struction. Aurangzeb sent an army to exterminate and destroy these unbelievers. The heroes of Islam charged with impetuosity and crimsoned their sabres with the blood of these desperate men. The struggle was terrible. At length the Satnamis broke and fled, but were pursued with great slaughter.

'General Khan Jahan Bahadur arrived from Jodhpur bringing with him several cartloads of idols taken from the Hindu temples which had been razed to the ground. Most of these idols, when not made of gold, silver, brass, or copper, were adorned with precious stones. It was ordered that some of them should be cast away in cut-offices and the remainder placed beneath the steps of the grand mosque to be trampled under foot. There they lay a long time until not a vestige of them was left.

' In 1090 A. H. (A. D. 1680) Prince Muhammad Azam and Khan Jahan Bahadur obtained permission to visit Udaipur. Two other officers at the same time proceeded thither to effect the destruction of the temples of the idolaters, which are described as the wonders of the age, erected by the infidels to the ruin of their souls. Twenty Rajputs had resolved to die for their faith. One of them slew many of his assailants before receiving his death blow. Another followed and another until all had fallen. Many of the faithful also had been dispatched when the last of these fanatics had gone to hell.

' Soon after Aurangzeb himself visited the Rana's lake and ordered all its temples to be levelled with the ground. Hasan Ali Khan then made his appearance with twenty camels taken from the Rana, and reported that the temple near the palace and one hundred and twenty-two more in the neighbouring districts had been

INTRODUCTION xlix destroyed. He was rewarded by the emperor with the title of Bahadur.

' When Aurangzeb went to Chitaur, still one of the most beautiful of all ancient cities, he caused sixty-three temples there to be demolished. The Rana had now been driven forth from his country and his home, the victorious Ghazis had struck many a blow, and the heroes of Islam had trampled under their chargers' hoofs the land which this reptile of the forest and his predecessors had possessed for a thousand years."

Aurangzeb's iconoclastic fury knew no bounds or moderation. Abu Turab, who had been commissioned by him to effect the destruction of the idol temples of Amber, the ancient capital of Jaipur, reported in person that three score and six of these edifices had been levelled with the ground." 1

We shall further on see that it was Aurangzeb who put Guru Teg Bahadur, the ninth Guru of the Sikhs, to death in Dihli. According to the author of the Dabistan the emperor ordered the Guru's body to be quartered and the parts thereof to be suspended at the four gates of the city. 2 Aurangzeb also persecuted Guru Gobind Singh, the tenth and last Guru of the Sikhs, and forced him to fly from the Panjab; and it was a result of the same monarch's tyranny that Guru Gobind Singh's four sons lost their lives and that none of his descendants survived.

Many earnest thinkers and reformers lived under the above and other Muhammadan emperors of India, but they were either executed and none dared record their teachings and their fate, or accounts of them belong to Hindu religious history, and lie beyond the scope of the present work.

1 On the conduct of the Muhammadan Emperors we have largely availed ourselves of the translations and narratives in Sir Henry Elliot's History of India. The original Persian histories are many of them difficult of access, and could not be consulted.

1 The Sikh chroniclers, as we shall subsequently see, give a different version of the mode of execution of Guru Teg Bahadur.

THE SIKH RELIGION
CHAPTER II

The great Pandits and Brahmans of Hinduism communi cated their instructions in Sanskrit, which they deemed the language of the gods. The Gurus thought it would be of more general advantage to present their messages in the dialects of their age. When Guru Amar Das was asked the reason for this, he replied: ' Well-water can only irrigate adjacent land, but rain-water the whole world. On this account the Guru hath composed his hymns in the language of the people, and enshrined them in the Gurumukhi characters, so that men and women of all castes and classes may read and understand them." A Brahman urged: That religious instruction ought not to be communicated to every one, it being forbidden to instruct Sudars and women in the sacred lore. 1 The Guru thus oracularly replied:â 0 father, dispel such doubts.

It is God who doeth whatever is done; all who exist shall be absorbed in Him.

The different forms, O God, which appear are ever Thine, and at the last they shall all be resolved in Thee.

He who is absorbed in the Guru's word, shall thoroughly know Him who made this world.

Thine, O Lord, is the word; there is none but Thee; where is there room for doubt?

2

Guru Nanak spoke of himself as neither continent nor learned, and was in every respect the essence of humility. His advent was heralded by no prophecies, and conse quently he was not obliged to make or invent incidents in 1 It is laid down in the twelfth chapter of the Institutes of Gautam that if a Sudar even hear the Veds his ears must be stopped either with molten lead or wax; if he read the Veds, his tongue must be cut out; and if he possess the Veds, his body must be cut in twain.

In the eighteenth slok of the ninth chapter of the Institutes of Manu it is laid down that women may not take part in any Vedic rites. Their doing so, or having any concern with Vedic texts, would be con trary to dharm. Women were therefore deemed as Sudars, and beyond the pale of religion.

INTRODUCTION li his life conformable thereto. He preached against idolatry, caste distinction, and hypocrisy, and gave men a most comprehensive ethical code; but in so doing he never uttered a word which savoured of personal ambition or an arrogation of the attribuies. oi. the Creator. He appears to have been on fairly good terms with Muhammadans, but his disregard of caste prejudices and his uncompro- mising language led him into occasional difficulties with the Hindus, though he was never embroiled in violent scenes. On the whole he was generally beloved during his life, and at his death Hindus and Muhammadans quarrelled as to which sect should perform his obsequies.

The Granth- Sahib contains the compositions of Guru Nanak y-Gura Angad, Guru Amar. Das, Guru Ram Das, Guru Arjan, Guru Teg Bahadur (the ninth Guru), a couplet of Guru Gobind Singh (the tenth Guru), panegyrics of bards who attended on the Gurus or admired their characters, and hymns of mediaeval Indian saints, a list of whom will subsequently be given. The cardinal principle of the Gurus and Bhagats whose writings find place in the sacred books of the Sikhs was the unity of God. This is everywhere inculcated in the Sikh sacred writings with ample and perhaps not unnecessary iteration, considering the forces Sikhism had to contend with in an age of ignorance and superstition.

The hymns of the Gurus and saints are not arranged in the holy volume according to their authors, but according to the thirty-one rags or musical measures to which they were composed. The first nine Gurus adopted the name Nanak as their nom de plume, and their compositions are distinguished by Mahallas or quartiers. The Granth Sahib is likened to a city and the hymns of each Guru to a ward or division of it. Thus the compositions of Guru Nanak are styled Mahalla one, that is, the first ward; the compositions of Guru Angad the second ward, and so on. After the hymns of the Gurus are found the hymns of the Bhagats under their several musical measures.

The Granth which passes under the name of Guru

Gobind Singh, contains his Japji, the Akal Ustat or praise of the Creator, the Vachitar Natak or Wonderful Drama, in which the Guru gives an account of his parentage, his divine mission, and the battles in which he had been engaged. Then come three abridged translations of the Devi Mahatamya, an episode in the Markandeya Puran, in praise of Durga the goddess of war. Then follow the Gyan Parbodh, or awakening of knowledge; accounts of twenty-four incarnations of the Deity, selected because of their warlike character; the Hazare de Shabd; quatrains called sawaiyas, which are religious hymns in praise of God and reprobation of idolatry and hypocrisy; the Shastar Nam Mala, a list of offensive and defensive weapons used in the Guru's time, with special reference to the attributes of the Creator; the Tria Charitar, or tales illustrating the qualities, but principally the deceit of women; the Zaf ar-nama, containing the tenth Guru's epistle to the Emperor Aurangzeb; and several metrical tales in the Persian lan guage. This Granth was compiled by Bhai Mani Singh after the tenth Guru's death.

There are two great divisions of Sikhs, Sahijdharis and Singhs. The latter are they who accept the baptism in augurated by Guru Gobind Singh, which will be described in the fifth volume of this work. All other Sikhs are called Sahijdharis. The Singhs, after the time of Guru Gobind Singh, were all warriors, the Sahijdharis those who lived at ease, as the word denotes, and practised trade or agricul ture. 1 In the Singhs are included thenirmalas andnihangs. The Sahijdharis include the Udasis founded by Sri Chand, son of Guru Nanak; the Sewapanthis founded by a water-carrier of Guru Gobind Singh; the Ramraiyas, followers of Ram Rai, son of Guru Har Rai; the Handalis, to be sub sequently described, and other sects of minor importance.

The Sikh religion differs as regards the authenticity of 1 Some say that the Sahijdharis received their name from the promises of certain Sikhs in the time of Guiu Gobind Singh, that they would not accept his baptism at the time, but that they would gradually do so.

INTRODUCTION liii its dogmas from most other great theological systems. Many of the great teachers the world has known have not left a line of their own composition, and we only know what they taught through tradition or second-hand informa tion. If

Pythagoras wrote any of his tenets, his writings have not descended to us. We know the teaching of Sokrates only through the writings of Plato and Xenophon. Budha has left no written memorials of his teaching, Rung fu-tze, known to Europeans as Confucius, left no documents in which he detailed the principles of his moral and social system. The Founder of Christianity did not reduce his doctrines to writing, and for them we are obliged to trust to the Gospels according to Matthew, Mark, Luke, and John. The Arabian Prophet did not himself reduce to writing the chapters of the Quran. They were written or compiled by his adherents and followers. But the compositions of the Sikh Gurus are preserved, and we know at first hand what they taught. They employed the vehicle of verse, which is generally unalterable by copyists, and we even become in time familiar with their different styles. No spurious compositions or extraneous dogmas can, therefore, be represented as theirs.

It is not clear, however, that this contributes to the success of the Sikh religion. It appears that the very authenticity of the sacred books of a religion may militate against its general or permanent acceptance. The teach ings of which there is no authentic record, are elastic and capable of alteration and modification to suit foreign countries and the aspirations and intellectual conditions of ages long subsequent to those in which they arose. No religion in its entirety is permanently adopted by a foreign country; and no religion when it spontaneously migrates can escape the assimilation of local ideas or super stitions. The followers of all religions are prone to indulge in the luxury of eclecticism. By a universal law they adhere to the dogmas most suitable for themselves, and reject what they deem the least important or the least practicable enjoined by the founders of their faiths.

It is curious that the greatest religious reforms have been effected by the laity. The clergy, apart from their vested interests, are too wedded to ancient systems, and dare not impugn their utility or authority. Pythagoras, who founded a religio-philosophical school and taught the transmigra tion of souls, was the son of a gem-engraver and not a priest by early training or association. Isaiah, the Hebrew poet, who gave consistency and splendour to Jewish sentiments, was not an ecclesiastic by profession. Moses had a brother who was a high priest, but he was not himself designed for the priesthood. Sokrates was a profound thinker and moral guide, but still a member of the laity who had emerged from the schools of the sophists. Budha was a prince brought up without any sacerdotal instruction. He conceived ideas of reform by profound contemplation and introspection. Christ was by trade a carpenter, and was never intended to expound the law, or play the part of a Jewish Rabbi. Muhammad of Makka was born an idolater, herded sheep and goats in early life, and appears to have had no religious instruction whatever until he had met the Hanif Waraka, his wife's cousin. The renowned Indian teacher Kabir was a weaver, who was so little of a professional priest that he denounced the Hindu and Muhammadan preachers of his age. And, as we shall see, Guru Nanak was not a priest either by birth or education, but a man who soared to the loftiest heights of divine emotionalism, and exalted his mental vision to an ethical ideal beyond the conception of Hindu or Muhammadan.

The illustrious author of the Vie de Jesus asks whether great originality will again arise or the world be content to follow the paths opened by the daring creators of ancient ages. Now there is here presented a religion totally un affected by Semitic or Christian influences. Based on the concept of the unity of God, it rejected Hindu formularies and adopted an independent ethical system, ritual, and standards which were totally opposed to the theological beliefs of Guru Nanak's age and country. As we shall see hereafter, it would be difficult to point to a religion of greater originality or to a more comprehensive ethical system.

CHAPTER III

India contains a population who profess many religions. It would be a great mistake to put them all on the same footing. Some make for loyalty and others for what we may call independence. Some religions appear to require State support, while others have sufficient vitality to dispense with it. The Jewish religion has survived for many centuries without a temporal head and in the face of endless persecutions. Islam has spread in many lands, and does not solicit or require much support from temporal power. Muhammadans only claim the free exercise of their religion, and this is allowed them in India. Many members of other religions, believing that they are direct emanations from heaven, may not suppose that they require State countenance or support, but the student of comparative theology must be allowed to entertain a different opinion.

Our little systems have their day; They have their day and cease to be.

To enumerate a few instances. When Constantine, the Roman Emperor of the West, after his conversion to Christianity, withdrew his support from the ancient religion of his country, it rapidly declined. Then vanished, in the words of Coleridge,

The intelligible forms of ancient poets, The fair humanities of the old religion, Its power, its beauty, and its majesty.

Budhism flourished in India, its parent home, many centuries ago, but the successors of the renowned Asoka, who were not so spiritual or enlightened as he, allowed their religion to be completely banished from Indian soil, like an exile, to find in foreign lands the repose and accept- ance it had vainly sought in its own country. The great Emperor Akbar, by an eclectic process, evolved what he considered a rational religion from Islam, Hindusim, and Zoroastrianism, but it perished when it received no support but rather opposition from his son Jahangir. The religion of the Cross was banished from its parent home of Judaea and supplanted by the religion of the Crescent. Christianity, however, or the civilization which passes under its name, gained in other countries much more than it lost in its own. Organization and the material forces by which it is main tained have obviously contributed to that result.

The Emperor Akbar's historian, Abul Fazl, very clearly saw the advantage of State support to a religion. He says in his Ain-i-Akbari: 'Men of deep insight are of opinion that even spiritual progress among a people would be impossible, unless emanating from the king, in whom the light of God dwells."

As Budhism without State support completely lost its hold in India, so it is apprehended that without State sup port Sikhism will also be lost in the great chaos of Indian religious systems.

The dialects and languages of the Gurus are now largely forgotten. There are no readable or trustworthy com mentaries or translations of their compositions in any lan guage, and the Sikhs find it difficult or impossible to under stand them. Added to this is the custom of writing the sacred hymns without any separation of words. As there is no separation of words in Sanskrit, the gyanis, or inter preters of the Gurus' hymns, deem it would be a profanation to separate the words of their sacred writings. It cannot be said that the object of the gyanis has been to keep all divine knowledge to themselves, but at any rate the result is, that the Sikh laity have now thrust aside the gyanis and their learning, and are content to dispense with both.

The sequel is a general relapse to Hinduism, which is princi pally a system of domestic ritual. Hinduism has six philo sophical systems, two of which, the Sankhya and Mimansa, if pushed to their legitimate consequences, are practically atheistical. The followers of the Hindu god Shiv may curse the followers of the Hindu god Vishnu, and the followers of Vishnu may retaliate on the followers of Shiv. To be deemed an orthodox Hindu it is only necessary to be born in Hinduism and to conform to certain external observances, such as not eating or touching what its followers believe to be unclean, avoiding contact with persons who are deemed of lower caste, cooking food in a particular manner, and not allowing the shadow of strangers to fall on it. The old Levitical Law of Moses and its accessory regulations were sufficiently strict, but Hinduism surpasses all the religions that have ever been invented in a social exclusiveness which professes to be based on divine sanction. Truly wonderful are the strength and vitality of Hinduism. It is like the boa constrictor of the Indian forests. When a petty enemy appears to worry it, it winds round its opponent, crushes it in its folds, and finally causes it to disappear in its capacious interior. In this way, many centuries ago, Hinduism on its own ground disposed of Budhism, which was largely a Hindu reformation; in this way, in a prehistoric period, it absorbed the religion of the Scythian invaders of Northern India; in this way it has converted uneducated Islam in India into a semi-paganism; and in this way it is disposing of the reformed and once hopeful religion of Baba Nanak. Hinduism has embraced Sikhism in its folds; the still comparatively young religion is making a vigorous struggle for life, but its ultimate destruc tion is, it is apprehended, inevitable without State support. Notwithstanding the Sikh Gurus' powerful denunciation of Brahmans, secular Sikhs now rarely do anything without their assistance. Brahmans help them to be born, help them to wed, help them to die, and help their souls after death to obtain a state of bliss. And Brahmans, with all the deftness of Roman Catholic missionaries in Protestant countries, have partially succeeded in persuading the Sikhs to restore to their niches the images of Devi, the Queen of Heaven, and of the saints and gods of the ancient faith.

CHAPTER IV

A few brief paragraphs, unburdened with detail, on the origin and progress of religion until it received its mono theistic consummation accepted by Guru Nanak appear to be necessary.

Statius, the Latin poet, expressed his opinion that it was fear which first made gods in the world. 1 Miserable and resourceless primitive man felt the inclemency and fury of the elements, and prayed and sacrificed to avert their wrath or to gain their favour. But as there were malignant, so there were benignant natural agencies which received devout and earnest worship. The Sun, which gives light and heat, appears to have been worshipped by all primitive peoples. He was, however, distant and non-tangible; but when fire was discovered, long ages after man had appeared on the surface of the earth, it appears to have received the greatest homage from the human race in all parts of the globe. By its means men warmed themselves, cooked their food, and smelted metals. It was to fire (Agni) the Indians of the Vedic period addressed some of their sublimest hymns; and its discovery and importance led the ancient Greeks to suppose that it must have been stolen from heaven, which had so long been parsimonious of its gifts.

As civilization progressed and the fruits of agriculture were added to the spontaneous gifts of nature, the bounty of the heavens was deemed necessary for man's comfort and sustenance. It was then that the sky, under the various names of Dyaus, Zcik, and Varuna, Ovpavos, was invoked, both in India and Greece, to shed its choicest blessings on crops and men. 2 Other deities arose as prompted or required by human necessities. Prithwi, the earth, as the parent of sustenance, logically and necessarily received, as the 1 ' Primus in orbe decs fecit timor Theb. iii. 661.

2 For long years after the discovery and study of Sanskrit there was no doubt whatever cast on the identity of Varuna with Ouranos. Doubts have now arisen in the minds of some persons on account, it is stated, of phonetic difficulties.

INTRODUCTION lix spouse of the sky, divine honours both in India and Europe. 1 Each deity addressed received all the homage and adoration that poetic fancy could lavish or imagine. His worshippers endeavoured to make him feel that he was the great god who ruled the world and controlled man and nature; and they hoped that by judicious flattery and plenteous sacrifice he would listen to and grant their passionate supplica tions.

The gods as well as their votaries appear to have lived in friendly contiguity both in India and in Greece. Jupiter had his temple near that of Venus as they are found to-day in the disentombed city of Pompeii. Near Delphi Apollo had exclusive sway even to the extent of relegating Jupiter into a subordinate position. Each province selected in the wide domain of Olympus some deity which it worshipped to the exclusion of all others. In India, though the worship of Shiv, which is associated with knowledge, is different from that of Vishnu, which is associated with devotion, and though the worshippers of both gods frequently quar relled and addressed each other in injurious language, yet they were united by the common bond of Hinduism, and sometimes celebrated their worship in harmony. 2

When man extended his horizon, the sufficiency and omnipotence of the gods ordinarily invoked began to be canvassed. In Greece the minor deities became completely subordinated to Zeus, the great ruler of Olympus. They could do everything but regulate human fate and action. That was reserved for the supreme deity alone: â 7rar)i fleouri yap ouris eori 7ra. T)i Ato's. 3

In India a belief in an infinite, illimitable, and supreme power was gradually evolved by seers and philosophers 1 Tacitus wrote of the ancient Germans â ' Herthum, id est terram matrem, colunt eamque intervenire rebus hominum, invehi populis arbitrantur Germania, cap. xl.

2 An idol in a temple, Harihareshwar, on the outskirts of the Maisur (Mysore) State contains the conjoint emblems of Vishnu and Shiv. 3 Aesch. Prom. Vine. 49.

ages before the emigration of the Aryans to Europe. Pra-japati, who was represented as the father of the gods, the lord of all living creatures, gradually received excep tional human homage. There was also Aditi, who appears under various guises, being, in one passage of the Rig Veda, identified with all the deities, with men, with all that has been and shall be born, and with air and heaven. In this character she corresponded to the Greek Zeus;

Zevs eorti; al6r)p, Zeus 6e y? j, Zevs rot TO. TTCLVTOL TI Tcoi5' and to the Latin Jupiter: â lupiter est quodcunque vides, quocunque moveris. 2

But there appears again to have been even a more ex alted concept of a divinity who was inexpressible and who could only be described by a periphrasis. He was bright and beautiful and great. He was One, though the poets called Him by many names.

Before there was anything, before there was either death or immortality, before there was any distinction between day and night, there was that One. It breathed breathless by itself. Other than it nothing has since been. Then was darkness, everything in the beginning was hidden in gloom, all was like the ocean, without a light. Then that germ which was covered by the husk, the One, was produced. 3 Guru Nanak, as we shall see, gave expansion to this conception of the one God: â 1 Aesch. Frag. 2 Lucan, Pharsalia ix.

3 Rig Veda, X, 129. Tacitus indicates one God worshipped under different names by the Germans, and only perceived by the light of faith: ' Deorum nominibus appellant secretum illud quod sola reve-rentia vident It may be here noticed that Tacitus' account of Germany and its people is much more trustworthy than that of Caesar, who was a less philosophical writer. Caesar states that the Germans worshipped the sun, fire, and the moon, and them only.

In the beginning there was indescribable darkness;
Then was not earth or heaven, naught but God's unequalled order.
Then was not day, or night, or moon, or sun; God was meditating on the void.
Then were not continents, or hells, or seven seas, or rivers, or flowing streams.
Nor was there paradise, or a tortoise, or nether regions;
Or the hell or heaven of the Muhammadans, or the De stroyer Death;
Or the hell or heaven of the Hindus, or birth or death; nor did any one come or go.
Then was not Brahma, Vishnu, or Shiv;
No one existed but the One God.
Then was not female, or male, or caste, or birth; nor did any one feel pain or pleasure.
There was no caste or religious garb, no Brahman or Khatri.
No horn, no sacred feasts, no places of pilgrimage to bathe in, nor did any one perform worship.
There was no love, no service, no Shiv, or Energy of his;
Then were not Veds or Muhammadan books, no Simritis, no Shastars;
The Imperceptible God was Himself the speaker and preacher; Himself unseen He was evei
When He pleased He created the world;
Without supports He sustained the sky.
He created Brahma, Vishnu, and Shiv, and extended the love of Mammon.
He issued His order and watched over all. 1

For many centuries thinking men in India have rejected gods and goddesses, and made no secret of their faith in the sole primal Creator, by whatsoever name called.

An important question arose how the Supreme Being should be represented. He could not be seen, but He was believed to exist. The highest conception that primitive man could form of Him was that He was in man's own image, subject to the human passions of wrath, jealousy, revenge, love of praise, and adoration. This conception is what has been termed anthropomorphism â that is, that 1 The Indian words in this hymn will subsequently be explained.

God is in man's image, or, conversely, that God made man in his own image. 1

When man's conception of God extended, and it was admitted that He had created the heavens and the earth, and held control over His boundless creation, it became difficult for the philosopher to imagine Him in human form. Were He such, it would appear to be a limitation of His omnipotence and omnipresence, and, moreover, the belief that God is infinite and governs His infinite creation, but at the same time is not included in it, though possibly intelligible to faith, is not equally so to reason. To over come this difficulty the belief arose that God is diffused through all matter, and that it is therefore a part of Him. This belief is known as pantheism.

In India, pantheism may be said to be the creed of intel lectual Hindus, but it cannot be held to be a generally satisfying or useful cult to the world. When a man believes that he is a part of God, and that God, who pervades space, pervades him also, moral obligation must obviously be relaxed. Nor can supplications be satisfactorily addressed to nature, with its elemental forces, even though God be held to reside therein. Pantheism is too cold and too abstract to satisfy the reasonable aspirations of the human soul. And the fact admitted by most philosophers, that men are endowed with free will, must make them pause before they accept the pantheistic philosophy in its entirety. Moreover, to gratify his emotional instinct, man must have access in spirit to a personal God to appeal to in order to grant him favours, to afford him solace in affliction, to love him as a son, and as a kind and merciful friend to take an interest in him when he needs assistance. According to the Sikh Gurus, God was a being to be approached and 1 The ancient Greeks also believed that God made man in the divine image. Thus Platoâ 'Os Se Kwqgev avrb KCU Â tov evo cre rv cu'Siw 0â oiv yeyovos ayaxfjia 6 yevvrjo-as Traryp, rjyda-Or) re KCU evav â ts en. 8r) jmaxXov ox-otov? rpos TO Trapdsclyfjla ctrevorjfv d-rrepydcraa-Oal (' The creative Father seeing that this image of the immortal gods had both motion and life was pleased, and in his delight considered how he might fashion it still more like its prototype'), Timaeus.

loved as a fond and faithful wife loves her spouse, and human beings were to be regarded with equality as brothers, and not to be considered as divided into castes which were at variance with or despised one another.

But though the Sikhs believe in a personal God, He is not in man's image. Guru Nanak calls Him, Nirankarâ that is, without form. Gur Das speaks of Him as formless, without equal, wonderful, and not perceptible by the senses. At the same time all the Gurus believed that He was diffused throughout creation. Guru Nanak wrote, 1 Think upon the One who is contained in everything." This same belief was again enunciated by Guru Ram Das, 'Thou, O God, art in everything and in all places." And, according to Guru Gobind Singh, even God and His worshipper, though two, are one, as bubbles which arise in water are again blended with it. This belief, according to the Guru, admitted of no doubt or discussion. 1 It is the error of men in supposing distinct existence, together with the human attributes of passion and spiritual blindness, which produces sin and evil in the world and renders the soul liable to trans migration.

No religious teacher has succeeded in logically dissociating theism from pantheism. In some passages of the Guru's writings pantheism is, as we have seen, distinctly implied, while in other texts matter is made distinct from the Creator, but an emanation from Him. Although anthropomorphic theism is a religion, while pantheism is a philosophy, and anthropomorphic theism is generally held orthodox and pantheism heterodox, yet, on account of the difficulty of describing the Omnipresent and Illimitable in suitable human language, both religion and philosophy are inextricably
1 Compare 'Ai po7rov yÂ Xn- e Trep TL KOL oaAo roiv avopniirivuv) TOV 0â tov xcrcxet, Xenoph. Memor.; ' Humanus autem animus decerptus ex divina mente cum alio nullo nisi cum ipso Deo, si hoc est fas dictu, comparari potest Cicero, Tusc. Disp.

Compare also the expressions attributed to Christ in the Gospel according to St. John, ' I and My Father are One," ' I am in the Father and the Father in Me and again, 'I am in My Father, and ye in Me and I in you."

blended by sacred as well as profane writers. Let us take a few examples:â

Doth not the Lord fill heaven and earth?â JEREMIAH.

God in whom we live, and move, and have our being.â ST. PAUL.

Spiritus intus alit totamque infusa per artus
Mens agitat molem, et magno secorporemiscet.â VIRGIL.

Estne Dei sedes nisi terra, et pontus, et aer, Et caelum et virtus? Superos quid quaerimus ultra? lupiter est quodcunque vides, quocunque moveris!â â

LUCAN.

All in all and all in every part.â COWLEY.

Lives through all life, extends through all extent. Spreads undivided, operates unspent.â POPE.

Deum rerum omnium causam immanentem, non vero transeuntem statuo.â SPINOZA.

Se Dio veder tu vuoi, Guardalo in ogni oggetto; Cercalo nel tuo petto; Lo troverai in te!â METASTASIO.

An indefinite number of such examples might be cited.

CHAPTER V

In the hymns of the Gurus, Nirvan, or absorption in God, is proposed as the supreme object of human attainment; but a paradise called Sach Khand is also promised to the blest. There they recognize one another and enjoy ever lasting beatitude. Several learned Sikhs, however, maintain that Nirvan and Sach Khand are practically the same.

Contrary to the practice of the ancient Indian ascetics, the Gurus held that man might obtain eternal happiness without forsaking his ordinary worldly duties. Reunion with the Absolute should be the supreme object of all Sikh devotion and aspirations.

My soul, seek shelter in God's holy name; Pondering on this should'st thou all thought employ. No more thou'lt grieve, hemmed in by mortal frame, But gain in God Nirvana's final joy.

Nirvan, from nir out and va to blow, means in Sikh literature the cessation of individual consciousness caused by the blending of the light of the soul with the light of God. The Sikhs compare it to water blending with water:â
As water blends with water, when
Two streams their waves unite, The light of human life doth blend
With God's celestial light. No transmigrations then await
The weary human soul; It hath attained its resting-place,
Its peaceful crowning goal.
Nirvan is to be obtained by meditation on God, with sufficient attention and iteration, and by a life spent in conformity with the Guru's teachings. Individual con sciousness then ceases, and there is no further pain or misery.

A man may have performed good works on earth, but, if they be unattended with devout meditation and mental absorption in God, he cannot expect either Nirvan or Sach Khand, but must undergo purgation after death. After this the soul returns to a human body and begins anew its career, to end in either the supreme bliss of ultimate absorption or the supreme misery of countless trans migrations.

If man have done evil and laid up demerits, his punish ment after death must be severe. When the punishment corresponds to his misdeeds, his soul must enter some lower animal and pass through a greater or lesser number of the eight million four hundred thousand forms of existence in creation, until its turn comes to enter the offspring of human parents. The soul thus reborn in a human being has again to proceed in its long struggle to obtain the boundless reward of Nirvan.

Longa dies, perfecto temporis orbe, Concretam exemit labem, purumque reliquit Aetherium sensum atque aurai simplicis ignem. 1

Mind, whether known as reason or instinct of a greater or less degree, and whether an attribute of the brain, of the nervous system, or of the heart, is common to all animals. It is held in most religious systems to be distinct from the soul. 2 It induces the soul, under the impulse of goodness or passion, to perform good or evil acts. Both the mind and the soul are concomitants of life, which is a particular com bination of certain elements existing in the body, and abides as long as the bodily mechanism is in order and harmonious operation. When the mechanism has fallen out of gear by illness, accident, or old age, life departs, and with it the soul, which in some religious systems is held to perish with the body, in others to be immortal and individual, and in others again to transmigrate from one living creature to another. We are in this work only con cerned with the soul in its migratory aspect.

In the Mosaic system God is represented as jealous and visiting the sins of the fathers upon the children even to future generations. The Indian philosopher feels that this belief is derogatory to God, and holds that the state of the soul after the death of the body depends on its acts (called Karma) while contained in the body. These acts attach to the soul, follow it, and determine its next abode.

Hindus, and all who have sprung from them, have never entertained any doubt as to the possibility of the wanderings of the soul in the bodies of all created animals. And not only Hindus, but some Europeans of exquisite intellectual fibre have accepted or coquetted with this belief, as if the 1 Virgil, Aeneid vi. 745.

2 In the Tusculan Disputations Cicero quotes a paragraph he had written in a work on Consolation, in which he appears to treat soul and mind as identical. After referring to the soul as that which possesses feeling, understanding, life, and vigour (' quicquid est illud, quod sentit, quod sapit, quod vivit, quod viget'), he states that the human mind is of the same kind and nature (' Hoc e genere atque eadem e natura est humana mens'), Tusc. Disp. i. 27.

minds of men of vivid imagination were of necessity recalling from the misty pastâ gathering from the fount of original knowledgeâ ideas evolved by primitive man long anterior, not only to European civilization, but to all Semitic history. Many persons have thought on beholding for the first time, in this life at any rate, scenes in foreign lands, that they had been previously familiar with their beauties and derived no new gratification from them. The tenacity with which the Greek philosopher Pythagoras held this doctrine, which he called metempsychosis, is well known. Well known, too, is the success with which he and his followers for a long time imparted their views to the Dorian aristocracy on this and kindred subjects, such as, for instance, the non-destruction of life. And according to the Phaedo of Plato, Sokrates appears to have proved the doctrine of Pythagoras to his own satisfaction.

To some of our English poets the belief has been one of curious interest and satisfaction. Thus Wordsworth:â

Our birth is but a sleep and a forgetting; The soul that rises with us, our life's star Hath had elsewhere its setting, And cometh from afar;

Thus, too, Browning:â

At times I almost dream
I too have spent a life the sages' way,
And tread once more familiar paths.

And also Rossetti:â

I have been here before,
But how or when I cannot tell.

The soul when it separates from the body is likened in ancient Indian works to the moon on the day when it is invisible on account of its conjunction with the sun. The soul exists as the moon exists, though it is not perceptible; and as the moon shines again when it progresses in its motion, so does the soul when it moves into another body.

The soul being in a state of mobility, and at the same time immortal, seeks a body for the performance of its functions, and, as it were, enters into a matrimonial alliance with it for the completion and perfection of both. As the same thread will penetrate a gold bead, a pearl, or an earthen ball, so the soul, bearing its burden of acts, will enter any body with which it conies in contact. This the soul is enabled to do by its possession of a covering of finer or grosser texture, which it takes with it from the last body it has inhabited. The soul thus passes from body to body in a revolving wheel, until it is purged of its im purities and deemed fit to blend with the Absolute, from which it originally emanated.

Paramatama, the primal spirit, is the Supreme Being considered as the pervading soul of the universe. It is represented as light. Jlvatama, the soul of each living being, is also light, an emanation from the Paramatama and not material.

The lines of Milton may be accepted as a definition of the deity according to the Sikh conception:â . Since God is light
And never but in unapproached light
Dwelt from eternityâ Bright effluence of bright essence increate.
And of Thomas Campbell nearly to the same effect:â
This spirit will return to Him Who gave its heavenly spark.

The Paramatama is likened to an illimitable ocean, the Jivatama to a glass of water immersed in it. The glass is the subtile body or covering of the soul. If the glass itself be broken or taken away, the water in it, which corresponds to the jivatama, blends with the water of the ocean. This is an exemplification of Nirvan.

According to Sikh ontology all animals have two bodies, one a solid material body and the other a subtile intangible body. 1 The jivatama is separated from the former at the 1 St. Paul speaks of a spiritual body (i Cor. xv. 44) time of death, but not from the latter unless the state oi Nirvan supervenes. While the jivatama is encased in a subtile body, it is susceptible of punishment.

Sokrates, in discussing the possibility of a separate existence after death, dilates on the pleasure it would afford to meet such men as Homer, Hesiod, c.; but Plato has not recorded what Sokrates' sensations would be on meeting his tormentors and persecutors in the same happy region. John Stuart Mill, too, thought that the most serious loss which would result to mankind from a disbelief in an after existence would be the despair of reunion with those dear to us who have ended their earthly life before us. An aspiration for such a reunion is easy to understand, and the hope of its realization has soothed the death-bed of many a believer in the soul's immortality. But all people are not equally dear to us, and it did not apparently occur to that eminent philosopher that, granted the hope of meeting those we love beyond the grave, there is also the possibility of meeting those who are not equally the objects of our affectionâ those who have perhaps embittered or even abridged our terrestrial existence, and who, it may be as the result of predestination or elective grace, are admitted to the sempiternal joys of paradise. To the believer in Nirvan there is no apprehension of such associations. Only those who are sufficiently purified can be absorbed in the Absolute, in the all-dazzling fount of God's infinite perfection and love. Here individual consciousness ceases, the supreme goal of existence is attained, and neither sorrow, misery, nor remembrance of earthly evils can be apprehended.

CHAPTER VI

About thirty miles south-west of the city of Lahore, the capital of the Panjab, and on the borders of the present civil districts of Gujranwala and Montgomery, stands the town of Talwandi, deep in a lonely forest. It is on the margin 1 Kssay on the Utility of Religion.

of the Bar or raised forest tract which occupies the centre of the Pan jab. The town is still girdled by a broad expanse of arborescent vegetation, which, when not w r hitened by the sand blown by the winds of the desert, wears through all seasons a cheerful appearance. The jal (Salvadora Persica) predominates, but there are also found the phulahi (Acacia modesta) and the jand (Prosopis spicigera). The wild deer is seen occasionally to appear startled at the traveller who disturbs the solitude of its domain, and the hare and the partridge cower cautiously among the thickets, deprecating molestation.

In this retreat was born Guru Nanak, the founder of the Sikh religion. His birth took place on the third day of the light half of the month of Baisakh (April-May) in the year 1526 of the Vikramaditya era, corresponding to A. D. 1469. As to the month in which he was born there are strange diversities of statement, which we shall subsequently notice. Guru Nanak's father was Kalu of the Bedi l section of the Khatri caste. He was by profession a village accountant, but added the practice of agriculture to this avocation. Kalu's father was Shiv Ram and his mother Banarasi. Kalu had one brother called Lalu, of whom little is known besides his name. Kalu was married to Tripta, daughter of Rama, a native of the Manjha 2 country. Tripta had a brother called Krishan, of whom history is as silent as of Lalu. Tripta bore to Kalu one daughter, Nanaki, and one son, Nanak. Nanaki married Jai Ram, a revenue official of high repute at Sultanpur, which is in the present native state of Kapurthala, and was then the capital of the Jalandhar Doab.

When Taimur had spread anarchy and devastation over Northern India, a dynasty of Saiyids, or descendants of the Prophet Muhammad, aspired to rule in Dihli in the name of the Mughal conqueror. To Dihli there was hardly any territory attached, and Ala-ul-din, the last of the Saiyid 1 The meaning of this name will be explained when we come to the writings of the tenth Guru.

2 The Manjha is the country between the rivers Ravi and Bias.

rulers, in contemptuous disregard for the small and trouble some dominion meted out to him by destiny, retired to the distant city of Badaun to end his days in religious and political tranquillity. He left Dihli and the fortunes of empire to Bahlol Khan Lodi, a man whose ancestors had been enriched by commerce, and whose grandfather had been Governor of Multan under the famous monarch Firoz Shah Tughlak.

Bahlol Khan Lodi reigned from A. D. 1450 to A. D. 1488, and it was consequently near the middle of his reign that Guru Nanak, the founder of the Sikh religion, was born.

After the accession of Bahlol Khan Lodi, Daulat Khan, a relative of his, obtained power in the Panjab, and governed under the paramount authority of his kinsman. He lived in state at Sultanpur till defeated and deprived of his possessions by the Emperor Babar. The Panjab appears to have been already parcelled out to Musalman chiefs who were retainers of the sovereigns of Dihli. One of these chiefs, called Rai Bhoi, a Musalman Rajput of the Bhatti tribe, had been Zamindar or proprietor of Talwandi. After his death his heritage descended to his son Rai Bular, who governed the town at the birth and during the youth of Nanak.

Talwandi is said to have been originally built by a Hindu king called Raja Vairat. It was sacked and destroyed by fire and crowbar, like most Hindu towns and cities, during the Musalman invasions. Rai Bular restored it and built a fort on the summit of the tumulus, in which he lived the secure and happy ruler of a small village, some limited acres of cultivated land, and a boundless wilderness.

Although the age was one of religious intolerance and persecution, Rai Bular appears to have been the very reverse of a bigot. His father and he were converted Hindus, doubtless added to the ranks of Islam by a hasty circumcision and an enforced utterance of some Arabic sentences which they did not perfectly comprehend. 1 1 The descendants of Rai Bular still exist in that part of the country.

In such a solitude Rai Bular could not have been under the less worthy influences of Islam; and indifference, the parent of toleration, appears to have supervened on his Muhammadan religious training. But the human mind is so constituted, and the religious or emotional instinct so dominant in human nature, that most men at some period of their lives are irresistibly impelled to religious speculation. Something, too, must be allowed for Rai Bular's patriotic prejudices for a suffering though renounced faith. Talwandi shared not the tumults and excitements of the outer political world. It was a theatre meet for the training of a prophet or religious teacher who was to lead his countrymen to the sacred path of truth, and disenthral their minds from the superstitions of ages. Rai Bular in his little realm had ample time for reflection, and when he heard of Nanak's piety and learning, felt a mysterious interest in the clever and precocious son of Kalu.

The house in which Nanak was born lay a little distant from the fort. Probably Rai Bular and his family alone inhabited the ancient tumulus, while his tenants dwelt in the town of Talwandi on the plain. The town has now lost its old name, and is known as Nankana, in memory of the religious teacher to whom it had the honour of giving birth. When the Sikh religion had gained prominence, there was a temple erected on the spot where the Guru was born. It was afterwards rebuilt and enlarged by Raja Tej Singh, at the time when the Sikh arms had attained their greatest power and the Sikh commonwealth its widest expansion. Within the temple is installed the Granth Sahib, or sacred volume of the Sikh faith, intoned by a pro fessional reader. The innermost shrine contains some cheap printed pictures of the Guru, and musicians beguile the day chanting the religious metrical compositions of the Gurus.

CHAPTER VII

We shall now examine the principal current accounts of Guru Nanak and give brief notices of their authors.

The oldest authentic account of the Guru was written by Bhai Gur Das, who flourished in the end of the sixteenth and the beginning of the seventeenth century, dying in A. D. 1629. He was first cousin of the mother of Guru Arjan, the fifth Guru of the Sikhs. He was Guru Arjan's amanuensis, and wrote out from his dictation the Adi 1 Granth, or sacred book of the Sikhs, which then contained the hymns of the first five Sikh Gurus and of the saints who preceded them. He next wrote what he called Wars or religious cantos. These are forty in number. The first War begins with the Sikh cosmology, and ends with a brief account of Guru Nanak and the succeeding Gurus to the date of Gur Das's composition. Gur Das's object was essentially religious. He delighted in singing the greatness of God, the littleness of man, and the excellence of the Guru. Besides the Wars, Gur Das wrote Kabits, which contains the Sikh tenets and a panegyric of the Gurus.

The details which Gur Das has given of Guru Nanak will be utilized in the life of that Guru. It is a matter of regret that he did not write a complete life of the Guru, as its details could at that time have been easily obtained. The date of the composition of his work is not given, but it is admitted on all hands that it was during the time of Guru Arjan. Making due allowance for Gur Das's pro tracted employment in copying and collating the sacred volume for Guru Arjanâ a task which was completed in A. D. 1604â it may fairly be assumed that Gur Das wrote his own work not much more than sixty years after the demise of Guru Nanak, when some of his contemporaries 1 The epithet Adi, which means primitive or first, was bestowed on the Granth Sahib of Guru Arjan to distinguish it from the Grantli of Guru Gobind Singh, the tenth Guru, which was subsequently com piled by Bhai Mani Singh.

were still alive, and one of them at least retained the vigour of his intellectual faculties.

There was then living in the village of Ramdas 1 about twenty miles north of Amritsar, Bhai Budha, who had embraced the Sikh religion under Guru Nanak at Kartarpur, and who used to attend him on some of his peregrinations. This man was in the prime of life when Gur Das copied the Granth Sahib for Guru Arjan, and the latter made him reader and custodian of the sacred volume at Amritsar. Bhai Budha subsequently lived until the Guruship of Guru Har Gobind, when he died at the ripe age of one hundred and seven years. In such estimation was he held that he was specially appointed to impress the saffron tilak, or patch of Gurudom, on the foreheads of the Gurus of his time; and his descendants had the same honoured privilege as long as legitimate Gurus remained to be thus distinguished. He, however, has left no memoirs of the founder of his religion.

Mani Singh was the youngest of five sons of Bika of Kaibowal, in the Malwa country, and belonged to the Dullat section of the Hindu Jats. The ruins of Kaibowal may now be seen near the village of Laugowal. When Guru Gobind Singh was going to Kurkhetar on a preaching excursion, Bika and his son Mani went to a place called Akoi to meet him and offer him their homage. Bika in due time returned home, leaving his son with the Guru. The Guru one day asked Mani to wipe the vessels from which the Sikhs had eaten, and, as an inducement, promised that as the vessels became bright so should his under standing. Mani wiped the dishes with great humility and devotion, and received baptism from the Guru as his reward. He remained a celibate and devoted his life to the Guru's service.

1 This was Bhai Budha's original name, and the village was called after him. The name Bhai Budha was given him by Guru Nanak.

The word ' Bhai' means brother. Guru Nanak, who disregarded caste and preached the doctrine of the brotherhood of man, desired that all his followers should be deemed brothers, and thus he addressed them. The title ' Bhai ' is now bestowed on Sikh priests and others who have made a special study of the Sikh sacred writings.

When the tenth Guru found it necessary to go to the south of India, he took Mani Singh, among others, with him. At Nander, or Abchalanagar, as it is now called by the Sikhs, the Guru expounded to his followers, among whom Mani Singh was an enthusiastic listener, the recon dite language of the Granth Sahib or the book par excellence.

After the Guru's death Bhai Mani Singh remained as Grant hi, or reader of the Granth in the Har Mandar in Am-ritsar. 1 The Sikhs commissioned him, while so employed, to write them a life of Guru Nanak. They represented that the Minas, or descendants of Prithi Chand, had interpolated much incorrect matter in the biography of the Guru, whereby doubts were produced in the minds of orthodox Sikhs; and they commissioned Mani Singh to discriminate the true from the false, and compile a trustworthy life of the founder of their religion. He accordingly expanded the first of Bhai Gur Das's Wars into a life of Guru Nanak. It is called the Gyan Ratanawali. Mani Singh wrote another work, the Bhagat Ratanawali, an expansion of Gur Das's eleventh War, which contains a list of famous Sikhs up to the time of Guru Har Gobind. After the demise of Bhai Mani Singh the copyists interlarded several Hindu ideas in his works.

The hymns of the Adi Granth are arranged under the musical measures to which they were intended to be sung. Mani Singh thought it would be better and more con venient to compile the hymns of each Guru separately. He therefore altered the arrangement of the Granth Sahib, on which he was censured by the Sikhs. He apologized, and was subsequently pardoned by the members of his faith.

In A. D. 1738 Mani Singh asked permission of Zakaria Khan, the Viceroy of Lahore, to allow the Diwali 2 fair to 1 Bhai Gyan Singh's Panth Parkdsh.

2 The Diwali, originally a festival observed only by Hindus in honour of Lakshmi, their goddess of wealth, on the i th day of Kartik (Oct.-Nov.). It was the date on which Bhai Budha the first Granthi be held in Amritsar. The Viceroy gave permission on condition that Mani Singh undertook to pay a poll-tax for every Sikh who attended. Mani Singh accepted this con dition, and sent circulars to the Sikhs to attend and hold a special Sikh gathering. The Viceroy sent troops to watch the movements of the Sikhs, but the Sikhs, mistaking their intention, dispersed. The result was that Mani Singh was unable to pay the stipulated tax. Upon this he was taken to Lahore for punishment. Zakaria Khan asked his Qazi what the punishment should be. The Qazi replied that Mani Singh must either accept Islam or suffer disj ointment of his body. Mani Singh heroically accepted the latter alternative. The Viceroy adjudged this barbarous punishment, nominally on account of his victim's non payment of the tax, but in reality on account of his influence as a learned and holy man in maintaining the Sikh religion. Mani Singh manifested no pain on the occasion of his execution. He continued to his last breath to recite the Japji of Guru Nanak and the Sukhmani of Guru Arjan.

Bhai Santokh Singh, son of Deva Singh, was born in Amritsar in A. D. 1788. He received religious instruction in the Sikh faith from Bhai Sant Singh in his native city, and in the Hindu religion from a Pandit in Kaul in the Karnal district. He found a patron in Sardar Megh Singh of Buria, in the present district of Ambala in the Panjab, and under his auspices translated a work called Amar Kosh from the Sanskrit. In A. D. 1823 ne wrote the Nanak Parkash, an exposition of the life and teachings of Guru Nanak.

After this Bhai Santokh Singh entered the employ of Maharaja Karm Singh of Patiala. In A. D. 1825, Bhai Ude Singh of Kaithal obtained his services from the Maharaja. In Kaithal Bhai Santokh Singh, with the aid of the Brahmans whom Bhai Ude Singh had placed at his disposal, translated several works from the Sanskrit. He then set about writing the lives of the remaining Gurus, completed his perusal of the Granth Sahib, and it consequently became a Sikh holiday also.

and this task he completed during the rainy season of A. D. 1843 under the name of ' Gur Partap Suraj ', popularly known as the ' Suraj Parkash', in six ponderous volumes. The lives of the Gurus, from the second to the ninth, inclu sive, are divided into twelve ras or sections, corresponding to the signs of the Zodiac. The life of the tenth Guru is pre sented in six ruts, or seasons, corresponding to the six Indian seasons, and into two ains, the ascending and descending nodes. The whole work is written in metre, and in difficult Hindi, with a large admixture of pure Sanskrit words. Santokh Singh's other works are a paraphrase of the Japji of Guru Nanak and of the Sanskrit works Atam Pur an and Valmik's Ramayan.

Bhai Ram Kanwar, a lineal descendant of Bhai Budha, was specially favoured by receiving the pahul, or baptism by the dagger, from Guru Gobind Singh himself; and on that occasion the name of Bhai Gurbakhsh Singh was bestowed on him. 1 Bhai Gurbakhsh Singh survived by twenty-five years the tenth and last Guru, and dictated his history to Bhai Sahib Singh. To the writings of the latter, which are now no longer extant, Bhai Santokh Singh is said to have been indebted. It is, however, doubtful whether Bhai Santokh Singh had access to any trustworthy authority. From his early education and environment he was largely tinctured with Hinduism. He was unquestionably a poet, and his imagination was largely stimulated by copious draughts of bhang and other intoxicants in which he freely indulged. The consequence was that he invented several stories discreditable to the Gurus and their religion. Some of his inventions are due to his exaggerated ideas of prowess and force in a bad as well as in a good causeâ a reflex of the spirit of the marauding age in which he lived. His statements accordingly cannot often be accepted as even an approach to history.

1 The genealogy of Bhai Gurbakhsh Singh is as follows: Bhiii Budha, who lived from the time of Guru Nanak to that of Guru Har Gobind, begot Bhana, who begot Sarwan, who begot Jalal, who begot Jhanda, who begot Gurditta, who begot Bhai Ram Kanwar (Gurbakhsh Singh).

We shall now notice works called Janamsakhis, which profess to be biographies of Guru Nanak. These com positions were obviously written at very different epochs after the demise of the Guru, and give very different and contradictory details of his life. In all of them miraculous acts and supernatural conversations are recorded. The question of these Janamsakhis is of such supreme impor tance, as showing the extent to which pious fiction can proceed in fabricating details of the lives of religious teachers, 1 that we must devote some space to a considera tion of them.

One of the most popular Janamsakhis is a large volume of 588 folio pages lithographed at Lahore. It is plentifully embellished with woodcuts, and its editor states that in its compilation he has expended vast pains, having collated books which he had brought from great distances at vast trouble and expense. He boasts that no one can produce such a book. If any one dare reprint it without his per mission, he shall be sued and mulcted in damages in a court of justice. The work is apparently based on Bhai Santokh Singh's Nanak Parkash.

To gain credence for a biography it is of course necessary to have a narrator, and to be assured that the narrator is no fictitious person. In the present, and indeed in all the popular Janamsakhis, which no doubt have been compiled by altering some one original volume, a person called Bhai Bala is made the narrator. He is represented as having been three years younger than Guru Nanak, and as having accompanied him in the capacity of faithful and confidential 1 Compare the manner in which Janamsakhis or gospels were multiplied in the early Christian Church. ' Vast numbers of spurious writings bearing the names of apostles and their followers, and claiming more or less direct apostolic authority, were in circulation in the early Churchâ Gospels according to Peter, to Thomas, to James, to Judas, according to the Apostles, or according to the Twelve, to Barnabas, to Matthias, to Nicodemus, c.; and ecclesiastical writers bear abundant testimony to the early and rapid growth of apocryphal literature." Supernatural Religion, vol. i, p. 292. It may be incidentally men tioned that it was the Gospel according to Barnabas which Muhammad used in the composition of the Quran.

attendant in all his wanderings. Bala is said to have dictated the biography to Paira by order of Guru Angad, the Guru next in succession to Guru Nanak. What thr value of this Janamsakhi is we shall briefly consider.

It is generally written in the current Panjabi dialect, with a slight admixture of archaic words, and no more corresponds with the dialect of the age of Guru Nanak and Guru Angad, whose compositions have descended to us and can be examined, than the English of the present day corresponds with that of Chaucer or Piers Plowman. If Paira wrote from Bala's dictation, where is the original volume, w r hich of course was written in the language of the time? When Bala proffered to dictate the biography, Guru Angad, who was well acquainted with Guru Nanak, knew so little of Bala that he is represented as having asked him whose disciple he was, and if he had ever seen Nanak. This does not appear as if Bala, supposing him to have ever existed, had been an eye-witness of Guru Nanak's deeds, or a trustworthy authority for the particulars of his life. If he had been, his fitness for the duty of biographer would have been well known to Guru Angad, who was a constant companion of Guru Nanak in the end of his life.

In Gur Das's eleventh War is found a list of well-known Sikhs up to his time. He does not state what Sikhs were converted by or lived in the time of each Guru. Mani Singh, in the Bhagat Ratanwali, has given the same list with fuller particulars of the Sikhs. Among them Bhai Bala is not mentioned. This Janamsakhi professes to have been written in the Sambat year 1592,! when Guru Nanak was still alive, and three years before Angad had obtained the Guruship. An earlier recension of the same biography professes to have been written in Sambat 1582, or thirteen years before the demise of Guru Nanak.

There were three great schisms of the Sikh religion which led to the falsification of old, or the composition of new Janamsakhis. The schismatics were known as the Udasis, 1 The Sambat or Vikramaditya era is fifty-seven years prior to annus domini. the Minas, and the Handalis. The first schism of the Sikhs began immediately after the demise of Guru Nanak. 1 Some of his followers adopted Sri Chand, his elder son, as his successor, and repudiated the nomination of Guru Angad. The followers of Sri Chand were termed Udasis, or the solitary; and they now constitute a large body of devout and earnest men. Anand Ghan, one of their number, has in recent times written the life of Guru Nanak. It contains an apotheosis of Sri Chand, and states that he was an incar nation of God, and the only true successor of Guru Nanak.

The second schismatical body of the Sikhs were the Minas. Ram Das, the fourth Guru, had three sons, Prithi Chand, Mahadev, and Arjan. Prithi Chand proved unfilial and disobedient, Mahadev became a religious enthusiast, while Arjan, the youngest, followed in the steps of his father. To Arjan, therefore, he bequeathed the Guruship. Prithi Chand he stigmatized as Mina or deceitful, a name given to a robber tribe in Rajputana. Prithi Chand, however, succeeded in obtaining a following, whom he warned against association with the Sikhs of Guru Arjan. Consequently enmity between both sects has existed up to the present time. Miharban, the son of Prithi Chand, wrote a Janamsakhi of Guru Nanak in which he glorified his own father. Here there was ample opportunity for the manipulation of details. It is in this Janamsakhi of the Minas we first find mention of Bhai Bala.

The Handalis, the third schismatic sect of the Sikhs, were the followers of Handal, a Jat of the Manjha, who had been converted to the Sikh religion by Guru Amar Das, 1 There are now several sects of the religion of Guru Nanak. It appears from the testimony of St. Paul that the early Christian Church was similarly divided. ' For it hath been declared unto me of you, my brethren, by them which are of the house of Chloe, that there are contentions among you. Now this I say that every one of you saith, I am of Paul; and I of Apollos; and I of Cephas; and I of Christ. Is Christ divided? was Paul crucified for you? or were you baptized in the name of Paul?" (i Cor. i. 11-13). Schisms appear to be the law of all religions. They began in Islam after the death of the Prophet's companions. Islam, it is said, now numbers seventy-three different sects.

the third Sikh Guru. Bidhi Chand, a descendant of Handal, was a Sikh priest at Jandiala, in the Amritsar district. He took unto himself a Muhammadan woman, whom he attached to him rather by ties of love than of law, and upon this he was abandoned by his followers.

He then devised a religion of his own, and compiled a Granth and a Janamsakhi to correspond. In both he sought to exalt to the rank of chief apostle his father Handal, and degrade Guru Nanak, the legitimate Sikh Guru. For this purpose creative fancy was largely employed. To serve the double object of debasing Guru Nanak and justify ing himself to men, he stated that Nanak had also taken unto himself a Muhammadan woman bound to him by no bonds save those of lucre and ephemeral affection.

According to this biographer, Guru Nanak, on his journey to Sach Khand, the true region, or the Land of the Leal, met the Hindu saint Dhru. One day while on earth Dhru sat on his father's lap, and was removed by his step-mother. For this trivial slight he left his home and turned his thoughts to God. God accepted his worship, and in recognition thereof offered him the highest place in heaven. The pole, as not moving, is supposed to have the position of honour, and there Vishnu set him in the centre of the stars. Dhru began to converse with Guru Nanak, and told him that only one man, Kabir, had previously been able to visit that select and happy region. Here there was a covert depreciation of Guru Nanak. Kabir, a famous religious teacher, by caste a weaver, was his precursor, and the Handali's object was to show that Guru Nanak was a follower of Kabir and not an original thinker. Guru Nanak is then represented to have said that a third man, Handal, was approaching, and would be present in the twinkling of an eye.

Guru Nanak, proceeds the Handali writer, continued his journey to Sach Khand, and there found Kabir fanning God, who is represented as the four-armed Hindu deity

Vishnu. A rude drawing in the Handali Janamsakhi represents God and Kabir in truly anthropomorphic fashion as a priest and his attendant disciple.

SIKH. I f
Nanak informed God that he had not fully carried out the orders he had obtained prior to his departure to earth and his human manifestation. He had only promulgated God's message in three directions. The western portion of the world remained still ignorant and unvisited. He was there fore remanded by God to fully accomplish his mission. On his return to earth he met in one of the lower worlds a Jogi with whom, as was his wont, he entered into familiar conversation. The Jogi, in reply to Nanak's question, told him that he had been, in a previous state of existence in the Treta age, a servant of Raja Janak, King of Mithila, and father-in-law of the renowned deified hero Ram Chandar. Nanak is made to confess to him that he, too, had been a servant of Raja Janak, and that they had both served under the same roof in the same menial capacity. The Jogi then questioned Nanak as to his secular position in the Dwapar age. Nanak is represented as saying with the same unsuspecting frankness that he had been the son of a teli or oil-presser, a trade held to be offensive and degrading to Hindus. Thus was the depreciation of Guru Nanak complete.

Such were the fictitious narratives introduced into the Janamsakhis, and, the reins of fancy having once been let loose, it was difficult for the Handalis to know at what goal to pause. The result was a total transformation of the biographies of Guru Nanak which they had found in exis tence. This occurred about the year A. D. 1640. Bidhi Chand died in the year A. D. 1654. H 8 successor was Devi Das, whom his Musalman companion bore him.

The Handali heresy was opportune for its followers. Zakaria Khan Bahadur, the Muhammadan Governor of the Panjab, about a century afterwards, set a price on the head of every Sikh. At first he offered twenty-five, then ten, and finally five rupees. The heads of Sikhs were supplied in abundance by both Musalmans and Hindus, 1 1 It was, as we shall subsequently see, a Brahman who betrayed the sons of Guru Gobind Singh, and placed them at the disposal of the Muhammadan Governor of Sarhind, who barbarously murdered them.

INTRODUCTION lxxxiii and the price offered was consequently reduced by degrees. The Handalis protested to the officials of Zakaria that they were not Sikhs of Nanak, but a totally different sect who merited not persecution; and in proof of this they pointed to their Granth, and their Janamsakhi, and to the Musalman companion of Bidhi Chand. Notwithstanding these subter fuges, the Handalis were subsequently persecuted and deprived of their land by Maharaja Ran jit Singh, but they still exist as a small community, whose head quarters are at Jandiala, where the guardians of their temple enjoy a jagir or fief from the British Government. They are now known by the name of Niranjanie, or followers of the bright God (Niranjan).

In the present age, accustomed as we are to the use and multiplication of printed books, it is not at once easy to realize how records of every description could have been forged, altered, and destroyed in an age when manuscripts only existed. It must be remembered that books then were few, and that combinations among their possessors, especially if supported by political power or religious fanaticism, could easily be effected. The Handalis appar ently had sufficient influence to destroy nearly all the older accounts of the life of Guru Nanak.

But, apart from this altogether, there is no doubt that there was a great destruction of Sikh manuscripts during the persecution of the Sikh faith by the Muhammadan authori ties. Sikh works or treatises preserved in shrines became special objects of attack. Their existence was known and could not be denied by the Sikh priests, and systematic raids were organized to take possession of them. It was only copies preserved by private individuals, living at a distance from the scenes of persecution, which had any chance of escape from the fury of the Moslems. 1 1 This finds a parallel in the destruction of Christian writings by fanatical Romans prior to the time of the Emperor Constantine. The records of the Christian persecutions show that the Christian priests who surrendered their sacred writings subsequently received severe treatment at the hands of their co-religionists. Compare the manner

All the Handali and modern Janamsakhis give Kartik as the month in which Baba Nanak was born. In Mani Singh's and all the old Janamsakhis the Guru's natal month is given as Baisakh. The following is the manner in which Kartik began to be considered as the Guru's natal month: There lived in the time of Maharaja Ran jit Singh, at Amritsar, Bhai Sant Singh Gyani, who was held in high estimation by that monarch. Some five miles from Amritsar is an ancient tank called the Ram Tirath or place of pilgrim age of the Hindu god Ram. At that place a Hindu fair was and is still held at the time of the full moon in the month of Kartik. The spot is essentially Hindu, and it had the further demerit in the eyes of the Bhai of having been repaired by Lakhpat, the prime minister of Zakaria Khan Bahadur, the inhuman persecutor of the Sikhs. Bhai Sant Singh desired to establish an opposition fair in Amritsar on the same date, and thus prevent the Sikhs from making the Hindu pilgrimage to Ram Tirath. He gravely adopted the Handali date of Guru Nanak's birth, and proclaimed that his new fair at Amritsar at the full moon in the month of Kartik was in honour of the nativity of the founder of his religion.

There is no doubt that Guru Nanak was born in Baisakh. All the older Janamsakhis give that as Guru Nanak's natal month. As late as the Sambat year 1872 it was in Baisakh that the anniversary fair of Guru Nanak's birth was always celebrated at Nankana. And finally the Nanak Parkash, which gives the full moon in Kartik, Sambat 1526, as the time of Guru Nanak's birth and the tenth of the dark half of Assu, Sambat 1596, as the date of his death, states with strange inconsistency that he lived seventy years five months and seven days, 1 a total which is irreconcilable with these dates, but it is very nearly reconcilable with the date of the Guru's birth given in the old Janamsakhi.

in which the Gospel according to the Hebrews, the Memoirs of the Apostles, and other valuable Christian records used by the early fathers of the Church, have been destroyed and lost for ever to the world.

1 The usually accepted horoscopes and ages of the Gurus are given in a work called the Gur Parndli.

How the month of Kartik was subsequently ratified by orthodox Sikhs as the month of Guru Nanak's nativity is also a curious instance of the manner in which religious anniversaries and observances can be prescribed and adopted. Bhai Harbhagat Singh, of Shahid Ganj in Lahore, was a Sikh of high consideration. He long debated in his own mind whether he would accept Baisakh or Kartik as the month of Guru Nanak's nativity. At last he submitted the matter to the arbitrament of chance. He wrote the word Baisakh on one slip of paper and Kartik on the other, placed both papers in front of the Granth Sahib, and sent an unlettered boy, who had previously performed religious ablution in the sacred tank, to take up one of them. The boy selected the one on which Kartik had been written. 1

Other reasons, too, for the alterations of the date can easily be imagined. In the beginning of the month of Baisakh there have been large Hindu fairs held from time immemorial to celebrate the advent of spring. These fairs were visited by the early Sikhs as well as by their Hindu countrymen; and it would on many accounts have been very inconvenient to make the birth of Guru Nanak synchronize with them. The comparatively small number of Sikh visitors at a special Sikh fair in the early days of the Sikh religion would have compared unfavourably with the large number of Hindu pilgrims at the Baisakhi fair, and furthermore, the selection of the month of October, when few Hindu fairs are held, and when the weather is more suitable for the distant journey to Nankana, would probably lead to a large gathering of Hindus at a Sikh shrine.

One difference of opinion among the victims of priestcraft is apt to produce many. When the month of Kartik was adopted by the Handalis as Guru Nanak's birth time, a discussion arose as to whether it was the lunar or the solar 1 In the East sacred books are often employed in this way for purposes of divination. In the Middle Ages the Bible, and in earlier times the poems of Homer, Virgil, and others, were used for the same purpose.

Kartik, there being a considerable difference between these forms of chronology. The partisans of the lunar Kartik, however, prevailed, the lunar month being the earlier form of calculation, and consequently the most acceptable to all personswhosereligion is based on anyform of Hinduism. Generally the confusion of solar and lunar chronology is the cause of much perplexity and qualms of conscience to the pious. 1

The last Janamsakhi which we shall notice was written by a Sikh called Sewa Das. 2 Of this we have obtained several copies. One of them in our possession bears the date Sambat 1645 = A. D. 1588. It was therefore completed at least sixteen years before the compilation of the Granth Sahib by Guru Arjan, which is admitted to have taken place in A. D. 1604. Its language is that of Pothohar, the country between the Jihlam and the Indus, and its written character is unmistakably more ancient than that of any other Gurumukhi book now in existence.

This Janamsakhi appears to have escaped the notice of both Gur Das and Mani Singh. Had Gur Das seen it, he would doubtless have given a fuller account of the life of Guru Nanak; and, had it been known to Mani Singh, he would probably have referred to it or criticized its details. While persecutions of the Sikhs were raging south of Lahore, and the other detailed memoirs of Guru Nanak's life, including those of Bhai Mani Singh, were destroyed, this Janamsakhi was preserved in Pothohar, where Moslem bigotry was not then aggressively exercised.

In this biography there is no mention whatever of Bhai 1 The late Bhai Gurumukh Singh, who first gave the author these details, afterwards put himself at the head of a deputation to move the Government of the Panjab to declare the fictitious anniversary of Guru Nanak's birth a public holiday. That Government accord ingly added a second Sikh holiday to the already long list of Christian, Hindu, and Muhammadan holidays sanctioned in its calendar. The other special Sikh holiday is the Hola Mahalla, the day on which the tenth Guru held a mimic battle for the instruction of his troops.

2 The late Sir Atar Singh, Chief of Bhadaur, gave the author this information.
INTRODUCTION lxxxvii

Bala. There is, however, mention made of Mardana, who undoubtedly accompanied Baba Nanak as his minstrel in most, if not all, of his wanderings. This Janamsakhi again is deformed by mythological matter which Baba Nanak himself would have been the first to repudiate.

Notwithstanding exaggerations, such as occur in all religions which deal with avatars or incarnations, the Janamsakhi now under consideration is beyond dispute the most trustworthy detailed record we possess of the life of Guru Nanak. It contains much less mythological matter than any other Gurumukhi life of the Guru, and is a much more rational, consistent, and satisfactory narrative. At the same time it is, of course, the product of legend and tradition, but these have, in at least one memorable instance, been thought more trustworthy than written records in such cases. 1 We shall make this ancient Janamsakhi the basis of our own details of the life of Guru Nanak 2, supple menting it when necessary by cullings from the later lives of the Guru. At the same time we must premise that several of the details of this and of all the current Janamsakhis appear to us to be simply settings for the verses and sayings of Guru Nanak. His followers and admirers found dainty word-pictures in his compositions. They considered under what circumstances they could have been produced, and thus devised the framework of a biography in which to exhibit them to the populace.

The deeds that have been done, the prophecies that have been uttered, and the instruction that has been imparted by that great procession of holy men, the Sikh Gurus, will be found described in the following pages. In the Gurus the East shook off the torpor of ages, and unburdened itself 1 Papias, a father of the Christian Church, who flourished about A. D. 130, wrote that he considered what he obtained from the living and abiding voice of men would profit him more in obtaining accurate details of the life of Christ than what was recorded in the gospels.

2 That accomplished Sikh scholar and saintly man, the late Bhai Dit Singh, has also made the Janamsakhi that we use the basis of his Gurumukhi life of Guru Nanak.

of the heavy weight of ultra-conservatism which had para lysed the genius and intelligence of its people. Only those who know India by actual experience can adequately appreciate the difficulties the Gurus encountered in their efforts to reform and awaken the sleeping nation.

Those who, secure in their own wisdom and infallibility, and dwelling apart from the Indian people spurn all know ledge of their theological systems, and thus deem Sikhism a heathen religion, and the spiritual happiness and loyalty of its followers negligeable items, are men whose triumph shall be short-lived and whose glory shall not descend with the accompaniment of minstrel raptures to future genera tions. I am not without hope that when enlightened rulers become acquainted with the merits of

GURU NANAK, THE FOUNDER OF THE SIKH RELIGION

SIKH I P. I
LIFE OF GURU NANAK
CHAPTER I

To recapitulate what has been more fully stated in the Introduction, Guru Nanak. the founder of the Sjkh religion, was born, according to all ancient Sikh rprords. in the early morningjpf the third day ol thÂ light half of thp month of Raisakh (April-May) in the yÂ Sr Aid. 1469; but for convenience sake his anniversary is now observed by the Sikhs on the occasion of the full moon in the month of Kartik (October-November). F father, who was called Kalu, was accountant in the village of Talwandi in the presptit-JLahor-ft. District of the Panjab, and his mother was Tripta. memorable in Sikh writings for her devation to her son.

The Sikh biographers recount in minute detail all the circumstances of the birth of Guru Nanak. Daulatan, a midwife, assisted on the occasion. When next morning interrogated by the astrologer Hardial, who came to write the child's horoscope, as to the nature of the voice uttered by him at birth, she said it was as the laughing voice of a wise man joining a social gathering; and she expressed herself at her wits' end to comprehend the child's nature. The astrologer desired to see him, but his mother refused owing to the chillness of the weather. He pressed the matter, and the child was brought to him in his swaddling clothes. The astrologer on seeing the infant is said to have worshipped him with clasped hands. He declared the child should wear the umbrella, the symbol of regal or prophetic dignity in the East. At the same time he regretted that he should never live to see young Nanak's eminence, worshipped as he should be alike by Hindus and Musalmans, and not merely by Hindus

SIKH. I B as in the previous human manifestations of the Creator. The child's name should resound both in earth and heaven. Inanimate nature should cry out ' Nanak, Nanak! ' He should have power over matter so as to traverse unscathed the depths of the ocean. He should worship and acknowledge but one God, and the creature he should treat as a creature. In other words he should be a mono-theist, not a worshipper of minor deities and idols.

At the unripe age of five years Nanak is said to have begun to talk of divine subjects, and to have fully understood the meaning of his language. Great trust was reposed in him; and both Hindus and Musalmans lavished on him their characteristic language of religious adulation.

At Nankana 1 every place with which Nanak had any association is deemed sacred. On the spot where he used to play with children of his own age and subsequently spend nights in devotion, there was a small tank constructed by Rai Bular, the landlord of the village, in affectionate remembrance of the childhood of the Guru, at a time when his fame had extended far and wide. The tank was greatly enlarged by Kaura Mai, the Diwan or financial minister of Zakaria Khan, who was satrap of Lahore. Kaura Mai was an enthusiastic admirer of Guru Nanak, and lent his great material and political influence to the amelioration of the condition of the Sikhs. The spot is called Balkrira or the child's playground.

When Nanak was seven years of age, his father in the manner of Hindus asked the village astrologer to select an auspicious time for the commencement of the boy's education. The schoolmaster thought the time had arrived. The school appears to have been a humble one, and the tuition fees not exorbitant. Kalu's wife and not, as in modern times, the village money lender was the custodian of the wealth of the house. Kalu took from her a coin corresponding to three 1 By which name Talwandi is now known.

farthings of English money, some betel-nut, and rice, and presented them to the schoolmaster with his son. In India wooden tablets painted black are employed in teaching children the letters of their language. The schoolmaster writes the letters with a kind of liquid chalk on the tablet; and the children repeat their names aloud with much noise and energy. The schoolmaster wrote the alphabet for Nanak, and the latter copied it from memory after one day.

It is said that on that occasion the young Guru made an acrostic on his alphabet. As in similar compositions in other languages, the letters were taken consecutively, and words whose initials they formed were employed to give metrical expression to the Guru's divine aspirations, his tenets, and his admiration of the attributes of the Creator.

The acrostic called the patti or tablet in the Rag 1 Asa is as follows:â

S. The one Lord who created the world is the Lord of all. Fortunate is their advent into the world, whose hearts remain attached to God's service. O foolish man, why hast thou forgotten Him? When thou adjustest thine account, my friend, thou shalt be deemed educated.

I. The Primal Being is the Giver; He alone is true. No account shall be due by the pious man who understandeth by means of these letters.

1 Indian writers enumerate six principal Rags or musical measures, namely, Sri Rag, Bhairav, Malkaus, Hindol, Dlpak, Megh. To these are allotted ' wives ' and sons', which are modifications of the principal airs, and are often sung differently in different provinces of India. The hymns of the Granth Sahib were composed to as many as thirty-one such musical measures, the names of which are as follows:â Sri Rag, Majh, Gauri, Asa, Gujari, Devgandhari, Bihagra, Wadhans, Sorath, Dhanasari, Jaitsari, Todi, Baiiari, Tilang, Suhi, Bilawal, Gaund, Ramkali, Nat, Maligaura, Maru, Tukhari, Kedara, Bhairo, Basant, Sarang, Malar, Kanra, Kalian, Prabhati, Jaijawanti. For further information see Raja Sir Surindra Mohan Tagore's learned works on Indian music. The Rags in European musical notation will be found at the end of the fifth volume of this work.

U. Praise Him whose limit cannot be found.

They who practise truth and perform service shall obtain their reward.

N. He who knoweth divine knowledge is the learned pandit. 1 He who knoweth the one God in all creatures would never say ' I exist by myself '. K. When the hair groweth white, it shineth without soap. King Death's hunters follow him who is bound by the chain of mammon. 2 K1I. The Creator, Lord of the world, giveth sustenance to His slaves. All the world is bound in His bonds; no other authority prevaileth. G. He who hath renounced the singing of God's word, is arrogant in his language. He who fashioned vessels made kilns in which He put them and burnt them. GH. The servant who performeth the Guru's 3 work, who remaineth obedient to His commands, Who deemeth bad and good as the same, shall in this way be absorbed in Him. CH. He who made the four Veds, 4 the four mines, 5 and the four ages, 6

Hath been in every age a Jogi, a worldly man, or a learned pandit.

1 Pandit means a learned man, but the title is now appropriated by Brahmans versed in Sanskrit literature.

2 Maya. In the sacred writings of the Sikhs this word has two meaningsâ one is mammon, as the word is here translated; the other is illusion or God's mystic power by which He created matter.

3 The word Guru means great. Here it stands for God. In a secondary sense it is applied to a great religious teacher.

4 They are the Rig, Sam, Yajur, and Atharv, composed in the most ancient form of the Sanskrit language. In Sikh literature they are named the white, the red, the yellow, and the black Veds.

5 In the East four sources of life are enumerated. It is there said that animals are born from eggs, wombs, the earth, and perspiration.

6 The Sat, Treta, Dwapar, and Kal, corresponding to the golden, silver, brass, and iron ages of Greece and Rome.

CHH. God's shadow is over everything; doubt is His doing.

O God, having created doubt, Thou Thyself lead-est man astray. They whom Thou favourest meet the Guru.

J. Thy slave, who wandered in the eighty-four lakhs 1 of existences, beggeth and prayeth for divine knowledge. There is One who taketh, One who giveth; I have heard of none other. JH. Why die of grief, O mortal? What God hath to give He continueth to give. He giveth, beholdeth and issueth His orders how living things are to obtain sustenance. N. When I look carefully I see no other than God.- The one God pervadeth all places; the one God dwelleth in the heart. T. O mortals, why practise deceit? Ye shall have to depart in a ghari 2 or two. Lose not the play of your lives, run and fall under

God's protection. TH. Comfort pervadeth the hearts of those whose minds are attached to God's feet. They whose minds are so attached are saved, O

Lord, and obtain happiness by Thy favour. D. O mortal, why make display? all that existeth is transitory. Serve Him who pervadeth all things, and thou shalt obtain happiness. DH. He Himself destroyeth and buildeth; He acteth as He pleaseth.

He beholdeth the work of His hands, issueth His orders, and saveth those on whom He looketh with favour. N. He in whose heart God dwelleth singeth His praises.

1 It is believed in the East that there are 8,400,000 species of animal life through which the soul may wander in transmigration. A lakh is one hundred thousand.

2 A ghari is a period of twenty-four minutes.

The Creator blendeth men with Himself, and they are not born again. T. The terrible ocean 1 is deep, and none findeth its end. We have no boat or raft; we are drowning; save us, O Saviour King. TH. He who made all things is in every place.

What do men call doubt? What mammon?

That which pleaseth God is good. D. Impute not blame to any one, but rather to thine own karma. 2 I have suffered the consequences of my acts; I may blame no one else. DH. He who made things after their kinds holdeth the power in His own hands.

All receive what He giveth under His most bounti ful order. N. The Master ever enjoyeth pleasure; He cannot be seen or grasped. I am called a married woman, my sister, but in reality I have never met my Husband. 3 P. The King, the Supreme God, made the play of the world to behold it.

He seeth, understandeth, and knoweth everything; y He is within and without His creation. PH. The whole world is entangled with a noose and bound by Death's chain.

They who by the Guru's favour have run to God for protection, are saved.

1 In Sikh writings this world is likened to a terrible and stormy ocean which can only be traversed with difficulty, and in which man is ever liable to founder without spiritual guidance. The Guru supplies a boat for salvation.

2 Karma are acts which follow the soul in its transmigration and hinder its progress to Nirvan.

3 The Gurus speak of God as a husband and themselves as His wives; and spiritual happiness they liken to connubial bliss. This belief has to some extent a parallel in Greek mythology. Psyche, the human soul, having forfeited the love of Eros, the divine soul, endured various sufferings to regain the affection of her lover.

B. God began to play by making the four ages His chaupar board. 1 He made men and lower animals His dice, and began to throw them Himself. BH. They who search and feel fear by the favour of the Guru obtain the fruit thereof. The perverse, fools that they are, wander and heed not, and so transmigrate in the eighty-four lakhs of animals. M. God destroyeth worldly love; is it only at death man is to remember Him? Other thoughts possess man and he forgetteth the letter M. 2 Y. If man recognize the True One, he shall not be born again.

The holy man uttereth, the holy man understand-eth, the holy man knoweth but the one God. R. God pervadeth all the creatures He hath made. Having created creatures He appointed them all to their duties; they to whom He is kind take His name. L. He who appointed creatures to their duties, made worldly love sweet. He giveth eating and drinking equally to all, and ordereth them as He pleaseth. W. The Supreme Being who created the vesture of the world to behold it, Seeth, tasteth, and knoweth everything; He is contained within and without the world. R. Why quarrel, O mortal? meditate on God, under whose order is creation. Meditate on Him; be absorbed in the True One; and be a sacrifice unto Him.

H. There is no other Giver than He who created crea tures and gave them sustenance. Meditate on God's name; be absorbed in God's 1 Chaupar is the Indian draughts.

2 The initial of Madhusudan, one of the names applied to God. It may also be the initial of the Arabic word maut, death.

name, and thou shall night and day derive profit therefrom. A. What God who made the world hath to do He con- tinueth to do.

He acteth and causeth others to act; He knoweth everything; thus saith the poet Nanak.

Nanak appears to have continued to attend school for some time. One day he was observed to remain silent, and not apply himself to his books. The schoolmaster asked him why he was not reading. Nanak inquired, ' Art thou sufficiently learned to teach me? ' The schoolmaster replied that he had read everything. He knew the Veds and Shastars, 1 and he had learned to cast up accounts, post ledgers and daybooks, and strike balances. Upon this Nanak said, ' To your accomplishments I prefer the study of divine knowledge '. He then composed the following hymn:â

Burn worldly love, grind its ashes and make it into ink; 2 turn superior intellect into paper.

Make divine love thy pen, and thy heart the writer; ask thy guru and write his instruction.

Write God's name, write His praises, write that He hath neither end nor limit.

0 master, learn to write this account,

So that, whenever it is called for, a true mark may be found thereon.

There 3 greatness is obtained, everlasting joys, and ever lasting delights.

They in whose hearts is the true Name, have the marks of it on their brows.

1 Sanskrit works on the six philosophical systems of the Hindus. They areâ the Nyaya founded by Gautama, the Vaisheshika by Kanada, the Sankhya by Kapila, the Yoga by Patanjali, the Mimansa by Jaimini, the Vedant by Vyas. The six systems have been learnedly expounded by Max Miiller in his Indian Philosophy.

2 At that time in India ink was made from burnt almond-rind and gum.

3 Corresponding to e ei in Greek, the next world.

By God's mercy men obtain it and not by idle words.

One man cometh, another goeth; we give them great names. 1

Some men God created to beg, and some to preside over great courts.

When they have departed, they shall know that without the Name 2 they are of no account.

I greatly fear Thine anger; 0 God, my body pineth and wasteth away.

They who have been called kings and lords are beheld as ashes.

Nanak, 3 when man departeth all false affections are sundered. 4

Upon this the schoolmaster became astonished, did Nanak homage as a perfect saint, and told him to do what he pleased.

Nanak, having thus shown his scholastic proficiency, left school and took to private study and meditation. He remained for long periods in the same attitude, whether sleeping or waking, and associated continually with religious men.

The scholastic ignorance of the founders of great 1 Literallyâ we call them commanders. This refers to the custom of parents giving their sons high-sounding names.

2 In the Sikh writings the word Name is frequently used for God. A somewhat similar practice was known to the ancient Jews (Amos vi. 10). At a time too early to be traced the Jews abstained from pro nouncing the name Jehovah for fear of its irreverent use, and uttered instead Adonai or Lord. In connexion with this we may say that the repetition of God's name is one of the principal forms of Sikh wor ship. Set forms of prayer are apt to be repeated mechanically or ostentatiously; and it was believed that by the constant heartfelt repetition of God's name man should be eventually absorbed in Him, and thus obtain the supreme object of human birth after countless transmigrations.

3 In Oriental poetical works it is usual for the poet to insert his real or assumed nameâ akhallusâ 'm the end of a composition or section of a composition. This practice is unknown to European poets except in the case of professed imitators of Oriental poetry. Were we there fore to omit the word c Nanak' wherever it occurs, we should be consult ing the taste of European readers, but the Sikhs do not desire such an omission. 4 Sri Rag.

religions has been made the subject of many a boast on the part of their followers. The object, of course, is that the acquirements and utterances of the religious teachers may be attributed solely to divine inspiration. We see no reason for ascribing a want of education to the founder of the Sikh religion; and the manner in which his learning was acquired is not difficult to understand. Had he remained at the humble village school, there is no reason to suppose that he would have acquired any considerable knowledge, but in the dense forests around Talwandi were to be found ascetics and anchorets who sought the extreme retirement of the locality for the com bined objects of undisturbed prayer and escape from the persecution of bigoted Moslem rulers. All the Janamsakhis are unanimous in stating that Nanak courted the retirement of the forest and the society of the religious men who frequented it. Several of them were profoundly versed in the Indian religious literature of the age. They had also travelled far and wide within the limits of Hindustan, and met its renowned religious teachers. Nanak thus became acquainted with the latest teachings of Indian philosophers and reformers. The satisfaction which he derived from spiritual thought and religious association he thus expressed: â Let Jogis practise Jog, 1 let gluttons practise gluttony, Let penitents practise penance, and rub and bathe them selves at places of pilgrimage;

But let me listen to Thy songs, O Beloved, if any will sit and sing them to me.

The names of the men with whom Nanak associ ated in the forest and who sang to him the songs of the Lord are all lost, and their excellences merged as connected with the Greek Â uyov, originally meant the union of the soul with God, and may be compared with the etymo logical meaning of the word ' religion '. They who practised Jog were called Jogis. The word Jog is now applied to certain practices of the Jogis which are detailed in the Aphorisms of Patanjali.

by a process of nirvan in the religious splendour of the founder of the Sikh religion. But more perhaps than learning from the lips of religious masters were his own undisturbed communings with nature, with his own soul, and with his Creator. The voice that had spoken to many a seer again became vocal in that wilderness, and raised Nanak's thoughts to the summit of religious exaltation. In summer's heat and winter's frost, in the glory of the firmament, in the changeful aspects of nature, as well as in the joys and sorrows of the inhabitants of his little natal vil lage, he read in bright characters and repeated with joyous iteration the name of the Formless Creator. The Name henceforth became the object of his continual worship and meditation and indeed one of the distinctive features of his creed.

As a man soweth so shall he reap; as he earneth so shall he eat.

No inquiry shall be made hereafter regarding the utterers of the Name. With banners flying shall they go to heaven. 1

Men are judged according to their acts.

The breath drawn without the thought of God is wasted in vain.

I would sell this body if only I found a purchaser.
Nanak, the body which is not filled with the true Name is of no account. 2

There is also proof from the satisfactory internal evidence of his own compositions that Guru Nanak studied the Persian language. Kalu felt that the society of religious men was not likely to advance his son's secular interests. Rai Bular promised that if Nanak learned Persian, in which all state documents and accounts were then written, he would appoint him village accountant in succession to his father. Persian was never the tongue of Hindus, and was despised by them as the language of foreigners and conquerors 1 San nishanaijai. Also translatedâ if they bear Thy mark.

2 SQhi.

and of impure Musalman literature; 1 but Hindus in the age of Nanak applied themselves to it as they do nowâ for the simple purpose of obtaining a liveli hood. Nanak soon astonished his Persian as he had previously astonished his Hindu teacher. In reply to Rukn-ul-Din's injunctions he assumed the role of teacher in turn and composed the following acrostic on the letters of the Persian alphabet:â

ALIF. Remember God and banish neglect of Him from thy heart. Accursed the life of him in this world who breatheth without uttering the Name. BE. Renounce heresy and walk according to the Shariat. 2

Be humble before every one, and call no one bad. TE. Repent with sincerity of heart lest thou afterwards grieve. Thy body shall perish: thy mouth shall be buried with it; what canst thou do then? SE. Praise God very much; draw not thy breath with out doing so, Or thou shalt be offered for sale from shop to shop, and not an adh 3 shall be obtained for thee. JIM. Put together travelling expenses, and pack up where withal to go with thee:

Without the Lord thou shalt trudge about wearily. HE. Embrace humility, renounce the pride of thy heart; Restrain thy wandering mind, O Rukn-ul-Din, and every moment remember thy Creator. KHE. They were traitors who forgot their Creator; 1 In the institutes of Parasar there is found an injunction not to speak the language of the inhabitants of Yavanâ a word which originally meant Greece, but was afterwards applied to Arabiaâ even though it save life from issuing by the throat. Parasar possessed the Hindu abhorrence of strange countries and gave expression to it. His words are now understood by the Hindus to refer to the language of the Musalmans, though there were no Musalmans for centuries after his time.

2 Muhammadan law.

3 About an eighth of a farthing of English money.

Their minds were bent on the hoarding of wealth, and they bore loads of sin upon their heads. DAL. Be honest, O man, and sleep not during the eight watches of day and night.

Awake for one watch and hold converse with God. ZAL. Remember God, O man, vacillate not an iota;

So shall hell fire not touch thee at all, and thy covetousness and worldly love be at an end. RE. The advantage of faith thou shalt know when thou arrivest before Godâ Restrain the five evil passions, 1 O Rukn-ul-Din, and apply thy heart to God. ZE. Practise humility, the Lord is independent;

He doeth what he pleaseth; what certainty is there regarding His acts? SIN. Search thy heart; the Lord is in thee.

The body is a vessel which He wrought, and into which He infused His workmanship and skill. SHIN. Thou shalt obtain martyrdom if thou die for the love of the dear One. O Rukn-ul-Din, this human body shall depart; while in it pray to obtain God. SUAD. Let thy mind be contented when thou obtainest thine allotted food. God who gave thee the disease of hunger is thy physician. ZUAD. God's splendour is lost for those who associate themselves with worldly affairs. Arise, look before thee, and regard not the play of the world. TOE. Embrace tariqat and enter upon marafat; 2VX

This body of thine shall become a heap of dust in the grave. ZOE. They were tyrants who heeded not the Name: 1 Lust, anger, covetousness, worldly love, and pride. v 2 There are four stages of Sufiism: Shariat, the law or external ceremonies; Tariqat, walking in God's way; Marafat, Divine know ledge; Haqiqat, certainty or union with God. Many learned natives of India believe that the Sufi system is based on Vedant.

How can man obtain peace without his Master?. 'AIN. Practise good works to the best of thy power:

Without good works and virtues man shall die full of regret.

GHAIN. O Rukn-ul-Din, they are rich who know them selvesâ In this cage of the body God who hath neither mother nor father sporteth.

FE. Have done with the world, and think it not thine own: If thou deem it to belong to God, thou shalt not be confounded. QAF. They in whose hearts the love of God hath arisen shall have no rest till they find Him. The bodies of those who have met the Lord God have become refined gold.

KAF. Remember thy creed; in what else is there profit? O Rukn-ul-Din, be not excessively addicted to sensuality. GAF. Man's mind is wanton; if thou restrain it,

Thou shalt plant thy feet firmly on the way to haqiqat.

LAM. May curses rain on those who abandon their prayers! They lose whatever little or much they have earned. MIM. Wilfulness is prohibited; walk as thy religious guide directeth thee. The wealth of those, saith Nanak, who have not given alms shall slip away.

NUN. Look to truth alone, and know that the world is false. They who think the world is true shall die con founded. WAW. They become saints who associate with the true.

The more they remember God, the more they love
Him.

HE. Be in fear of that day when God will judge thee What order will He pass in our case, O Rukn-ul-Din?

LAM. They on whom He casteth His look of mercy have become worthy.
LIFE OF GURU NANAK 15-

What is desire for life if a man regulate not his own conduct? ALIF. God is in thee; why thinkest thou not on Him,

O ignorant man? By service to the guru God is found, and deliverance obtained at last. YE. Love God whose empire is everlasting.

He is unrivalled, O Nanak, and in need of no one. 1

There are numerous Persian words and some Persian verses of the Guru found in the Granth Sahib, and it may be accepted as a fact that he became a fair Persian scholar. It is highly probable that his habit of free thought and toleration for other men's opinions were assisted by his perusal of the Muham-madan writings with which the Persian language abounds.

It does not appear that even the acquisition of Persian tended to give Nanak's thoughts a more practical direction. His father thought him insane, and was sore distressed for his future. He, how ever, sent him to herd buffaloes in the adjoining forest. Matters progressed smoothly for one day, but the next day Nanak fell asleep, and his cattle trespassed on a neighbour's field. The owner remonstrated, but Nanak said that God would bless the field. The owner was not to be diverted by this unpractical defence. He complained to Rai Bular, and the latter, hearing that Nanak was insane, was not content to send for him, but also for his father to adjust the quarrel. Nanak said that no injury had befallen the field: it was blessed by God. Rai Bular sent his own messengers to inspect the spot. On their arrival they found that not one blade had been trampled on or eaten. The field where this miracle is said to have occurred is pointed out to 'â visitors. It is known as the Kiara Sahib, or the parterre par excellence.

1 This composition is not found in the Granth Sahib. Some Sikhs deny that it is the composition of Guru Nanak.

CHAPTER II

When Nanak had attained the age of nine years, his father determined to have him invested with the janeu, or sacrificial thread of the Hindus. Until a boy is so invested, he is deemed almost an out cast. When the members and relations of the family, and all the neighbours, secular and religious, had assembled, and all preliminary rites had been duly performed, Hardial, the family priest, pro ceeded to put the sacred thread on Nanak's neck. The boy caught the thread with his hand, and asked the priest what he was doing, and what advantage it was to put a thread of that description on him. The priest then explained that the janeu was the basis of the Hindu religion, that without it a man would only be a Sudar, 1 and that by putting it on greatness should be obtained in this world and happiness in the next. On hearing this the young Guru gave utterance to the following:â

Make mercy thy cotton, contentment thy thread, con tinence its knot, truth its twist.

That would make a janeu for the soul; if thou have it, O Brahman, then put it on me.

It will not break, or become soiled, or be burned, or lost.

Blest the man, O Nanak, who goeth with such a thread on his neck.

Thou purchasest a janeu for four damris, 2 and seated in a square puttest it on; 1 There are four great varans or castes of Hindusâ Brahmans, the priestly class; Kshatris, the militant class; Vaisyas, the trading class; and Shudars, the working class, the lowest of all. Of these castes there are now many subdivisions.

2 Four damris is one paisa of Indian, or a farthing of English money.

Thou whisperest instruction that the Brahman is the guru of the Hindus â

Man dieth, the janeu falleth, and the soul departeth without it. 1

The priest explained that the custom of wearing a janeu had descended from the Vedic ritual, and that no Hindu could be deemed religious without wearing it. The

Brahman then familiarly addressed the Guru, ' Thou art but a child of yesterday, and are we not as wise as thou? Unless thou wear this thread thou shalt be deemed a person without religion." Guru Nanak replied:â

Though men commit countless 2 thefts, countless adul teries, utter countless falsehoods and countless words of abuse;

Though they commit countless robberies and villanies night and day against their fellow creatures;

Yet the cotton thread is spun, and the Brahman cometh to twist it.

For the ceremony they kill a goat and cook and eat it, and everybody then saith ' Put on the janeu '.

When it becometh old, it is thrown away, and another is put on.

Nanak, the string breaketh not if it be strong.

The Brahman priest, on hearing this, became angry, and asked the Guru if everybody else was a fool, and he alone, who had abandoned the customs of his forefathers, was wise. He then called on the Guru to tell him what a proper janeu was. The Guru replied:â

By adoring and praising the Name honour and a true thread are obtained.

In this way a sacred thread shall be put on, which will not break, and which will be fit for entrance into God's court.

1 Asa ki War. This composition will subsequently be given in extenso, and the meaning of the word war explained.

2 Lakh. Here used for an indefinite number.

The Guru then wound up his instruction on the subject as follows:â

There is no string for the sexual organs, there is no string for women;

There is no string for the impure acts which cause your beards to be daily spat upon;

There is no string for the feet, there is no string for the hands;

There is no string for the tongue, there is no string for the eyes.

Without such strings the Brahman wandereth astray,

Twisteth strings for the neck, and putteth them on others.

He taketh hire for marrying;

He pulleth out a paper, and showeth the fate of the wedded pair.

Hear and see, ye people, it is strange 7 That, while mentally blind, man is named wise. 1

We have seen in the Introduction to this work that Sultanpur was then the capital of the Jalandhardoab. At that time and up to the period of British occupa tion, land revenue was generally collected in kind. 2 Surveyors and appraisers called Amils were dis patched from the capital to different districts. Amil Jai Ram was appointed to appraise the revenue demand of Talwandi. While one day surveying a corn-field, he observed Nanaki, sister of Nanak, draw ing water from a well, and saw that she was fair to look upon. A marriage between them was arranged through the kind offices of Rai Bular. The lady went and lived with her husband at Sultanpur.

Nanak's marriage must have taken place soon after his sister's. It is related in the Janamsakhi which bears the name of Mani Singh, that Nanak was married at the age of fourteen. His marriage, as is usual in the East, was arranged for him as a matter of religious duty by his parents. He was 1 Asa ki War.

2 Under the Emperor Akbar it was often optional for the husbandman to pay either in money or in kind. Ain-i-Akbari, Book III, Ain 13.

betrothed to Sulakhani, daughter of Mula, a resident of Batala 1 in the present district of Gurdaspur. It would appear that, owing to the distance between Nankana and Batala, which hindered frequent visits and negotiations, the marriage followed very soon after the betrothal. Nanak's sister was present at the wedding, but her husband could not obtain per mission to attend. He sent word that he was another person's servant, an apology that was perfectly understood.

Nanak appears to have been further trusted in the capacity of a herdsman. While one day herd ing his buffaloes, he lay down to sleep under a tree during the midday heat. Rai Bular passing by in the evening found him in that attitude, and observed that the protecting shadow of the tree had remained stationary over him, and not veered round like the 5 shadows of the other trees with the sun's progress. On another occasion, as Nanak lay asleep in the S pasture ground, it was observed that a large cobra watched over him, and protected the youthful saint with its hood. Rai Bular acknowledged the mira culous powers of the boy, and congratulated Kalu on being the father of such a son. Kalu ought no longer to be displeased with him for his indifference to his worldly affairs. He was a very great man. A jal-tree, 2 gnarled and maimed by the centuries, is still pointed out as the scene of the former miracle. It possesses a thick trunk, is still gratefully umbra geous, and its venerable branches depend to the earth in a fashion that suggests the pillared shade of the Indian fig-tree.

Nanak still persisted in doing no useful work, and his mother reproached him with his idleness. She counselled him to rise, work for his livelihood, and cease weaving unpractical discourses. She told him 1 Her place of birth in Batala is revenerced by the Sikhs. Maha raja Sher Singh erected a temple in her honour.

2 The Salvador a Oleoides.

that he was popularly credited with madness; but he paid no heed to her admonitions further than to compose the following hymn on the occasion:â

He who dieth in obstinacy shall not be accepted.
Even though man wear a religious garb and apply much ashes to his body,
Yet, if he forget the Name, he shall afterwards repent.
0 man, obey God and thou shalt be happy.
If thou forget the Name, thou shalt have to endure Death's torture.
They who apply distilled aloe-wood, sandal, and camphor to their bodies,
Are immersed in worldly love, and far from the supreme dignity of salvation.
They who forget the Name are the falsest of the false.
They who are guarded by lances, for whom bands play, who sit on thrones, and are objects of salutation,
Suffer from excessive avarice and lust.
Being without God they pray not for His service or His name.
God is found not by argument or by pride.
If man apply his mind he shall find the comforting Name. '
They who love mammon are painfully ignorant.

Without money goods cannot be had from a shop;
Without a boat man cannot cross the sea;
So, without serving the Guru, there is complete loss.
Hail, hail to him who showeth the road!
Hail, hail to him who communicateth the Word!
Hail, hail to him who blendeth us with God!
Hail, hail to Him to whom the soul belongeth!
Under the Guru's instruction separate the true from the false, and drink it as nectar.
The greatness of the Name is bestowed according to Thy pleasure, 0 God.
Without the Name how could I live, O mother?
Night and day 1 1 repeat it and remain, 0 Lord, under Thy protection.

Nanak, he who is imbued with the Name obtaineth honour. 2 1 Anudm, translated 'night and day' by the gyanis, is literallyâ every day. 2 Gauri Ashtapadi.

After this Nanak lay down, remained in one posi tion for four days, and declined all physical exertion.

Nanak appears to have become unfitted for all secular occupation. His idleness became notorious, and a serious source of anxiety to his parents. His mother sought to lead him with mild admonitions to secular duty, but fortunately failed. His father then addressed himself to the task. He represented that he required assistance in the culti vation of his land, and Nanak was now of an age to turn his attention to agriculture. Nanak replied:â

Make thy body the field, good works the seed, irrigate with God's name;

Make thy heart the cultivator; God will germinate in thy heart, and thou shalt thus obtain the dignity of nirvan. 1

His father and Rai Bular represented that that was not the way to become a husbandman, whose business ought to be manual labour, and whose object was to gain a livelihood. Upon this Nanak composed the following:â

Become a husbandman, make good works thy soil, and the word of God thy seed; 2 ever irrigate with the water of truth.

Faith shall germinate, and thus even a fool shall know the distinction between heaven and hell.

Think not that thou shalt find the Lord by mere words.

In the pride of wealth and the splendour of beauty life hath been wasted.

The sin of the body is a puddle, the mind is a toad therein, which valueth not at all the lotus.

The bumble-bee is the teacher, 3 who preacheth incessantly; but can the guru cause a man to understand who will not understand? 4 1 Sri Rag.

2 Also translatedâ Clear thy ground, make the Word thy seed.

3 That is, the Guru.

4 The body is compared to a puddle; the mind to a toad which loves the puddle, but sets no value on the beautiful lotus of spiritual wisdom. The spiritual guide, like the bee, unceasingly hums his message.

Preaching and listening are as the sough of the wind, when man's mind is tinctured by the illusions of the world.

The Lord casteth a look of favour, and is well pleased with those who meditate on Him alone.

Even though thou perform the thirty days' fast, and make the five prayers thy daily companions, yet he who is called Satan will cut the thread of thy thoughts. 1

Nanak saith, man must depart; why amass property and wealth? 2

On the same occasion the Guru uttered the fol lowing:â

Make thy mind the ploughman, good acts the cultiva tion, modesty the irrigating water, and thy body the field to till,

The Name the seed, contentment the harrow, and the garb of humility thy fence:

By the work of love the seed will germinate; thou mayest behold happy the homes of persons who thus act.

0 father, mammon accompanieth not man when he de-parteth:

Mammon hath allured this world, and few there are who understand it.

Then Nanak informed his father that he had sown his own field, and that its harvest was now ready. He had such confidence in his tillage, that, even after deduction of the portion paid in kind to the government as revenue, the full produce would still remain. Sons, daughters, beggars, brethren, and relations would all be profited thereby. He had done farming work for God, who had treated him as a lord does his tenants, and the day that he effected union with his Creator, his soul within him would be glad.

1 That is, make thy thoughts wander. For man in the old Panjabi life of the Guru the Granth Sahib has mat. The line may then be translatedâ Perform the thirty days' fast of the Musalmans, make their five daily prayers thy companions, and take care lest Satan destroy the effect of thy prayers. 2 Sri Rag.

On hearing this, his father told him to keep a shop, for a shop was as profitable as tillage. Nanak replied:â

Make the knowledge that life is frail thy shop, the true Name thy stock-in-trade;

Make meditation and contemplation thy piles of vessels; put the true Name into them.

Deal with the dealers of the true Name, and thou shalt gladly take home thy profits.

Then again Kalu said, ' If thou desire not to be a shopkeeper, take horses and deal in them. Thy heart is sad; but do something for thy livelihood, and visit foreign countries. We will say that thou hast gone to earn thy living, and that thou wilt soon return." Upon this Nanak uttered a third stanza:â

Make thy hearing of the sacred books thy merchandise, truth the horses thou takest to sell;

Tie up virtues as thy travelling expenses, and think not in thy heart of to-morrow.

When thou arrivest in the land of God, thou shalt obtain happiness in His abode.

Kalu in despair replied, ' Thou art lost to us; go and take government service. Jai Ram, Daulat Khan's revenue officer, is thy brother-in-law; go and take service with him; perhaps thou wilt like that place; we can dispense with thine earnings. If thou go elsewhere without any occupation, every body will say that my son hath become a faqir, and people will heap reproaches on me." Upon this, Guru Nanak uttered a fourth stanza:â

Make attention thy service, faith in the Name thine occupa tion;

Make the restraint of evil thine effort, so shall men con gratulate thee.

1 In which the Indian petty shopkeeper keeps his goods.

God will then look on thee, O Nanak, with an eye of favour, and thy complexion shall brighten fourfold. 1

Nanak then informed his father that God had granted him the object of his prayers. The gains of commerce, of government service, and of banking, had all been imparted to him. The astonished father said he had never seen or heard of a God who granted so many favours. Nanak replied that his God was the object of praise to those who had seen Him:â

As men have heard, O Lord, so all call Thee great;
But hath any one ever seen how great Thou art? 2
Thy worth cannot be estimated or described;
They who seek to describe it are absorbed in Thee.
0 my great Lord, deep and profound, brimful of excel lences,
None knoweth the extent of Thine outline.
Though all meditative men were to meet and meditate upon Thee,
Though all appraisers were to meet and appraise Theeâ
They who possess divine and spiritual wisdom, priests, and high priests 3 â
Yet could they not describe even a small portion of Thy greatness.
All truth, all fervour, all goodness,
The excellences of perfect men,
Cannot be obtained in their perfection without Thee.
If Thy grace be obtained none can be excluded;
Of what account is the helpless speaker?
Thy store-rooms are filled with Thy praises.
Who can prevail against him to whom Thou givest?
Nanak, the True One arrangeth all. 4

His father was not satisfied, but further remon- 1 Sorath.

2 Also translatedâ How great He is whoever hath seen Him could tell.

3 Gurhai, translated high priests, is really the Persian plural of guru. Compare the words Shaikh mashdtkh, so frequently found in the Granth Sahib. Mashaikh is, of course, the Arabic plural of shaikh.

4 Asa.

strated with Nanak. He enjoined him to abandon his whims and act like others, as no one could live without worldly occupation. Nanak was not con vinced, so his father in despair left him and went to attend to his ordinary business. Nanak's mother again attempted the worldly reformation of her son. She requested him to forget even for a few days his devotions and go abroad, so that the neighbours might be assured that Kalu's son had recovered his reason. Nanak then uttered the following verses in the Rag Asa:â

If I repeat the Name, I live; if I forget it, I die; 1
It is difficult to repeat the true Name.
If a man hunger after the true Name,
His pain shall depart when he satisfieth himself with it. 2
Then how could I forget it, O my mother?
True is the Lord, true is His name;

Men have grown weary of uttering
Even an iota of His greatness; His worth they have not discovered.
If all men were to join and try to describe Him,
That would not add to or detract from His greatness.
God dieth not, neither is there any mourning for Him;
He continueth to give us our daily bread which never faileth.
His praise isâ that there neither is,
Nor was, nor shall be any one like unto Him.
As great as Thou art Thyself, O God, so great is Thy gift.
Thou who madest the day madest also the night.
They who forget their Spouse 3 are bad characters; 4
Nanak, without His name they are naught. 5 1 Of course, spiritual life and death are meant.

2 Literallyâ the pain of that hungry man shall depart on eating the Name, that is, on receiving it as food. The verse is also translatedâ His pain shall depart; all his desires shall be merged in his hunger for the Name.

1 The allusion here is to men forgetting God.

4 A colloquial meaning of the word kamjdt, which literally means inferior caste.

5 Sana, a plural form of san, a year, or an age. The word was

Then his mother arose and told the household of Nanak's state. Upon this the whole family and relations grew sad, and said it was a great pity that Kalu's son had become mad.

His uncle Lalu among others exerted himself to console the young prophet. He represented to Nanak that all his relations had fixed on an occupa tion for him, but he had refused to adopt it. On the contrary, he would do nothing whatever, not even enjoy himself. Nanak then gave utterance to the following hymn, which, however, is not found in the Granth Sahib:â

All men are bound by entanglements; how can these be called good qualities?

Nay, O Lalu, listen to the following qualities:â Forgiveness is my mother, contentment my father, Truth by which I have subdued my heart my uncle, Love of God my brother, affection mine own begotten son,

Patience my daughterâ I am pleased with such relationsâ Peace my companion, wisdom my discipleâ This is my family in whom I ever rejoice. The one God who adorned us all is my Lord. Nanak, he who forsaketh Him and clingeth to another shall suffer misery.

Guru Nanak then became silent, lay down, and ate and drank nothing. The whole family repre sented to Kalu that something ought to be done for his son. A physician ought to be called, and medicine prescribed. ' Who knows but that behind a straw there is a lakh? ' that is, by a small expenditure Nanak may recover. Upon this, Kalu went and brought a physician. The physician came, and began to feel Nanak's pulse. He withdrew his arm, and, drawing in his feet, stood up and said, ' O applied to coin which had long circulated, and which had conse quently worn away and become worthless.

physician, what art thou doing? ' The physician said that he was diagnosing his disease. Upon this Nanak laughed, and then uttered the following verses:â

The physician is sent for to prescribe a remedy; he taketh my hand and feeleth my pulse.
The ignorant physician knoweth not that it is in my mind the pain is. 1
Physician, go home; take not my curse with thee.
I am imbued with my Lord; to whom givest thou medicine?
When there is pain, the physician standeth ready with a store of medicine:
The body is weeping, the soul crieth out, ' Physician, give none of thy medicine."
Physician, go home, few know my malady.
The Creator who gave me this pain, will remove it.
The physician asked Nanak what he himself thought his illness was. Nanak replied:â
I first feel the pain of separation from God, then a pang of hunger for contemplation on Him.
I also fear the pain which Death's powerful myrmidons may inflict.
I feel pain that my body shall perish by disease.
0 ignorant physician, give me no medicine.
Such medicine as thou hast, my friend, removeth not The pain I feel or the continued suffering of my body.
1 forgot God and devoted myself to pleasure; Then this bodily illness befell me.
The wicked heart is punished. Ignorant physician, give me no medicine. As sandal is useful when it exhaleth perfume, As man is useful as long as he hath breath in his body, So when the breath departeth, the body crumbleth away and becometh useless:
No one taketh medicine after that.
1 Malar ki War.
When man shall possess the Name of the Bright and Radiant 1 One,
His body shall become like gold and his soul be made pure;
All his pain and disease shall be dispelled,
And he shall be saved, Nanak, by the true Name. 2
The following was on the same subject:â
Pain is arsenic, the name of God is the antidote.
0 ignorant man, take such medicines As shall cure thee of thy sins.
Make contentment thy mortar, the gift of thy hands thy pestle:
By ever using these the body pineth not away,
Nor at the final hour shall Death pommel thee.
Make enjoyments thy firewood, covetousness thy clarified butter and oil.
Burn them with the oil of lust and anger in the fire 3 of divine knowledge.
Burnt offerings, sacred feasts, and the reading of the Purans, 4
If pleasing to God, are acceptable.
Empire, wealth, and youth are all shadows;
So are carriages and imposing mansions.
Hereafter neither man's name nor his caste shall be considered.
There is day, here all is night.
Let us make penitence the paper, 5 Thy name, 0 Lord, the prescription.
They for whom this priceless medicine is prescribed, 1 Also translatedâ When man possesseth even a portion of the name of the Bright One.

2 Malar.

3 It was intended by his parents to make a horn sacrifice or burnt offering for Nanak's recovery. The Sanskrit word horn is interpreted to mean casting into the fire, and correctly represents the oblation of clarified butter, sesames, butter, c., which forms part of the ceremonial.

4 Sacred books of the Hindus, eighteen in number. They are the principal authorities for the idolatry and superstition of the Hindus.

5 To write a prescription on.

Are fortunate when they reach their final home.

0 Nanak, blessed are the mothers who bore them. 1

Then the physician drew back, stood still, and said that Nanak was not ill. His relations and friends ought to feel no anxiety for him, for he was a great being. Upon this the physician worshipped him and took his leave.

There is very little known regarding Nanak's married life excepting that he begot two sons, Sri Chand and Lakhmi Das. It was related that he used to retire to the desert, and pass his time under trees in religious contemplation.

All the modern Janamsakhis make Nanak's marriage long subsequent to this, and after his departure to Sultanpur. They say that it was Jai Ram who had him married, and that his wife was a native of Pakkho, a town not far from Sultanpur. We have followed Mani Singh and the old Janamsakhi. If Nanak had been left to his own discretion, and if his marriage had not been made for him by his parents, it is most probable that he would not have turned his attention to that part of a man's duties after entering the service of the government in Sultanpur. This will subsequently be understood when we come to consider his mode of life at that capital.

CHAPTER III

The Guru, on one occasion seeing his parents and relations standing around him to consider his condition, composed a hymn in the Rag Gauri Cheti:-

Since when have I a mother? Since when a father? Whence have we come?

1 Malar.

2 Gauri is a ragini or consort of Sri Rag, and has nine varieties one of which is the Cheti.

From fire and bubbles of water are we sprung; for what object were we created?

My Lord, who knoweth Thy merits?

My demerits cannot be numbered.

How many shrubs and trees have we seen! how many beasts created by Thee!

How many species of creeping things, and how many birds hast Thou caused to fly!

Men break through the shops and great houses of cities and stealing therefrom go homewards.

They look before them, they look behind them, but where can they hide themselves from Thee?

The banks of streams of pilgrimage, the nine regions â of the earth, shops, cities, and market-places have I seen.

Becoming a shopkeeper I take a scale and try to weigh my actions in my heart.

My sins are numerous as the waters of the seas and the ocean.

Bestow compassion, extend a little mercy, save me who am like a sinking stone.
My soul is burning like fire; it is as though shears were cutting my heart.
Nanak humbly representethâ he who obeyeth God's order is happy day and night.
2

Kalu then desired that his son should embrace a mercantile life. He instructed him to go to Chuharkana in the present district of Gujranwala, and buy there salt, turmeric, and other articles to trade with. Nanak set out with a servant, and on the way met some holy men, whose vows obliged them to remain naked in all seasons. Nanak was struck with this peculiarity, and inquired of their head-priest Santren if they had no clothes to wear, or if, having clothes, they found it uncomfortable to

L The ancient Indian Geographers divided the earth into nine regions or continents.
2 Gauri.

wear them. Before he could receive an answer, Nanak was reminded by his servant of his more practical mission, and counselled to proceed to Chuharkana in obedience to his father's instructions. Nanak, however, was not to be thwarted in his object. He pressed the priest for an answer. The priest replied that his company required not clothes or food, except in so far as the latter was voluntarily bestowed on them. To avoid all luxury they dwelt in forests, and not in peopled towns and villages. Nanak thought he had found what he had sought for, and said to his servant that he had already obeyed his father's instructions, which were to spend his money to the best advantage. He therefore gave the holy men the money with which his father had provided him. Upon this they asked him his name, and he said that he was Nanak Nirankari, or Nanak the worshipper of the Formless One, that is, God. Nanak was prevailed upon to take the money to the nearest village to buy food jfor the holy men, who had not tasted any for some â days.

When the faqirs took their departure, Nanak was censured by his servant for his reckless prodigality. He then realized the nature of his act, and did not go home, but sat under a tree outside the village of Talwandi. He was there found by his father, who cuffed him for his dis obedience. The aged tree under which he sat is still preserved. A wall has been built around it for protection. Within the enclosure are found religious men in prayer and contemplation. The tree is known as the Thamb Sahib, or the holy trunk.

Jai Ram, during his yearly visits to Talwandi at the close of the spring harvest, had ample oppor tunities of cultivating Nanak's acquaintance, and appreciating his good qualities. Rai Bular, too, was no apathetic advocate of Nanak. It was agreed between him and Jai Ram that Nanak was a saint ill-treated by his father; and Jai Ram promised to cherish him and find him occupation in Sultanpur. Nanak's departure to his brother-in-law was pre cipitated by another act of worldly indiscretion. He had entered into companionship with a faqir who visited the village. Nanak told him, as he did the other faqirs, that his name was Nanak Nirankari; and a friendly intimacy sprang up between them. The faqir was probably a swindler, and coveted a brass lota, or drinking vessel, and a gold wedding ring which Nanak wore, and asked that they might be presented to him. Nanak acceded to the request, to the further sorrow and indignation of his parents. After that it was not difficult to induce Kalu to allow his son to proceed to Sultanpur to join Jai Ram and Nanaki.

The other members of Nanak's family also unanimously approved of his decision. Nanak's wife alone, on seeing him make preparations for his journey, began to weep, and said, ' My life, even here thou hast not loved me; when thou goest to a foreign country, how shalt thou return? ' He answered, ' Simple woman, what have I been doing here? ' Upon this she again entreated him, ' When thou satest down at home, I possessed in my estimation the sovereignty of the whole earth; now this world is of no avail to me." Upon this he grew compassionate, and said, ' Be not anxious; thy sovereignty shall ever abide." She replied, ' My life, I will not remain behind; take me with thee." Then Nanak said, ' I am now going away. If I can earn my living, I will send for thee. Obey my order She then remained silent.

When Nanak asked Rai Bular's permission to depart, the Rai gave him a banquet. The Rai then requested him to give him any order he pleased, that is, to state what favour he might grant him. Nanak replied:â

I give thee one order if thou wilt comply with it. When thine own might availeth not, clasp thy hands and worship God.

Jai Ram introduced Nanak as an educated man to the Governor, Daulat Khan, who appointed him storekeeper and gave him a dress of honour as a preliminary of service. Nanak began to apply himself to his duties, and so discharged them that everybody was gratified and congratulated him. He was also highly praised to the Governor, who was much pleased with his new servant. Out of the provisions which Guru Nanak was allowed, he devoted only a small portion to his own maintenance; the rest he gave to the poor. He used continually to spend his nights singing hymns to his Creator.

If Nanak, when weighing out provisions, went as far as the number thirteenâ tera â he used to pause and several times repeat the wordâ which also means ' Thine," that is, ' I am Thine, O Lord-before he went on weighing.

The minstrel Mardana subsequently came from Talwandi and became Nanak's private servant. Mardana was of the tribe of Dums, who are minstrels by heredity. He used to accompany Nanak on the rabab, or rebeck. 1 Other friends too followed. Nanak introduced them to the Khan and procured them employment. They all got a living by Nanak's favour, and were happy. At dinner-time they came and sat down with him, and every night there was continual singing. A watch before day, Nanak used to go to the neighbouring Bein river and perform his ablutions. When day dawned, he went to discharge the duties of his office.

One day after bathing Nanak disappeared in the

This instrument, which was of Arabian origin, has fallen into disuse in Northern India. It had from four to six strings of goat-gut with steel strings for resonance.

forest, and was taken in a vision to God's presence. He was offered a cup of nectar, which he gratefully accepted. God said to him, ' I am with thee. I have made thee happy, and also those who shall take thy name. Go and repeat Mine, and cause others to do likewise. Abide uncontaminated by the world. Practise the repetition of My name, charity, ablutions, worship, and meditation. I have given thee this cup of nectar, a pledge of My regard The Guru stood up and made a prostration. He then sang the following verses to the accompaniment of the spontaneous music of heaven:â

Were I to live for millions of years and drink the air for my nourishment;

Were I to dwell in a cave where I beheld not sun or moon, and could not even dream of sleeping, 1

I should still not be able to express Thy worth; how great shall I call Thy name?
O true Formless One, Thou art in Thine own placeâ
As I have often heard I tell my taleâ If it please Thee, show Thy favour unto me.
Were I to be felled and cut in pieces, were I to be ground in a mill;
Were I to be burned in a fire, and blended with its ashes, 1 should still not be able to express Thy worth; how great shall I call Thy name?
Were I to become a bird and fly to a hundred heavens;
Were I to vanish from human gaze and neither eat nor drink,
I should still not be able to express Thy worth; how great shall I call Thy name?
Nanak, had I hundreds of thousands of tons of paper and a desire to write on it all after the deepest research;
Were ink never to fail me, and could I move my pen like the wind,
That is, were I to lead even the most ascetic life possible.
I should still not be able to express Thy worth; how great shall I call Thy name? 1
Hereupon a voice was heard, ' O Nanak, thou hast seen My sovereignty." Then Nanak said, ' O Sire, what is anything that mortal can say, and what can be said or heard after what I have seen? Even the lower animals sing Thy praises." Upon this, the Guru uttered the preamble of the Japji:â

There is but one God whose name is True, the Creator, devoid of fear and enmity, immortal, unborn, self-existent, great, and bountiful. 2
The True One was in the beginning; The True One was in the primal age.
The True One is, was, O Nanak, and the True One also shall be.
When Nanak had finished, a voice was heard again: ' O Nanak, to him upon whom My look of kindness resteth, be thou merciful, as I too shall be merciful. My name is God, the primal Brahm, and thou art the divine Guru."
The Guru then uttered the following hymn:â
Thou wise and omniscient, art an ocean; how can I a fish obtain a knowledge of Thy limit?
Wherever I look, there art Thou; if I am separated from Thee, I shall burst.
I know neither Death the fisherman nor his net.
When I am in sorrow, then I remember Thee.
Thou art omnipresent though I thought Thee distant.
What I do is patent unto Thee;
Thou beholdest mine acts, yet I deny them.
I have not done Thy work or uttered Thy name;
Whatever Thou givest, that I eat.
There is no other gate than Thine; to whose gate shall I go?
Nanak maketh one supplicationâ
Soul and body are all in Thy power.

1 Sri Rag.
2 The ordinary translation of Gur par sad, 'By the Guru's favour," does not seem appropriate here.

Thou art near, Thou art distant, and Thou art midway.

Thou seest and hearest; by Thy power didst Thou create the world.

Whatever order pleaseth Thee, saith Nanak, that is acceptable. 1

After three days the Guru came forth from the forest. The people thought he had been drowned in the neighbouring river; and how had he returned to life? He then went home, and gave all that he had to the poor. A great crowd assembled, and Nawab Daulat Khan, the Governor, also came. He inquired what had happened to Nanak, but received no reply. Understanding, however, that the Guru's acts were the result of his abandonment of this world, the Governor felt sad, said it was a great pity, and went home.

It was the general belief at this time that Nanak was possessed with an evil spirit, and a Mulla or Muhammadan priest was summoned to exorcise it. The Mulla began to write an amulet to hang round Nanak's neck. While the Mulla was writing Nanak uttered the following:â

When the field is spoiled where is the harvest heap?

Cursed are the lives of those who write God's name and sell it.

The Mulla, paying no attention to Nanak's serious objurgation, continued the ceremony of exorcism and finally addressed the supposed evil spirit, ' Who art thou? ' The following reply issued from Nanak's mouth:â

Some say poor Nanak is a sprite, some say that he is a demon,

Others again that he is a man.

Those who were present then concluded that Nanak was not possessed, but had become insane.

On hearing this Nanak ordered Mardana to play the rebeck and continued the stanza:â 1 Sri Rag.

Simpleton Nanak hath become mad upon the Lord. 1 And knoweth none other than God. When one is mad with the fear of God, And recognizeth none other than the one God, He is known as mad when he doeth this one thingâ When he obeyeth the Master's orderâ in what else is there wisdom?

When man loveth the Lord and deemeth himself worthless, And the rest of the world good, he is called mad. 2

After this, Guru Nanak donned a religious cos tume and associated constantly with religious men. He remained silent for one day, and the next he uttered the pregnant announcement, ' There is no Hindu and no Musalman." The Sikhs interpret this to mean generally that both Hindus and Muham-madans had forgotten the precepts of their religions. On a complaint made by the Nawab's Qazi, or expounder of Muhammadan law, the Guru was summoned before Daulat Khan to give an explana tion of his words. He refused to go, saying, ' What have I to do with your Khan? ' The Guru was again called a madman. His mind was full of his mission, and whenever he spoke he merely said, 'There is no Hindu and no Musalman." The Qazi was not slow to make another representation to the Governor on the impropriety of Nanak's utter ance. Upon this the Governor sent for him. A footman went and told the Guru that the Governor had requested him to come to him. Then Guru Nanak stood up and went to the Governor. The Governor addressed him, ' Nanak, it is my misfor tune that such an officer as thou should have become a faqir." The Governor then seated him beside him, and directed his Qazi to ask, now that Nanak was in conversational mood, the meaning of his utterance. The Qazi became thoughtful, and smiled. He then asked Nanak, 'What hath happened to thee, that 1 S. colloquialism. 2 Mam.

38 THE SIKH RELIGION thou sayest there is no Hindu and no Musalman? ' The Guru, not being engaged in controversy with Hindus at the time, gave no answer to the first part of the question. In explanation of his statement that there was no Musalman he uttered the follow ing:-

To be 1 a Musalman is difficult; if one be really so, then one may be called a Musalman.

Let one first love the religion of saints, 2 and put aside pride and pelf 3 as the file removeth rust.

Let him accept the religion of his pilots, and dismiss anxiety regarding death or life; 4

Let him heartily obey the will of God, worship the Creator, and efface himself-
When he is kind to all men, then Nanak, shall he be indeed a Musalman. 5

The Qazi then put further questions to the Guru. The Guru called on Mardana to play the rebeck, and sang to it the following replies and instructions adapted for Muhammadans:â

Make kindness thy mosque, sincerity thy prayer-carpet, what is just and lawful thy Quran,

Modesty thy circumcision, civility thy fasting, so shalt thou be a Musalman;

Make right conduct thy Kaaba, 6 truth thy spiritual guide, good works thy creed and thy prayer,

The will of God thy rosary, and God will preserve thine honour, O Nanak.

1 In the original, ' to be called a Musalman The same idiom is found in Greek.

2 Also translatedâ (a) Let him first of all make his religion agree able to men; (Â) let him first love his saints and his religion.

3 Also translatedâ (a) which bring trouble; (6) to dispel pride and worldly love is to be filed or cleansed of impurities.

4 This verse is also translatedâ Being resigned to God, obedient. (din), and lowly (mahane), let man set aside all fear of birth and deathâ the transmigration which so exercises the oriental mind.

5 Majh ki War.

6 The great cube-like Muhammadan temple at Makka to which the. faithful make pilgrimages.

Nanak, let others' goods 1 be to thee as swine to the Musalman and kine to the Hindu; 2

Hindu and Musalman spiritual teachers will go bail for thee if thou eat not carrion. 3

Thou shalt not go to heaven by lip service; it is by the practice of truth thou shalt be delivered.

Unlawful food will not become lawful by putting spices 4 therein.

Nanak, from false words only falsehood can be ob tained.

There are five prayers, five times for prayer, and five names for them 5 â

The first should be truth, the second what is right, the third charity in God's name,

The fourth good intentions, the fifth the praise and glory of God.

If thou make good works the creed thou repeatest, thou shalt be a Musalman.
They who are false, O Nanak, shall only obtain what is altogether false.

The Qazi became astonished at being thus lectured. Prayers had become to him a matter of idle lip-repetition of Arabic texts, while his mind was occupied with his worldly affairs.

It was now the time for afternoon prayer. The whole company, including Nanak, went to the mosque. Up rose the Qazi and began the service. The Guru looked towards him and laughed in his face. When prayer was over, the Qazi complained to the Nawab of Nanak's conduct. The Guru said he had laughed because the Qazi's prayer was not 1 Literally â rights, or what is due to thy neighbour.

2 The Musalmans abstain from the flesh of swine, and the Hindus from the flesh of kine.

3 What is not thine own.

4 This means that, if wealth be improperly obtained, a portion of it bestowed in alms will be no atonement.

5 Prayers, or rather texts from the Quran, are repeated by strict Musalmans at dawn, at midday, in the afternoon, in the evening, and before going to sleep at night.

accepted of God. The Qazi asked Nanak to state the reason for his conclusion. The Guru replied that immediately before prayer the Qazi had unloosed a new-born filly. While he ostensibly performed divine service, he remembered there was a well in the enclosure, and his mind was filled with appre hension lest the filly should fall into it. His heart was therefore not in his devotions. The Guru in formed the Nawab also that while he was pretending to pray, he was thinking of purchasing horses in Kabul. Both admitted the truth of the Guru's statements, said he was favoured of God, and fell at his feet. The Guru then uttered the follow ing:-

He is a Musalman who effaceth himself, Who maketh truth and contentment his holy creed, Who neither toucheth what is standing, nor eateth what hath fallenâ

Such a Musalman shall go to Paradise.

The whole company of Musalmans at the capital â the descendants of the Prophet, the tribe of shaikhs, 1 the qazi, the muftis, 2 and the Nawab him self, were all amazed at Nanak's words. The Muham-madans then asked the Guru to tell them of the power and authority of his God, and how salvation could be obtained. Upon this the Guru addressed them as follows:â

At God's gate there dwell thousands of Muhammads, thousands of Brahmas, of Vishnus, and of Shivs; 3

Thousands upon thousands of exalted Rams, 4 thousands of spiritual guides, thousands of religious garbs; 1 Shaikhs are superiors of darweshes or Muhammadan monks, but the title has now in India a much more extended signification, and is very often adopted by Hindu converts to Islam.

2 Muhammadan jurists.

3 Brahma, Vishnu, and Shiv, form the Hindu trinity, and are respectively the gods of creation, preservation, and destruction.

4 Ram Chandar, king of Ayudhia, deified by the Hindus. He and his consort Slta will be found often mentioned.

Thousands upon thousands of celibates, true men, and Sanyasis; 1

Thousands upon thousands of Gorakhs, 2 thousands upon thousands of superiors of Jogis;
Thousands upon thousands of men sitting in attitudes of contemplation, gurus, and their disciples who make suppli cations;
Thousands upon thousands of goddesses and gods, thou sands of demons;
Thousands upon thousands of Muhammadan priests, prophets, spiritual leaders, thousands upon thousands of qazis, mullas, and shaikhsâ
None of them obtaineth peace of mind without the instruc tion of the true guru.
How many hundreds of thousands of sidhs 3 and strivers, 4 yea, countless and endless!
All are impure without meditating on the word of the true guru.
There is one Lord over all spiritual lords, the Creator whose name is true.
Nanak, His worth cannot be ascertained; He is endless and incalculable. 5

It is said that Daulat Khan, the Musalman ruler, on hearing this sublime hymn, fell at Guru Nanak's feet. The people admitted that God was speaking through Nanak's mouth, and that it was useless to catechize him further. The Nawab, in an outburst l The Sanyasis are anchorets who have abandoned the world, and are popularly believed to have overcome nature. The word sanyas means renunciation.

2 Gorakh was a famous Jogi who lived many centuries ago. His followers slit their ears, and make Shiv the special object of their worship. The name Gorakh, meaning Supporter of the earth, is often used for God in the sacred writings of the Sikhs.

3 Sidhs, in Sanskrit Simhs t are persons who by the practice of Jog are popularly supposed to acquire extended life and miraculous powers.

4 Sadhik, persons aspiring to be Sidhs.

5 Banno's Granth Sahib. An account of Banno will be found in the life of Guru Arjan.

of affectionate admiration, offered him a sacrifice of his authority and estate. Nanak, however, was in no need of temporal possessions, and went again into the society of religious men. They too offered him their homage, and averred that he was desirous of the truth and abode in its performance. Nanak replied:â

My beloved, this body, first steeped in the base of worldliness, 1 hath taken the dye of avarice.

My beloved, such robe 2 pleaseth not my Spouse; How can woman thus dressed go to His couch?

I am a sacrifice, O Benign One, I am a sacrifice unto Thee.

I am a sacrifice unto those who repeat Thy name.

Unto those who repeat Thy name I am ever a sacrifice.

Were this body, my beloved friends, to become a dyer's vat, the Name to be put into it as madder,

And the Lord the Dyer to dye therewith, such colour had never been seen.

0 my beloved, the Bridegroom is with those whose robes are thus dyed.

Nanak's prayer is that he may obtain the dust of such persons' feet.

God Himself it is who decketh, it is He who dyeth, it is He who looketh with the eye of favour.

Nanak, if the bride be pleasing to the Bridegroom, he will enjoy her of his own accord. 3

Upon this the faqirs kissed the Guru's feet, the Governor also came, and all the people, both Hindu and Musalman, attended to salute and take final leave of him. Some complaints had been made of his extravagance as storekeeper; but, when the Governor made an investigation, he found the 1 A metaphor from the dyer's trade. Clothes before the process of dyeing are steeped in alum as a base or mordant the better to retain the dye.

2 Cholra, a coat which reaches to the knees; choli, its diminutive, is a woman's bodice.

' That is, man will be happy if he by good works make himself acceptable to God. The hymn is from Tilang.

storehouse full and all the Guru's accounts correct. Nay, it was discovered that money was due to him from the State. The Guru, however, refused to receive it and requested the Nawab to dispose of it in relieving the wants of the poor

CHAPTER IV

After a short stay with the holy men with whom he had recently been consorting, the Guru, in company with Mardana, proceeded to Saiyidpur, the present city of Eminabad, in the Gujranwala district of the Panjab. Nanak and his companion took shelter in the house of Lalo, a carpenter. When dinner was ready, Lalo informed the Guru, and asked him to eat it within sacred lines. 1 The Guru said, ' The whole earth is my sacred lines, and he who loveth truth is pure. Wherefore remove doubt from thy mind." On this Lalo served dinner, and the Guru ate it where he was seated. After two days the Guru desired to take his departure, but was prevailed on by Lalo to make a longer stay. The Guru consented, but soon found himself an object of obloquy because he, the son of a Khatri, abode in the house of a Sudar. After a fortnight, Malik Bhago, steward of the Pathan who owned Saiyidpur, gave a great feast, to which Hindus of all four castes were invited. A Brahman went and told the Guru that, as all the four castes had been invited, he too should partake of Malik Bhago' s bounty. The Guru replied, ' I belong not to any of the four castes; why am I invited?" The Brahman replied, ' It is on this account people call thee a heretic. Malik Bhago will be displeased with thee for refusing his hospitality." On this the Brahman went away, and 1 Enclosures, generally smeared with cow-dung to make them holy, within which Hindus pray and cook their food.

Malik Bhago fed his guests, but the Guru was not among them.

When subsequently Malik Bhago heard of the Guru's absence from the feast, he ordered him to be produced. Bhago inquired why he had not responded to his invitation. The Guru replied, that he was a faqir who did not desire dainty food, but if his eating from the hands of Malik Bhago afforded that functionary any gratification, he would not be found wanting. Malik Bhago was not appeased, but charged the Guru, who was the son of a Khatri, while refusing to attend his feast, with dining with the low-caste Lalo. Upon this the Guru asked Malik Bhago for his share, and at the same time requested Lalo to bring him bread from his house. When both viands arrived, the Guru took Lalo's coarse bread in his right hand and Malik Bhago's dainty bread in his left, and squeezed them both. It is said that from Lalo's bread there issued milk, and from Malik Bhago's, blood. The meaning was that Lalo's bread had been obtained by honest labour and was pure, while Malik Bhago's had been obtained by bribery and oppression and was there fore impure. The Guru hesitated not to accept the former.

After this the Guru and Mardana proceeded to a solitary forest, nowhere entering a village or tarrying on the bank of a river. On the way they were overtaken by hunger, and Mardana complained. The Guru directed him to go straight on and enter a village where the Upal Khatris dwelt. He had only to stand in silence at the doors of their houses, when Hindus and Musalmans would come to do him homage, and not only supply him with food, but bring carpets and spread them before him to tread on. Mardana did as he had been directed, and succeeded in his errand.

Mardana subsequently received an order to go to another village. He there also received great homage.

The villagers came and fell at his feet, and offered him large presents of money 1 and clothes. These he tied up in bundles and took to the Guru. On seeing them the Guru laughed, and asked Mardana what he had brought. He answered that the vil lagers had made him large presents of money and clothes, and he thought that he would bring them to his master. The Guru replied that they did not belong to either of them. Mardana inquired how he was to dispose of them. The Guru told him to throw them away, an order which he at once obeyed. The Guru explained to him the disastrous effects of offerings on laymen. ' Offerings are like poison and cannot be digested. They can only bring good by fervent adoration of God at all hours. When man per-formeth scant worship and dependeth on offerings for his subsistence, the effect on him is as if he had taken poison

The Guru and Mardana are said to have visited a notorious robber called Shaikh Sajjan. With extreme impartiality he had built for his Hindu guests a temple, and for his Muhammadan guests a mosque; and he otherwise ostensibly provided them with everything necessary for their comfort. His hospitality, however, was as false as that of the famous Greek robber, Procrustes. When night came on, Sajjan dismissed his guests to sleep. He then threw them into a well in which they perished. Next morning he took up a pilgrim's staff and rosary, and spread out a carpet to pray in the true spirit of an ancient Pharisee. Shaikh Sajjan, seeing the Guru, interpreted the look of spiritual satisfaction on his countenance into a consciousness of worldly wealth, and expected much profit from such a wind fall. He as usual invited his guests to go to sleep. The Guru asked permission to recite a hymn to God, and having obtained it, repeated the following:â 1 Literallyâ twenty-fives, because it used to be the Indian custom to count money in heaps of twenty-five each.

Bronze is bright and shining, but, by rubbing, its sable blackness appeareth,
Which cannot be removed even by washing a hundred times.
They are friends l who travel with me as I go along,
And who are found standing ready whenever their accounts are called for.
Houses, mansions, palaces painted on all sides,
When hollow within, are as it were crumbled and use less.
Herons arrayed in white dwell at places of pilgrimage;
Yet they rend and devour living things, and therefore should not be called white. 2
My body is like the simmal tree; 3 men beholding me mistake me. 4

Its fruit is useless: such qualities my body possesseth.
I am a blind man carrying a burden while the moun tainous 5 way is long.
I want eyes which I cannot get; how can I ascend and traverse the journey?
Of what avail are services, virtues, and cleverness?
Nanak, remember the Name, so mayest thou be released from thy shackles. 6

Shaikh Sajjan, on hearing this warning and heart-searching hymn, came to his right understanding. He knew that all the faults were his own, which the Guru had attributed to himself. Upon this he made 1 The name Sajjan also means friend. There is here a pun on the word.

! The heron, though white, has a black heart.

3 The Bombax heptaphyllum. It bears no fruit in the true sense of the word. Its pods yield cotton, which is unfit for textile purposes. Its wood is very brittle, and almost useless for carpentry.

4 Like birds which peck at what they suppose to be the fruit of the simmal tree, but find none. The gyanis exercise their ingenuity on this line, and translateâ The parrots (mat jan looking at it make a mistake.

5 Dugar, thence the tribe of Dogras in the Kangra and adjacent districts. Dogra literally means hillman.

6 Suhi.

him obeisance, kissed his feet, and prayed him to pardon his sins. Then the Guru said, ' Shaikh Sajjan, at the throne of God grace is obtained by two things, open confession and reparation for wrong Shaikh Sajjan asked him to perform for him those things by which sins were forgiven and grace ob tained. Then the Guru's heart was touched, and he asked him to truly state how many murders he had committed. Shaikh Sajjan admitted a long catalogue of the most heinous crimes. The Guru asked him to produce all the property of his victims that he had retained in his possession. The Shaikh did so, where upon the Guru told him to give it all to the poor. He obeyed the mandate, and became a follower of the Guru after receiving charanpahul. 1 It is said that the first Sikh temple 2 was constructed on the spot where this conversation had been held.

The Guru, hearing of a religious fair at Kurkhetar 3 near Thanesar, in the present district of Ambala, on the occasion of a solar eclipse desired to visit it with the object of preaching to the assembled pil grims. Needing refreshment, he began to cook a deer which a disciple had presented to him. The Brahmans expressed their horror at his use of flesh, upon which he replied:â

Man is first conceived in flesh, he dwelleth in flesh.
When he quickeneth, he obtaineth a mouth of flesh; his bone, skin, and body are made of flesh.

1 Also called charanamrit. This was a form of initiation by drink ing the water in which the Guru's feet had been washed. The pre amble of the Japji was read at the same time. The ceremony was inaugurated by Guru Nanak.

2 Dharmsal In modern times this word means a charitable rest-house where the Granth Sahib is kept and divine worship held, where travellers obtain free accommodation, and children receive religious instruction. A temple at a place visited by a Guru is now called Gurd ara.

3 The ancient Kurukshetra, the scene of the great battle between the Pandavs and Kauravs. In Hindu books it is called the Navel of the earth, and it is held that worldly beings were there created. Khuldsal-ul- Tawarikh.

When he is taken out of the womb, he seizeth teats of flesh.
His mouth is of flesh, his tongue is of flesh, his breath is in flesh.
When he groweth up he marrieth, and bringeth flesh home with him.
Flesh is produced from flesh; all man's relations are made from flesh.
By meeting the true Guru and obeying God's order, everybody shall go right.

fhou suppose that man shall be saved by himself, he shall not; Nanak, it is idle to say so.

The following is also on the same subject:â
Fools wrangle about flesh, but know not divine know ledge or meditation on God.
They know not what is flesh, or what is vegetable, or in what sin consisteth.
It was the custom of the gods to kill rhinoceroses, roast them and feast.
They who forswear flesh and hold their noses when near it, devour men at night.
They make pretences to the world, but they know not divine knowledge or meditation on God.

Nanak, why talk to a fool? He cannot reply or under stand what is said to him.
He who acteth blindly is blind; he hath no mental eyes.
Ye were produced from the blood of your parents, yet ye eat not fish or flesh.
When man and woman meet at night and cohabit,
A foetus is conceived from flesh; we are vessels of flesh.

O Brahman, thou knowest not divine knowledge or meditation on God, yet thou callest thyself clever.

Thou considerest the flesh that cometh from abroad 1 bad, O my lord, and the flesh of thine own home good.

All animals have sprung from flesh, and the soul taketh its abode in flesh.
1 The flesh of animals.

They whose guru is blind, eat things that ought not to be eaten, and abstain from what ought to be eaten.

In flesh we are conceived, from flesh we are born; we are vessels of flesh.
O Brahman, thou knowest not divine knowledge or meditation on God, yet thou callest thyself clever.

Flesh is allowed in the Purans, flesh is allowed in the books of the Musalmans, flesh hath been used in the four ages.

Flesh adorneth sacrifice and marriage functions; flesh hath always been associated with them.

Women, men, kings, and emperors spring from flesh.
If they appear to you to be going to hell, then accept not their offerings.
See how wrong it would be that givers should go to hell and receivers to heaven.
Thou understandest not thyself, yet thou instructest others; O Pandit, thou art very wise!!

0 Pandit, thou knowest not from what flesh hath sprung. Corn, sugar-cane, and cotton are produced from water; 2 from water the three worlds are deemed to have sprung.

Water saith, ' I am good in many ways '; many are the modifications of water.

If thou abandon the relish of such things, thou shalt be superhuman, saith Nanak deliberately. 3

The Guru succeeded in making many converts at Kurkhetar. When departing, he thus addressed his Sikhs: ' Live in harmony, utter the Creator's name, and if any one salute you therewith, return his salute with the addition true, and say " Sat Kartar ", the True Creator, in reply. There are four ways by which, with the repetition of God's name, men may reach Him. The first is holy companionship, the second truth, the third contentment, and the fourth restraint of the senses. By whichsoever of these 1 Said ironically.

2 Water assists the growth of vegetables, and on vegetables animals are fed.

3 Malar ki War.

doors a man entereth, whether he be a hermit or a householder, he shall find God

The Guru next visited Hardwar in pursuance of his mission. A great crowd was assembled from the four cardinal points for the purpose of washing away their sins. The Guru saw that, while they were cleansing their bodies, their hearts remained filthy; and none of them restrained the wanderings of his mind or performed his ablutions with love and devotion. While they were throwing water towards the east for the manes of their ancestors, the Guru went among them, and, putting his hands together so as to form a cup, began to throw water towards the west, and continued to do so until a large crowd had gathered round him. Men in their astonishment began to inquire what he was doing, and whether he was a Hindu or Muhammadan. If the latter, why had he come to a Hindu place of pilgrimage? If he were a Hindu, why should he throw water towards the west instead of towards the rising sun? And who had taught him to do so? In reply, the Guru asked them why they threw water towards the east. To whom were they offering it, and who was to receive it? They replied that they were offering libations to the manes of their ancestors. It would satisfy them, and be a source of happiness to themselves.

The Guru then asked how far distant their ances tors were. A learned man among them replied that their ancestors were thousands of miles distant. The Guru, upon this, again began to throw palmfuls of water towards the west. They reminded him that he had not answered their questions, or vouch safed any information regarding himself. He replied that, before he had set out from his home in the west, he had sown a field and left no one to irrigate it. He was therefore throwing water in its direction, that it might remain green and not dry up. His field was on a mound where rain-water would not rest, and he was obliged to have recourse to this form of irrigation. On hearing this, the spectators i thought he was crazed, and told him he was sprink-; ling water in vain, for it would never reach his field. Where was his field and where was he, and how could the water ever reach it? ' Thou art a great fool, thy field shall never become green by what thou art doing The Guru replied, ' Ye have forgotten God. Without love and devotion your minds have gone astray. My field, which you say this water cannot reach, is near, but your ancestors are very far away, so how can the water ye offer them ever reach them or profit them? Ye call me a fool, but ye are greater fools yourselves

The Guru after a little time again broke silence, and said, ' The Hindus are going to hell. Death will seize and mercilessly punish them A Brahman replied, ' How can they who repeat God's name go to hell? Thou hast in the first place acted contrary to our custom, and now thou hast the audacity to tell us that we are going to hell The Guru replied, It is true that, if ye repeat the Name with love, ye shall not be damned. But when ye take rosaries in your hands, and sit down counting your beads, ye never think of God, but allow your minds to wander thinking of worldly objects. Your rosaries are therefore only for show, and your counting your beads is only hypocrisy. One of you is thinking of his trade with Multan, another of his trade with Kabul, another of his trade with Dihli, and the gain that shall in each case accrue The people, on hearing the Guru thus accurately divine their thoughts, began to think him a god, and prayed him to pardon them and grant them salvation by making them his disciples.

The Guru, requiring fire to cook his food, went into a Brahman's cooking-square for it. The Brahman charged him with having defiled his viands. The Guru replied that they had already been denied. Upon this the following was com posed:â

Evil mindedness is a low woman, 1 cruelty a butcher's wife, a slanderous heart a sweeper woman, wrath which ruineth the world a pariah woman.

What availeth thee to have drawn the lines of thy cooking place when these four are seated with thee?

Make truth, self-restraint, and good acts thy lines, and the utterance of the Name thine ablutions.

Nanak, in the next world he is best who walketh not in the way of sin. 2

While at Hardwar the Brahmans pressed the Guru to return to his allegiance to the Hindu religion. They pointed out the spiritual advantages of sacri fices and burnt-offerings, and of the worship of cremation-grounds, gods, and goddesses. The Guru replied that the sacrifices and burnt-offerings of this age consisted in giving food to those who repeated God's name and practised humility. And where the Guru's hymns were read, there was scant worship of places of burial or cremation, or of gods, god desses, and ignorant priests. As to the homage paid the latter, the Guru said that men were ruined thereby, as sweetmeats are spoiled by flies settling on them.

Guru Nanak and Mardana departed thence, and proceeded to Panipat, a place famous in Indian history as the scene of three great decisive battles. At that time a successor of Shaikh Sharaf 3 was the 1 Dumni, the wife of a Dum.

2 Sri Rag Id War.

3 Shaikh Sharaf, whose patronymic was Abu Ali Qalandar, received instruction at the age of forty years from Khwaja Qutub-ul-Dm, who was also spiritual guide of Shaikh Farid and of the Emperor Shams-ul-Din Altmish. Shaikh Sharaf says of himself, ' Learned men gave me a licence to teach and to pronounce judicial decisions, which offices I exercised for twenty years. Unexpectedly I received a call from God, and throwing all my learned books into the Jamna, I set out on travel. In Turkey I fell in with Shams-ul-dm Tabrezi and Maulana Jalal-ul-Din Rumi, who presented me with a robe and turban and with many books, which in their presence I threw into the river.

Muhammadan priest of the place. A disciple called Tatihari went to fetch a pot of water for his spiritual guide from the well near which the Guru and Mar-dana had sat down to rest. The Guru wore a Persian hat and a nondescript costume, which Tatihari took for that of a Persian darwesh. He addressed the Guru with the Muhammadan salutation, ' Salam Alaikum ' (the peace of God be with you). Nanak replied, ' Salam Alekh ' (salutation to the Invisible). Tatihari was astonished, and said that until then nobody had distorted his salutation. He went and told his religious superior, the Shaikh, that he had met a darwesh who had taken the liberty of punning on the Muhammadan salutation. The Shaikh at once resolved to go himself to see the man who had saluted the Invisible One, and inquire what he knew regarding Him.

The Shaikh, on arriving, asked the Guru what religious denomination his head-dress denoted, and why he did not shave his head in orthodox fashion. The Guru replied:â

When man hath shaved his mind he hath shaved his head j 1
Without shaving his mind he findeth not the way.
Let him cut off his head and place it before his guru.
If he resign his own wisdom, he shall be saved by the wisdom of his guru.
To become the dust of the feet of all is to shave the head.
Such a hermit appreciateth the words of the guru;
That is the way in which the head is shaved, O brother.
Few are there who shave their heads according to the instruction of their guru.
Nanak having abandoned all pleasures, affections, and egotism,
Hath put on a hat of this fashion. 2
Subsequently I came to Panipat and there lived as a recluse." His tomb is there. 1 That is, has laid aside egotism.

2 This and the following hymns bearing on the Jog philosophy express Guru Nanak's ideas on the subject. These hymns are not found in the Granth Sahib.

The Shaikh then asked the Guru to what religious sect he belonged. The Guru replied:â

Under the instructions of my Guru 1 I remain His disciple.
My stole and my hat consist in grasping the Word in my heart.
I have turned the flowing river into a streak of sand. 2
I sit there at mine ease and am happy. 3
I have dispelled joy and sorrow.
Having put on my stole I have killed all mine enemies; 4
I have settled in the silent city and abide therein:
There I learned how to wear this stole.
Having forsaken my family I live aloneâ
Nanak having put on this stole is happy.

The Shaikh next inquired to what sect the Guru's loin-cloth belonged. The Guru replied:â

By the word and instruction of the Guru my mind hath obtained peace;
I restrain my five senses and abide apart from the world;
I close mine eyes and my mind hath ceased to wander.
I have locked up the ten gates 5 of my body,
And I sit in contemplation in its sixty-eight chambers. 6
With this loin-cloth I shall neither grow old nor die.
Putting on a loin-cloth I dwell alone

And drink from the waterfall 7 of the brain.
I discard my low intelligence for the lofty wisdom of my Guru.
In this way Nanak weareth a loin-cloth.

1 Nanak's Guru was God. See Sorath xi, Mahalla I, and Gur Das's War, xiii, 25.
2 My brain is in a state of repose.
3 The wanderings of the mind hither and thither have ceased.
4 Dusht, literally, ill-wishers, then man's evil passions.
5 The apertures or openings of the body frequently mentioned in Oriental medical and theological sciences. Nine of them can be easily enumerated, the tenth is the brain.
6 In Jog philosophy the breath is supposed to wander in sixty-eight chambers of the body.
7 Jogis believe that nectar falls or trickles from the brain in a state of exaltation.

Then again the Shaikh desired to know what sect the Guru's slippers denoted. The Guru replied:â

By associating with those who go the right way I have obtained all knowledge.
I have reduced my mind to the caste of fire and wind; l
I abide in the manner of the earth or a tree;
I can endure the cutting and digging of my heart; 2 1 desire to be as a river or sandal
Which whether pleased or displeased conferreth advantage on all.
Having churned the churn 3 of this world I am exalted,
And having abandoned evil I appear before my God.
To those, who put on their slippers while meditating on Him,
O Nanak, mortal sin shall not attach.

Again the Shaikh said, ' Explain to me what a darwesh is." The Guru, ordering Mardana to play the rebeck, composed the following hymn:â

He who while he liveth is dead, while he waketh is asleep, 4 who knowingly alloweth himself to be plundered, 5
And who having abandoned everything meeteth his Creator, is a darwesh.
Few servants of Thine, 0 God, are darweshes at heart,
Who feel not joy, sorrow, anger, wrath, pride, or avarice;
Who look on gold as dross, and consider what is right to be lawful;
Who obey the summons of God and heed none other;
Who seated in a contemplative attitude in the firma ment 6 play spontaneous musicâ
Saith Nanak, neither the Veds nor the Quran know the praises of such holy men.

That isâ I have no more caste than fire and wind.
2 Cutting, as applied to a tree, and digging to earth. That isâ I can endure every form of torture.
3 Having extracted all pleasures from this world, 4 Who takes no heed of the world.
5 That is, who effaces himself.
0 That is, in the brain in a state of exaltation.

The Shaikh finally said, ' Well done! why make a further examination of him who beareth witness to God? Even to behold him is sufficient." Then he shook hands with the Guru, kissed his feet and departed.

Guru Nanak journeyed on and arrived in Dihli. An elephant belonging to the reigning sovereign Ibrahim Lodi had just died; and the keepers, regretting the loss of the animal whose service had afforded them maintenance, were bewailing its death. The Guru inquired whose the elephant was. They replied in Oriental fashion, that it was the Emperor's, but that all things belonged to God. The Guru said that the elephant was alive, and bade them go and rub its forehead with their hands, and say at the same time, ' Wah Guru 'â hail to the Guru! 1 It is said that the elephant stood up to the astonish ment of all. The Emperor, having received informa tion of the miracle, sent for the animal, mounted it, and went to the Guru, and asked if it was he who had restored it to life. The Guru replied, ' God is the only Destroyer and Re-animater. Prayers are for faqirs, and mercy for Him." The monarch then asked, if the elephant were killed would the Guru again restore it. The Guru, not wishing to be treated as an itinerant showman, replied:â

It is He (pointing on high) who destroyeth and destroying re-animateth;
Nanak, there is none but the one God.

The animal then died, the inference of the chroni clers being that it died at the will of the Guru, as it had been previously called to life by him. The Emperor ordered him to again revivify it. The Guru replied, ' Hail to your Majesty! Iron when heated in the fire becometh red, and cannot be held for a moment in the hand. In the same way faqirs 1 Wahguru generally means God. We here merely give its apparent meaning.
become red in the heat of God's love, and cannot be constrained." The Monarch, it is said, was pleased at this reply, and requested the Guru to accept a present from him. The Guru replied:â

Nanak is hungry for God, and careth for naught besides. I ask for God, I ask for nothing else.

The king returned to his palace, and the Guru continued his wanderings.

The Guru next proceeded to Bindraban, where he saw enacted the play called Krishanlila, in which the exploits of Krishan are represented. Krishan appears making love to milkmaids, stealing their clothes while they were bathing, and killing his uncle Kans. The Guru expressed his dissatisfaction with the subject of the performance:â

The disciples play, the gurus dance,
Shake their feet, and roll their heads.
Dust flieth and falleth on their hair;
The audience seeing it laugh and go home.
For the sake of food the performers beat time,
And dash themselves on the ground.
The milkmaids sing, Krishans sing,
Sitas and royal Rams sing.
Fearless is the Formless One, whose name is true,
And whose creation is the whole world.
The worshippers on whom God bestoweth kindness worship Him;
Pleasant is the night for those who long for Him in their hearts.

By the Guru's instruction to his disciples this knowledge is obtained, 1 Krishan son of Vasudev, by his wife Devaki, was born, according to Indian tradition, 3185 B. C. Cattle-grazing was the original calling of the family, and Krishan is celebrated for his adventures among the milkmaids of Mathura. In the Bhagavat Glta, an episode of the Sanskrit epic Mahabharat, he declared himself to be God, the supreme Soul, the Creator of the world, and its Destroyer; and he has been accepted as such by Hindus, who deem him an in carnation of Vishnu.

vxThat the Kind One saveth those on whom He looketh with favour.
Oil-presses, spinning-wheels, hand-mills, potters' wheels,
Plates, 1 whirlwinds, many and endless,
Tops, churning-staves, threshing-frames,
Birds tumble and take no breath.
Men put animals on stakes and swing them round.
0 Nanak, the tumblers are innumerable and endless.
In the same way men bound in entanglements are swung round;
Every one danceth according to his own actsâ
They who dance and laugh shall weep on their departure,
They cannot fly or obtain supernatural power.
Leaping and dancing are mental recreations;
Nanak, they who have the fear of God in their hearts have also love. 2

CHAPTER V

The Guru set out towards the east, having arrayed himself in a strange motley of Hindu and Muham-madan religious habiliments. He put on a mango-coloured jacket, over which he threw a white safa or sheet. On his head he carried the hat of a Musalman Qalandar, 3 while he wore a necklace of bones, and imprinted a saffron mark on his forehead in the style of Hindus. This was an earnest of his desire to found a religion which should be acceptable both to Hindus and Muhammadans without conforming to either faith. As the Guru and his attendant proceeded, they met a Muhammadan notable called Shaikh Waj id. The Shaikh alighted under a tree, and his bearers began to shampoo and fan him. This afforded matter for contemplation to Mardana, and he asked the Guru whether there was not one God for the rich and another for the poor. The Guru replied that there 1 Thai, plates poised on a stick and spun round.

2 Asa ki War.

3 A Muhammadan anchoret who abandons all worldly ties and possessions. He corresponds to the Indian Sanyasi.

was only one God. Mardana then put his question in another form: ' Who created this man who rideth in a sedan of ease while the bearers have no shoes to their feet? Their legs are naked while they shampoo and fan him." The Guru replied with the following verses:â

They who performed austerities in their former lives, are f now kings and receive tribute on earth.

They who were then wearied, are now shampooed by others.

The Guru continued in prose: ' O Mardana, whoever is born hath come naked from his mother's womb, and joy or misery is the result of actions in previous states of existence." Upon this, Mardana fell at the Guru's feet.

As Guru Nanak and Mardana journeyed on, they arrived at Gorakhmata, or temple of Gorakh, some twenty miles north of Pilibhit, in the United Provinces of India. 1 There they observed a pipal-tree 2 of many a religious reminiscence. Years previously it had withered from age, but it is related that when the holy man sat beneath it, it suddenly became green. The biographer of the Guru states that Sidhs came on that occasion and addressed him: ' O youth, whose disciple art thou, and from whom hast thou obtained instruction? '

Guru Nanak, in reply, composed the following hymn:â

What is the scale? What the weights? What weighman 3 shall I call for Thee?

Who is the guru from whom I should receive instruction, and by whom I should appraise Thy worth?

0 my Beloved, I know not Thy limit.

Thou fillest sea and land, the nether and upper regions; it is Thou Thyself who art contained in everything.

1 The place is now known as Nanakmata, in memory of the Guru's visit. 2 The Ficus religiosa.

3 This line appears to mean that God cannot be weighed or estimated.

My heart is the scale, my understanding the weight, Thy service the weighman I employ.

I weigh the Lord in my heart, and thus I fix my attention.

Thou Thyself art the tongue of the balance, the weight, and the scales; Thou Thyself art the weighman;

Thou Thyself beholdest, Thou Thyself understandest, Thou Thyself art the dealer with Thee-

A blind man, a low-born person, and a stranger come but for a moment, and in a moment depart.

In such companionship Nanak abideth; how can he, fool that he is, obtain Thee? 2

Then the Sidhs said, ' O youth, become a Jogi, and adopt the dress of our order, so shalt thou find the true way and obtain the merits of religion." The Guru replied with the following hymn:â

Religion consisteth not in a patched coat, or in a Jogi's staff, or in ashes smeared over the body;

Religion consisteth not in earrings worn, or a shaven head, or in the blowing of horns. 3 . Abide pure amid the impurities of the world; thus shalt thou find the way of religion.

Religion consisteth not in mere words;

He who looketh on all men as equal is religious.

Religion consisteth not in wandering to tombs 4 or places of cremation, or sitting in attitudes of contemplation; 5

Religion consisteth not in wandering in foreign countries, or in bathing at places of pilgrimages.

Abide pure amid the impurities of the world; thus shalt thou find the way of religion.

On meeting a true guru doubt is dispelled and the wander ings of the mind restrained.

It raineth nectar, slow ecstatic music is heard, and man is happy within himself.

1 In the Granth Sahib God is the wholesale merchant from whom all grace and good gifts proceed, and men are the dealers who receive from Him. 2 SQhi 3 The j ogis blow deers hornst 4 Marhi, a structure raised over the ashes of the dead. ' Tari lagdna is to sit cross-legged in contemplative attitude as Buddha is represented.

LIFE OF GURU NANAK 61
Abide pure amid the impurities of the world; thus shalt thou find the way of religion.
Nanak, in the midst of life be in death; practise such religion.
When thy horn soundeth without being blown, thou shalt obtain the fearless dignityâ
Abide pure amid the impurities of the world, thus shalt thou find the way of religion.
1

On hearing this the Sidhs made Guru Nanak obeisance. The Guru, having infused sap into the pipal-tree by sitting under it, necessarily became a great being in their estimation.

The Guru and his musical attendant proceeded to Banaras, 2 the head quarters of the Hindu religion, and the birthplace of the renowned Kabir, then dead but not forgotten. The Guru and Mardana sat down in a public square of the city. At that time the chief Brahman of the holy city was Pandit Chatur Das. On going to bathe he saw the Guru and made the Hindu salutation, ' Ram Ram! ' On observing the Guru's dress, he twitted him with possessing no salagram 3 though he called himself a faqir, with wearing no necklace of sacred basil and no rosary. ' What saintship hast thou obtained?" The Guru replied:â 0 Brahman, thou worshippest and propitiatest the salagram, and deemest it a good act to wear a necklace of sweet basil. 4

Why irrigate barren land and waste thy life? Why apply plaster to a frail tottering wall? Repeating God's name, form a raft for thy salvation; may the Merciful have mercy on thee!

1 Suhi.

2 Banaras, in Sanskrit Baranasi, is derived from Barna and Asi, two tributary streams of the Ganges.

3 A quartzose stone bearing the impression of ammonites and believed by the Hindus to represent Vishnu petrified by a curse of Brinda for possessing her in the guise of her spouse. Salagrams are found in the Gandaka and Son rivers.

Chatur Das replied: ' O saint, the salagram and the necklace of sweet basil may indeed be useless as the irrigation of barren land, but tell me by what means the ground may be prepared and God found." The Guru replied:â

Make God the well, string His name for the necklace of waterpots, and yoke thy mind as an ox thereto.

Irrigate with nectar and fill the parterres therewith; thus shalt thou belong to the Gardener.

The Pandit inquired: ' The soil is irrigated, but how can it yield produce until it hath been dug up and prepared for the seed? ' The Guru explained how this was to be done:â

Beat both thy lust and anger into a spade, with which dig up the earth, O brother:

The more thou diggest, the happier shalt thou be: such work shall not be effaced in vain.

The Pandit replied: ' I am the crane, and thou art the primal swan of God. My understanding is overcome by my senses The Guru replied:â

If thou, O Merciful One, show mercy, a crane shall change into a swan.

vNanak, slave of slaves, supplicateth, O Merciful One have mercy. 1

The Pandit then admitted that the Guru was a saint of God, and asked him to bless the city and sing its praises. The Guru inquired in what the specialty of the city consisted. The Pandit said it was learning, by which wealth was acquired. ' The world admireth the ground on which the possessor of wealth treadeth. By applying the mind to learning, thou shalt become a high priest." The Guru replied in a series of metaphors:â

The city 2 is frail, the king 3 is a boy and loveth the wicked;
He is said to have two mothers 4 and two fathers 5; O Pandit, think upon this.
1 Basant. The body. 3 The heart.
4 Hope and desire. 5 Love and hate.
O, sir Pandit, instruct me
How I am to obtain the Lord of life.
Within me is the fire, 1 the garden 2 is in bloom, and I have an ocean 3 within my body.
The moon and sun 4 are both in my heart; thou hast not obtained such knowledge?
He who subdueth mammon knoweth that God is every where diffused;
He may be known by this mark that he storeth con tentment as his wealth. 5
The king dwelleth with those who listen not to advice, and who are not grateful for what they receive.
Nanak, slave of slaves, representeth, 0 God, in one moment makest the small great and the great small. 6

Chatur Das requested further information. ' Sir, shall the name of God be to any extent obtained by what we teach the people and what we learn ourselves? ' The Guru inquired in return: ' O reli gious teacher, what hast thou read? What teachest thou the people, and what knowledge dost thou communicate to thy disciples? ' The Pandit replied: ' By the will of God I teach the people the fourteen sciences â reading, swimming, medicine, alchemy, astrology, singing the six rags and their raginis, the science of sexual enjoyment, grammar, music, horsemanship, dancing, archery, theology, and states manship The Guru replied that better than all these was knowledge of God. Upon this he repeated the long composition called the Oamkar in the Rag 1 The fire of evil passions. 2 Of my youth.

3 Of desires. Man is here the measure of infinity. The ocean is supposed to contain fire which consumes it and hinders its increase. This fire is called barwtinal, and is supposed to be near the Equator.

4 Meditation and divine knowledge.

5 Also translated â He who hoardeth mercy instead of wealth recognizeth God.

6 Literally â in a moment thou canst make a tola a masha, and in a moment a masha a tola. A tola is 180 grains avoirdupois, the weight of a rupee. A masha is the twelfth part of a tola. The hymn is from Basant.

Ramkali, the first two pauris or stanzas of which are as follow:â
It is the one God who created Brahma; 1
It is the one God who created our understanding;
It is from the one God the mountains and the ages of the world emanated;
It is the one God who bestoweth knowledge.
It is by the word of God man is saved.

It is by the name of the one God the pious are saved.
Hear an account of the letter Oâ 2
O is the best letter in the three worlds.
Hear, O Pandit, why writest thou puzzles?
Write under the instruction of the Guru the name of God, the Cherisher of the world.
He created the world with ease: in the three worlds there is one Lord of Light.
Under the Guru's instruction select gems and pearls, and thou shalt obtain God the real thing.
If man understand, reflect, and comprehend what he readeth, he shall know at last that the True One is every where. 3
The pious man knoweth and remembereth the truthâ that without the True One the world is unreal.
On hearing the whole fifty-four stanzas of the Oamkar, the Pandit fell at the Guru's feet, and became a Sikh and possessor of God's name.
During the Guru's stay at Banaras Krishan Lai and Har Lai, two eminent young pandits, went to visit him, and he explained to them the tenets and principles of his religion.
From Banaras the Guru proceeded to Gaya, the famous place of pilgrimage, where Buddha in days long past made his great renunciation and per formed his memorable penance. There the Guru uttered the following in reply to Brahmans who had
This means that the true God is superior to all other gods.- The symbol of the eternal God. It is here used instead of the Name. 3 Nirantar, pervades creation uninterruptedly.
urged him to perform the ceremonies usual among Hindus for the repose of the souls of ancestors.
The Name alone, is my lamp, suffering the oil I put therein.
The lamp's light hath dried it up, and I have escaped meeting Death.
0 ye people, make me not an object of derision.
The application of a particle of fire will destroy even hundreds of thousands of logs heaped together. 1
God is my barley rolls 2 and leafy platters, 3 the Creator's name the true obsequies. 4
In this world and the next, in the past and the future, that is my support.
Thy praises are as the Ganges and Banaras to me; my soul laveth therein.
If day and night I love Thee, then shall my ablution be true.
Some rolls are offered to the gods, some to the manes 5; but it is the Brahman who kneadeth and eateth them.
Nanak, the rolls which are the gift of God are never exhausted. 6
The Guru and Mardana in the course of their travels found themselves at a grain-dealer s house. A son had just been born to one of the partners, and several people had come to offer him congratula tions. Some threw red powder 7 in token of joy, and voices of blessing and congratulation filled the neighbourhood. Mardana sat down and gazed on the 1 That is, God's name will remove hundreds of thousands of sins.

2 Find this word also means the body which is supposed to be put together by the offering of these rolls.

3 Paital, literally, plates of leaves generally of the palas (Butea frondosa) in which food is placed.

4 Kiriya, the ceremonies performed on the thirteenth day after death.

5 Chhamchari, those who walked the earth, the manes of ancestors.

6 Asa.

7 Red powder is thrown on passers-by in India on occasions of festivity. The practice is particularly resorted to on the occasion of the Holi, a Hindu saturnalia.

spectacle. In the evening, when the grain-dealer's entertainment was at an end, he stood up and went to his private apartments without taking any notice of Mardana. The latter went to the Guru, who sat at some distance, informed him of the birth of the child, and gave him an account of the entertainment. The Guru smiled, and said it was not a son who had been born in the grain-dealer's house, but a creditor who had come to settle his account. He would remain for the night and depart in the morning. Then the Guru ordered Mardana to play the rebeck, and sang to its strains the following hymn:â

In the first watch of night, my merchant friend, the child by God's order entereth the womb.

With body reversed it performeth penance within, O merchant friend, and prayeth to the Lord-It prayeth to the Lord in deep meditation and love. It cometh naked into the world, and again it departeth naked. Such destiny shall attend it as God's pen hath recorded upon its forehead.

Saith Nanak, in the first watch the child on receiving the order entereth the womb.

In the second watch of night, O merchant friend, it for-getteth to meditate on God.

It is dandled in the arms, O merchant friend, like Krishan in the house of Yasodha. The child is dandled in the arms, and its mother saith, This is my son."

Think on this, O thoughtless and stupid man, 1 nothing shall be thine at last.

Thou knowest not Him who created thee; meditate upon Him in thy heart.

1 Man in the original might be translated mind, but the word includes the heart in the next line.

Saith Nanak, the child hath forgotten to meditate at the second watch.

At the third watch of night, O merchant friend, man's thoughts are of woman and the pleasures of youth;

He thinketh not of God's name, O merchant friend, which would release him from his bondage.

Man thinketh not of God's name, but groweth beside himself with worldly love.

Devoted to woman and intoxicated with his youth he wasteth his life in vain.

He hath not traded in virtue or made good acts his friends.

Saith Nanak, in the third watch man's thoughts are of woman and the pleasures of youth.

In the fourth watch of night, 0 merchant friend, the reaper cometh to the field;

The secret hath been given to none when Death shall seize and take away his victim.

Think upon God; the secret hath been given to none when Death shall seize and take man away.

Hollow are the lamentations around. In one moment man's goods become another's. He shall obtain those things on which he hath set his heart. 1

Saith Nanak, O mortal, in the fourth watch the reaper hath reaped the field. 2

When morning came, the grain-dealer's child died, and the grain-dealer and his relatives came forth weeping and wailing. Mardana asked the Guru what sudden change of fortune had come to those who yesterday had been engaged in their rejoicings 1 It is supposed that man shall receive in the next world the things which formed the object of his last thoughts in this. He who has not fixed his thoughts on God at the last moment shall not find Him, but begin anew a course of transmigration. See Trilochan, Gujari, vol, vi. 2 g r i R 5 Pahare.

and saturnalia. Then the Guru uttered the following on the vicissitudes of human life:â

They to whose faces were uttered gratulations and hundreds of thousands of blessings,

Now smite their heads in grief; and their minds and bodies suffer agony.

Of the dead some are buried, others are thrown into rivers. 1

The gratulations have passed away; but even so do thou, O Nanak, praise the True One.

As the Guru and Mardana pursued their way they saw a small enclosed field of gram. 2 The watchman of the field began to roast some for his dinner, while the Guru and Mardana gazed at him at a distance. As the watchman was preparing to eat, he saw them, and it occurred to him that they wanted something more dainty than gram, so he would go to his house and bring them better fare and comfortable bedding. As he stood up, the Guru, who did not wish to trouble him, asked whither he was going, and, on being informed, uttered the following verses:â

Thy pallet is a coverlet and mattress for me; thy love is my dainty dish.

Nanak is already satiated with thy good qualities; come back, O monarch.

In due time the watchman obtained spiritual dignity in return for his kind intentions towards the Guru.

There was at that time a shopkeeper whose mind had taken a religious bent, and who desired to meet a religious guide. He heard of Guru Nanak's arrival, and vowed that he would not eat or drink until he had had an interview with him. Having 1 The Musalmans bury their dead. The Hindus cremate them, or throw them into their sacred streams.

2 Ghana, Cicer an'etinum, chick peas, on which horses are fed in India. It is called gram by Europeans. When roasted green it is sometimes eaten by the poorer classes.

once visited the Guru he continually went to him to receive religious instruction. A neighbouring shopkeeper heard of his friend's visits, and said that he too would go to see the holy man. They proceeded together, but on the way the second shopkeeper saw a woman of whom he became enamoured, and his visit to Nanak was indefinitely postponed. It was the custom of both to set out together, one to visit his mistress, and the other to visit the Guru. The second shopkeeper desired to put the fortunes of both to the test, and said, ' Thou practisest good works, while I practise bad works. Let us see what shall happen to each of us to-day. If I arrive first, I will sit down and wait for thee; and if thou arrive first, then wait for me This was agreed upon. The second shopkeeper went to the house of his mistress as usual, but did not find her. He then proceeded to the spot where his: friend had agreed to meet him, but his friend, who on that day tarried long with the Guru, had not yet arrived. The second shopkeeper needing some occupa tion in his solitude, drew out his knife and began to whittle the ground with it, when he found a shining gold coin. He continued his excavations with the weak delving implement he possessed, when, to his disappointment, he only discovered a jar of charcoal. He had, however, obtained some reward for his labour.

Meanwhile the first shopkeeper arrived in doleful case. Having left the Guru, a thorn pierced his foot. He bound up the wound, and proceeded sore limping to the trysting-place. His friend told him of his better fortune. They both saw that he who went daily to commit sin prospered, while he who went to his religious teacher to pray and meditate on God, suffered; and they agreed to refer to Guru Nanak for an explanation of their unequal and unmerited fates.

The Guru explained that the sinful shopkeeper had in a former birth given a gold coin as alms to a holy man. That coin was converted into many gold coins as a reward for the alms-giver, but, when he entered on his career of sin, the gold coins were turned into charcoal. The original gold coin was, however, restored. The shopkeeper who visited the Guru, had deserved to die by an impaling stake for the sins of deceit and usury, but, as he continued to progress in virtue, the impaling stake was reduced in size till it became merely a thorn. Having been pierced by it, he had fully expiated the sins of a former birth. Thus may the decree of destiny be altered by the practice of virtue. Both men were thoroughly satisfied with this explanation of unequal retribution. The sinful as well as the virtuous man fell at Guru Nanak's feet, and both became true worshippers of God. The Guru then uttered the following verses:â

The heart is the paper, conduct the ink; l good and bad are both recorded therewith.
Man's life is as his acts constrain him; there is no limit to Thy praises, O God.
O fool, why callest thou not to mind Thy Creator?
Thy virtues have dissolved away by thy forgetfulness of God.
Night is a small net, day a large one; there are as many meshes as there are gharis in the day.
With relish thou ever peckest at the bait, and art ensnared; O fool, by what skill shalt thou escape?
The body is the furnace, the mind the iron therein; five fires 2 are ever applied to it.
Sin is the charcoal added thereto, by which the mind is heated; anxiety is the pincers.
The mind hath turned into dross, but it shall again become gold when it meeteth such a Guru
As will bestow the ambrosial name of the one God; then, Nanak, the mind shall become fixed. 3 1 Literallyâ Conductâ heart being the paperâ is the ink.
2 The deadly sins. 3 Maru.

The Guru then took the opportunity of discoursing on the immoral shopkeeper's peculiar vice: Man is fickle when he beholdeth a courtesan; he then hath a special desire for love's play, and can in no way be restrained. On meeting her he loseth his human birth. Bereft of his religion he falleth into hell, where he undergoeth punishment and profusely lamenteth. Wherefore look not on her, but pass thy time among the holy."

After this they all separated, and the Guru and Mardana continued their wanderings. On the way they were encountered by robbers. On seeing Guru Nanak, they said to themselves that he on whose face shone such happiness could not be without wealth. They accordingly went and stood around the Guru. As they beheld him morning dawned, so they were able to examine him more closely. He asked them who they were, and what they wanted. They candidly replied that they were thags, 1 and had come to rob him. The Guru gave them spiritual instruction, and said that their sins should be wiped out when they had abandoned their evil career, turned to agriculture, and bestowed charity out of the spoils in their possession. They acted on his suggestions, began to repeat the Name, and reform their lives. The Guru on that occasion composed the following:â

Covetousness is a dog, falsehood a sweeper, food obtained by deceit carrion;

Slander of others is merely others' filth in our mouths; the fire of anger is a sweeper. 2

Pleasures and self-praiseâ these are mine acts, O Creator.

My friends, doth any one obtain honour by mere words?

Call them the best, who are the best at the gate of the Lord; they who do base acts sit and weep.

1 Indian robbers who generally effect their purpose by the use of stupefying and poisonous drugs.

2 Also translatedâ Slander of others is our neighbour's dirt, filthy language a sweeper, anger fire.

There is pleasure in gold, pleasure in silver and in women, pleasure in the perfume of sandal;

There is pleasure in horses, pleasure in couches and in palaces, pleasure in sweets, and pleasure in meats.

When such are the pleasures of the body, how shall God's name obtain a dwelling therein?

It is proper to utter the words by which honour is obtained.

Injury resulteth from uttering harsh words; hearken, O foolish and ignorant man.

They who please God are good; what more can be said?

They in whose heart God is contained possess wisdom, honour, and wealth.

What need is there of praising them? What further decoration can they obtain?

Nanak, they who are beyond God's favouring glance love not charity or His name. 1

By the following the Guru recommended agricul tural labour:â

The oxen are disciples, 2 the ploughman is their Shaikh; 3 The earth is a book, the furrow the writing. The sweat of the ploughman's brow falleth to his heels, And every one eateth of his earning. 4 They who eat the fruit of their earning and bestow a little from it,

O Nanak, recognize the true way.

Then the Guru departed thence.

1 Sri Rag.

2 Mushaiq. This is the Arabic mashshaq, a striven 3 Their spiritual guide.

4 Compareâ ' On its oxen and its husbandmen An empire's strength is laid."

CHAPTER VI

The Guru and Mardana went to Kamrup, 1 a coun try whose women were famous for their skill in incantation and magic. It was governed by a queen called Nurshah in the Sikh chronicles. She with several of her females went to the Guru and tried to obtain influence over him.

Then the Guru uttered the following verses:â

You buy saline earth, 2 and want musk into the bargain: Without good works, Nanak, how shall you meet your Spouse?

The Guru continued as follows:â

The virtuous wife enjoyeth her husband; why doth the bad one bewail?

If she become virtuous, then shall she too go to enjoy her husband.

My Spouse is an abode of sweetness; why should He enjoy other women?

If a woman become virtuous and turn her heart into a thread,

She shall string her Spouse's heart thereon like a priceless gem.

I show the way to others, but walk not in it myself; 3 I say I have already traversed it.

If thou, 0 my Spouse, speak not to me, how shall I abide in Thy house?

Nanak, excepting One there is none besides.

If Thy wife, O Spouse, remain attached to Thee, she shall enjoy Thee. 4

Nurshah observed that her people's spells were of no avail, however much they tried. The Guru, on 1 In the time of the Guru it is believed that Kawaru, or Kamrdp, included at least the present districts of Goalpara and Kamrup.

2 Kallar, impure nitrate of soda found in sandy soils in India.

3 Compareâ ' Fungar vice cotis, acutum Reddere quae ferrum valet, exsors ipsa secandi."â HORACE.

4 Wadhans.

beholding their fruitless efforts, uttered the following hymn in the Suhi measure entitled Kuchajji, or the woman of bad character:â

I am a worthless woman; in me are faults; how can I go to enjoy my Spouse?

My Spouse's wives are one better than the other; O my life, who careth for me? 1

My female friends who have enjoyed their Spouse are in the shade of the mango. 2

I do not possess their virtues; to whom can I attribute blame? 3

What attributes of Thine, O Lord, shall I blazon abroad? What names of Thine shall I repeat?

I cannot even attain one of Thy many excellences: I am ever a sacrifice unto Thee.

Gold, silver, pearls, and rubies which gladden the heartâ

These things the Bridegroom hath given me, and I have fixed my heart on them. 4

I had palaces of brick fashioned with marble.

In these luxuries I forgot the Bridegroom and sat not near Him.

The kulangs cry in the heavens, 5 and the cranes have come to roost. 6

The woman goeth to her father-in-law's; 7 how shall she show her face as she proceedeth?

As morning dawned she soundly slept, and forgot her journey.

She separated from Thee, O Spouse, and therefore stored up grief for herself.
1 Literallyâ who knoweth my name?
2 That is, they are fortunate. The mango is an evergreen, and its leaves always afford shelter.
3 It is my own fault that I possess not virtue.
4 And forgotten the Giver.
5 The Orientals believe that very old men hear noises in their heads. The kulang is a large stately Indian bird.
6 Grey hair has come.
7 In the Granth Sahib the present world is called one's father's house, and the next world one's father-in-law's.

In Thee, 0 Lord, are merits; in me all demerits: Nanak hath this one representation to make.

Every night is for the virtuous woman; may I though unchaste obtain a night also! 1

Nurshah grew weary of her efforts. She felt that her ill success was the result of her sins. Her women then, beating drums, stood in front of the Guru, and began to dance and sing. He on that occasion com posed the following hymn:â

The impulses of my heart are my cymbals and madiras. 2
The world is my drum; this is the music that playeth for me.
Saints like Narad dance under the influence of this Kal age. 3
They who call themselves continent and virtuous also enter the dance.
Nanak, I am a sacrifice to the Name.
The world is blind in the opinion of those who know the Lord.
Contrary to custom, a disciple eateth from the hand of his guru,
And goeth and dwelleth with him only for the sake of food. 4
If man were to live and eat hundreds of years,
Only that day would be acceptable in which he recognized the Lord.
Compassion is not exercised by merely beholding a suitor; 5
There is no one who receiveth or giveth not bribes.
The king dispenseth justice when his palm is filled.
If a man make a request for God's sake nobody heedeth him. Nanak, men nowadays are men only in shape and name: 1 She has grown grey in sin, and is not desirable to her Husband.

2 The madiras were struck with a stick, and somewhat corre sponded to European triangles.

3 Even saints dance for pleasure, and not for the love of God in this age.

1 This is described as a custom of this degenerate age. The proper course would be for the disciple to feed his master. 5 A bribe must be paid to the judge.

In action they are dogs; shall they be accepted at God's gate?
If man by the favour of his guru deem himself a guest in this world,
He shall acquire some honour in God's court. 1
Again the Guru uttered the following verses:â
In words we are good, but in acts bad.

We are impure-minded and black-hearted, yet we wear the white robes of innocence.²

We envy those who stand and serve at His gate.
They who love the Bridegroom and enjoy the pleasure of His embraces,
Are lowly even in their strength, and remain humble.
Nanak, our lives shall be profitable if we meet such women. 3

When the Guru had uttered these verses, Nurshah thought she would tempt him with wealth. Her attendants brought pearls, diamonds, gold, silver, coral, sumptuous dresses, all things precious the state treasury contained, and laid them at his feet. The Guru rejected all the proffered presents, and uttered the following hymn, which he sang to Mar-dana's rebeck:â 0 silly woman, why art thou proud?

Why enjoyest thou not the love of God 4 in thine own home?
The Spouse is near; O foolish woman, why searchest thou abroad?
Put the surma 5 needles of God's fear into thine eyes, and wear the decoration of love.
Thou shalt be known as a devoted happy wife 6 if thou love the Bridegroom.
1 Asa.
2 Literallyâ we are white outside. 3 Sri Rag ki War. 1 The Indian husband is deemed as a god by his wife.
5 A species of collyrium.
6 Suhdgan, from the Sanskrit su, good, and bhag, fortune, is applied to a wife whose husband is alive. Her lot is happy, and her state deemed holy in comparison with that of a widow.

What shall a silly woman do if she please not her Spouse?
However much she implore, she may not enter His chamber.
Without God's grace she obtaineth nothing, howsoever she may strive.
Intoxicated with avarice, covetousness, and pride, she is absorbed in mammon.
It is not by these means the Bridegroom is obtained; silly is the woman who thinketh so.

Go and ask the happy wives 1 by what means they obtained their Spouseâ ' Whatever He doeth accept as good; have done with cleverness and orders.
' Apply thy mind to the worship of His feet by whose love what is most valued is obtained. 2
Do whatever the Bridegroom biddeth thee; give Him thy body and soul; such perfumes apply." 3
Thus speak the happy wives: 4 ' O sister, by these means the Spouse is obtained.
' Efface thyself, so shalt thou obtain the Bridegroom; what other art is there? '
Only that day is of account when the Bridegroom looketh with favour; the wife hath then obtained the wealth of the world.
She who pleaseth her Spouse is the happy wife; Nanak, she is the queen of them all.
She is saturated with pleasure, intoxicated with happi ness, 5 and day and night absorbed in His love.
She is beautiful and fair to view, accomplished, and it is she alone who is wise. 6
1 Who have God for their spouse.

2 That is, salvation. Also translatedâ from whom the wealth of love is obtained.

3 That is, let these be thy blandishments.

4 This is the reply of the favourite wives showing how they won God as their Spouse.

5 Sahij. This word has many meanings in the Granth Sahib. It means natural disposition, easily, slowly, divine knowledge, divine tranquillity, God, c. In some of its meanings it is derived from sah, with, andy'a, born. 6 Tilang.

Nurshah and her women, on hearing this hymn, twisted their head-dresses around their necks in token of submission, and fell at the Guru's feet. They asked how they could obtain salvation. The Guru told them to repeat God's name, conscientiously perform their domestic duties, renounce magic, and they should thus secure future happiness. It is said that they became followers of Guru Nanak, and thus secured salvation

The Guru, on leaving Kamrup, entered a wilderness. There Kaljug 1 came to tempt him. Mardana became sore afraid. The Guru remonstrated with him; asked why he was afraid of Kaljug; if he felt fear it ought to be the fear of God.

The Guru then sang the following hymn:â

Put the fear of God 2 into thy heart; then the fear of Death shall depart in fear.

What is that fear by fearing which the fear of Death may take fright?

0 God, there is no other abode than in Thee; Whatever happeneth is according to Thy pleasure. Fear if thou have any other fear than that of God: Fear is mental disturbance.

The soul dieth not, neither is it drowned; it is saved through fear of God.

'He who made something will make something.

By His order man cometh; by His order man goeth;

Before and behind us His order prevaileth.

The swan of the heart aspireth to fly to heaven;

But on the way it is a target for great hunger which restraineth it.

Let the swan make fear its eating, drinking, and support;

Without such food the stupid bird would die.

Who hath a helper let anybody say.

Everybody is Thine; Thou art the helper of all.

1 Kaljug here means Satan.

2 Dar ghar, the abode of fear, is explained by the gyanis to mean God.

Nanak, to name and meditate on Him to whom belong Men, lower animals, wealth, and property, is difficult. 1

Mardana inquired who Kaljug was, by what signs he was known unto men, and what prerogative he exercised? The Guru replied:â

When true men speak the truth and suffer for it; when penitents fail to perform penance in their homes;

When he who repeateth the name of God meeteth obloquyâ these are the signs of the Kaljug. 2

Kaljug offered the Guru the wealth of the world if he would abandon his mission. He said, ' I possess everything. Say but the word, and I will build thee a palace of pearls, inlay it with gems, and plaster it with fragrant aloes and sandal. I will bring thee very beautiful women, and give thee the wealth of the world, the power of working miracles, and confer upon thee the sovereignty of the East and of the West. Take whatever pleaseth thee The Guru informed him that he himself had renounced all sovereignty. What could he do with what Kaljug offered him, which moreover belonged to others? Then the Guru uttered the following stanza:â

Were a mansion of pearls erected and inlaid with gems for me;
Perfumed with musk, saffron, fragrant aloes and sandal to confer delight;
May it not be that on beholding these things I may forget Thee, 0 God, and not remember Thy name!
My soul burneth without Thee.
I have ascertained from my Guru that there is no other shelter than in God.
Were the earth to be studded with diamonds and rubies, and my couch to be similarly adorned;
Were fascinating damsels whose faces were decked with jewels to shed lustre and enhance the pleasure of the scene; 1 Gauri. 2 Ramkali.
May it not be that on beholding them I may forget Thee and not remember Thy name I
Were I to become a Sidh and work miracles; could I command the wealth of the universe to come to me;
Could I disappear and appear at pleasure, and were the world to honour me;
May it not be that on beholding these things I may forget Thee and not remember Thy name!
Were I to become a monarch on my throne and raise an army;
Were dominion and regal revenue mineâ O Nanak, they would be all worthlessâ
May it not be that on beholding these things I may forget Thee and not remember Thy name! 1

Then Kaljug went round him in adoration, fell at his feet, and took his departure.
On the way Guru and Mardana sought shelter in a village, but were not allowed to remain there. The villagers began to play practical jokes on them. The Guru on that occasion uttered the following verses:â

When I remain silent, they say I have no understanding in my heart;
When I speak, they say I chatter too much;
When I sit, they say I have spread my pallet to stay;
When I go away, they say I have thrown dust on my head; 2
When I bow down, they say I perform my devotions through fear.
I can do nothing by which I may spend my time in peace.
Both here and hereafter may the Creator preserve Nanak's honour!
Then the Guru composed the following hymn in the Rag Malar:â 1 Sri Rag.
2 That is, I have become a faqlr and dishonoured my family.

Death is forgotten amid eating and drinking, laughter and sleep.
By forgetting the Lord man hath ruined himself and ren dered his life accursed; he is not to tarry here.
O man, ponder on the one Name,
And thou shalt go to thy home with honour.
What do they who worship Thee give Thee? Nay, they cease not to beg of Thee.

Thou conferrest gifts on all creatures; Thou art the life within their lives.
The pious who meditate on God receive nectar; it is they who are pure.
Day and night repeat the Name, 0 mortal, that thine impurities may be washed away.
As is the season so the comfort of the body, and so the body itself. 1 0 Nanak, that season is agreeable in which God's name is repeated; but what is any season without the Name?

The Guru and Mardana did not remain long in that village. Mardana asked the Guru what his decision was regarding its inhabitants. He replied, ' O Mardana, may they remain here! '

The inhabitants of the next village at which they arrived showed them great attention. They remained there, however, for only one night, and departed next morning. The Guru when leaving said that the village should be abandoned. Then Mardana re marked, ' Sir, the village in which we were not allowed to sit down, thou hast blessed; and that which bestowed great attention and kindness on us thou hast cursed." The Guru replied, ' Mardana, if the people of the former village remove to another, they shall ruin it; but if the people of the latter village remove to another, they shall save it."

The Guru returned from Kamrup by the great river Brahmaputra, and then made a coasting voyage to Puri on the Bay of Bengal, where Vishnu or 1 That is, the condition of the body is as changeable as the seasons.

Krishan, under the name of Jagannath, lord of the world, is specially worshipped. When the lamps were lit in the evening the Guru was invited by the high priest to stand up and join in the god's worship, which was of a gorgeous and imposing character. In that rich temple offerings to the god were made on salvers studded with pearls. On the salvers were placed flowers and censers. A fan was employed to excite the flames of the incense, while the lamps around threw light over the temple. But the use of these articles showed artificial worship, while the expanse of the firmament, the sun and the moon, the procession of the stars, the natural incense of the sandal, the winds and forests, were the fitting acces sories of Nanak's purer worship of the God of creation. The Guru therefore, instead of accepting the high priest's invitation to adore the idol, raised his eyes to heaven, and gave utterance to the following hymn:â

The sun and moon, O Lord, are thy lamps; the firmament, Thy salver; the orbs of the stars, the pearls enchased in it.

The perfume of the sandal l is Thine incense; the wind is Thy fan; 2 all the forests are Thy flowers, O Lord of light. 3 1 Malianlo, literallyâ the wind from the Malay tree.

2 In the original, chauri, a flapper made from the tail of the yak or Thibetan cow, and used in India to brush away flies.

J The following is Dr. Trumpp's translation of these two verses:â

The dish is made of the sky, the sun and moon are made the lamps, the orbs of stars are, so to say, the pearls.

The wind is incense-grinding, the wind swings the fly-brush, the whole blooming wood is the flames (of the lamps).

While the present author was engaged in translating the sacred writings of the Sikhs at their request, one Bhai Gurumukh Singh projected a rival translation, which was to surpass all others. His modus operandi was to alter Dr. Trumpp's words here and there, and thus produce what he perhaps deemed would be an original version. He circulated the following as his translation of these lines:â

The sky is for my plate (for arti); the sun and moon are for lamps; (and) rows of stars are as it were for pearls.

The air of sandal wood for perfumary smoke, the wind (for my) fan and all the rows of blooming forests (for flowers), O Lord of light.

What worship is this, O Thou Destroyer of birth? l Un beaten strains of ecstasy are the trumpets of Thy worship.

Thou hast a thousand eyes and yet not one 2 eye; Thou hast a thousand forms and yet not one form; 3

Thou hast a thousand pure feet and yet not one foot; Thou hast a thousand organs of smell and yet not one organâ I am fascinated by this play of Thine.

The light which is in everything is Thine, O Lord of light.

From its brilliancy everything is brilliant;

By the Guru's teaching the light becometh manifest.

What pleaseth Thee is the real arati. 5

O God, my mind is fascinated with Thy lotus feet as the bumble-bee with the flower: night and day I thirst for them.

Give the water of Thy grace to the sarang 6 Nanak, so that he may dwell in Thy name. 7

L That is, of transmigration.

2 Thou hast many spiritual eyes, but no material eye.

3 Thy manifestations are many, yet Thou hast no bodily form.

4 Also translatedâ In this way Thou hast enchanted the world.

5 In memory of the circumstance recorded in the text the Sikhs repeat several prayers in the evening. The prayers are collectively called Arati, and consist of this hymn and some others, which will be noted in their proper place. The word Arati originally meant waving lamps at night before an idol.

5 The Sarang, or pied Indian cuckoo, the Cuculits Melanoleukos is supposed to drink water only when the moon is in the mansion of Arcturus, so, when its time comes to drink, it is naturally thirsty. This bird is also known under the names cha-trik and paplha. Its love is celebrated in song and story. It is in full voice on the ap proach of the Indian monsoon, when its plaintive strains are beard clearest at night. It is said that they make love's unhealed wounds bleed anew. 7 Dhanasari.

While at Jagannath, Guru Nanak met a Brahman who kept his eyes and nose closed so as to receive no pleasure from these organs. He averred that in that state he with his mental eyes saw the secrets of the world. Nanak hid his lota and the Brahman could not find it, so Nanak by the following hymn in the Dhanasari measure twitted him on his want of omniscience:â

This is not the age, there is no longer acquaintance with Jog; this is not the way of truth.

The holy places in the world have fallen; the world is thus ruined.

In this Kal age God's name is the best thing.
Thou closest thine eyes and boldest thy nose to deceive the world.
Thou boldest thy nose with thy thumb and first two fingers, and sayest that thou seest the three worlds.
But thou seest not what is behind thee, this is a wonderful thing. 1

CHAPTER VII

The Guru and Mardana after their travels in Eastern India returned to the Panjab, and proceeded on a visit to the shrine of Shaikh Farid, a Moslem saint, at a place then called Ajodhan, but now Pak Pattan, in the southern part of that province. A saint called Shaikh Brahm (Ibrahim) was then the incumbent of the shrine. He was the first to speak. On seeing the Guru, whom he knew to be a religious man, dressed in ordinary secular costume, he said:â

Either seek for high position 2 or for God.
Put not thy feet on two boats lest thy property founder. 3

The Guru replied:â 1 Also translatedâ lo! this is thy devotional attitude. Padam asan is one of the Jogis' attitudes.

2 Muqaddami, literally, the headship of a town.

3 The meaning isâ lead either a secular or a religious life. Do not combine both.

Put thy feet on two boats and thy property also on them: 1 One boat may sink, but the other shall cross over. 2 For me there is no water, no boat, no wreck, and no loss. Nanak, the True One is my property and wealth, and He is naturally everywhere contained.

Shaikh Brahm replied:â 0 Farid, the world is enamoured of the witch 3 who is found to be false when her secret is known.

Nanak, while thou lookest on, the field 4 is ruined.

Upon this the Guru urged:â 0 Farid, love for the witch hath prevailed from the very beginning.

Nanak, the field shall not be ruined if the watchman be on the alert.

Then Shaikh Brahm:â

Farid, my body faileth, my heart is broken, and no strength whatever remaineth me.

Arise, beloved, become my physician and give me medicine.

Then the Guru exhorted him:â My friend, examine the truth, lip-worship is hollow. Nanak, the Beloved is not far from thee; behold Him in thy heart.

Then Shaikh Brahm uttered the following:â When thou oughtest to have made thy raft, thou didst not do so; When the full river 5 overfloweth, it is difficult to cross over.

1 That is, enjoy the world and also remember God. 1 The body may perish, but the soul shall be saved.

3 Worldly love.

4 Man's body.

5 When the body has completed its measure of sin. Sarwar is, literally, a tank or lake, but Shaikh Brahm refers to the broad river Satluj, near which he lived.

Put not thy hand into the fire or it will burn, 1 my dear.
Some have obtained honour for themselves by uttering God's name.
As milk will not return to the udder, so the soul will not again enter the same body.

Saith Farid, O my companions, when the Spouse calleth you,
The soul shall depart in perplexity, and the body become a heap of dust. 2
The Guru replied by a hymn in the same measure:â
Make a raft of devotion and penance, so mayest thou cross the stream. 3
There is no lake, no overflowing; such a road is easy.
0 Lord, Thy name alone is the madder with which my robe is dyed.
Such colour is everlasting, O my dear.
If thou, my beloved, go not thus arrayed to meet the Bridegroom, how canst thou meet Him?
If thou possess virtues, He will meet thee.
If He become united with thee, He will not part from thee; that is, if union be really effected.
It is the True One who putteth an end to transmigration.
She who hath abandoned egotism hath sewed for herself a garment to please the Bridegroom.
Under the Guru's instruction she obtaineth her reward in the ambrosial converse of her Lord.
Nanak saith, O female companions, the Lord is thoroughly dear.
We are His slaves, true is our Spouse.
Then Shaikh Brahm uttered the following:â
They who have heart-felt love for God are the true; But they who have one thing in their hearts and utter another are accounted false.

1 Also translatedâ Touch not safflower: its dye will depart.
2 Suhi.
3 Wahela, also translatedâ comfortably.

They who are imbued with the love of God and a longing to behold Him are also true.
They who forget God's name are a burden to the earth.
God hath attached to His skirt those who were darweshes at His gate.
Blest the mothers who bore them; profitable was their advent into the world.
0 Cherisher, Thou art illimitable, unapproachable, and endless.
1 kiss the feet of those who recognize the True One.
I seek Thy shelter, O God; it is Thou who pardonest. Grant Thy worship as charity to Shaikh Farid. 1
On this the Guru uttered the hymn called Suchajji, the fortunate, in the Suhi measure:â
When I have Thee I have everything; Thou, O Lord, art my treasure.
In Thee I dwell in peace, in Thee to dwell is my pride;
If it please Thee, Thou bestowest a throne and greatness; if it please Thee, Thou makest man a forlorn mendicant;
If it please Thee, rivers flow over dry land, and the lotus bloometh in the heavens;
If it please Thee, man crosseth the terrible ocean; if it please Thee, he is drowned therein; â If it please Thee, Thou art my merry Spouseâ I am absorbed in Thy praises, 0 Lord 2 of excellences.

If it please Thee, O Lord, Thou terrifiest me, and then I am undone with transmigration.

O Lord, Thou art inaccessible and unequalled; I am exhausted uttering Thy praises.

What can I ask of Thee? What can I say to Thee? I hunger and thirst for a sight of Thee.

Under the instruction of the Guru I have obtained the Lord; Nanak's prayer hath been granted.

1 Asa.

2 Task is a Persian word meaning Lord. The gyanis translate it vessel.

The Guru and Shaikh Brahm remained together that night in the forest. A kindhearted and charit able villager who had seen them, took them a basin of milk before daylight. The Shaikh separated his own share from that of the Guru, and uttered these verses:â

Devotion in the beginning of the night is the blossom, in the end of the night l the fruit. They who watch obtain gifts from the Lord. 2

The Guru responded:â

Gifts are the Lord's; what can prevail against Him? 3 Some who are awake receive them not; others who are asleep He awaketh, and confereth presents upon them. 4

The Guru then asked Shaikh Brahm to put his hand into the milk and feel what was in it. Farid found that it contained four gold coins. Upon this the villager, deeming that he was in the hands of magicians, went away without his basin. The Guru uttered the following hymn:â

O thou with the beautiful eyes, in the first watch of a dark night

Watch thy property, O mortal; thy turn shall come next.

When thy turn cometh, who will awake thee? Death shall taste thy sweets as thou sleepest.

The night is dark; what shall become of thee when the thief breaketh into and robbeth thy house?

O inaccessible, incomparable Protector, hear my suppli cation.

â O Nanak, the fool hath never thought of God; what can he see in a dark night?

1 That is, the end of life.

2 Farid's Sloks.

3 No one can force Him to bestow His gifts.

4 Sri Rag ki War.

It is the second watch; awake, O heedless one.

Watch thy property, O mortal; thy field is being eaten up.

Watch thy field, love God's praises; while thou art awake, the thief shall not touch thee.

Then shalt thou not go the way of Death, nor suffer from him; the fear and dread of him shall depart.

The lamps of the sun and moon shall shine for thee, if thou under the Guru's instruction ponder on the True One in thy heart, and utter His name with thy lips.

Nanak, the fool heedeth not even now; how shall he obtain happiness in the second watch?

It is the third watch, thou art wrapt in slumber.

By wealth, children, and wives men are afflicted with sorrow:

Yet wealth, children, wives, and worldly possessions are dear to man; he nibbleth at the bait, and is continually caught.

If man under the Guru's instruction meditate on the Name, he shall obtain rest, and Death shall not seize him. 1

Transmigration and death never forsake us; without the Name we are afflicted.

Nanak, in the third watch men, under the influence of the three qualities, 2 feel worldly love.

1 Death only seizes the soul which has to undergo further trans migration. He does not harass the emancipated soul.

2 The three gunas or qualities of goodness, passion, and darknessâ or reality, impulse, and ignorance â are frequently mentioned in Sikh as well as Hindu sacred literature. The Mosaic and Zoroastrian systems recognized two principles, good and evil, in the economy of nature. It was the Indian sage Kapila who discerned the three prin ciples or qualities above stated. He beheld good, moderately good, and evil everywhere in creation. He believed that these qualities, but in different degrees, pervade all things, and are the distinguishing characteristics of matter implanted in it by the Creator Himself.

The demigods possess goodness in excess, the demons darkness, and men passion. Manu thus defines the three qualities: ' It ought to be known that the three gunas or fetters of the soul are goodness, passion, and darkness. Restrained by one or more of these it is ever

It is the fourth watch; the sun riseth.

They who night and day are watchful have saved their homes.

Night is pleasant for those who under the Guru's instruc tion watch and apply themselves to the Name.

They who act according to the instruction of the Guru shall not be born again; the Lord will befriend them.

In the fourth watch hands shake, feet and frames totter, eyes grow dim, and men's bodies become like ashes.

Nanak, without God's name abiding in the mind man is unhappy during the four watches.

The knot of life is open; arise, thine allotted time hath come.

All pleasures and happiness are at an end; Death will lead thee captive away.

Without being seen or heard he will lead thee captive, when it so pleaseth God.

His turn shall come to every one; the ripe field shall ever be cut down.

An account of every ghari and moment shall be taken, and the soul shall obtain punishment or reward.

Nanak, God made everything, demigods and men are herein agreed. 1

When the Guru and Shaikh Brahm left the forest the villager returned to fetch his basin. On lifting it up, it is said, he found that it had become gold, and was filled with gold coins. Then he began to repent of his suspicions, and confessed to himself that they were religious men. If he had come with attached to forms of existence. Whenever any one of the three qualities predominates, it causes the embodied spirit to abound in that quality The aim of the soul apparently should be to divest itself

of all three qualities. Compare Plato's distinction of the three parts of the mind corresponding to the three classes of his ideal state. 1 Tukhari Chhant.
his heart disposed towards God, he would have gained holiness. ' I came with worldliness, and worldliness have I found." Upon this he took up his basin and departed.

Shaikh Brahm remarked that it was difficult for those who attached themselves to mammon to obtain salvation, and inquired what aid besides God's name was ordinarily necessary for future happiness. The Guru replied with the following hymn:â

The union of father and mother produceth a body, On which the Creator hath written its destiny, The gifts, the divine lights, and the greatness allotted it â But on associating with mammon it loseth remembrance of God.

0 foolish man, why art thou proud?
Thou shalt have to depart when it pleaseth the Lord.
Abandon pleasures, and peace and happiness shall be thine.
Thou shalt have to leave thy home; no one is permanent here.
Eat a little and leave a little,
If thou art again to return to this world. 1
Man decketh his body, dresseth it in silk,
And issueth many orders;
He maketh a couch of ease and sleepeth thereon.
Why weepeth he when he falleth into the hands of Death? 2
Domestic entanglements are a whirlpool, O brother;
Sin is a stone which floateth not over.
Put thy soul on the raft of God's fear, and thou shalt be saved.
Saith Nanak, such a raft God giveth but to few. 3

Then the people brought them bread, but Shaikh Brahm said that he had already dined. The people, annoyed that their offerings were thus spurned, said 1 That is, to practise great economy would be useless for him who is not to return to this world.

2 If man disregard the present opportunity of doing good works, why should he afterwards weep when Death seizes him for punishment?

3 Maru.

to him: ' You must be a liar from that country where Farid, who wore a wooden cake on his stomach, held religious sway. Whenever any one offered him food he used to say he had taken dinner 1 Upon this Shaikh Brahm said: ' What shall be my condition, who am ever saying that I have dined, when I am only fasting? ' The Guru was pleased to observe the Shaikh's tender conscience, and said to him: ' Shaikh Brahm, God is in thee." The Shaikh then asked the Guru to tell him of God, and by what virtues and merits He was to be found. The Guru replied as follows:â

Come, my sisters and dear companions, embrace me.
Having embraced me, tell me tales of the Omnipotent Spouse.
In the true Lord are all merits, in us all dements.
0 Creator, every one is in Thy power.
Meditate on the one Word; where Thou, 0 God, art, what more is required?
Go ask the happy wife by what merits she enjoyeth her Spouseâ
Composure, contentment, and sweet discourse are mine ornaments.

' I met my Beloved, who is an abode of pleasure, when I heard the Guru's word."
How great, O God, is Thy power! how great Thy gifts!
How many men and lower animals utter Thy praises day and night!
How many are Thy forms and colours! how many castes high and low!
When the true Guru is found, truth is produced, and man becoming true is absorbed in the truth.
When man is filled with fear through the Guru's instructions, then he obtaineth understanding, and honour re-sulteth.
Nanak, the true King then blendeth man with Himself. 2 1 An account of Farid will be found in the sixth volume of this work.
2 Sri Rag.

The Guru, after his pleasant visit to Shaikh Brahm and his district, where he made several converts, proceeded to a country called Bisiar, probably the state of Bushahir in the Himalayas, where he was ill received. The inhabitants, deeming his presence pollution, purified every place he had stood on. One man alone, Jhanda, a carpenter, was found to treat him with hospitality. He took him to his house, washed his feet, and drank the water used for the purpose. While drinking, it was revealed to him that Nanak was a Guru. He joined him in his wanderings.

The Guru and his companions directed their steps to the East. They went to an island in the ocean where they could obtain no food. There the Guru composed the Jugawali, a poem (no longer extant) on the four ages of the world. Jhanda committed it to writing and circulated it. With the new composition in his possession he returned to his own country, leaving the Guru and Mardana to continue their pilgrimage.

Not long after they found themselves in a lonely desert. Mardana began to feel the pangs of hunger, and thus addressed his master: ' We are lost in this great wilderness, from which God alone can extricate us. Here I shall fall into the clutches of some wild animal which will kill and eat me The Guru asked him to take care, and nothing should come near him. He further consoled him by stating that they were not in a desert, as the place where God's name was uttered was always inhabited. ' Many better men than we', said the Guru, 'have endured greater hardships." Upon this he composed the following:â

The demigods in order to behold Thee, O God, made pilgrimages in sufferings and hunger.
Jogis andjatis 1 go their own ways, and don ochre-coloured garbs.
1 Jatis, men vowed to perpetual continence.
For Thy sake, O my Lord, the darweshes are imbued with love.
Thy names are various, Thy forms are various, the number of Thy merits cannot be told.
Men leaving houses and homes, palaces, elephants and horses go abroad.
Priests, prophets, holy and sincere men leave the world to obtain salvation.
They abandon good living, rest, happiness, and dainties; they doff clothes, and wear skins.
Imbued with Thy name they in anguish and pain become darweshes at Thy gate.
They don skins, carry begging bowls, staves, and wear hair-tufts, sacrificial threads, and loin-cloths.

Thou art the Lord, I am Thy player; Nanak repre-senteth, what is caste? 1

The Guru further remonstrated with his attendant: ' We cannot succeed without God's word. Think of some hymn and play the rebeck." Mardana replied that his throat was collapsing for want of food, and he had no strength to move, much less to play. The Guru then pointed to a tree and told him to eat his fill of its fruit, but take none with him. Mardana accordingly began to eat, and so much enjoyed the flavour of the fruit, that he thought he would eat what he could, and also take some with him, lest he might soon again find himself in a similar plight.

As they continued their wanderings, Mardana again felt hungry, so he drew forth his stock of fruit. Directly he tasted it he fell down.' The Guru inquired what had happened. Mardana confessed his dis obedience of his master's instructions in having brought with him and eaten some of the forbidden fruit. The Guru remonstrated with him for his disregard of orders. The fruit was poisonous, but the Guru had blessed it for the occasion and made 1 Asa.

it wholesome. The Guru put his foot on Mardana's forehead as he lay stretched on the ground, and he at once revived.

CHAPTER VIII

Mardana had by this time had enough of travel, hardship, and hunger, and thus addressed his mas ter: ' Blessings on thy devotion and thy deeds! Thou art a holy man who hast abandoned the world, who neither eatest nor drinkest, and who never enterest a village. How can I remain with thee? ' The Guru asked him on what conditions he would change his mind and continue to accompany him. He replied, ' I will remain with thee if thou satisfy my hunger in the same way as thou satisfiest thine own; and if thou also promise not to take notice of anything I do The Guru agreed to these conditions, and told him he should be happy in this world and the next. Mardana then fell at his feet.

It would appear, however, that Mardana soon represented to the Guru the duty and propriety of returning home, and seeing his parents after twelve years' wandering. The Guru adopted his suggestion, and they both directed their steps towards Talwandi. They halted in the forest some three miles from the village. Mardana asked permission to go home and inquire if his people were dead or alive. The Guru replied, ' Since thou desire it, go and see thy people. Go also to my father Kalu's house, but mention not my name. Return quickly."

When Mardana reached his house he found several persons assembled there. They all affectionately greeted him, and said he had grown like Nanak. He was a great man now, and no longer the humble person he had been before. Mardana, having seen his people, proceeded to the house of Kalu, and sat down in his courtyard. The Guru's mother, on seeing him, arose, embraced him, and wept for joy. She asked for some account of her son Nanak. By that time a great crowd had assembled, and every one wanted to hear about him. Mardana evaded all inquiries, only telling people that he had been with Nanak. He then went away. The Guru's mother at once suspected that he must have had some ob ject in departing so quickly, and that her son could not be far off. She again arose, and taking some clothes and sweets for Nanak, followed Mardana and overtook him. She earnestly requested him to take her to her son. Mardana made no answer, but went on his way, she following.

Nanak arose on seeing his mother, and respect fully saluted her. She kissed his forehead and began to weep, saying, ' I am a sacrifice unto thee. I am a sacrifice unto the ground thou treadest on. Seeing thy face hath made me happy. Now I desire that thou shouldst abandon thy wanderings, abide with us, and turn thine attention to commerce for thy livelihood The Guru, who was in turn delighted to see his mother, called on Mardana to play the rebeck while he himself sang the following:â

Drunkards abandon not stimulants, nor fishes water:
So God is pleasing beyond all others to those who are imbued with their Lord. 1
I am a sacrifice, I would be cut in pieces, O Lord, for Thy name.
The Lord is a fruit-bearing tree whose name is ambrosia.
They who have partaken of it are satisfied; I am a sacrifice unto them.
Why appearest Thou not unto me, 0 Lord, since Thou abidest with all?
1 These two lines are also translatedâ
If drunkards obtain not stimulants, and fishes water, they are pleased with nothing else,
So all who are imbued with their Lord are content with none but Him.
How shall my thirst abate when there is a screen between the Tank l and me?
Nanak is Thy dealer; Thou O Lord, art his capital.
Illusion leaveth my mind when I praise and pray to Thee. 2

His mother placed before Nanak the new clothes and sweets she had brought for him, and asked him to eat. He said he required no food. His mother inquired where he had eaten. He again called on Mardana to play an accompaniment to the following hymn:â

To obey God's word is all sweet flavour; to hear it is salt flavour;
To utter it with the mouth is acid flavour, and to sing it is spices.
The love of the one God is thirty-six dishes 3 for those on whom He looketh with favour.
O mother, other viands afford ruinous happiness;
By eating them the body is pained, and sin entereth the mind.

His mother asked him to take off the faqir's jacket he wore, and put on the new becoming clothes she had brought him. His reply was the following:â

To be imbued with God is as red, truth and charity as white clothing;
To cut away the blackness of sin is blue, to meditate on God's feet is the real raiment;
Contentment is the waistband: Thy name, 0 Lord, is wealth and youth.
Mother, other dress affordeth ruinous happiness;
By putting it on, the body is pained and sin entereth the mind.

By this time his father Kaluhad heard of Nanak's arrival, and went on horseback to meet him. Nanak 1 God. 2 Wadhans.

3 Indian gourmets enumerate thirty-six palatable dishes.

bowed to him, and fell at his feet. Meantime Kalu continued to weep for joy. He asked his son to mount the horse on which he had come, and go home with him. Nanak replied that he had no need of a horse, and then sang the following:-

To know Thy way, 0 God, is as horses with saddles made of gold.
To pursue virtue is as quivers, arrows, bows, spears, and sword-belts.

To be honourably distinguished is as bands and lances; Thy favour, O God, is as caste for me.

Father, other conveyance affordeth ruinous happiness;

By mounting it the body is pained, and sin entereth the mind.

The father again pressed the son to return with him, if only for once. He said he had built a new house which he should like to show him after his long absence. Nanak ought also to visit his wife, and then, if he felt so disposed, he might continue his wanderings. Nanak replied:â

The pleasure of the Name is as mansions and palaces; Thy favouring glance, O Lord, is as family for me.

To please Thee is mine empire; to say more were alto gether useless.

Nanak, true is the King; He decideth without taking others' counsel.

Father, other intercourse affordeth ruinous happiness;

By indulging in it the body is pained, and sin entereth the mind. 1

Kalu again said: ' My son, tell me at what thou art offended. If thou desire it, I will find thee another wife." The Guru replied as follows:â

He who made the world watcheth over it, and appointeth His creatures to their various duties.

Thy gifts, O Lord, are as light to the mind, and as the moon and lamps to the body.

1 Sri Rag.

Thy gifts are as the moon and lamps to the body, by which the pain of darkness is dispelled.

The bridal procession of attributes which accompany the Bridegroom who hath chosen His bride, appeareth beautiful.

The marriage hath been performed with splendour to the accompaniment of the five musical instruments. 1

I am a sacrifice to my unchanging companions and friends.

I have exchanged hearts with those to whom my body is attached.

Why should I forget those friends with whom I have exchanged hearts?

Let those whose sight giveth pleasure be clasped to the heart.

All merits and not one demerit is theirs for ever and ever.

If one have a casket of virtues, let him extract odour from it.

If our friends possess virtues, let us go and become partners with them.

Let us form a partnership with virtue and abandon vice.

Let us wear silk, go in state, and take possession of our arena. 2

Wherever we go, let us sit down, speak civilly, and skim and drink nectar.

If one have a casket of virtues, let him extract odour therefrom.

It is God Himself who acteth; to whom should we complain? No one else acteth.

Go and complain to Him if He forget.

If He forget, go and complain to Him; but why should the Creator Himself forget?

He heareth, seeth, giveth His gifts without asking or praying for.

The Giver, the Arranger of the world giveth His gifts, Nanak, and true is He.

1 The voice, stringed instruments, wind instruments, leather instru ments, as drums, and metallic instruments as cymbals, bells, c. Panch sabd may also mean the five species of breath enumerated by Jogis.

2 That is, the company of saints.

When He Himself acteth, to whom should we complain? No one else acteth. 1

Nanak continued to address Kalu: ' Father dear, it is God who arrangeth marriages. He maketh no mistake, and those whom He hath once joined He joineth for ever By these words the Guru perhaps meant to establish monogamy. 2 The Guru's mother then interposed, and asked her son to stand up and go with them, and cease his nonsense. He would obtain wealth by attending to his worldly duties. The Guru replied with the following hymn:â

In the end of the night call upon the name of the Lord,

And tents, umbrellas, pavilions, and carriages shall appear ready for your celestial journey.

They are ever obtained by those who meditate on Thy name, 0 Lord.

Father, I am without good works and false; I have not meditated on Thy name.

My mind is blind, led astray by superstition.

The pleasures I have had have blossomed into pain by primal destiny, O mother.

The pleasure was little; the pain great; in much pain have I passed my life.

What separation is there from those who have separated from God? and what meeting is there with those who have met Him?

Praise that Lord who made and beholdeth this play.

By good destiny men meet God and enjoy pleasures even in this life.

By evil destiny they who meet separate, O Nanak, but even so they meet again by God's favour. 3

Suhi Chhant.

2 Bhai Gur Das, so understood the Guru's words when he wroteâ Be chaste with one wife (War, vi, 8). In the Prem Sumarag, a work containing the supplementary teaching of Guru Gobind Singh, is found the injunction: 'Be satisfied with one wife. That befits a good man."

3 Maru.

Kalu, finding his arguments vain, appealed to his son on the score of his health and safety, and pointed out how regardless of them he had been. The following was the Guru's reply:â

I have no anxiety regarding death, and I have no desire for life.

Thou, 0 God, art the Cherisher of all living things; our breathings l are taken into account.

Thou dwellest in the holy; as it pleaseth Thee, so Thou decidest.

O my soul, by uttering God's name the heart is satisfied.

Under the Guru's instruction divine knowledge is obtained, and the burning of the heart extinguished. 2

The Guru again addressed his parents: ' Father dear, mother dear, I have returned home. I have been until now a hermit. Obey God's order and let me again depart." His mother replied: ' My son, how shall I console myself, seeing that thou hast only now returned after an absence of twelve years? ' Then the Guru urged, ' Mother, agree to what I say; con solation shall come to thee. 1 She then became silent, thinking it was useless to make further remonstrance.

CHAPTER IX

The Guru and Mardana again set out on their travels. It is said that they went to the west and crossed the rivers Ravi and Chanab, and, after a long circuitous route through a desert country, made their way again to Pak Pattan to pay another visit to Shaikh Brahm. They sat down to rest about four miles from the city. Shaikh Kamal, a pious and God-fearing disciple of Shaikh Brahm, who had gone 1 Sas giras, expiration and inspiration. 2 Sri Rag.

into the forest for firewood, observed the Guru and his attendant. The latter was playing his rebeck and singing the following:â

Thou art the tablet, 0 Lord, Thou art the pen, and Thou art also the writing.
Speak of the one God; O Nanak, why should there be a second? 1

Shaikh Kamal went and, after obeisance, sat down near them, and asked to have the couplet repeated. This was done, and he learned it by heart. He then took up the firewood he had collected and went home. He told his master of his adventure, and repeated the couplet for him. Shaikh Brahm was highly pleased that the Guru had again visited his country, and he promptly proceeded to welcome him. After mutual salutations, the Guru thanked God for having again granted him a sight of Shaikh Brahm. After some friendly conversation, the Shaikh asked the Guru to explain the couplet. ' Nanak, thou sayest, "There is only one God; why should there be a second? " I say:â

There is one Lord and two ways; Which shall I adopt, and which reject? '
The Guru replied:â
There is but one Lord and one way; Adopt one and reject the other.
Why should we worship a second who is born and dieth? Remember the one God, Nanak, who is contained in sea and land.

The Muhammadan priest then said in turn:â
Tear thy coat into tatters and wear a blanket instead; Adopt a dress by which thou mayest obtain the Lord. 2

The Guru traversed this instruction: ' It is not 1 Malar ki War. 2 Faiid's Sloks.

necessary for me to tear my coat or adopt a religious garb. Men who reside at home and work in their ordinary costume shall find the Lord if they fix their hearts on Him;' 1

A young wife sitteth at home, her Beloved is abroad; she continually thinketh of Him and pineth away.
She shall have no delay in meeting Him if she have good intentions. 2

Shaikh Brahm replied to the latter couplet:â
When she was little, she enjoyed not her Spouse; when she grew up she died. Lying in the grave she calleth out, ' I have not met Thee, O Lord." 3

Guru Nanak then gave utterance to the following, to the effect that salvation depends upon virtue and not on a pleasing exterior or the possession of accomplishments:â

A woman may be stupid, untidy, black, and impure-minded;
Yet, if she possess merits, she meeteth her Beloved; otherwise, Nanak, the woman is to blame.

The Shaikh then put the following questions:â
What is that word, what that virtue, what that priceless spell â

What dress shall I wear by which I may captivate the Spouse? 4 1 This reply of the Guru was subsequently versified by Guru Amar Das:â

Why tear thy coat, Nanak, and why wear a blanket? Seated at home thou shalt find the Lord if thine intentions be good.

2 Wadhans ki War. 3 Farid's Sloks. 4 Farid's Sloks.

The Guru replied:â

Humility is the word, forbearance the virtue, and civility the priceless spell.

Make these three 1 thy dress, O sister, and the Spouse shall come into thy power. 2

The Spouse shall be hers who serveth Him.

Forsaking all His other companions He will go to her.

The Shaikh then said he wanted a knifeâ ' Give me such a knife as will make those who are killed with it acceptable to God. With the ordinary knife in use the lower animals are killed, and if a man's throat be cut with it he becomes carrion." The Guru replied: ' Dear Shaikh, here it is:â

Truth is the knife, truth is pure steel;

Its fashion is altogether incomparable.

Put it on the hone of the Word,

And fit it into the scabbard of merit.

If any one be bled with that, O Shaikh,

The blood of avarice will be seen to issue forth.

If man be slaughtered with it, he shall go to meet God,

O Nanak, and be absorbed in the sight of Him." 3

On hearing this the Shaikh raised his head in amazement and said, ' Well done. Thou hast seen God, and art dear to Him. God hath been very kind to me in that I have met thee. It would be rude to ask any further questions of those who are so beloved by Him." The Guru then volunteered the following:â

There is friendship between beauty and love, alliance between hunger and dainty viands;

Companionship between greed and wealth, between a sleepy man and a bed and coverlet.

1 Tewar, three pieces forming an Indian woman's dress 2 Fand's Sloks. 3 Ram'ali ki War.

The anger which barketh is despised; it is vain to worry with worldly occupations.

To be silent, O Nanak, is good; without the Name the mouth is defiled. 1

The Shaikh asked the Guru to let him hear a strain in praise of the one God. ' My idea is ', said the Shaikh, ' that adoration cannot be performed without two beings, that is, God and the Prophet; Let me see whom thou makest man's intercessor The Guru called upon Mardana to play the rebeck and recite the first slok and pauri 2 of the Asa ki War.

I am a sacrifice, Nanak, to my Guru a hundred times a day,

Who without any delay made demigods out of men.

Nanak, they who, very clever in their own estimation, think not of the Guru,

Shall be left like spurious sesames in a reaped fieldâ

They shall be left in the field, saith Nanak, without an owner.

The wretches may even bear fruit and flower, but these shall be as ashes within their bodies.

God Himself created the world and Himself gave names to things.

He made Maya by His power; seated He beheld His work with delight.

0 Creator, Thou art the Giver; being pleased Thou bestowest and practisest kindness.

Thou knowest all things; Thou givest and takest life with a word. 3

Seated Thou beholdest Thy work with delight. 4 1 Malar ki War.

2 A shlok in Sanskrit is a distich or couplet, but in modern Indian poetry it may extend to the length of an English sonnet. The word pauri is literally a ladder. In the Granth Sahib it means a stanza of five lines, and always follows a slok.

3 Also translatedâ Thou givest and takest life from the body.

4 Asa ki War.

Shaikh Brahm asked the Guru for further instruc tion. The Guru then spoke on the subject of humility, and said that as water, which resteth lowly on the earth, riseth under pressure into the air in sparkling fountains, so they who preserve a humble mind mount to God's highest pinnacle.

The Shaikh then rose to take his leave, and said, ' O Nanak, thou hast found God. There is no difference between Him and thee. Kindly grant that I too may be on good terms with Him The Guru replied, ' Shaikh Brahm, God will cause thy cargo also to arrive safe." By this the Guru meant that God would accept the Shaikh's devotion. The Shaikh requested the Guru to give him a certain promise of this, and the Guru complied. They then shook hands and parted.

The Guru next proceeded to Dipalpur. During his journey a Sanyasi asked him to define the word udas. The Guru replied: ' To make use of all things in this world and not deem them one's own, but only God's property, and ever to possess a desire to meet Him is udas."

The Guru then visited Kanganpur, Kasur, and Patti in the Lahore District. He thence proceeded to Windpur, not far from the present town of Cholha, in the sub-collectorate of Tarn Taran in the Amritsar District. He met some Khatris who dwelt there; but when they saw him dressed as a faqir and heard his minstrel Mardana sing, they were displeased at what they considered the masquerade he had adopted, and said to him, ' What dress is this which thou hast assumed? Having become a faqir, thou hast dis graced thy tribe, and led the world astray. Quit this place." The Guru represented that he would only remain for the night, and would depart next morning. He added that he was not leading people the wrong way, but guiding them to salvation. They replied that they would not allow him to remain for a moment in their village. He must depart at once, or they would forcibly expel him. The Guru, complying with this insulting order, said that the Guru's place should ever be permanent.

The Guru thence proceeded to a village on the site of the present Goindwal, where he desired to stay, but no one except a poor leper would receive him or allow him to remain there. The leper took him to his hut, and entertained him for the night. The leper thanked God that he had at last seen a human face, for even the lower animals had fled from him. When he began further to bemoan his fate, the Guru uttered the following:â

My mind is ever and ever troubled.

In many troubles my body pineth away and ever groweth worse.
The body which forgetteth God's word,
Screameth like a real leper.
To make many complaints is to talk folly â 'Without our complaining everything is known to God,
Who made our ears, our eyes, and our noses;
Who gave us tongues wherewith to speak;
Who preserved us in the fire of the womb;
And through whom the breath moveth and speaketh every where.
Worldly love, affection, and dainties
Are all blackness and stains.
If man depart with the brand of sin on his face,
He will not be allowed to sit in God's court.
If he meet Thy favour, 0 God, he repeateth Thy name. v By attaching himself to it he is saved; he hath no other resource.
Even if he be drowning in sin, God will still take care of him. Nanak, the True One is beneficent to all. 1

The Guru further warmed towards the leper and blessed him. The leper was cured of his malady, fell at the Guru's feet, and began to utter the Name.

1 Dhanasari.

The Guru then travelled through Sultanpurâ his old head quarters when he was a Government officialâ Vairowal, and Jalalabad, until he arrived at a place called Kari Pathandi in the Amritsar District. In Kari Pathandi he made many Pathan converts. They used to serenade him with instru mental music, interspersed with cries of ' Hail to King Nanak!" The Guru there composed the fol lowing:â

He who made the world watcheth over it; what shall we say, O brother?
He Himself who hath laid out its garden knoweth and acteth.
Sing the praises of the Beloved; sing His praises by which happiness is ever obtained.
She who enjoyeth not her Spouse with love shall after wards repent.
She shall wring her hands, and beat her head as the night passeth away.
She shall not be able to repent when the whole night is at an end;
But she may again enjoy her Husband when it cometh to her turn. 1
The wife whom the Spouse hath chosen is better than I.
I have not her merits; whom shall I blame?
I will go and ask the female companions who have enjoyed their Spouse;
I will touch their feet, implore them, and induce them to show me the way.
Nanak, she who obeyeth her Spouse's order, applieth fear as her sandal,
And performeth the incantation of merits, shall find her Beloved.
She who meeteth Him with her heart shall continue to meet Him; that is called a real meeting.
However much one may desire it, a meeting is not effected by words.

1 That is, in a future birth.

Metal blendeth with metal and love hasteneth to love.
Know the Guru's favour, and thou shalt find the Fearless One.

A garden of betel may be in the house, but the donkey knoweth not its merits.
When one is a judge of perfume, then may one appreciate flowers.
He who drinketh nectar, 1 Nanak, putteth an end to his doubts and transmigration; He easily blendeth with God, and obtaineth the undying dignity. 2

The Guru continued his wanderings and visited Batala in the Gurdaspur District. Thence he pro ceeded a second time to Saiyidpur, where he again visited Lalo. Lalo complained to him of the oppres sion of the Pathans. The Guru replied that their dominion should be brief, as Babar was on his way to the conquest of India. The Guru then addressed the following threnody to his host:â

As the word of the Lord cometh to me, so I make known, O Laloâ

Bringing a bridal procession of sin, Babar hath hasted from Kabul and demandeth wealth as his bride, O Lalo.

Modesty and religion have vanished; falsehood marcheth in the van, O Lalo.

The occupation of the Qazis and the Brahmans is gone; the devil readeth the marriage service, 3 O Lalo.

Musalman women read the Quran, and in suffering call upon God, O Lalo.

Hindu women whether of high or low caste, meet the same fate as they, O Lalo.

They sing the paean of murder, O Nanak, and smear themselves with the saffron of blood.

Nanak singeth the praises of the Lord in the city of corpses, and uttereth this commonplace â 1 He who performs heartfelt devotion. 2 Tilang, Ashtapadi.
5 This refers to the licentiousness of Babar's army.

no THE SIKH RELIGION

He who made men assigned them different positions; He sitteth apart alone and regardeth them.

True is the Lord, true His decision, true the justice He meteth out as an example.

Bodies shall be cut like shreds of cloth; Hindustan will remember what I say.

They shall come in '78, depart in '97, and then shall rise another disciple of a hero. 1

Nanak uttereth the word of the True One, and will pro claim the truth at the True One's appointed time. 2

Lalo asked the Guru what he meant by saying that God had assigned men different positions. The Guru replied as follows:â

God can cause lions, hawks, kestrels, and falcons to eat grass;

And the animals which eat grass He can cause to eat meat â such a custom can He establish.

He can cause hills to appear in rivers, and unfathomable rivers in sandy deserts.

He can appoint a worm to sovereignty, and reduce an army to ashes.

What wonder would it be if God caused to live without breath all the animals which live by breathing?

Nanak, as it pleaseth the True One, so He giveth us sustenance. 3

A Brahman came to the Guru, offered him a basket of fruit, and said, ' My friend, thou art uttering hymns of wrath The Guru replied, 'Remain not here; there is a pool three miles distant; go thither with thy family. All who remain here will be put 1 That is, the Mughals shall come in Sambat 1578, and depart in Sambat 1597 (A. D. 1540).

The Sambat year is fifty-seven years in ad vance of annus Domini. The departing monarch was Humayun. The disciple of a hero is understood to be Sher Shah Sun, vho dispossessed him. This line appears to be an answer to a question put to the Guru by Lalo.

to death." The Brahman acted on his advice. After some days Babar assaulted and destroyed the city. He also devastated the neighbouring villages. There was a general massacre of the people, and Pathan as well as Hindu habitations were plundered and razed to the ground.

The lives of the Guru and Mardana were spared, probably because they were strangers, but they were imprisoned and placed under the superinten dence of Mir Khan, an officer of Babar's army. Mir Khan, on seeing them, ordered, ' Take away these slaves to work The Guru was condemned to carry loads on his head, and Mardana to do the work of a groom. The Guru upon this uttered the fol lowing:â

I am a purchased slave, my name is Lucky.

I have sold myself in the shop for God's word; where He placed me, there am I placed.

What cleverness hath Thy slave?

He cannot obey the Lord's order.

My mother was a slave, my father a slave, I was born a slave.

My mother danced, my father sang, I perform Thy service, O King. 1

If Thou drink I will fetch Thee water, O Lord; if Thou eat I will grind Thee corn.

I will fan Thee, I will shampoo Thy limbs, and continue to repeat Thy name.

Saith Nanak, ungrateful is Thy slave; if Thou pardon him, it will be to Thy glory.

In the beginning, in every age, Lord of mercy, Bestower, without Thee salvation is not obtained. 2

When the Guru had finished this hymn, Mardana saw some women weeping and shrieking as they passed along, and asked his master what had hap pened to them. The Guru told Mardana to play the 1 That is, I am a hereditary servant of God. 2 Maru.

rebeck. Mardana replied that he could not do so, as he was holding a horse. The Guru bade him utter ' Wah Guru ' and let go the horse. Mardana obeyed and played the Rag Asa, to which the Guru sang the following hymn:â

They who wore beautiful tresses and the partings of whose hair were dyed with vermilion,

Have their locks now shorn with the scissors, and dust is thrown upon their heads.

They dwelt in their private chambers; now they cannot find a seat in publicâ

Hail, Father! hail!

0 Primal Being, Thy limit is not known; Thou makest and beholdest the different phases of existence â

When they were married, they appeared beautiful near their spouses;

They came in their sedans adorned with ivory;

Water was waved round their heads, 1 and glittering fans over them.

They had hundreds of thousands waiting on them sitting, and hundreds of thousands waiting on them standing.

Eating coco-nuts and dates they sported on their couches;

But now chains are on their necks, and broken are their strings of pearls.

The wealth and beauty which afforded them pleasure have now become their bane.
The order was given to the soldiers to take and dishonour them.
If it please God, He giveth greatness; and if it please Him, He giveth punishment.
If they had thought of Him before, why should they have received punishment?
But they had lost all thought of God in joys, in spectacles, and in pleasures.
When Babar's rule was proclaimed no Pathan prince ate his food.
1 The bridegroom's mother or elder sister waves water around the head of a bride and then drinks it, so as to take all her ills on herself.
Some lost their five times of prayer, others their hours of worship.
How shall Hindu women now bathe and apply frontal marks without their sacred squares?
f They who never thought of Ram 1 are not now allowed even to mention Khuda. 2
One may return to her home; another may meet and in quire after the safety of a relation;
But others are destined to sit and weep in pain. v What pleaseth God, O Nanak, shall happen; what is man? 3

After this, Mir Khan, the governor of the jail, arrived. He saw that the Guru's bundle was raised a cubit over his head without any apparent support, and that the horse entrusted to Mardana followed him while he played sacred music on his rebeck. The governor communicated this information to Babar. The Emperor replied that, if he had known the city contained such holy men, he would not have destroyed it. At the governor's suggestion he went to the prison, which was two miles distant. There were Pathan and Hindu women huddled pro miscuously together, grinding corn. The Guru had also been supplied with a hand-mill for the same purpose. It is said that the mill revolved of its own accord while he put in the corn. The Emperor addressed the Guru, but he was in a trance, thinking of the slaughter of his unoffending countrymen. On awaking he uttered the following hymn, which, however, is not found in the Granth Sahib:â 1 The Hindu name of God.

2 The Muhammadan name of God, which Hindus shrink from pronouncing.

3 Compare â

God of our fathers! what is man, That thou towards him with hand so various, Or might I say contrarious,
Temper'st thy providence through his short course, Not evenly, as thou rulest
The angelic orders, and inferior creatures mute, Irrational and brute?
MILTON, Samson Agomstes.
No one can kill him, O Kind One, whom Thou preserves!.
How can Thy praises be numbered? Thou savest countless beings.
Preserve me, O Beloved, preserve me! I am Thy slave.
My true Lord pervadeth sea and land, the nether and the upper regions.
Thou didst preserve Jaidev and Nama, Thy beloved saintsâ
Thou didst save those on whom Thou didst bestow Thy nameâ
Thou didst preserve Sain, Kabir, and Trilochan who loved Thy name.
Thou didst preserve Ravdas, the tanner, who is numbered among Thy saints. 1
Nanak, who is without honour or family, uttereth suppli cation.

Extricate him, O Lord, from the ocean of the world, and make him Thine own.

It is said that the Emperor, on hearing this, fell at Nanak's feet, and declared that God appeared on his face. Upon this all the courtiers saluted Nanak. The Emperor asked him to accept a present from him. The Guru replied that he wanted nothing for himself, but he requested that the captives of Saiyidpur might be released. Upon this the Emperor ordered that they should be set free and their pro perty restored to them. The captives, however, refused to depart without the Guru. He was then allowed to go with them, and they went to their homes in the city. They found that all the people who had remained in Saiyidpur had been put to death. Mardana told his master that it had all hap pened as God had willed it. Upon this the Guru, to the accompaniment of Mardana's rebeck, sang the following lamentation:â

An account of the saints mentioned in this hymn, with their com positions contained in the Granth Sahib, will be given in the final volume of this work.

Where are those sports, those stables, and those horses? Where those bugles and clarions?

Where are those who buckled on their swords and were mighty in battle? where those scarlet uniforms?

Where those mirrors and fair faces? we see them no longer here.

This world is Thine, O Lord of the earth.

In one ghari Thou establishest and disestablishest; Thou distributest wealth as Thou pleasest.

Where are those houses, those mansions, and those palaces? where those beautiful seraglios?

Where are those easy couches and those women a sight of whom banished sleep?

Where is that betel, those betel-sellers, and those fair ones? They have vanished.

For wealth many are ruined; this wealth hath disgraced many.

It is not amassed without sin, and it departeth not with the dead.

Him whom the Creator destroyeth He first depriveth of virtue.

Millions of priests tried by their miraculous power to restrain the emperor when they heard of his approach.

He burned houses, mansions, and palaces; he cut princes to pieces, and had them rolled in the dust.

No Mughal hath become blind; no priest hath wrought a miracle.

There was a contest between the Mughals and Pathans; the sword was wielded in the battle.

One side aimed and discharged their guns, the other also handled their weapons:

They whose letter hath been torn in God's court must die, my brethren.

There were the wives of Hindus, of Turks, of Bhattis, and of Rajputs.

1 In India when announcing the death of a relation it is usual for the writer to tear the top of the letter. The reference here is to that custom.

The robes of some were torn from head to foot; the dwellings of others were their places of cremation.

How did they whose husbands came not home pass the night?

The Creator acteth and causeth others to act; to whom shall man complain?

Misery and happiness are according to Thy pleasure; to whom shall we go to cry?

The Commander is pleased issuing His orders; Nanak, man obtaineth what is allotted him. 1

A propos of the change of circumstances in India the Guru uttered the following:â

God-hath given fixed time for all events, and fully estab lished the nine regions, the seven seas, the fourteen worlds, 2 the three qualities, and the four ages.

He put four lamps 3 one by one into the hands of the four ages.

0 kind God, such is Thy power.

The dwellers at every hearth are Thy slaves, and religion is their ruler.

The earth is Thy cooking-pot, Thou gavest once for all; destiny is Thy storekeeper.

Instigated by their hearts 4 men lose patience and beg again and again to their ruin.

Covetousness is a black dungeon, demerits the fetters on the feet.

Wealth ever beatei; h the soul with its mallet, while sin sitteth as judge.

Man shall be either good or bad, O Lord, as Thou lookest on him.

1 Asa.

2 The Hindus and the Muhammadans agree in believing that there are fourteen worlds, seven above and seven, including the earth itself, below. According to the Hindus these worlds emerged from the mundane egg when divided into two equal parts.

3 The Veds.

4 Narad the Muni is here understood by the gyanis to mean the human heart. Some furiher account of Narad will be given.

The Primal Being is now called Allah; the turn of the Shaikhs hath come.

There is a tax on the shrines of the gods; such is the practice established.

There are ablution-pots, calls to prayer, five daily prayers, prayer-carpets, and God appeareth dressed in blue. 1

In every house all say ' Mian '; 2 your language hath been changed.

Since Thou, who art Lord of the earth hast appointed Babar a Mir, 3 what power have we?

In the four directions men make Thee obeisance, and Thy praises are uttered in every house.

The profit which is obtained from pilgrimages, repeating the Simritis, 4 and bestowing alms all day long,

Is, O Nanak, obtained in one ghari by remembering the Name which conferreth greatness. 5

The Hindus and the Musalmans who returned to Saiyidpur began to dispose of their dead, and there was weeping and mourning in every house. People said, ' Such and such was the deceased Upon this the Guru fell into a trance, and uttered the following hymn:â ' As herdsmen stay for a short time in the pasture-ground, 6 so do men stay in this world.

Men by the exercise of falsehood build houses for themselves.

Awake, awake, ye sleepers; lo! the soul the dealer departeth.

If ye are to remain here for ever, then build houses.

The body shall fall and the soul depart, if any one desire to know the truth.

The Muhammadans frequently vcar blue clothes, a custom which has descended from the ancient Egyptians.

2 Mian, a title of respect addressed to Muhammadans. In the hill districts of India it is given to the sons of Rajput princes.

3 Mir, a lord or master.

4 Simrifit, the traditional ceremonial and legal institutes of the Hindus. The principal Simritis are twenty-seven in number.

f) Basant Ashtapadi.

' This refers to the nomadic life which prevailed around the Guru's natal village.

Why criest thou ' Alas! alas! ' 1 God is and shall be.
Ye weep for others, but who will weep for you?
Ye worry with worldly occupations, my brethren, and practise falsehood.
The dead hear not at all; ye only cry to be heard of others.
He who laid them to sleep, Nanak, will awake them.
If man know his own home in God, then shall he not sleep.
If any one know of any one at his departure taking any thing with him,
Then let him with open eyes amass wealthâ know and consider this.
Do thy dealing; gain thine object; be not sorry here after.
Thou shalt be known as a true dealer if thou take profit with thee.
Sow the seed of truth in the soil of honesty; in that way practise tillage.
Forsake vice, practise virtue, so shalt thou obtain the Real Thing.
If it be God's favour, man shall meet the true Guru, understand his instruction,
Repeat the Name, hear the Name, and deal in the Name.
As is the profit so the loss; that is the way of the world.
What pleaseth Him, O Nanak, is my glory. 2

One day Mardana took it into his head to ask the Guru to explain the cause of the Saiyidpur massacre, and said, ' Sir, some Pathans have done wrong; but why have so many been killed on their account? ' The Guru pointed out a tree, and told Mardana to go and sleep under it. When he awoke, the Guru would give him an answer. Mardana accordingly went and lay down to sleep under the tree. A drop of honey fell on his naked breast. As he slept, ants came to drink it, and the sleeper half unconsciously crushed them to death with his hand. The Guru asked him on awaking what he had done. He replied 1 Ohi, ohi! There is a pun on the word ohi. It means, Alas! and He (God) is. 2 Asa Ashtapadi.

that one insect had bitten him, and so he had killed them all. The Guru replied, It is in that very way the people of Saiyidpur were killed Upon this Mardana fell at his feet, and the remnant of the inhabitants of Saiyidpur became his disciples.

After this the Guru returned to the Emperor's camp with the object of obtaining another interview with him. He visited the prison and sang hymns for the prisoners whose treatment he deplored. Under the influence of such feelings he composed the following:â

Babar ruled over Khurasan and hath terrified Hindustan.

The Creator taketh no blame to Himself; it was Death disguised as a Mughal who made war on us.

When there was such slaughter and lamentation, didst not Thou, O God, feel pain?
Creator, Thou belongest to all.
If a tyrant slay a tyrant, one is not angry;

But if a ravening lion fall on a herd, its master 1 should show his manliness.

The dogs of Lodi 2 have spoiled the priceless inheritance; when they are dead no one will regard them.

0 God, Thou Thyself joinest and Thou Thyself separatest â lo! this is Thy greatness.

If any one give himself a great name and enjoy himself to his heart's content,

In God's view he is as a worm which nibbleth corn;

But he who while alive is dead, may gain something, O Nanak, by repeating the Name. 3

When Babar had heard this hymn, he ordered the Guru to be sent for. When the Guru appeared, the Emperor asked him to sing the hymn again, and 1 The master of Hindustan at the time was Sultan Ibrahim Lodi. He only met Babar's force at Panipat, where he was defeated.

2 The Pathan dynasty of the Lodis who ruled in India prior to the advent of the Mughal Babar.

3 Asa.

the Guru did so. Upon this, it is said, Babar's brain opened for the reception of spiritual truths. He praised the Guru, and opening his bhang-pouch, offered him some. The Guru replied that he had already taken bhang whose intoxication would never subside. JBabar asked what bhang that was. The Guru replied with the following hymn:â 0 God, fear of Thee is my bhang, my heart its pouch; 1 am an intoxicated hermit.

My hands are the cup; it is for a sight of Thee, 0 God, I hunger,

And ever beg at Thy doorâ

For a sight of Thee I crave.

I beg at Thy door; grant me Thine alms.

Saffron, flowers, musk, gold, and sandal are all applied to the body;

So the bright perfume of the saints rendereth all souls fragrant.

No one calleth clarified butter or silk impure;

Such is a saint in regard to caste.

May Nanak obtain alms at the doors

Of those who are imbued with Thy name and continue to love Thee! 2

The Emperor was so pleased with the Guru that he asked him to accompany him. The Guru would at first only promise to remain one day with him, but, on being pressed to remain three days, at last consented. The Guru was always distressed as he looked towards the prisoners. For the third time he sang the preceding hymn, and then fell into a trance and became unconscious. The Emperor stood over him, and asked the bystanders what had happened. They replied that the faqir, on beholding God's wrath, was in suffering, and had fallen into a trance. Babar became alarmed for the Guru's safety, and asked the people to pray to God for his re- 1 That is, no one despises them. 2 Tilang.

covery. Upon this the Guru stood up, and there then shone such light as if a thousand suns had arisen. Babar saluted, and asked the Guru to be gracious unto him. The Guru replied, ' If thou, O Emperor, desire kindness, set all thy captives free." He agreed, on one conditionâ that the Guru should promise that his empire should continue from generation to generation. The Guru replied, ' Thine empire shall remain for a time."

The Emperor on this ordered that all his prisoners should be clothed with robes of honour, a matter which gave great pleasure and satisfaction to the Guru. The Emperor asked the Guru for instruction suitable to his position. The Guru said, ' Deliver just judgements, reverence holy men, forswear wine and gambling. The monarch who indulgeth in these vices shall, if he survive, bewail his misdeeds. Be merciful to the vanquished, and worship God in spirit and in truth."

At the final parting, the Emperor pressed the Guru to embrace Islam, which recognized only one God, as the Guru himself had been preaching, so he would not have far to go on his spiritual journey and his progress to salvation. Moreover, on embracing Islam he would have the advantage of the mediation of God's holy and last prophet Muhammad. The Guru replied:â

There are hundreds of thousands of Muhammads, but only one God.
The Unseen is true and without anxiety.
Many Muhammads stand in His court.
So numberless they cannot be reckoned.
Prophets have been sent and come into the world.
Whenever He pleaseth He hath them arrested and brought before Him.
The slave Nanak hath ascertained
That God alone is pure and all else impure.

The Emperor, instead of being incensed at this outspoken language, invited the Guru to ask him a favour. The Guru replied to the accompaniment of Mardana's rebeck:â

It is the one God Who hath commissioned me.
Every one partaketh of His Gifts.

(He who looketh for human support Loseth both this world and the next. There is but one Giver, the whole world are beggars.

They who forsake Him and attach themselves to others lose all their honour.

Kings and Emperors are all made by Him. There is none equal to Him. Saith Nanak, Hear, Emperor Babar, He who beggeth of thee is a fool.

CHAPTER X

The Guru then departed for Pasrur, and thence to Sialkot, the fortress of the Sial tribe, now a can tonment in the northern part of the Pan jab. He rested under a wild caper tree, which still exists outside the city. Having taken refreshment, he sent Mardana to the market-place for a paisa, or a farthing's worth of truth and a paisa worth of falsehood. Nobody understood what the messenger meant till Mardana reached Mula, who was a Karar, or petty shopkeeper. The latter said that death was true and life false. Mardana returned with this message to the Guru. Upon this a great friendship sprang up between the Guru and Mula, and Mula afterwards accompanied him to Kabul. On a subsequent occasion when Guru Nanak and Mardana visited Sialkot, Mardana went to Mula. His wife, thinking her husband would again leave her, concealed him, and told Mardana to say he was not at home. In his concealment, he was bitten by a snake and died. On this Guru Nanak composed the following:â

Friendship with Karars is false, and false is its foundation.
Mula saw not whence death would come to him. 1 1 Additional Sloks of Guru Nanak.

When his work was accomplished in Sialkot, the Guru proceeded to the south of the Pan jab as far as Mithankot (in the present district of Dera Ghazi Khan), where Mian Mitha, a famous Muhammadan priest, resided. The Guru took up his quarters in a garden near the town. When Mian Mitha heard of the Guru's arrival he said, ' Nanak is a good faqir; but, if I meet him, I will squeeze the juice out of him as if he were a lemon. Mardana, when reporting his speech to the Guru, said, ' Mian Mitha is thine automaton, and will play as thou causest him to play." Mian Mitha continued his boasting: ' I will go to see Nanak, and, if I meet him, I will take the cream off him as I would skim milk." Mian Mitha met the Guru and, after saluting him in the Muhammadan fashion, sat down. He challenged the Guru by the following slok:â

The first name is that of God, the second that of the Prophet.

O Nanak, if thou repeat the Creed, 1 thou shalt find acceptance in God's court.

The Guru replied:â

The first name is that of God; how many prophets are at His gate!

O Shaikh, form good intentions, and thou shalt find acceptance in God's court.

The Guru continued: ' Mian Mitha, at God's gate there is no room for a prophet. He who dwelleth there is God alone." Mian Mitha then put the Guru two questions: ' How can a lamp burn without oil? and, How shall man obtain a seat in God's court? '

The Guru replied as follows:â

Act according to the Quran and thy sacred books. Put the wick of fear into thy body; Burn in it the knowledge of truth; 1 That is, if thou become a Muhammadan.

Thus shall thy lamp burn without oil.

Make such a light, and thou shalt find the Lord.

When God's words leave an impression on man

And service is performed, happiness is obtained.

All worlds come and go:

While abiding in this world perform worship;

Thus shalt thou obtain a seat in God's court,

And, saith Nanak, triumphantly swing thine arm. 1

Mian Mitha then put to the Guru the question con tained in the first line of the following hymn. He also inquired the condition of the souls of the wicked after death. The Guru replied as follows:â

My brother, salam alaikum! for God's sake tell the truth; how shall man obtain distinction in God's court? '

As man soweth so shall he reap; he shall eat what he obtaineth from the Commander.

Nanak, without the true Name man shall be bound and endure suffering.

Praise be to the Creator; when man goeth down to the wretched dark grave, God's power shall be manifested.

The angels, the heralds of the Almighty, shall come with His orders.

They shall hold quivers, maces, battle-axes, two-edged swords, bows,

Lances, and shields made of fire; and put chains on men's necks.

By God's order they shall bind and lead away the back biter as well as the man without a priest.

Nanak, the true Name, the source of consolation in this last age, shall procure man's acceptance in God's court.

Ye fear lions, jackals, and snakes; but they shall make their dwellings in your graves.
Oxen shall root up your graves, and even your enemies' hatred of you shall cool.
1 Sri Rag.
Brethren, friends, and lovers read the fatiha, 1 and say prayers for the departed.
Nanak, such things are false, and God alone is true.
The sinners who have committed transgressions are bound and led away.
Their luggage of sins is so heavy that they cannot lift it.
The steep road ahead is dark, while the executioner walketh behind them.
In front is a sea of fire; how shall they cross it?
Ravens stand on men's skulls, and peck at them fast as a shower of sparks.
Nanak, where shall man escape when the punishment is by God's order?
The eyes of the sinful shall be torn out; they shall be come blind, and terrible darkness prevail.
Their ears shall be pressed as if they were the sockets of oil-presses, 2 and storms of filth shall assail their noses.
Their tongues shall be cut out for breaking their promises and forgetting the True One.
They shall cry aloud when their skulls are burning in the fire.
No one can save the ignorant man who is covetous and hath no priest;
But they whose demerits are pardoned through their merits shall be, O Nanak, of the elect.
As sesame is heated and pressed, or cotton carded by means of a thong, so shall sinners be punished.
Like paper they shall be beaten with mallets, and put into presses;
They shall be heated like iron; they shall burn and cry aloud;
The wretched beings' heads shall be taken up with tongs and placed on anvils, 1
The introductory prayer of the Quran. Its secondary meaning is prayers offered up for a deceased person.
2 The Indian oil-press is a primitive machine. A beam is made to revolve in a socket in which the seeds to be pressed are placed. The meaning here is, that the ears shall be tortured as if the beams of oil-presses revolved in them as sockets.
On which they shall be beaten with hammers in time according to the smith's 1 lead.
Nanak, without the true Name they shall have no rest either in this world or the next.
Iron spikes shall be driven into their feet, and the sun shall burn their heads.
They who are captivated with the strange woman's flesh, shall lose their manhood and their honour;
They shall be bound to a heated pillar, and no one will go near them;
They shall be unloosed and again tied to it; they shall repent and implore pityâ
Everybody, Nanak, is an enemy of the sinnerâ
They shall be put into a furnace and bodkins of fire thrust into their eyes;
They shall be burnt by sand under which fire hath been kindled;

They shall be roasted in a caldron like rice, and shall then crackle and make a report.

God Himself pardoneth, O Nanak; whom else shall we address?

As the juice of sugar-cane is expressed by putting great weight on it,

So man is weighed down by eating, drinking, dressing, and pleasures which degrade his mind.

An account shall be demanded from the soul which hath dealt in such things.

Feet and legs perform the duties the soul ordereth them.

The tongue which tasted sinful savours shall stand up in court and cry out against the soul;

The ears shall also depose that it is the soul which is false and deceitful.

The nose and eyes shall also plead not guilty, and it is the poor soul which shall suffer.

The soul under arrest in Death's court pleadeth, 'It is the senses which have led the whole world astray:

The senses united have thrown man into misery as the smith putteth iron on the anvil."

1 Dharmraj, the Pluto of Greek mythology.

Nanak, he who meeteth not the true Guru and obtaineth not divine knowledge, shall find no rest in this world or the next.

The soul shall be filed seventy times like an arrow;

It shall be melted like gold in a mould; O soul, thou shalt suffer for what thou hast done.

The soul shall have to bear a prodigious saddle and be driven like a steed.

Nanak, it shall be bound by Death, and have to suffer transmigration again and again.

How many enemies shall it have on sea and land! the forests and glades shall cause it to suffer.

Every house shall bear it enmity; Nanak, the real thing is to meditate on the Eternal.

Death with the three bloodshot and terrible eyes shall lie in wait for the soul.

The whole world is Death's provender; merciless is the god of death.

He seizeth men, Nanak, and hurrieth them away in obedience to the Commander.

My body is before Thee; Thou art Master; Thou mayest preserve or destroy it.

There shall be no mother, father, kinsman, wife, or brother,

Son, or wealth to assist us; how shall we have conso lation?

There shall be no quiver, or bow, or shield, or sword to protect us,

But a seething caldron day and night; consider this under the Guru's instruction.

vxmake honesty thy steed, truth thy saddle, continence thine equestrian armour; vxthe five virtues 1 thine arrows, and truth thy sword and shield.

Nanak, pious men who have truth in their hearts, shall obtain honour in God's court.

1 Contentment, compassion, piety, patience, morality. The list of the five virtues is somewhat arbitrary. Truth is generally included in them, but here the Guru makes it a separate virtue.

v' Brahma who came into the world repeating the Veds cannot describe God. What is poor Krishan who by God's order descended upon earth?

Shiv and countless gods and goddesses standing at Thy gate praise Thee.

He who turneth from God shall pine away and die; the True One is ever the Pardoner. 1

Mian Mitha then spoke: ' What is that one Name which thou praisest so much? ' The Guru replied, ' Hath any one ever known the worth of that Name? ' Mian Mitha asked him to be good enough to explain it to him. The Guru then took his arm, led him aside, and said to him, ' Shaikh, hearest thou the Name of the one God? ' While they were speaking, the name of the Prophet vanished amid the sounds of divine ecstasy, and when they looked again there appeared instead of it only a heap of ashes. Then came a voice from heaven which only repeated ' Allah ', God's Arabic name. Upon this Shaikh Mitha got up and kissed the Guru's feet. The Guru then fell into a trance, and in that state gave utterance to the following:â v N ASIH AT NAM A 2

The present are favoured; the absent are not.

Faith is a friend, want of faith an infidel;

Pride is ruin, wrath is unlawful;

Concupiscence is Satan, conceit is infidelity;

The slanderer's face is black.

The man without faith is unclean; he who is tender hearted is pure.

Knowledge is gentleness. The non-avaricious are holy; the avaricious are impatient.

The honest man hath a bright, the ungrateful man a yellow face.

1 Banno's Granth Sahib. It must be noted that this hymn is not generally accepted by the Sikhs.

2 Instruction. This too is not found in the Granth Sahib.

Truth is heaven, falsehood is hell.

Mildness is victuals.

Force is oppression, justice is pure.

God's praises are ablutions, the call to prayer is noise.

Theft is greed, adultery uncleanness.

Patience is humility, impatience deceit.

The right way is that of spiritual advisers; the wrong way is for those who have none.

Compassion is wealth, want of compassion useless.

The sword is for warriors, justice for monarchs.

He who knoweth and causeth others to know these things,

Is, O Nanak, called a wise man.

Upon this the Guru and Mian Mitha separated.

CHAPTER XI

The Guru proceeded to the river Ravi and thence to Lahore. The Lahore territory was then farmed from the Emperor by a millionaire Khatri, whose name was Duni Chand. He was performing the ceremony of shradh 1 for his father, when he heard of the devout Nanak's arrival. He took the Guru to his house, and treated him with great affection. When everything was ready for the anniversary feast, Duni Chand began to feed the Brahmans. The Guru, on being summoned, asked what the matter was. Duni Chand replied that it was his father's shradh, and that he had fed one hundred Brahmans in his name. The Guru replied, ' It is now two days since thy father hath eaten anything, and yet thou sayest thou hast fed one hundred Brahmans for him." Duni Chand asked where his father was. The Guru replied that he had become incarnate in a wolf, which was now in a clump of trees six miles distant. The reason 1 Shrddhs are oblations of cakes and libations of water made to the spirits of deceased ancestors: Vide Monier Williams's Indian Wisdom, passim.

his father's soul had entered a wolf was, that while he was in human birth he had coveted meat which a Sikh was cooking, and had died in that desire.

The Guru, on seeing several flags over Duni Chand's door, asked what they were. It was explained that each flag denoted a lakh of rupees which Duni Chand had acquired. On this the Guru gave him a needle, and told him to keep it until he asked for it in the next world. Duni Chand took the needle to his wife, and told her to put it by for the purpose indicated. She believed him crazed, and asked how a needle could go to the next world. She accordingly charged him to return it to the Guru. Duni Chand took the needle with his wife's message to the Guru, who said, ' If such a small and light thing as a needle cannot go to the next world, how can thy wealth reach there? ' Upon this Duni Chand fell at his feet, and prayed him to tell him by what means his wealth should reach the next world. The Guru replied, ' Give some of thy wealth in God's name, feed the poor, and thy wealth shall accompany thee." Upon this Duni Chand distributed seven lakhs of treasure, for he understood that disobedience to the Guru's order would militate against his salvation. He then became a disciple of the Guru, and began to repeat the Name. Guru Nanak uttered the following on the occasion:â

False are kings, false their subjects, false the whole world;
False are mansions, false palaces, false those who dwell therein;
False is gold, false silver, false he who weareth them;
False the body, false raiment, false peerless beauty;
False husbands, false wives; they pine away and become dust. 1
Man who is false loveth what is false, and forgetteth the Creator.
1 Instead of chhar, dust, the Granth Sahib has khwdr, despised.
With whom contract friendship? The whole world passeth away.
False is sweetness, false honey, in falsehood shiploads are drownedâ
Nanak humbly assertethâ Except Thee, 0 God, everything is thoroughly false. 1

The Guru went in a north-east direction, and took up his post on the bank of the Ravi. His arrival there caused great excitement, and every one went to see him. He was universally held to be a man of God. All who visited him went away pleased. Every verse that he composed was at once pub lished abroad. He used to compose verses like the following, which faqirs sang to the accompaniment of reeds:â

Falsehood is at an end; Nanak, truth at last prevaileth. 2

There was only the one Name mentioned in the Guru's dwelling, and he became the object of great popular admiration.

A millionaire official who dwelt in a neighbouring village began to depreciate the Guru. He said," Who is this person whose name is repeated by every one, as if he were a god, though he is only a mortal like ourselves? The Hindus are being perverted, and even the Musalmans are losing their faith. Come, let us imprison him." When the speaker mounted on horseback, the animal shied and threw him. Next day he again mounted, but, as he proceeded on his way, became blind and had to alight. Those who witnessed his calamity were afraid to make any remark save that Nanak was a great saint. They, however, suggested to the millionaire that he should do homage to the Guru. Upon this he began to praise the Guru; and those who were with him bowed towards the Guru. The millionaire again 1 Asa ki War. 2 Ramkali ki War I.

mounted his horse, intending this time to go and supplicate the Guru, but immediately fell down. His companions addressed him, ' Thou hast made a mistake in going on horseback. Go on foot, that thou mayest be pardoned He took this advice. On arriving at a spot whence the Guru's residence could be seen, he recovered his sight, and began to make salutations in the Guru's direction. On arriving in his presence he fell at his feet. The Guru was pleased and made him his guest for three days. The millionaire, in honour of the Guru, founded a village, which he called Kartarpur, on the margin of the Ravi, and built a Sikh temple therein, both of which he dedicated to the Guru.

One day a fanatical Brahman came to the Guru and begged for alms. The Guru, who was at his break fast, invited the Brahman to join him. The Brahman replied that he would not eat food in that way. He would only eat what he had cooked himself. He would first dig up the earth to a depth of a cubit so that all impurity of the surface might be removed, and he would also make a cooking square into which none but himself might enter. He would then dig a span deeper, and make a fireplace on which he would put firewood which he had washed, so that no insects might be burned in it. The Guru had not attended to these formalities, and the Brahman spurned food otherwise cooked. The Guru told him he would give him uncooked viands which he might cook himself. He then went outside and began to dig up the earth, but wherever he dug he only turned up bones, which he deemed a still greater abomination than the Guru's food. He continued digging all day, but with the same result. At last, overcome by hunger, he went and threw himself at Nanak's feet, and asked for the cooked food he had previously rejected. The Guru was pleased to gratify him, and then composed the following:â

Cooking places of gold, vessels of gold, Lines of silver far extended, Ganges water, firewood of the karanta l tree, Eating rice boiled in milk â 0 my soul, these things are of no account Until thou art saturated with the true Name. Hadst thou the eighteen Purans with thee, Couldst thou recite the four Veds,

Didst thou bathe on holy days and give alms according to men's castes,

Didst thou fast and perform religious ceremonies day and night;

Wert thou a qazi, a mulla, or a shaikh,

A Jogi, a jangam, 2 didst thou wear an ochre-coloured dress.

Or didst thou perform the duties of a householderâ

Without knowing God, Death would bind and take all men away.

The duties of all creatures are recorded on their heads;

They shall be judged according to their acts.

Foolish and ignorant men issue ordersâ Nanak, the True One hath storehouses of praises. 3

The Guru initiated the practice of singing hymns in the end of the night. A boy seven years of age used to come to listen and stand behind him. When the singing was over, he used quietly to depart. One day the Guru ordered his servants to detain the boy in order to discover the object of his continual attendance. He was accordingly brought before the Guru, who asked him, ' O boy, why comest thou so early in the morning to listen to hymns? This is the time of life for thee to eat, play, and sleep The boy replied, ' Sir, one day my mother bade me light the fire. When I put on the wood, I observed that the little sticks burned first and afterwards the big ones. From that time I have been afraid of early death. It is very 1 The Carissa Carandas.

2 A class of faqirs with matted hair and thin chains to their feet. They generally go about ringing bells. 3 Basant.

doubtful whether we shall live to be old, and so I attend thy religious gatherings The Guru was much pleased on hearing this wisdom from the child's lips, and said he spoke like an old man (budha). On that occasion the Guru composed the following:â

In the briny unfathomable ocean the fish did not recognize the net. 1

Why did the very clever and beautiful fish have so much confidence?

It was caught through its own doing; death cannot be averted, 0 my brethren; know that in like manner death hangeth over your heads.

Man is like the fish upon which the net falleth unawares.

The whole world is bound by death; without the Guru death cannot be destroyed.

They who are imbued with the True One, and have abandoned worthless mammon, are saved.

I am a sacrifice unto those who are found true at the gate of the True One.

Death is like the hawk among the birds, or the huntsman with the noose in his hands.

They whom the Guru preserved have been saved; all others have been entrapped by the bait.

They who possess not God's name shall be rejected; no one will assist them.

God is the truest of the true, and His place is the truest of the true.

They who obey the True One meditate on Him in their hearts.

Even the perverse who obtain divine knowledge under the Guru's instruction are pure.

Make supplication to the true Guru to unite thee with the Friend.

When man meeteth the Friend he obtaineth happiness, and the myrmidons of death poison themselves.

1 The worldly man does not remember death.

I abide in the Name, and the Name abideth in my heart.

Without the Guru all is darkness; without the Word nothing can be known.

By the Guru's instruction light shineth, and man con-tinueth to love the True One.

Death entereth not where the soul's light is blended with God's.

Thou, 0 God, art the Friend; Thou art wise; it is Thou who unitest men with Thee.

Under the Guru's instruction, O man, praise Him who hath no end or limit.

Death entereth not where there is the incomparable Word of the Guru.

By God's order all sentient beings were produced; by God's order they perform their functions.

By God's order they are in the power of death; by God's order they are absorbed in the True One.

Nanak, what pleaseth God shall happen; there is nothing whatever in the power of His creatures. 1

The boy to whom the above hymn was addressed was subsequently known as Bhai Budha on account of the complimentary expression of the Guru. He was held in such high estimation that he was commissioned to confer the tilaks or patches of Guruship on the first five successors of Guru Nanak.

Kalu with all his people proceeded to where his son the Guru had fixed his habitation. Sikh societies then began to be formed. The Guru took off his extraordinary costume and dressed in a more con ventional manner. With a cloth around his waist, a sheet over his shoulder, and a turban on his head, he looked the impersonation of holiness. The string of his fame rose to heaven, it was said, like that of a kite. Every one addressed him, ' Hail, Nanak! a great saint hath been born in the world."

1 Sri Rag, Ashtapadi.

At Kartarpur, a watch before day, the Japji and the Asa ki War were repeated. Then followed reading and expounding of the Guru's hymns, until a watch and a quarter after sunrise. This was succeeded by singing and the reading of the Arati (Gagan mai thai). After this, breakfast was served. In the third watch there was again singing, after which in the evening the Sodar was read. Then the Sikhs all dined together. The repast ended with further singing. After a watch of night had elapsed the Sohila was read, and every one then retired.

The Guru when not engaged in prayer occupied himself during the day in Kartarpur in giving instruction to all who sought it. He thus delivered himself to Malo and Bhago on the subject of Hindu penances: ' To burn in fire, to abide long in water, to fast, to endure heat and cold, to hold up one's arm permanently, to do penance with body reversed, to stand for a long time on one leg, to live on forest tubers and roots, to abide on the margins of rivers, to wander over the world as a pilgrim, to fast at full moonâ all such penances are works of darkness."

The Guru thus expressed himself on the subject of the devotional exercises of the Sikhs: ' To recall the wandering mind from the distraction of the senses, and then employ it in pious discourses and in devoutly singing and listening to songs of praise of the Almightyâ know that these are merito rious acts which may be easily performed. They involve but little labour and bring great reward. The Hindu penances on the contrary involve great trouble while only small recompense is obtained therefrom."

The Guru replied to a man called Kalu who had asked him for a definition of a holy man: ' Recognize him as holy in whom are to be found friend ship, sympathy, pleasure at the welfare of others, and dislike of evil company. In the first place, the intentions of holy men are pure. Secondly, they are pleased on hearing the praises of others. Thirdly, holy men serve the virtuous. Fourthly, they honour those who can impart to them learning and good counsel. Fifthly, as there is a periodical craving for food or intoxicants, so they feel a craving for the Guru's word and for divine knowledge. Sixthly, they love their wives, and renounce other women. Seventhly, they avoid subjects from which quarrels may arise. Eighthly, they serve those who are superior to themselves in intelligence or devotion. Ninthly, even if strong, they're not arrogant, and trample not on others. Tenthly, they abandon the society of the evil, and only associate with the holy Two Sikhs, called Bhagta and Ohri, asked Guru Nanak how rest was to be obtained, and transmigra tion avoided. The Guru replied as follows: ' You shall find rest by avoiding manmukh karm (perverse acts)." Being asked to define manmukh karm more particularly, the Guru replied: ' It is to be heartily envious of every one, to desire that worldly wealth and all happiness should forsake others and come to oneself, to suffer great pain as one beholdeth the houses and property of others, to believe all men one's enemies, and do good to no one. Expel all this evil from your hearts. In the second place, the perverse man is proud and relentless to every one. When he seeth such and such a person inferior to himself, he never adviseth him; nay, he laugheth at him, and treateth him with contempt, saying, "His is not equal to my lofty intellect." In the third place, the perverse man is addicted to slander; but do you renounce it and never utter it. If any one praise another who is superior to him, he cannot endure it, nay he becometh wroth, saying, "O! I am well acquainted with him." In this way he uttereth slander. How can he who is proud of his efforts and envious of others ever possess excellence? In the fourth place, if the perverse man receive advice, he will not act on it through obstinacy; nay, he will perversely do the very reverse. These vicesâ envy, pride, slander, and obstinacyâ belong to the perverse. Relinquish them, acting as trees do when they drop their leaves in autumn

The Guru was asked why the words Sat Namâ the True Nameâ were always written as an intro duction to his hymns. He replied, ' The Name is the God of all gods. Some propitiate Durga, 1 some Shiv, some Ganesh, 2 and some other gods; but the Guru's Sikhs worship the True Name and thus remove all obstacles to salvation. Accordingly, the prefatory words, the True Name, are written in all compositions

It was here the Guru composed his poem on the Twelve Months of the year. The description is of course suited to the climate of the Panjab, his native country. We here give a translation in extenso 3:â

Hear Thou, 0 God â according to men's acts in previous states of existence
The weal or woe which Thougivest to each individual is just.

0 God, the Creation is Thine; what is my condition? I cannot live for a moment without Thee.

1 am miserable without my Beloved; I have no friend; yet from the Guru's instruc tion I drink nectar.

The Formless One continueth His creation; 4 to obey God is the best of human acts.

1 Durga is the energy or consort of Shiv.

2 Ganesh is an elephant-headed god of the Hindus, who in one of his attributes presides over literature, and is specially invoked in the prefaces to literary works.

3 The Indian seasons and months areâ i, Spring, which includes the months Chet and Baisakh; 2, the hot weather, Jeth and Har; 3, the rainy weather, Sawan and Bhadon; 4, the temperate weather, Assu and Kartik; 5, the cold weather, Maghar and Poh; 6, Autumn, Magh and Phagan. These seasons are in Sanskrit and Hindi called respec tivelyâ Basant, Grikham, Pawas, Sard, Him, and Sisar. The latter season, when the leaves fall, is contemporaneous with the European early spring. The Indian lunar year

begins with Chet, which is movable, and the Indian solar year with Baisakh about the i2th of April.

4 In Indian sacred writings several creations and destructions of the world are alluded to.

Nanak, the woman is waiting for Thee; hear Thou, O Omnipresent Spirit.

The chatrik l crieth ' Prio! ' and the kokil 2 also singeth its lays.

The woman who is embraced by her Spouse enjoyeth every happiness.

She whom God in His pleasure hath embraced is a happy woman.

God established the nine mansions of the body; the tenth which is superior to them all, is His home.

Everything is Thine; Thou art my Beloved; I delight in Thee night and day.

Nanak, the chatrik crieth ' Prio, prio! ' and sweet is the kokil's song.

0 God, filled with delight, my Beloved, hear Thou me. Thou art contained in my soul and body; I forget Thee not for an instant.

Why should I forget Thee for an instant? I am a sacrifice unto Thee; I live by singing Thy praises.

1 have no one; whose am I? I cannot abide without God.

I have sought the shelter of His feet, and dwell there; and my body hath become pure.

Nanak, he on whom God looketh with favour obtaineth peace in his home, and his mind is consoled with the Guru's teaching.

It raineth a torrent of nectar, whose drops are de lightful,

When the friend, the kindly Guru meeteth one, and love is established with God.

God entereth the temple of the body when it pleaseth Him, and the woman riseth up and repeateth His praises.

1 Its cry is ' prio', a word which also means beloved. Hence it is said the bird calls to God and lives in His worship.

2 The black Indian cuckoo. Its name is derived from its cry, which increases in volume of sound as it progresses. It is larger than the chatrik.

In every house the spouse enjoyeth his happy wife; why hath my Spouse forgotten me?

Lowering clouds have overspread the heavens; it raineth pleasantly and love comforteth my soul and body.

Saith Nanak, Thou who rainest ambrosial speech, graciously come to mine abode.

In Chet agreeable is the spring; the bumble-bee is pleasing.

In the Bar the forests are flowering; may my Beloved return to me!

When her beloved returneth not home, how can a wife obtain comfort? Her body wasteth away with the pain of separation.

The kokil singeth sweetly on the mango-tree; why should I endure pain of body?

The bumble-bee is flitting on the flowering branches; how shall I survive? I am dying, O mother.

Nanak, in Chet comfort is easily obtained if woman obtain God in her home as her Spouse.

The month of Baisakh is pleasant; the trees are in blossom;

The woman is waiting for God at her gate, saying, ' Come, take compassion on me.

' Come home, my Beloved, make me cross the difficult ocean; without Thee I am worthless.

' Who can appraise Thy worth, my Darling? If it please Thee, I shall look at Thee and show Thee to others.

' I know that Thou art not distant; I acknowledge that Thou art in my heart, and I recognize Thy mansion."

Nanak, in Baisakh God is found by him who meditateth on the Word and whose mind is thus happy.

The month of Jeth is pleasant; why should the Beloved be forgotten?

The land is burning like a furnace; woman is making supplicationâ

Woman is making supplication and praising His qualities: ' I shall be pleasing to the Lord if I utter His praises.

' The Bairagi 1 liveth in the true palace; if He allow me to go to Him, I will go.

' Without God I am without honour and strength; how shall I obtain comfort in His palace?"

Nanak, in Jeth if a woman know God and embrace virtue, she shall by His favour become like unto Him.

The month of Har is sultry; 2 the sun is burning in the sky;

The earth is suffering; it is parched and heated like fire;

The heat is drying up moisture; men die in anguish, yet the sun wearieth not of his toil.

When his chariot turneth towards the south, 3 woman looketh for the shade; the grasshoppers chirp in the forest.

She who hath departed with her sins shall suffer in the next world, while she who remembereth the True One shall obtain comfort.

Nanak, with God, to whom I gave my heart, are death and life.

In Sawan be happy, O my soul; it is the season of clouds and rain.

' I love my Spouse with my soul and body, but the Dear One hath gone abroad; ' My Spouse cometh not home; I am dying with the pang of separation; the flash of the lightning terrifieth me.

' I am alone on my couch and greatly grieved; O mother, my pain is as bad as death.

'Say how can sleep and appetite come to me without God? Raiment affordeth my body no comfort."

1 God, in the sense that He loves not the sinner. The word Bairagi ordinarily means a man without love for the world. The Bairagis now form a special sect who worship Vishnu and wear sacrificial threads. They are distinguished from the Sanyasis who worship Shiv and dis pense with sacrificial threads.

2 We are obliged here to take a liberty with the word bhala, which means good. 3 After the summer solstice.

Nanak, she is the happy wife who is embraced by her beloved Spouse.

In the month of Bhadon woman in the bloom of youth is led astray by doubt, but afterwards repenteth.

The lakes and the meadows are filled with water; it is the rainy seasonâ the time for pleasure.

It raineth during the dark night; how can the young wife have comfort without her mate? Frogs and peacocks are croaking.

'Prio, prio' crieth the chatrik; serpents go abroad biting;

Mosquitoes sting; lakes are filled to the brim; how shall man obtain comfort without God?

Nanak, I will ask my Guru and go where the Lord is.

In Assu come, O Beloved; the wife is pining and dying for Thee.

Man can meet the Lord when He granteth him an inter view; but love of mammon ruineth him.

When woman is spoiled by falsehood, her husband putteth her away; then bloom the kukah and the kahi reeds. 1

The heat is over, the cool season is approaching; on seeing this my mind is uneasy. 2

On all sides the trees are green and verdant; that which slowly ripeneth is sweet.

Nanak, the true Guru hath become my mediator; may I meet my Beloved in Assu!

In Kartik what pleaseth God is recorded in man's destiny.

The lamp which is lit by divine knowledge easily burneth.

Love is the oil of the lamp; the woman and her Beloved have met; 3 she is overwhelmed with delight.

She whom sin killeth shall not be acceptable at her death, while she whom virtue killeth shall really die. 4

God hath given His name and service to those who dwell in their own homes; ever their prayer isâ 1 Kukah is supposed to be the Saccharum munja, and kahi the Sac char um spontaneum.

2 That is, so much time has passed away, that I fear I shall never meet my Beloved.

3 Guided by the lamp's light. 4 Shall not suffer transmigration.

' Meet us, O God, and open the doors of our understand ing; otherwise one hour shall be as six months."

The month of Maghar is pleasant for those who are blended with God's person by singing His praises.

The virtuous woman through her virtues enjoyeth her spouse; my Spouse is ever pleasing to me.

While the whole world is movable, He is immovable, clever, wise, the Arranger.

They who possess the merits of divine knowledge and meditation shall be blended with God. They are pleasing to God, and God is pleasing to them.

The songs, music, and poems of bards have I heard; but it is at the name of God sorrow fleeth away.

Nanak, that wife is dear to her spouse who in his pre sence doeth him hearty service.

In Poh it freezeth; the moisture of the forest and of the grass drieth up.

Why comest Thou not? Thou dwellest in my body, in my soul, and in my mouth. 1

The Life of the world pervadeth my soul and body; I enjoy pleasure through the instruction of the Guru.

The light of God is contained in the hearts of animals born from eggs, wombs, perspiration, and earth.

Lord of compassion, beneficent One, grant me a sight of Thee, and give me understanding that I may obtain salva tion.

Nanak, the Enjoyer enjoyeth her with pleasure who beareth Him love and affection.

In Magh woman becometh pure when she knoweth the place of Pilgrimage 2 within her.

I have easily met the Friend, and, by adopting His attributes, have become blended with Him.

Hear me, O beloved and beautiful God, I made Thine attributes mine ornaments; if it please Thee, I shall bathe in Thy tank.

1 That is, I ever think of Thee and repeat Thy name, but am unworthy to receive Thee. 2 God.

The Ganges, the Jamna, the meeting of the three rivers at Tribeni Priyag, 1 the seven oceans,

Alms, charity, and worship are all contained in God's name. I recognize Him as the One God in every age.

Nanak, in the month of Magh, if I repeat God's name with great delight, I bathe at the sixty-eight places of pilgrimage. 2

In Phagan the hearts of those to whom God's love is pleasing are happy.

Night and day are pleasant to him who effaceth himself.

When it pleased God, I effaced worldly love from my heart; O Lord, mercifully come to my home.

Though I deck myself in various garbs, yet without the Beloved I shall not obtain a place in heaven.

I decorated myself with necklaces, strings of pearls, per fumes, 3 silks, and satins, when my Beloved desired me.

Nanak, my Guru hath blended me with God, and I have obtained Him as my Spouse.

The twelve months, the seasons, the lunar days, and the week days,

The gharis, the mahurats, 4 the moments, are all pleasant when the True One cometh and meeteth me of His own accord.

1 A famous place of Hindu pilgrimage, near Allahabad. The third river is the Saraswati, which is supposed to meet the Ganges and Jamna underground. The Saraswati, though no longer seen, was at one time an actual river. From a legend in the Mahabhdrat it would appear that it took its rise with other great rivers in the Himalayas, that it thence flowed through Rajputana, where it occasion ally disappeared in the sands of that country, and that it finally de bouched north of Dwaraka into the Arabian Sea.

2 Sixty-eight is the number of sacred places of pilgrimage in the estimation of the Hindus. 3 Ras really means relishes.

4 The following is the Hindi time-table:â 60 visias = i chasia 60 chasias = i pal 60 pals = i ghari 2 gharis = i muhurat 4 muhurats = i pahar 8 pahars = i day and night.

When the dear Lord is obtained, everything is arranged; the Creator knoweth everything.

I am dear to Him who decorated me; I have met Him and am happy.

The couch of my home is beautiful when my Beloved enjoyeth me; the holy have good fortune written on their foreheads.

Nanak, the Beloved enjoyeth me day and night; having obtained God as my Spouse, I am a permanent bride.

At that time there was a man in very straitened domestic circumstances who had a daughter to marry. He appealed to Guru Nanak to assist in procuring her a wedding outfit. The Guru told him to give him a list of the things he required, and he would send for them. The man did so. The Guru called a servant of his, named Bhagirath, and ordered him to go to Lahore and fetch what was required. He warned him at the same time not to spend a night in that city. 1 Bhagirath, on arriving in Lahore went to a shopkeeper, and asked him to supply the articles at once. The shopkeeper bade him remain for a day and everything should be ready. Bhagirath said it was impossible. The shopkeeper told him that everything should be ready on that day, but the bride's bracelets could not be made and coloured before nightfall. Bhagirath explained the order that had been given him. The shopkeeper inquired what sort of master he had who had issued such an order. Bhagirath replied that his master was the Guru. The shopkeeper inquired who the gurus of this generation were. Bhagirath could only reply that his master was a great Being. The shopkeeper rejoined, ' Wretch, where canst thou find a great being in this age? ' After further colloquy and further praise of the Guru by Bhagirath, the shop keeper decided that he would go with him to his 1 Which he characterized as a city of poison and wrathâ Lahaur shahr zahir qahir. By this the Guru meant the intemperance and licentiousness of that city.

master. He had a set of coloured bracelets in his private house, which he would take and give the Guru. ' If he be a great being continued the shop keeper, ' he shall be my Guru as well as thine, and he shall have the bracelets for nothing; but, if he be not a great being, I will exact the full price from him When the shopkeeper saw the Guru and heard his gentle remonstrance with Bhagirath for his delay, he became convinced that he was a great being and searcher of hearts, and he accordingly fell at his feet and was made happy. He remained three years with the Guru, during which time he committed to memory many of his hymns.

When the shopkeeper returned to Lahore, he sent for merchants and bankers and sold them every thing he had in his shop. He then sailed to Ceylon to extend his commerce. There he took up his residence and began to trade. At the same time he led a religious life, and did not forget the Guru's hymns. He used to sing them late into the night, and again rise before day for his devotions and ablutions. On the subject of bathing the Guru had taught him that whoever bathed a watch before day in cold water and repeated God's name with love and devotion, shouldreceive nectar at God's door, and be blended with Him who is unborn and self-existent.

After bathing, the shopkeeper used to repeat the Japji and read the Guru's hymns. He was wont to take breakfast at daybreak, and then go to discharge his worldly duties. Though the people of Ceylon were said to corrupt strangers who went among them, they had no influence over the shopkeeper, who con tinued to adhere rigidly to the teachings of the Guru. The king of the country, whose name accord ing to the Sikh annals was Raja Shivnabh, hearing that the shopkeeper would not conform to the religious customs of his country, summoned him to his presence. The shopkeeper presented the Raja with a coco nut in token of his loyalty. In reply to the Raja's questions, he said that he had already obtained what others sought to obtain by fasting, religious cere monies, and austerities; so why should he perform them? The Raja asked him what it was he had obtained. The shopkeeper replied that he had beheld a great being and thus secured salvation. The Raja inquired if he had really obtained spiritual comfort by seeing the great being. The shopkeeper replied, ' Sire, when one hath met God, what further comfort is necessary? ' The king asked, ' In this Kal age who is there, a sight of whom can confer salvation? ' The shopkeeper replied, ' Such a per son is Guru Nanak; the mere repetition of his name can confer salvation." He then translated for him one of the Guru's hymns. The Raja on hearing it was satisfied, and joy thrilled through his frame. He then requested the shopkeeper to take him to where Nanak lived, so that he too might behold him. The shopkeeper replied, ' Sire, meditate on him in thy heart, and thou shalt meet him here."

The shopkeeper loaded his ship with the products of Ceylon, and returned to India. Raja Shivnabh remained at home, thinking of the Guru and yearning to behold him.

CHAPTER XII

Meanwhile the Guru made a journey to the south of India. He wore wooden sandals, took a stick in his hand, twisted a rope round his head as a turban, and on his forehead put a patch and a streak. On that occasion he was accompanied by Saido and Gheho of the Jat tribe. He proceeded to the Dra-vidian country now named Madras.

His companions, seeing his morning ablutions, thought that he worshipped the river god, Khwaja Khizir, 1 and derived his power from him. They 1 Le mot de Khedher, signifiant en Arabe verd et verdoyant, on determined to worship the same god, and advance themselves if possible to a higher spiritual eminence than the Guru had attained. While travelling one night for the purpose of their worship they met a man carrying a fish in his hand. After mutual interrogations he said that he was the river god taking an offering to the Guru, and that it was from the Guru he had obtained his power, and not the Guru from him. He added: ' I am water, he is air, a superior element; I am often contained in him Saido and Gheho then went and prostrated them selves before the Guru. He asked them why they had come to him at that hour. They used formerly only to come after sunrise. They then confessed to him the whole story of their attempted worship of Khwaja Khizir, and begged his forgiveness. The Guru composed the following on that occasion:â

He who batheth in the immortal water of divine know ledge taketh with him the sixty-eight places of pilgrimage.

The Guru's instruction is jewels and gems; by serving him his disciples find them.
There is no place of pilgrimage equal to the Guru;
The tank of consolation is contained in that Guru.
The Guru is a river whence pure water is ever obtained, and by which the filth of evil inclinations is washed away.

He who findeth the True Guru hath obtained perfect bathing, which maketh him a god out of a beast or a ghost.

He who is imbued with the true Name obtaineth it; that Guru is called sandal.
Fix thine attention on His feet by whose odour vegetables are perfumed.

pretend que ce nom fut donne a ce prophete a cause qu'il jouit d'une vie florissante et immortelle depuis qu'il cut bu de l'eau de la Fontaine. Plusieurs le confondent avec le prophete Â lie, que nous disons faire sa demeure dans le Paradis terrestre et jouir de l'immortalite'. Parce que l'arbre de vie e'toit dans ce Paradis, et qu'il y avoit aussi une Fontaine, les Musalmans donnent a cette Fontaine le nom de Fontaine de Vie, et croyent que c'est de la boisson de son eau, aussi bien que du fruit de l'arbre de vie, qu'filie entretient son immortalite. (D'Herbelot.)

Through the Guru man obtaineth real life, and through the Guru man departeth to God's home.

Nanak, through the Guru man is absorbed in the True One; through the Guru man obtaineth the special dignity of deliverance

On the same occasion the Guru composed the following:â

They who forget the Name go astray in worldly love and superstition;

They let go the stem and cling to the branches; what shall they obtain? Ashes.

How can man be saved without the Name? If any one know, let him tell it.

If man be holy he shall be saved; the perverse shall lose their honour.

Perfect is the wisdom of those who serve the one God.

Servants of God, take shelter in Him who was in the beginning, in every age, and who is the Bright One.

My Lord is one; there is none other, my brethren.

By the favour of the True One happiness is obtained.

Without the Guru no one hath obtained God, however much the matter be debated.

He Himself showeth the way and fixeth true devotion in the heart.

Even though thou advise the perverse man, he will still go to the wilderness;

But without God's name he shall not be saved; he shall die and go to hell.

He who repeateth not God's name shall wander in birth and death.

God's worth cannot be known without serving the true Guru.

Whatever service God causeth men to do, that will be done.

It is God Himself who acteth; whom besides shall I men tion? God beholdeth His own greatness.

He whom God inspireth serveth the Guru.

1 Prabhati.

Nanak, they who give their lives shall be saved, and shall obtain honour in God's court. 1

The Guru arrived at a Saravagi or Jain temple, which was much frequented. Narbhi, the Jain priest, went with his disciple to visit him. The Jains attach an exaggerated value to life in every form. The Jain priest heard that the Guru had not the same tender scruples on the subject, and began to catechize him. ' Eatest thou old or new corn? ' (that is, dost thou eat corn with worms in it or not?) ' Drinkest thou cold water; shakest thou the trees of the forest to eat their fruit? Who is thy guru, and what power hath he to pardon thee since thou violatest all rules and destroyest life? ' The Guru in reply uttered the following pauri:â

When the True Guru is merciful, faith is perfected.

When the True Guru is merciful, man shall never grieve.

When the True Guru is merciful, man shall know no sorrow.

When the True Guru is merciful, man shall enjoy divine pleasure.
When the True Guru is merciful, what fear hath man of Death?
When the True Guru is merciful he ever bestoweth happi ness.
When the True Guru is merciful, man obtaineth the nine treasures. 2
When the Guru is merciful, man is absorbed in the True One. 3
After this the Guru launched out into a satire on the Jains:â

They have their hair plucked out, they drink dirty water, they beg and eat others' leavings; 1 Asa Ashtapadi.

2 Nau nidhi. This expression is used in ihe sacred writings of the Sikhs to denote unlimited wealth and prosperity. In the sacred books of the Hindus the expression has a more definite numerical signification. 3 Majh ki War.

They spread out their ordure, they inhale its smell, they are shy to look at water;

They have their heads plucked like sheep; the pluckers' hands are smeared with ashesâ

They spoil the occupations of their parents; their families weep and wail for them.

They give not their deceased relations lamps or perform their last rites, or place anywhere barley rolls and leaves for them. 1

The sixty-eight places of pilgrimage grant them no access; the Brahmans will not eat their food.

They are ever filthy day and night; they have no sacri ficial marks on their foreheads.

They ever sit close as if they were at a wake, and they enter no assembly.

They hold cups in their hands; they have brooms 2 by their sides; they walk in single file.

They are not Jogis, or Jangams, or Qazis, or Mullas.

God hath ruined them; they go about despised; their words are like curses.

God killeth and restoreth animals to life; none else may preserve them.

The Jains make not gifts or perform ablutions; dust lighteth on their plucked heads.

From water gems arose when Meru was made the churning staff. 3

The gods appointed the sixty-eight places of pil grimages, and holy days were fixed accordingly by their orders.

1 The Jains conform in many ways to Hindu customs. The Guru here censures them for not being altogether consistent.

2 To brush away insects and thus avoid treading on them.

3 According to the Hindus, Vishnu in his Kurmavatar assumed the shape of a tortoise which supported the mountain Mandara â in the Sikh writings called Meru â the Olympus of the Hindus, with which the gods churned the ocean. From the ocean were produced the fourteen gems or jewels here referred to. They are Lakhsmi, wife of Vishnu, the moon, a white horse with seven heads, a holy physician, a prodigious elephant, the tree of plenty, the all-yielding cow. c.

After ablution the Muhammadans pray; after ablution the Hindus worship; the wise ever bathe.

The dead and the living are punned when water is poured on their heads.

Nanak, they who pluck their heads are devils: these things I please them not.

When it raineth there is happiness; animals then perform their functions.

When it raineth, there is corn, sugar-cane, and cotton, the clothing of all.

When it raineth, kine ever graze, and women churn their milk.

By the use of the clarified butter thus obtained burnt offerings and sacred feasts are celebrated, and worship is ever adorned

All the Sikhs are rivers; the Guru is the ocean, by bathing in which greatness is obtained.

If the Pluckedheads bathe not, then a hundred handfuls of dust be on their skulls. 2

The Jain priest asked the Guru why he travelled in the rainy season, when insects are abroad and there is danger of killing them under foot. The Guru replied as follows:â

Nanak, if it rain in Sawan, four species of animals have pleasureâ

Serpents, deer, fish, and sensualists who have women in their homes.

Nanak, if it rain in Sawan, there are four species of animals which feel discomfortâ

Cows' calves, the poor, travellers, and servants.

The Jain priest went and fell at his feet and be came a convert to his faith. On that occasion the Guru completed his hymns in the Majh ki War, and Saido and Gheho wrote them down from his dictation.

It is said that the Guru then went to an island in the ocean, governed by an inhuman tyrant. The name of the island has not been preserved. Besides 1 That is, water and bathing. 2 Majh ki War.

Saido and Gheho a third Jat called Siho accompanied him thither. On seeing them the tyrant resolved to put them to death for trespassing on his domain. He seized the Guru as the first victim of his rage. The Guru fell into a trance and sang the following:â

He to whom the Lord is compassionate and merciful, will do the Master's work.

That worshipper whom God causeth to abide by His order, will worship Him.

By obeying His order man is acceptable, and shall then reach his Master's court.

He shall act as pleaseth his Master, and obtain the fruit his heart desireth;

And he shall be clothed with a robe of honour in God's court. 1

It is said that on hearing this hymn the tyrant desisted from his intention, and prostrated him self before the Guru. Saido gave him water to drink in which the Guru had washed his feet, and thus made him a Sikh, and ensured him deliverance.

The Guru on that occasion met a successor of Pir Makhdum Baha-ul-Din Qureshi, who had an extrava gant idea of his own spiritual and temporal impor tance. On being assured of the man's hypocrisy, the Guru uttered the following:â

The heart which relinquisheth God's praises and magnifica tion and attacheth itself to a skeleton, 2

Receiveth a hundred reproaches by day and a thousand by night. 3

The Pir then fell at his feet, invited the Guru to abide with him and desist from his wanderings, upon which the Guru uttered the following reflection and instruction:â 1 Asa ki War. 2 That is, to the filth of the world.

3 Suhi ki War.

Rest, sit at home, there is trouble in ever travelling.

A place of rest is recognized when men dwell there per manently.

What manner of resting-place is the world?

Tie up the practice of sincerity as thy travelling expenses, and remain attached to the Name.

Jogis sit in devotional postures, mullas dwell at places of rest;

Pandits read books; sidhs sit in the palaces of the gods;
Demigods, sidhs, heavenly musicians, munis, saints, shaikhs, pirs, and commanders
Have gone, stage by stage, and others too are departing.
Emperors, kings, princes, nobles have marched away.
Man must depart in a ghari or two; O my heart, under stand that thou too must go.
This is told in hymns, yet few are they who understand it.
Nanak humbly asserteth, God is contained in sea and land, in the upper and lower regions;
He is unseen, inscrutable, omnipotent, the kind Creator.
The Merciful alone is permanent; the whole world beside is transitory.
Call Him permanent on whose head no destiny is recorded.
The heavens and the earth shall pass away; He the one God alone is permanent.
By day the sun travelleth, by night the moon; hundreds of thousands of stars pass away.
The one God alone is our resting-place, Nanak saith verily. 1
Upon this the Pir was convinced that the Guru was an exalted spiritual leader.

CHAPTER XIII

The Guru then turned his thoughts towards Ceylon, and succeeded in reaching that country, where he took his seat in Raja Shivnabh's garden.

1 Sri Rag, Ashtapadi.

At that time it was barren, but it is said to have become green on the Guru's arrival. The gardener requested the king to go and see the faqir who had caused the withered garden to bloom anew. The king sent beautiful damsels to dance before the Guru and tempt him with their charms. The Guru, wrapped up in his own thoughts, neither spoke to them nor noticed them. The king came and inquired his name, caste, and whether he was a Jogi. The Guru replied as follows:â

The Jogi who is associated with the Name and is pure, hath not a particle of uncleanness.

He who keepeth with him the name of the Beloved, which is ever true, hath escaped birth and death.

The king asked if he were a Brahman. The Guru replied:â

He is a Brahman who hath divine knowledge for his ablutions, and God's praises for the leaves 1 of his worship.

There is but One Name, One God, One Light in the three worlds.

The king asked if he were a shopkeeper. The Guru replied:â

Make thy heart the scale, thy tongue the beam, and weigh the inestimable Name.

There is but one shop, one Merchant above all; the dealers are many.

The king again inquired if he were a Hindu or a Muhammadan. The Guru continued his enigmati cal replies:â

The True Guru hath solved the problem of the two ways. It is he who fixeth attention on the One God, and whose mind wavereth not, who can understand it.

1 Brahmans use sweet basil and bel (Aegle Marmelos) leaves in iheir worship, the former in the worship of Vishnu and the latter in the worship of Shiv.

He who abideth in the Word and ever worshippeth day and night, hath ended his doubts.

The king then asked if he were Gorakhnath. The Guru showed no inclination to directly gratify his curiosity.

Above us is the sky, Gorakh is above the sky; His inaccessible form dwelleth there; By the favour of the Guru, whether I am abroad or at home is the same to me; Nanak hath become such an anchoret. 1

When the Guru had ended, the king invited him to go to his palace and see his queen. He gave him an opportunity of expounding his doctrines to her.

It was during Guru Nanak's visit to Ceylon that he composed the Pransangali, which contained an account of the silent palace of God, the manner of meditating on Him, the private utterances of the Guru, and the nature of the soul and body. The following are its opening verses:â

The supreme state is altogether a void, 2 all people say; In the supreme state there is no rejoicing or mourning; In the supreme state there are felt no hopes or desires; In the supreme state are seen no castes or caste-marks; In the supreme state are no sermons or singing of hymns;

In the supreme state abideth heavenly meditation; In the supreme state are those who know themselves. 3 Nanak, my mind is satisfied with the supreme state.

Saido and Gheho subsequently wrote out the Pransangali from memory.

1 Maru.

2 The Greek KOL OV, the Latin caelum, heaven.

3 The meaning of this expression is totally different from that of yvui0i o-favrov. To know oneself, in the Sikh sacred writings, means to know God who is within one.

On his return to India the Guru, having heard of the fair of Shivrat l, went to Achal Batala 2 to preach his doctrines. The whole country crowded to see and hear him, and showered offerings on him. The Jogis on witnessing his success became very jealous and determined to humble him. Bhan-garnath, their superior, asked him why he mixed acid with his milk, that is, why he a holy man led a family life. ' When the milk becometh sour said Bhangarnath, ' no butter is produced by churning. Why hast thou doffed thy hermit's dress, and donned ordinary clothes? '

The Guru replied: ' O Bhangarnath, thy mother was an unskilful woman. She knew not how to wash the churn, and so spoilt the butter in producing thee. Thou hast become an anchoret after abandoning thy family life, and yet thou goest to beg to the houses of family men. When thou doest nothing here, what canst thou obtain hereafter? '

Bhangarnath made no reply to the Guru's ques tion but broached another subject: ' O Nanak, thou hast exhibited miracles to the world; why art thou slow to exhibit them to us also? ' The Guru replied: ' I have nothing worth showing you. Man hath absolutely no shelter except in the com panionship of the hymns of the Guru. Were man to move the earth, that would not induce God to grant him undeserved favours. Hear the Word; I speak verily, I have no miracle except the True Name:â 1 A festival in honour of the god Shiv held on the I4th day of the dark half of Phagan (February-March). It was usual for Jogis to congregate on the occasion of this festival. In the Ain-i-Akbari it is stated that the Emperor Akbar used then to hold meetings of all the Jogis of the Empire and eat and drink with them. Under the in fluence of such carousals they used to promise him that he should live three or four times as long as ordinary mortals.

2 Achal, about three miles from Batala, contains the shrine of Samkartik, son of Shiv. For a full account of Batala see the Khuldsat-id-Tawdrikh, whose author was born there.

Were I to put on a dress of fire, construct a house of snow and eat iron;
Were I to turn all my troubles into water, drink it, and drive the earth as a steed;
Were I able to put the firmament into one scale and weigh it with a tank; 1
Were I to become so large that I could be nowhere con tained; and were I to lead every one by the nose; 2

Had I such power in myself that I could perform such things or cause others to perform them, it would be all in vain.

As great as the Lord is, so great are His gifts; He bestoweth according to His pleasure.

Nanak, he on whom God looketh with favour obtaineth the glory of the True Name." 3

In Batala the Guru vanquished in argument all priests who attended the fair, and obliged the followers of the six schools of philosophy to bow before him. The Jogis finally complimented him on his success and said: ' Hail, O Nanak, great are thy deeds! Thou hast arisen a great being, and lit a light in this last age of the world It was the time the Jogis took their daily wine, and the goblet was accordingly passed around. On its reaching the Guru he asked what it was. They said it was the Sidhs' cup. He inquired what it contained. They said molasses and the flower of the dhava 4 plant, of which Indian spirits are made. The Guru then uttered the following hymn:â

Make divine knowledge thy molasses, meditation thy dhava flowers, good actions thy fermenting bark 5 to put into them.

Make the love of God thy furnace, devotion the sealing of the still; in this way shall nectar be distilled.

1 In Hindi apothecaries' weight a tank is equal to four mashas, a masha is eight rattis, and a ratli is the weight of eight grains of rice.

2 As a camel is led. 3 Majh ki War. 4 The Bassia lafifolia. 5 This is generally the bark of the ktkar, or Acacia Arabica.

Father, by quaffing the divine juice the mind becometh intoxicated and easily absorbed in God's love.

I have arranged to fix my attention on God day and night, and heard the unbeaten sound.

God is true, His cup is pure; He giveth it to drink to him on whom He casteth a favouring glance.

Why should he who dealeth in nectar feel love for paltry wine?

The Guru's word is a nectar-speech; by drinking it man becometh acceptable.

When man performeth service at God's gate l to obtain a sight of Him, what careth he for salvation or paradise?

He who is dyed with God's praises never loveth the world, and loseth not his life in the game.

Saith Nanak, hear, Jogi Bharthari, I am intoxicated with the nectareous stream. 2

The Jogis inquired if he lived by begging. The Guru replied, ' Why should he who is absorbed in the Formless go to beg alms? ' They then asked if he were an Udasi or hermit. The Guru replied:â

He who taketh the sword of knowledge and wrestleth with his heart;

Who knoweth the secrets of the ten organs of action and perception 3 and of the five evil passions;

Who can knot divine knowledge to his mind;

Who maketh pilgrimage on each of the three hundred and sixty days of the year;

Who washeth the filth of pride from his heartâ

Nanak saith, he is a hermit.

1 Sikhs and Moslems use the expression ' Gate. of God' for God's throne or God's court. The latent allusion is to a king who removes himself from his subjects' gaze. It is at his gate those who appeal to him for justice wait, and it is at his gate when he goes forth his subjects can obtain a sight of him.

2 Asa.

3 The organs of action are the mouth, the hands, the feet, and the generative and excretory organs. The organs of perception are the five senses.

The Jogis then asked the Guru if he were an Audhut. The Guru told them what an Audhut ought to be:â

He is a servant of the Guru who restraineth his sexual organs,

Whose heart is free from worldly desires, whose words are true,

And who receiveth as his alms the glance with which the Merciful One beholdeth him.

Know him to be meek whose heart is meek,

And whose instruction is the profitable Word.

Nanak saith, he is an Audhut

Whose mind is not fickle, who goeth not to spectacles,

Or to gamble or play chaupar,

Who attacheth not his mind to things bad or good,

Who weareth on his body whatever is given by the Guru,

Who, when he goeth to another's house, talketh not scandal,

Who observeth the restraint put on him by the true Guru,

And who receiveth the Guru's instructionsâ O holy man,

Nanak saith, such a man is an Audhut.

The Jogis then desired to know if he were a Jogi, and the Guru replied:â

To remain seated without support, To collect and restrain the five evil passions, To sleep little and take scant food, To keep guard over the saintly body, To be constant in devotion, penance, self-restraint, and remembrance of Godâ

Nanak saith, these are the marks of a Jogi.

When he speaketh, he uttereth divine wisdom;

He day and night waketh in the contemplation of God;

He attacheth a string to the vacant sphere, 1

And by the Guru's favour never dieth.

All the gods do obeisance to him 1 That is, he fixes his attention on God.

Who in this way performeth the Guru's service, And who alloweth not his tongue to taste daintiesâ Nanak saith, these are the marks of a Jogi.

He who effaceth wrath, avarice, and greed;
Who quencheth the fire of the five evil passions within his heart;
Who day and night flieth the kite
By which divine knowledge is produced and evil inclina tions depart;
Who cherisheth holiness, restraineth his evil passions
And repeateth no spell but the Guru'sâ
The habits of that good man are the bestâ
Nanak saith, these are the marks of a Jogi.
He who maketh his body the vessel, remembrance of
God his milk,
Who putteth pure truth into it as his acid, Who by contrivance and effort easily curdleth the milkâ Without contrivance it would be spoiled â Who useth divine knowledge as his churning staff and the Name as its string;
Who in this way repeateth only the Name,
And who by rolling and rolling extracteth the butterâ
Nanak saith, these are the marks of a Jogi.
The Jogis wondered if he were a Bairagi. The Guru defined the word for them:â

He is a Bairagi who is sold to God, Who in the presence of God subdueth mammon, Who performeth the work of God and mammon, 1 Who beareth an unbearable and intangible thing, Who hath abandoned wrath, avarice, and prideâ Nanak saith, such a man is a Bairagi.

He who abideth lonely in the house of enjoyment, And dwelleth in the house of worshipâ 1 That is, who performs his worldly avocations and thinks of God at the same time.

Where the cat fleeth at the sound of a mouse 1 â Nanak saith, is a Bairagi.

He is a Bairagi who embraceth contentment, Who reverseth his breath and is absorbed in God, Who subjecteth to himself the five sensesâ Such a Bairagi shall rise higher than Shiv. He who renounceth evil ways and fixeth his attention on the one God,

Nanak saith, is a Bairagi.

Upon this the followers of Gorakhnath pressed the Guru to adopt the style of a Jogi. The Guru asked them to describe a Jogi. They replied:â

A Jogi weareth earrings, a patched coat, carrieth a wallet, a staff,
And a deer's horn which soundeth through the world.

The Jogis were proceeding to give a further de scription of their sect when the Guru interrupted and offered spiritual substitutes for all the externals of a Jogi:â

Put the Guru's word into thy heart for the rings in thine ears; wear the patched coat of forbearance;

Whatever God doeth consider as good; in this way shalt thou easily obtain the treasure of jog.

0 father, in this way the soul which hath been a pilgrim in every age, uniteth with the Supreme Essence.

He who obtaineth the ambrosial name of the Pure One, and maketh reflection his Jogi's cup,

Divine knowledge his staff, and the Omnipresent the ashes he smear eth on his body, shall enjoy the great elixir of divine knowledge.

Make God's praise thy prayer, the Guru's instruction thy sect of Atits, 2

The renunciation of desires and quarrels thy sitting in contemplation in God's citadel 3 â 1 Where hypocrisy flees before humility.

2 By Atits here is meant a sect of Jogis who consider themselves liberated from worldly restraints. 3 The brain.

From the sound of thy horn a melody shall thus be pro duced which day and night shall fill thee with music.

In everything is Thy light contained, 0 God, and many and various are its colours.

Saith Nanak, hear, Jogi Bharthari, the Primal God is the sole object of my love. 1

During his residence in Batala the Guru composed the Sidh Gosht, a treatise from which the Jogis are said to have derived spiritual consolation.

CHAPTER XIV

The Guru continued his journey to the north. He wore leather on his feet and on his head, twisted a rope round his body, and on his forehead stamped a saffron tilak. He was accompanied by Hassu, a smith, and Sihan, a calico-printer. The party went as far as Srinagar in Kashmir, where they stayed some time and made many converts.

Brahm Das was then the most eminent of the Kashmiri pandits. On hearing of the Guru's arrival, he went to pay him a formal visit. The better to impress the Guru with his piety and learning, he wore an idol suspended from his neck, and took with him two loads of Sanskrit books. On seeing the Guru's dress he said, ' Is that the sort of faqir thou art? Why wearest thou leather, which is unclean? Why twistest thou a rope round thy body? Why hast thou abandoned the observances of thy religion? And why eatest thou flesh and fish? ' The Guru, not paying much attention to these impertinent questions, thus unburdened him self of the thoughts which filled his mind: â

There is but one road, one door; the Guru is the ladder to reach one's home.

Beautiful is God; Nanak, all happiness is in His name.

1 Asa. M 2

PAURI

God Himself created and recognized His creation.

He separated the earth from the sky and spread a canopy over it.

He fixed the heavens without pillars by the utterance of a word.

Having created the sun and moon, He infused His light into them.

He made the wonderful play of night and day.

Pilgrimage, religion, meditation, and bathing on holy daysâ

None of these is equal to Thee, O God; how can I describe Thee?

Thou sittest on a true throne; all else are subject to birth and death.

After a pause the Guru again burst forth in God's praises:â

Thou, 0 God, who didst diffuse truth, art the truest of the true.

Thou sittest in an attitude of contemplation concealed in the lotus of the heart.

Brahma called himself great, but he found not Thy limit.

Thou hast no father or mother; who begot Thee?

Thou art devoid of all form, outline, or caste.
Thou feelest not hunger or thirst; Thou art satisfied and satiated.
The great God is contained in Himself, and hath diffused His word.
They who are satisfied with the True One are absorbed in Him. 1

Brahm Das then recognizing the Guru's piety and genius fell at his feet, and asked him what existed before creation? The Guru in reply uttered the following hymn known as Solaha 2 in Rag Maru:â 1 Malar ki War. 2 A hymn containing sixteen stanzas.

In the beginning 1 there was indescribable darkness;
Then was not earth or heaven, naught but God's unequalled order.
Then was not day, or night, or moon, or sun; God was meditating on the void.
Then were not the mines of production, or voices, or wind, or water;
Neither creation nor destruction, nor coming nor going,
Then were not continents, or hells, or seven seas, or rivers, or flowing streams,
Nor was there paradise, or a tortoise, 2 or nether regions;
Or the hell or heaven of the Muhammadans, or the destroyer Death;
Or the hell or heaven of the Hindus, or birth, or death; nor did any one come or go.
Then was no Brahma, Vishnu, or Shiv:
No one existed but the One God.
Then was no female, or male, or caste, or birth; nor did any one feel pain or pleasure.
There was no Jati, Sati, 3 or dweller in the forest;
There was no Sidh, or Striver, or dweller at ease;
No Jogi, or Jangam, or religious garb; nor did any one call himself a Nath; 4
No devotion, penance, austerity, fasting, or worship;
Nor did any one speak or tell of duality. 5
God Himself having created was pleased, and valued what He had done.
There was no purification, or self-restraint, or necklace of sweet basil;
There was no milkmaid, or Krishan, or cow, or herdsman; 1 Arbad is here understood to be for aramlh. Arbud in Sanskrit means a number of one hundred millions, so arbad narbad may also meanâ for countless years.

2 Which some Hindus believe supports the earth.

3 Sati means a faithful wife, especially one who cremates herself with her deceased husband.

4 A superior of Jogis.

6 Dwait, duality, in the Sikh writings means the worship of other than God.
No incantations or spells, no hypocrisy, nor did any one play on the flute. 1
There were no acts attaching to the soul, or religion, or the gadfly of mammon.
No one saw caste or birth with his eyes.
There was not the net of pride, nor was death written on man's brow, nor did man meditate on aught created. 2
There was no slander, no seed, no soul, no life.
There was no Gorakh or Machhindar. 3
Nor was there divine knowledge, or meditation, or nobility; nor did any one have conceit of himself.

There was no caste or religious garb, no Brahman or Khatri;

No demigod, no temple, no cow, no gayatri, 4

No horn, no sacred feasts, no places of pilgrimage to bathe in, nor did any one perform worship.

There was no Mulla or any Qazi;

No Shaikh, no Disciple, no Haji; 5

No subject or king; nor was pride in the world, nor did any one give himself a great name.

There was no love, no service, no Shiv, or energy of his; o

No friend, no helper, no seed, no blood. 7

God Himself was the merchant, Himself the dealerâ such was the will of the True Oneâ 1 One of Krishan's youthful accomplishments.

2 Literallyâ nor did any one meditate on any one else. That is, no one then worshipped the gods or idols of the Hindus.

3 Machhindar is described in a verse attributed to Gorakhnath as his father.

4 The gayatri is the spell of the Hindus. It is now recited as follows: Oam, bhur, bhuvas, svar, tat savitur varenyam, bhargo devasya, dhlmahi dhiyo yo nah prachodyat ' Oam, earth and air and sky, let us meditate on that excellent sun the bright god, which stimulateth our intellects." The late Professor Max Miiller gave the following translationâ ' We meditate on the adorable light of the divine Savitri, that he may rouse our thoughts 5 This word is applied to Muhammadans who have made the pilgrimage to Makka.

6 Shiv's energy or consort was variously named Parbati, Durga, c.

7 ' No seed, no blood': this refers to the male and female func tions of generation.

Then were no Veds or Muhammadan books, 1 no Simritis, no Shastars;

No reading of the Purans, no sunrise, no sunset.

The Imperceptible God was Himself the speaker and preacher; Himself unseen He saw everything.

When He pleased He created the world;

Without supports He sustained the sky.

He created Brahma, Vishnu, and Shiv, and extended the love of mammon.

He communicated the Guru's words to some few persons.

He issued His order and watched over all.

He began with the continents, the universe, and the nether regions, and brought forth what had been hidden.

His limit no one knoweth.

From the True Guru I have learned,

Nanak, that they who are imbued with the truth are wonderful, and delight in singing God's praises.

Upon this Brahm Das again fell at the Guru's feet, cast away the idol from his neck, and, becoming a worshipper of God, performed service for the Guru. His evil desires, however, departed not. Whatever service he performed was brief and per functory, for he thought to himself that he had performed similar service before; but whatever he did was of no avail on account of his pride.

At one of their meetings the Guru told him to take a guru. He inquired, ' What guru shall I take?" The Guru bade him go to a certain house in the wilderness where he should find four faqirs, and they would inform him. The pandit went to them, and they, after some delay, pointed out a temple in which they said he should find his guru. The pandit pro ceeded thither, but instead of receiving a courteous reception, was shoe-beaten in a piteous manner by a woman in red who guarded the temple. Crying bitterly he returned to the four men who had dis- 1 They are described as the Psalms of David, the Old Testa ment, the New Testament, and the Quran.

patched him on the unpleasant errand. They inquired if he had found a guru, and in reply he told them his painful story. They explained to him that the woman was Maya, or worldly love; and that she for whom he had so longed was his guru. The pandit returned to the Guru, and fell at his feet. He then cast away his two loads of books, began to repeat God's name, and became so humble as to be, as it were, the dust of the earth. The pandit inquired who were happy in this world. The Guru replied with the following sloks, which Hassu and Sihan committed to writing:â

Indar wept after his thousandfold punishment; l

Paras Ram wept on his return home; 2

King Ajai 3 wept after eating what he had obtained as almsâ

Such is the punishment meted out in God's courtâ

Ram wept when he was expelled from his kingdom,

And separated from Sit a and Lachhman. 4

Rawan, who took away Sita with beat of drum,

Wept when he had lost Lanka; 5

The Pandavs 6 though their master 7 had been with them,

Became slaves and wept; 1 Indar was the god of the firmament. His punishment was for his effort to seduce Ahalya, the wife of the sage Gautama.

2 Paras Ram. Ram with the axe was the sixth avatar of Vishnu and preceded the Ram of Indian popular worship. He is said to have cleared the earth twenty-one times of the Kshatriyas. He then gave it to the sage Kashyapa and retired to the Mahendra mountains. The text alludes to his subsequent homeward return.

3 Aj was grandfather of Ram Chandar. One day when hunting he dipped a cloth in the blood of a deer which he had shot, and in order to test his wife's affection sent it to her with a dying message that he had been killed in the hunting-field. She, believing the mes senger, at once cremated herself with the cloth she had received. King Aj on returning home found out what had occurred, and was so overcome with grief and sorrow, that he abandoned his throne and retired from the world to do penance for his crime.

4 Lachhman was Ram's brother.

5 Lanka. This was the ancient name of Ceylon, where Rawan ruled.

6 The opponents of the Kauravs in the great war which forms the subject of the Mahdbharat. 1 Krishan.

Janameja l wept when he went astray; â For one offence he was deemed a sinner- Shaikhs, Disciples and Pirs 2 weep For fear of suffering at the last moment; Kings wept when their ears were torn, 3 And they went to beg alms from door to door; The miser wept at his departure from the wealth he had amassed;

The pandit wept when he had lost his learning; The young girl who hath no husband weepethâ Nanak, the whole world is in misery. He who revereth the Name is victorious; No other act is of any avail. 4

The Guru, leaving Srinagar, penetrated the Hima laya mountains, and scaled numerous lofty peaks 1 Janameja, king of Hastinapura, who listened to the long Sanskrit epic Mahdbhdrat in expiation of the sin of killing Brahmans.

2 Pirs are Muhammadan saints.

3 The reference is to Gopi Chand and Bharthari. Bharthari was king of Ujjain. In his stale there lived a Brahman who by his austeri ties had obtained the fruit of immortality. Not deeming it useful to himself he presented it as a fitting offering to his monarch. He being in love with his queen presented it to her. She being in love with the head police officer of the state presented it to him. He being in love with a favourite courtesan presented it to her. She being in love with the king presented it to him. On being informed of the strange vicis situdes of the fruit of immortality, and pondering on the instability of love and friendship, Bharthari abdicated and became a religious men dicant.

Gopi Chand was king of Bengal, whose capital, according to legend, was then Doulagarh. His mother Menawati was Raja Bharthari's sister. One day as Gopi Chand was bathing, his mother, seated in an upper chamber, admired his beauty, but at the same time felt that he was not so handsome as his father, her late husband. Death had taken him, it would also take Gopi Chand. Gopi Chand as he bathed felt moisture falling on him, and was told in reply to his inquiries that it was his mother's tears. He tried to console her and said that death was the way of the world, and one must not endeavour to resist Nature's primordial law. On reflection she decided that Gopi Chand should become a faqlr under the spiritual guidance of Jalandharnath. Gopi Chand abdicated, proceeded to him, and after many troubles received, it is said, instruction how to overcome death.

4 Ramkali ki War.

until he arrived at Mount Sumer. He there met many renowned Sidhs. When the Guru had made his obeisance and sat down, they inquired whence he had come and in what state he had left Hindustan. He replied:â

The Kal age is a knife, kings are butchers; justice hath taken wings and fled.

In this completely dark night of falsehood the moon of truth is never seen to rise.

I have become perplexed in my search:

In the darkness I find no way.

Devoted to pride, I weep in sorrow:

Saith Nanak, how shall deliverance be obtained? 1

On this the Sidhs requested the Guru to join them in praising God. Having done so he put his subse quent conversation with them into the following form:â

The Sidhs holding an assembly sat in religious attitude â hail to the assembly of the saints!

I offer my prayer to Him who is the true and Infinite One.

I will cut off my head and lay it before Him; I will place before Him my soul and body.

Nanak, by meeting a holy man the True One is found, and honour is easily obtained.

Is the True and Pure One obtained by wandering?
There is no salvation without the True Word
The Sidhs asked:â 1 Who art thou? What is thy name? What is thy sect and what thine object?
' Speak the truth; this is what we urge; we are a sacrifice to saintly men.
' Where is thy seat; where dwellest thou, O youth? Whence hast thou come, and whither goest thou?
' Hear, O Nanak," said the Sidhs, ' What are thy tenets? ' 1 Majh ki War.
Nanak â ' I dwell in God who hath His seat in every heart; I act according to the will of the True Guru.
' I came in the course of nature, and according to God's order shall I depart. Nanak is ever subject to His will.
' To be fixed in God is my prayerful attitude; such know ledge have I obtained from the Guru.
' If one understand the Guru's instruction and know him self, then he being true shall be absorbed in the True One."
A Sidh called Charpat asked:â ' The world is an ocean, and is said to be difficult to cross; how shall man traverse it? '
Saith Chaipat, ' O Audhut Nanak, give a true reply."
Nanak â ' Thou sayest so; thou thyself understandest; What answer can I give thee?
' I speak truly; thou hast reached the distant shore; how can I argue with thee?
' As a lotus in the water remaineth dry, as also a water fowl in the stream, ' So by meditating on the Word and repeating God's name," ' shalt thou be unaffected by the world."
Nanak is a slave to those who remain apart from the world, in whose hearts the one God abideth, who live without desires in the midst of desires,
And who see and show to others the inaccessible and incomprehensible God. 1
The Sidhs then said ' All hail! ' The Guru replied, ' All hail to the Primal Being! '
Several Sikhs suppose that Guru Nanak com posed the Sidh Gosht on that occasion when he found leisure and retirement for composition.

CHAPTER XV

After his sojourn with the Sidhs the Guru returned to the plains of the Panjab and travelled in a north westerly direction until he reached Hasan Abdal, 1 Sidh Gosht. then a great centre of Muhammadan religious enthusiasm.

There abode on a small hillock a bigoted and selfish priest known as Bawa Wali of Kandhar. The Guru and his minstrel needed water for their evening repast, and it could only be obtained from the Wali. Mardana told him that he and Guru Nanak had arrived, and he advised him to see the Guru, who was a great saint of God. Bawa Wali, who claimed exclusive holiness for himself, became offended on hearing the Guru's praises, and refused the required water. He said if Mardana's master were such a holy man, he ought to provide water for himself. When this reply was communicated to the Guru, he sent Mardana back to the Wali with the message that he himself was a very poor creature of God, and laid no claims to the character of a saint. The Wali paid no heed to this protestation, but persisted in his refusal to afford water to the Guru and his minstrel. The Guru was then com pelled to bore a hole near where he had taken shelter, and a stream of water immediately issued forth. Upon this, the Wali's well dried up, there being only a limited supply of water in the locality. The Wali's rage naturally increased, and it is said that he hurled the hillock upon Guru Nanak's un offending head. The Guru, on seeing the descend ing volume of earth, raised his right arm to protect himself. It is related that upon this the fall of the hillock was arrested. The impression of the palm of the Guru's hand was left on the descending mass, which is now known as 'Panja Sahib' and held in reverence by the Sikhs.

After a brief residence in Hasan Abdal the Guru proceeded to Gorakh-Hatari, a quarter of the city of Peshawar on the frontier of the Panjab where there is an ancient temple of Gorakhnath. The Jogis having heard of his fame were anxious to discover how he had acquired such moral and spiritual influence, and, when the Guru was seated, put him the questions contained in the first four verses of the following hymn. The Guru's replies follow:â

What callest thou that gate at which thou sittest? Who can see the gate within it?
Let some one come and describe to me that gate to attain which the Udasi wandereth.
How shall we cross the ocean?
How shall we be dead when alive?
Sorrow is the gate, wrath the porter, hope and anxiety its folding-doors.
Mammon is a moat, domestic life its water; man abideth by taking his seat on truth.
How many names hast Thou, 0 God! Their limit cannot be known; there is none equal to Thee.
Man ought not to call himself exalted, but dwell in his own thoughts; what God deemeth proper, He doeth.
As long as there is desire, so long is there anxiety; how can one who feeleth it speak of the one God?
When man in the midst of desires remaineth free from desires, then, O Nanak, he meeteth the one God.
In this way shall he cross the ocean,
And thus be dead while alive. 1

On uttering this hymn the Guru was pressed to adopt the style and religion of a Jogi. The principles of the Jogis' sect were explained to him. The Guru replied:â

The Word is my meditation, divine instruction the music of my horn for men to hear;
Honour is my begging-wallet, and uttering the Name my alms.
Father, Gorakh awaketh.
Gorakh is He who lifted the earth and fashioned it without delay; 1 Ramkali.
Who enclosed water, breath, and life in the body, and made the great lights of the moon and sun;
Who gave us the earth as our abode, but whose many favours we have forgotten.
Sidhs, Strivers, Jogis, Jangams, and Pirs are many.
If I obtain the Name from them, I will sing their praises, and serve them heartilyâ
Paper and salt melt not in clarified butter; the lotus remaineth unaffected by waterâ
What can Death say to them, O Nanak, who meet such saints? 1

After his successful discussion with the Jogis the Guru decided to visit Makka, the pole star of Muham-madan devotion. He disguised himself in the blue dress of a

Muhammadan pilgrim, took a faqir's staff in his hand and a collection of his hymns under his arm. He also carried with him in the style of a Musalman devotee a cup for his ablutions and a carpet whereon to pray. And when an oppor tunity offered, he shouted the Muhammadan call to prayer like any orthodox follower of the Arabian prophet. As usual in his peregrinations, he was accompanied by his faithful minstrel and rebeck-player Mardana. It is recorded that whenever he met children on his journey he joined in their sports. He accidentally found a Muhammadan faqir also bent on the Makkan pilgrimage, and passed a night with him in pleasant spiritual converse. The pilgrim offered him his bhang-pouch, and asked whether he was a Hindu or a Musalman. The Guru replied with the hymn he had previously addressed to the Emperor Babar when he inquired what intoxication that was whose effects should never depart.

As they proceeded on the road to Makka, it is said, a cloud they saw over their heads accompanied them. The pilgrim became alarmed at the unusual occur- 1 Ramkali.

rence, and said to the Guru, ' No Hindu hath ever yet gone to Makka. Travel not with me; either go before or after." The Guru told the pilgrim to precede him. When the pilgrim turned round to see where his companion was, it is said he could see neither him nor the cloud. The pilgrim then began to wring his hands, and said, ' It was God who was with me, but I could not endure the sight of Him. He worked illusion on me."

When the Guru arrived, weary and footsore, in Makka, he went and sat in the great mosque where pilgrims were engaged in their devotions. His disregard of Moslem customs soon involved him in difficulties. When he lay down to sleep at night he turned his feet towards the Kaaba. An Arab priest kicked him and said, ' Who is this sleeping infidel? Why hast thou, O sinner, turned thy feet towards God? ' The Guru replied, ' Turn my feet in a direction in which God is not." 1 Upon this the priest seized the Guru's feet and dragged them in the opposite direction, whereupon, it is said, the temple turned round, and followed the revolution of his body. Some understand this in a spiritual sense, and say it means that Guru Nanak made all Makka turn to his teaching. Those who witnessed this miracle were astonished and saluted the Guru as a supernatural being.

The Qazis and the Mullas crowded round the Guru, and interrogated him on the subject of his religion. They admitted that he had accomplished a great feat, but the source of his power was not apparent. They opened his book, and seeing that it was on religious subjects, inquired which was 1 Curious it is to find the same expression in an Italian operatic writer of the eighteenth century.

E se, dov' ei dimora, Non intendesti ancora, Confondimi, se puoi; Dimmi dov' ei non e.

(Metastasio.) superior, the Hindu or the Muhammadan religion. The Guru replied, ' Without good acts the professors of both religions shall suffer. Neither the Hindus nor the Muhammadans shall obtain entrance into God's court. All their devotions shall vanish like the fleeting dye of safflower. Both sects are jealous of each other. The Hindus insist on saying Ram and the Moslems Rahim, but they know not the one God. Satan hath led them both along his own flowery way On that occasion the Guru uttered the following hymn in the Tilang measure:â

Thy fasting and worship shall be acceptable
When thou, O man, keepest watch over the ten apertures of thy body, hatest the world,
Chastenest thy mind, restrainest thy sight, and fleest worldly desires and wranglings.
Every day of the month offer thy love to the Lord; thus shalt thou be recognized as pure and gentle.
Keep the fast of meditation, and let the renunciation of pleasure be thy dance;
Keep watch over thy heart, so shalt thou be a really learned man;
Abandon delights, ease, evil speaking, mental anxiety, and vexation;
Treasure kindness in thy heart, and renounce the devices of infidelity;
Extinguish the fire of lust in thy heart, and thus become cool.
Saith Nanak, thus practise fasting, and thy faith shall be perfect. 1
When the Guru had finished, the Qazi said, ' Well done! I have to-day for the first time seen a real saint of God The Qazi then went and told the high priest that the darwesh Nanak had arrived. The high priest went to see him, shook hands with him,

1 This hymn is not found in the Granth Sahib.

and sat down beside him. He thanked God that Nanak had come.

The high priest asked Nanak if the Hindus who read the Veds, and the Musalmans who read the Quran, should or should not find God. The Guru courageously replied with the following outspoken hymn of Kabir:â

O brethren, the Veds and the Quran are false, and free not the mind from anxiety.
If for a moment thou restrain thy mind, God will appear before thee.
0 man, search thy heart daily, that thou mayest not again fall into despair.
This world is a magic show which hath no reality.
Men are pleased when they read falsehood, and quarrel over what they do not understand.
The truth is, the Creator is contained in the creation; He is not of a blue colour in the guise of Vishnu.
Thou shouldst have bathed in the river which floweth in heaven. 1
Take heed; ever fix thine eyes on Him who is every where present. 2
God is the purest of the pure; shall I doubt whether there is another equal to Him? 3
Kabir, he to whom the Merciful hath shown mercy, knoweth Him.

The high priest then asked how God might be obtained by men. The Guru replied that it was by humility and prayer. He added the following hymn in the Persian language:â 1 make one supplication before Thee; lend Thine ear, O Creator.

1 In the brain instead of the Ganges and other sacred streams of the Hindus.
2 Also translatedâ Embrace perpetual poverty, fix thy mental eyes on God, and thou shalt behold Him everywhere present.
3 Also translatedâ If there be another like Him, then entertain doubt.

SIKH. 1 N 0 God, Thou art great and merciful; Thou art the fault less Cherish er.
The world is a perishable abode; O my heart, know this as the truth.
Azrail l seizeth me by the hair of my head; yet thou knowest it not, O my heart.
There shall be no wife, no son, no father, no brother, no one to take my hand.
There shall be no one to hinder my falling at last when my fate 2 cometh.

I have passed my nights and days in vanity, and my thoughts have been evil.

I have never done a good actâ this is my condition;

I am unfortunate, I am also miserly and negligent; I see not, and I fear not.

Nanak saith, I am Thy slave, and the dust of the feet of Thy servants. 3

The high priest then asked the Guru to tell him the composition of matter, the nature of the God he adored, how He was to be found, and in what con sisted the essence of his religion. The Guru replied again in the Persian language:â

Know that according to the Musalmans everything is produced from air, fire, water, and earth;

But the pure God created the world out of five elements. 4

However high man may leap, he shall fall on the earth again.

Even though a bird fly, it cannot compete in endurance with the torrent and the wind which move by God's will.

How great shall I call God? to whom shall I go to in quire regarding Him?

1 Azrall is frequently mentioned in the Sikh sacred writings. In the Muhammadan dispensation he is the minister of Death who separates men's souls from their bodies by violently tearing them asunder. The Quran, Suras 32 and 79.

1 Takbir is understood to be for the Arabic taqdir, destiny.

3 Tilang. 4 Akash, or ether, being the fifth.

He is the greatest of the great, and great is His world; men depart in their pride.

I have consulted the four Veds, but these writings find not God's limits.

I have consulted the four books of the Muhammadans, but God's worth is not described in them.

I have consulted the nine regions of the earth; one improveth upon what the other saith.

Having turned my heart into a boat, I have searched in every sea;

I have dwelt by rivers and streams, and bathed at the sixty-eight places of pilgrimage;

I have lived among the forests and glades of the three worlds and eaten bitter and sweet;

I have seen the seven nether regions and heavens upon heavens.

And , Nanak, say man shall be true to his faith if he fear God and do good works. 1

In due time the Guru proceeded to Madina, where he vanquished the Muhammadan priests in argu ment. Thence he journeyed to Baghdad, and took up his position outside the city. He shouted the call to prayer, on which the whole population became wrapt in silent astonishment. 2 The high priest of Baghdad, on meeting face to face the enthusiastic stranger, inquired who he was and to what sect he belonged. The Guru replied, ' I have appeared in this age to indicate the way unto men. I reject all sects, and only know one God, whom I recognize in the earth, the heavens, and in all directions."

Upon this the Guru began to repeat the Japji. As the high priest listened to its doctrines he said, ' This is a very impious faqir. He is working 1 Banno's Granth Sahib.

2 It is certain that the Guru omitted the words Muhammad ar rasul Allah of the creed, and substituted Arabic words of a similar sound to express his own ideas. Hence the astonishment of the people.

miracles here, and informing us, contrary to the authority of our holy Quran, that there are hundreds of thousands of nether and upper regions, and that at last men grow weary of searching for them The high priest then called upon the Guru to give a manifestation of his power. Upon this, it is said, the Guru laid his hand on the high priest s son and showed him the upper and lower regions described in the Japji. 1

The Guru having accomplished his mission in the West resolved to return to his own country. When he arrived in Multan, the local high priest presented him with a cup of milk filled to the brim. By this he meant it to be understood that the city was full of holiness already, and that there was no room for another religious teacher. The Guru, in no wise disconcerted, took the milk and laid on it an Indian jasmin flower. The cup did not overflow. This typified that there was still room for the Guru in the midst of the Multanis, as there is still room for the ever flowing Ganges in the ocean.

The Guru, after a brief sojourn in Multan, set out for Kartarpur. His reputation daily increased in the world, and men meditated on his name. He insisted that praying for anything except God's name merely conferred on man a crown of sorrow. By this time the Guru had founded a pure religion and made his coin current in the world.

In due time the Guru and his minstrel arrived at Kartarpur on the right bank of the river Ravi, opposite the present town of Dehra Baba Nanak. There he doffed his pilgrim's dress, and donned worldly garments in order to show that he did not desire men to devote themselves exclusively to an ascetic life. At the same time he sat on his re ligious stool, and began to preach to the people.

During Guru Nanak's stay at Kartarpur he con- 1 Japji, Pauri xxiii.

tinued to compose hymns which diffused spiritual light and dispelled mental darkness. He ever con versed on religious subjects, and divine measures were ever sung in his presence. The Sodar and the Sohila were chanted in the evening and the Japji repeated at the ambrosial hour of morning. 1

At Kartarpur, Mardana, the Guru's faithful minstrel, advanced in years and wearied with his long wanderings and physical privations, fell ill. He felt that he had no hope of longer life, and resigned himself to man's inevitable fate. He had originally been a Muhammadan, but, being now a Sikh, the question arose as to how his body should be disposed of after death. The Guru said, ' A Brahman's body is thrown into water, a Khatri's is burnt in the fire, a Vaisya's is thrown to the winds, and a Sudra's is buried in the earth. Thy body shall be disposed of as thou pleasest." Mardana replied, Through thine instruction the pride of my body hath totally departed. With the four castes the disposal of the body is a matter of pride. I deem my soul merely as a spectator of my body, and am not concerned with the latter. Where fore dispose of it as thou pleasest." Then the Guru said, ' Shall I make thee a tomb and render thee famous in the world." Mardana replied, ' When my soul hath been separated from its bodily tomb, why shut it up in a stone tomb? ' The Guru answered, ' Since thou knowest God and art therefore a Brah man, we shall dispose of thy body by throwing it into the river Ravi and letting it go with the stream. Sit down therefore on its margin in prayerful posture, fix thine attention on God, repeat His name at every inspiration and expiration, and thy soul shall be absorbed in the light of God." Mardana accordingly sat down by the river, and his soul separated from its earthly enclosure the following morning at a watch 1 A translation of these divine services will be found in this volume.

before day. The Guru then, by the aid of his Sikhs, consigned Mardana's body to the river Ravi, 1 caused the Sohila to be read for his eternal repose, and con cluded the obsequies by distributing karah parshad z (sacred food). The Guru counselled Mardana's son Shahzada and his relations not to weep. There ought to be no lamentation for a man who was returning to his heavenly home, and therefore no mourning for Mardana. 3

The Guru bade Shahzada remain with him in the same capacity as his father, and he would be held in equal honour. Accordingly Shahzada, the Guru's faithful friend and minstrel, accompanied him to the time of his death.

In the Granth Sahib are found three sloks of the Guru, dedicated to Mardana, against the use of wine. The following, which may conveniently be given here, will suffice as a specimen:â

The barmaid is misery, wine is lust; man is the drinker.

The cup filled with worldly love is wrath, and it is served by pride.

The company is false and covetous, and is ruined by excess of drink.

Instead of such wine make good conduct thy yeast, truth thy molasses, God's name thy wine;

Make merits thy cakes, good conduct thy clarified butter, and modesty thy meat to eat.

Such things, O Nanak, are obtained by the Guru's favour; by partaking of them sins depart. 4

CHAPTER XVI

There lived in a town called Khadur a Sikh named Jodha who used to repeat God's name while 1 It is stated in several Sikh works that Mardana's body was cremated.

2 The recipe for the preparation of karah parshad, or Sikh sacred food, will be given in the life of Guru Gobind Singh, vol. v.

3 Gydn Ratanawali. 4 Bihagre ki War.

the rest of the inhabitants worshipped Durga. Their priest was a man called Lahina. One day when Jodha was repeating Guru Nanak's Japji, Lahina heard him and inquired whose composition it was. Jodha duly informed him, and they became intimate. On being introduced to the Guru, Lahina told his name, upon which the Guru said, 'Thy lahina is here, where else can it be found?" In the Panjabi language the word lahina means to take or receive, and the Guru meant, ' What thou de-sirest to receiveâ salvationâ is here, and nowhere else." After some spiritual instruction from the lips of the Guru, Lahina threw away the tinkling bells he wore on his hands and feet to dance before the goddess, and began to repeat God's name. He made it a practice afterwards to perform menial service for the Guru. 1

It is said that Lahina in a vision saw a female in a red dress shampooing the Guru. Lahina asked her who she was. She replied that she was Durga, and that she came once a week to do service for the Guru. On this Lahina became convinced of the divine mission of Guru Nanak.

A Jogi went to visit the Guru and congratulate him on the large number of converts he had made The Guru replied that he had few real Sikhs, as the Jogi himself would see. The Guru and the Jogi determined to proceed into the forest and there make trial of the Sikh converts who accompanied them in numbers. For this purpose the Guru assumed a terrible guise. He put on dirty, tattered clothes, took a knife in his hand, and proceeded with some hunting dogs into the forest, ostensibly in quest of game. On this several of his Sikhs fled. It was on that occasion the Guru composed the following:â 1 A fuller account of Jodha's influence on Lahina will be given in the Life of Guru Angad, Vol. II.

I have a dog 1 and two bitches 2 with me;
Every morning they bark at the wind. 3
Falsehood is my hunting-knife and carrion its handle.
0 Creator, I remain in the guise of a huntsman; 1 do not follow my Master's counsel or do His work. I appear deformed and terrible.
Thy Name alone saveth the world;
It is my support; to obtain it is my desire.
I utter calumny day and night;
I am base and worthless; I covet my neighbour's house.
Lust and anger, which are pariahs, dwell in my heart.
0 Creator, I remain in the guise of a huntsman; In saint's dress I meditate to entrap others.
1 am a cheat in a country of cheats. 4 deem myself very clever, and bear a great load of sin. O Creator, I remain in the guise of a huntsman. Ungrateful that I was, I did not appreciate what Thou didst for me.

How can I, who am wicked and dishonest, show my face? Humble Nanak expresseth his thoughtsâ 0 Creator, I remain in the guise of a huntsman. 5

As the party proceeded they found the road covered with copper coins. Some Sikhs took them up and departed. Further on were found silver coins. Several Sikhs took up the silver coins and returned home. As the Guru's party proceeded further, they saw gold coins on the road. Several of the remaining Sikhs took up the gold coins and quickly vanished. Only the Jogi, two Sikhs, and the Guru's attendant Lahina now remained.

On proceeding further they found a funeral pyre. Near the corpse were four lighted lamps. A sheet was stretched over it as it lay on the ground and emitted an offensive smell. The Guru said, ' Let 1 Avarice. 2 Desire and covetousness.

3 The line means that desire and covetousness call in vain to the saint.
4 Also translatedâ I am a cheat and cheat the country.
5 Sri Rag.

whoever wisheth to accompany me eat of this." The Sikhs quailed at the dreadful proposal, but Lahina remained staunch in his faith in the Guru. Without more ado he clasped his hands and asked the Guru if he should begin to eat the head or the feet of the corpse. The Guru told him to begin at the waist. Lahina lifted the winding-sheet in order to begin to eat, when lo! it is said, a dish of sacred food appeared instead of the corpse! Lahina offered the sacred food to the Guru first, and said he would partake of his leavings. The Guru replied, ' Thou hast obtained this sacred food because thou didst desire to share it with others. The wealth given by God which man useth himself or burieth in the earth, is like carrion; but the wealth which man shareth with others is as sacred food. Thou hast obtained my secret; thou art in mine image. I will tell thee the real thing, the spell which is the essence of religion, and by which thou shalt have happiness here and hereafter. The following, which is the preamble of the Japji, is the spell meant by the Guru: â

There is but one God whose name is True, the Creator, devoid of fear and enmity, immortal, unborn, self-existent, great, and bountiful. Repeat His name.

The True One was in the beginning; The True One was in the primal age;

The True One is, was, O Nanak; the True One also shall be.

The Guru instructed Lahina to utter the spell with a pure heart. It would fulfil all his desires, bestow happiness in this world and salvation in the next; and by the continual practice of it the light of God should dawn in his heart. Upon this the Jogi said, ' O Nanak, he shall be thy Guru who is produced from thy body â ang." Upon this the Guru embraced Lahina, addressed him as Angad, and promised that he should be his successor. The Jogi and the Guru then went to their respective homes.

The Sikhs who had deserted the Guru, afterwards bitterly regretted their conduct. They who had found the copper money said, that if they had gone further they would have found the silver money; and they who had found the silver money said that if they had gone further, they would have found the gold money. Upon this the Guru composed the following:â

The words man speaketh shall be taken into account; the food he eateth shall be taken into account;

Man's movements shall be taken into account; what he heareth and seeth shall be taken into account;

Every breath he draweth shall be taken into account; why should I go and ask the learned?

O father, attachment to Maya is deceitful.

He who being spiritually blind forgetteth God's name, shall gain neither this world nor the next.

Life and death are for everything that is born; death devoureth everything here.

Where the Judge sitteth and decideth, thither no one shall accompany thee.

All who weep for thee tie up, as it were, a bundle of refuse. 1

Everybody saith that God is great; nobody detracteth from Him;

But no one hath found His price; He becometh not great by what man saith.

O True Lord, Thou art one Lord; how many other worlds in which creatures dwell!

Nanak is with those who are low-born among the lowly;

Nay, who are lowest of the low; how can he rival the great?

Where Thou, O Lord, watchest over the lowly, Thy look of favour shall be their reward. 2

The successor of Pir Baha-ul-Din, the Musalman prelate of Multan, went accompanied by several of his followers to visit Guru Nanak. On meeting him he said, ' I have loaded the load; do something 1 That is, they weep in vain. 2 Sri Rag.

for me' â that is, pray that I may have a successful journey to the next world. The Guru replied:â

He who filleth the sack shall load it on himself; 1 the will of God is over all;

Nanak, they who have acted honestly shall depart with bright faces.

The Guru, seeing the Pir prepared for death, said he would soon follow him himself. The Guru upon this composed the following hymn:â

Wealth, youth, and flowers are guests 2 only for four days; 3
They wither and fade like the leaves of the water lily.
Enjoy God's love, O dear one, in the freshness of youth.
Few are thy days; thou art wearied and the vesture of thy body hath grown old.
My merry friends have gone to sleep in the grave.
I too shall depart in sorrow, and weep with a feeble voice.
O fair one, 4 why not attentively listen to this message?
Thou must go to thy father-in-law's; thou mayest not dwell for ever in thy father's house.
Nanak, know that she who sleepeth 5 in her father's house, is robbed at an untimely season.
She hath lost her bundle of merits and departed with a load of demerits. 6

CHAPTER XVII

The Guru, knowing that his end was approaching, appointed Angad his successor. The Guru's sons had not obeyed him. Their minds were insincere, and they had rebelled and deserted him. Wherefore he subsequently placed the umbrella 1 Man shall take with him the result of his acts.

2 Ndthiare is connected with the Panjabi nathna, to run away.

3 Four days is a common Oriental expression for a short period. The soul is here meant.

Who awakes not in God's service. 6 Sri Rag.

of spiritual sovereignty over Angad's head, and bowed to him in token of his succession to the Guruship. Then it became known to his people that Guru Nanak was about to die. Whole troops of Sikhs, Hindus, and Musalmans went to bid him J farewell. Angad stood up before him in an attitude of supplication. When Guru Nanak had invited him to speak, he said, ' O king, be pleased to attach again to thy skirt those who have seceded from thee." By this Angad meant the Sikhs whose faith had been tried and found wanting. Guru Nanak replied, ' I have forgiven them all for thy sake Upon this Angad fell at his feet.

Guru Nanak went and sat under a withered acacia tree, when lo! it became green, and produced leaves and blossoms. Angad again fell at his feet in adoration. Guru Nanak's family, relations, and disciples began to weep. On that occasion he composed the following:â

Hail to the Creator, the True King, who allotted to the world its various duties!
When the measure 1 is full, the duration of life is at an end; the soul is led away;
When the destined hour arriveth, the soul is led away and all one's relations weep.
The body and soul are separated, O my mother, when one's days are at an end.
Thou hast obtained what was allotted thee, and reaped the fruit of thy former acts.
Hail to the Creator, the True King, who allotted to the world its various duties!
Remember the Lord, O my brethren; all must depart.
The affairs of this world are transitory, only for four days; we must assuredly proceed onwards:
We must assuredly proceed onwards like a guest; why should we be proud?

1 Pai. This is an Indian corn measure.

Repeat the name of Him by whose worship thou shalt obtain happiness in His court.

In the next world thou canst in no wise enforce thine authority; every one shall fare according to his acts.

Remember the Lord, my brethren, every one must depart.

That which pleaseth the Omnipotent shall come to pass; this world is an illusion.

The true Creator pervadeth sea and land, the nether regions, and the firmament.

The true Creator is invisible, unequalled; His limit cannot be found.

Profitable is their advent into this world who have medi tated with their whole hearts upon Him.

The Adorner by His order demolisheth and again con-structeth.

That which pleaseth the Omnipotent shall come to pass; this world is an illusion.

Saith Nanak, O Father, they shall be considered to have wept who weep through love.

If men weep for the sake of worldly things, all their weeping, O Father, shall be in vain:

All their weeping shall be in vain; the world is not mindful of God, and weepeth for mammon.

They know not good from evil, and thus lose their human lives.

All who come into this world must depart; false are you who practise pride.

Saith Nanak. men shall be considered to have wept, O Father, if they weep through love. 1

After this the assembled crowd began to sing songs of mourning, and the Guru fell into a trance. When he awoke therefrom, his sons, on seeing a stranger appointed to succeed their father, inquired what provision had been made for themselves. Guru Nanak replied, ' O my sons, God giveth to His creatures; you shall obtain food and clothing in 1 Wadhans, Alahanian.

abundance, and if you repeat God's name you shall be saved at last."

The Musalmans who had received God's name from the Guru, said they would bury him after his death. His Hindu followers on the contrary said they would cremate him. When the Guru was invited to decide the discussion he said, ' Let the Hindus place flowers on my right, and the Musal mans on my left. They whose flowers are found fresh in the morning, may have the disposal of my body."

Guru Nanak then ordered the crowd to sing the Sohila:â

In the house in which God's praise is sung and He is meditated on,

Sing the Sohila and remember the Creator.

Sing the Sohila of my fearless Lord; I am a sacrifice to that song of joy by which everlasting comfort is obtained.

Ever and ever living things are watched over; the Giver regardeth their wants.

When even Thy gifts cannot be appraised, who can appraise the Giver?

The year and the auspicious time for marriage are re corded; O relations, meet and pour oil on me the bride. 2 0 my friends, pray for me that I may meet my Lord. This message is ever sent to every house; such invita tions are ever issued.

Remember the Caller; Nanak, the day is approaching. 3

The concluding slok of the Japji was then sung. The Guru drew a sheet over him, uttered 1 Wahguru ', made obeisance to God, and blended his light with Guru

Angad's. The Guru remained the same. There was only a change of body pro duced by a supreme miracle.

1 Death is here considered a marriage as among the ancient Greeks.
2 Before marriage the bride's relations anoint her with oil.
3 Rag Gauri Dlpaki. Guru Nanak caused this hymn to be repeated for him in token of rejoicing when he was dying. It is still read as a funeral service.

When the sheet was removed next morning, there was nothing found beneath it. The flowers on both sides were in bloom. The Hindus and the Musal-mans removed their respective flowers. All the Sikhs reverently saluted the spot on which the Guru had lain. He breathed his last on the tenth day of the light half of the month of Assu, Sambat 1595 (A. D. 1538) at Kartarpur in the Panjab.

The Sikhs erected a shrine and the Muhammadans a tomb in his honour on the margin of the Ravi. Both have since been washed away by the river, perhaps providentially, so as to avoid idolatrous worship of the Guru's last resting-place.

Bhai Gur Das, a brief account of whom we have given in the Introduction, draws a gloomy picture of the wickedness of the world at the rise of the Sikh religion:â Men's ideas and aspirations were low. Mammon fascinated the world and led every one astray. Good acts no longer commended themselves to men. They burned with pride, and respected not one another. The high and the low forgot their mutual duties. Monarchs were unjust, and their nobles were butchers who held knives to men's throats.

Everybody thought he possessed knowledge, but none knew in what knowledge or ignorance consisted. Men did what pleased themselves. Alchemy and thaumaturgy were professed, incantations and spells practised, and men indulged in strife, wrath, and mutual jealousies. In the general disorder every one adopted a religion of his own. Out of one God they made many, and carved gods attractive and unat tractive from wood and stone. Some worshipped the sun or moon, others propitiated the earth, sky, wind, water, or fire, and others again the god of death, while the devotion of many was addressed to cemeteries and cremation grounds. Thus did mankind go astray in vain religions and vain worship.

Men despised one another and hence caste received religious sanction. The Brahmans set the Veds, the Purans, and the Shastars at variance. The professors of the six schools of Hindu philosophy quarrelled with one another, and while so employed indulged to their hearts' content in hypocrisy and superstition.

Not only were the Hindus divided into four castes, but the Muhammadans were divided into four sects, 1 and while the Hindus worshipped the Ganges and Banaras, the Muhammadans addressed their devo tions to Makka and the Kaaba. The devil fascinated the members of both religions; they forgot their holy books; they went astray on every road; and truth was the one thing they failed to discover.

There was no guru or religious guide, and without one the people were pushing one another to their destruction. Sin prevailed throughout creation. Pure religion was weeping day and night, and finally began to disappear from men's gaze beneath the earth. She was weighed down by human trans gressions. In lowly attitude she appealed to God for a guide. God observing men's anguish and hearing their piteous cries, conferreot supernatural attributes on Guru Nanak. He bestowed on him the supreme wealth of the Name and humility, and sent Mm into the world to relieve its sufferings. When Guru Nanak contemplated the world, he everywhere saw spiritual darkness, and heard the cry of pain. He endured the greatest privations and travelled to different countries in order to regenerate the human race.

He pointed out to men the straight wayâ that there was but one God, the primal and omnipreaent. He restored the three legs which religion had lost, and reduced to one the four castes of the Hindus. He placed the king and the beggar on a spiritual equality, and taught them to respect each other.

1 Hanifi, Shafai, Maliki, and Hanbali.

He preached to all a religion of the heart as distin guished from a religion of external forms and unavailing ritual.

He found that the acts and austerities practised by professedly religious men of his age and country were without divine love or devotion, and conse quently contained no merit before God. He satisfied himself that Brahma, the reputed author of the Veds, did not include love in them, nor was it men tioned in the Simritis. He declared that God who has no form or outline was not found by wearing religious garbs, but by humility, and that if men rejected caste and worshipped God in spirit they should be accepted in His court.

The Guru examined all religious sects, contem plated the gods, goddesses, and spirits of earth and heaven, and found them all immersed and perishing in spiritual pride. He scrutinized Hindus, Moslems, priests, and prophets, and found not one godly person among them. They were all groping in the blind pit of superstition.

Religious men who ought to be guiding their flocks, had retreated to the solitude of mountains. There was no one left to instruct and save the world. Though hermits rubbed ashes night and day on their bodies, they possessed no knowledge, and the world was rushing to its ruin for want of a divine guide. Rulers were everywhere oppressive. The fence began to eat the field instead of protecting it. Guardians proved faithless to their trusts and con sumed the wealth of their wards. Some disciples played while their spiritual guides danced. Other disciples sat at home while, contrary to all custom, their spiritual guides waited on them. Judges took bribes and perpetrated injustice. Women only paid regard to their husbands for the wealth they pos sessed, and sin was diffused throughout the world.

When Guru Nanak appeared, the fog of spiritual ignorance dispersed, and light shone in the world, as when the sun rises the stars disappear and dark ness fades away, or as when the lion roars in the forest the timid deer incontinently disappear. Wherever the Guru planted his foot, there was established a seat of worship. Every house of his followers became a temple in which the Lord's praises were ever sung and the Lord's name continually repeated. The Guru established a separate religion, and laid out an easy and simple way of obtaining salvation by the repetition of God's name. The Guru extri cated men from the terrible ocean of the world, and included them in the boon of salvation. He cut off the fear of transmigration, and healed the malady of superstition and the pain of separation from God. Until the Guru's advent death's mace ever impended over men's heads, and the apostate and the evil spent their lives in vain. When men grasped the feet of the divine Guru, he gave them the true Word and effected their deliverance. He inculcated love and devotion, the repetition of God's name, and the lesson that as men sow so shall they reap. The four castes of the Hindus he reduced to one. Whether a Sikh had a caste or not, he was distin guished in the society of the holy. The six schools of philosophy are like the six seasons of the year, but the sect of the Guru is the sun which shines over them all. Guru Nanak having abolished all sects shed great splendour on his own. Setting aside the Veds and the books of Islam, he taught his sect to repeat the name of the infinite God who surpasses all conception. By falling at one another's feet and by practising humility are the Guru's Sikhs recognized. They live as hermits among their fami lies, they efface their individuality, they pronounce the ineffable name of God, and they transgress not the will of the Creator by uttering blessings or curses upon their fellow-creatures. Thus were men saved in every direction and Guru Nanak became the true support of the nine regions of the earth.

DIVINE SERVICES BY GURU NANAK AND OTHER GURUS

THE JAPJI 1

THERE is but one God whose name is true, the Creator, 2 devoid of fear and enmity, immortal, unborn, self-existent; 3 by the favour of the Guru. 4

REPEAT His NAME

The True One was in the beginning; the True One was in the primal age.

The True One is 5 now also, O Nanak; the True One also shall be. 6 1 The Japji is considered by the Sikhs a key to their sacred volume and an epitome of its doctrines. It is silently repeated by the Sikhs early in the morning. Every Sikh must have it by heart, otherwise he is not deemed orthodox. It is the duty of all Sikhs, even if they cannot read, to have themselves taught this great morning divine service. The composition appears to have been the work of Guru Nanak in advanced age.

2 Karta pumkh. It is perhaps not necessary to translate the word puriikh. It means male or creative agency. The all-pervading spirit in union with a female element uttered a word from which sprang creation.

8 Saibhan is derived from the Sanskrit swayambhu, which we have found in this passage in a very ancient Sikh MS.

4 Gur Par sad. We have translated these words in deference to the opinions of the majority of the Sikhs; but with several learned gyanis we have no doubt that they were intended as epithets of Godâ the great and bountiful. Guru Nanak had no human guru; as we have already seen, his guru was God. It was during the spiritual supremacy of his successors the favour of the Guru was invoked, and deemed indis pensable for deliverance. Moreover, though gur par sad does sometimes in the Granth Sahib mean the Guru's favour, this appears to be more often expressed by gur parsddi.

6 Bhi. There are two this in this line which some say are idiomatic. We have very little doubt that the first bhi is an obsolete past tense of the defective verb bhu, and that the verse ought to be translatedâ 1 The True One is, was, and also shall be." Compare â ' Guru Nanak, Shahu hai, bhi, hosi."â Suhi Ashtapadi i.

6 Also translatedâ

God was true in the beginning, He was true in the primal age;

He is true now also, Nanak, and He also will be true.

By thinking I cannot obtain a conception of Him, even though I think hundreds of thousands of times.

Even though I be silent and keep my attention firmly fixed on Him, I cannot preserve silence.

The hunger of the hungry for God subsideth not though they obtain the load of the worlds.

If man should have thousands and hundreds of thousands of devices, even one would not assist him in obtaining God.

How shall man become true before God? How shall the veil of falsehood be rent? 1

By walking, O Nanak, according to the will 2 of the Com mander as preordained.

By His order bodies are produced; His order cannot be described.

By His order souls 3 are infused into them; by His order greatness is obtained.

By His order men are high or low; by His order they obtain preordained pain or pleasure.

By His order some obtain their reward; 4 by His order others must ever wander in transmigration.

All are subject to His order; none is exempt from it.

He who understandeth God's order, O Nanak, is never guilty of egoism. 5

Who can sing His power? Who hath power to sing it? 6

Who can sing His gifts or know His signs? 7

This translation appears to be unmeaning, for it is not doubted that God was true in all ages. With the translation in the text compare 'Eyw etxi TTOLV TO yeyovos, KOL ov, KOL e(roxeyoi, I am all that was, and is, and will be."â Inscription on a Greek temple.

1 Also translatedâ How shall the line of falsehood be broken?

2 Rajdi, the Arabic razd, the divine pleasure.

3 In these two lines some suppose akdr to refer to the non-sentient, jiv to the sentient world. 4 That is, to be blended with God.

5 Literallyâ would not be guilty of saying haun main, i. e. I exist by mvself independently of God. This is the sin of spiritual pride.

6 Also translatedâ Whoever has the power.

7 Also translatedâ He who knows his signs.

Who can sing His attributes, His greatness, and His deeds? 1

Who can sing His knowledge whose study is arduous?

Who can sing Him, who fashioneth the body and again destroyeth it?

Who can sing Him, who taketh away life and again restoreth it?

Who can sing Him, who appeareth to be far, but is known to be near.

Who can sing Him, who is -seeing and omnipresent? 2

In describing Him there would never be an end.

Millions of men give millions upon millions of descriptions of Him, but they fail to describe Him.

The Giver giveth; the receiver groweth weary of receiving.

In every age man subsisteth by His bounty.

The Commander by His order hath laid out the way of the world.

Nanak, God the unconcerned is happy.

True is the Lord, true is His name; it is uttered with endless love. 3

People pray and beg, Give us, give us '; the Giver giveth His gifts;
Then what can we offer Him whereby His court may be seen?
What words shall we utter with our lips, on hearing which He may love us?
At the ambrosial hour of morning meditate on the true Name and God's greatness.

1 Char is understood to be a contracted form of achar. Some translate the word ' excellent," and make it an epithet of wadidi.

2 This and the preceding lines of this pauri are also translatedâ
Some sing His power according to their abilities;
Some sing His gifts according to their knowledge of His signs;
Some sing His attributes, His greatness, and His deeds;
Some sing His knowledge whose study is arduous;
Some sing that He fashioneth the body and again destroyeth it;
Some that He taketh away the soul and again restoreth it;
Some that He appeareth far from mortal gaze;
Some that He is all-seeing and omnipresent.

3 Also translatedâ His attributes are described in endless languages.

The Kind One will give us a robe of honour, and by His favour we shall reach the gate of salvation. 1
Nanak, we shall thus know that God is altogether true. 2
He is not established, nor is He created.
The pure one existeth by Himself.
They who worshipped Him have obtained honour.
Nanak, sing His praises who is the Treasury of excellences.
Sing and hear and put His love into your hearts.
Thus shall your sorrows be removed, and you shall be absorbed in Him who is the abode of happiness. 3
Under the Guru's instruction God's word is heard; under the Guru's instruction its knowledge is acquired', under the Guru's instruction man learns that God is everywhere contained. 4
The Guru is Shiv; the Guru is Vishnu and Brahma; the Guru is Parbati, Lakhshmi, 5 and Saraswati. 6

1 This verse is also translatedâ By our former acts we acquire this human vesture, and by God's favour reach the gate of salvation.

The body is first formed, and then the soul from another body enters it. God decides in what body the soul is to have residence until the body perishes. The acts of previous births are adjusted when the soul attains a human body. It is the acts done in a human body which accompany the soul to future states of existence.

2 This verse is commonly translatedâ we shall then know that God is all in all Himself; but this translation does not appear to harmonize with the preceding part of the pauri.

3 Also translatedâ and you shall take happiness to your homes.

4 This very difficult verse is also translatedâ (a) Under the Guru's instruction God's word is heard â under the Guru's instruction the knowledge of it is acquired '; it is contained in the Guru's instruction.

() The voice of God is found as well in other compositions as in the Veds; the voice of God is all-pervading.

(c) The pious know the Guru's instruction, that God is every where contained.

(d) The voice of the Guru is as the Veds for the holy; they are absorbed in it.

5 The Hindu goddess of wealth and riches, consort of Vishnu, and mother of Kam the god of love.

1 The goddess of eloquence and learning and patroness of arts and sciences.

This verse is also translated—

If I knew Him, should I not describe Him? He cannot be described by words.

My Guru hath explained one thing to me—

That there is but one Bestower on all living beings; may I not forget Him!

If I please Him, that is my place of pilgrimage to bathe in; if I please Him not, what ablutions shall I make?

What can all the created beings I behold obtain without previous good acts?

Precious stones, jewels, and gems shall be treasured up in thy heart if thou hearken to even one word of the Guru.

The Guru hath explained one thing to me—

That there is but one Bestower on all living beings; may I not forget Him!

Were man to live through the four ages, yea ten times longer;

Were he to be known on the nine continents, and were everybody to follow in his train; 1

Were he to obtain a great name and praise and renown in the world;

If God's look of favour fell not on him, no one would notice him.

He would be accounted a worm among worms, and even sinners would impute sin to him.

(a) He is greater than Shiv; greater than Vishnu and Brahma; greater than Parbati, Lakhshmi, and Saraswati.

(6) For the holy the Guru is Shiv; the Guru is Vishnu and Brahma; the Guru is Parbati, Lakhshmi, and Saraswati.

The tenth Guru says:—

Khanda prithme saj ke Jin sab sansdr upaiya —

God first created the sword, the emblem of Death, and then the world.

So here Shiv obtains precedence as the agent of destruction. The word uttered by God became the source of knowledge of Him through the Guru in the three forms of Shiv, Vishnu, and Brahma.

1 That is, to show him respect.

Nanak, God may bestow virtue on those who are devoid of it, as well as on those who already possess it;

But no such person is seen as can bestow virtue upon Him.

VIII

By hearing the name of God men become Sidhs, Pirs, Surs, 1 and Naths;

By hearing the Name man understandeth the real nature of the earth, its supporting bull, 2 and Heaven;

By hearing the Name man obtaineth a knowledge of the continents, the worlds, and the nether regions.

By hearing the Name death doth not affect one. 3

Nanak, the saints are ever happy.
By hearing the Name sorrow and sin are no more.
By hearing the Name man becometh as Shiv, Brahma, and Indar.
By hearing the Name even the low become highly lauded. 4
By hearing the Name the way of Jog and the secrets of the body are obtained.
By hearing the Name man understandeth the real nature of the Shastars, the Simritis, and the Veds.
Nanak, the saints are ever happy.
By hearing the Name sorrow and sin are no more.
By hearing the Name truth, contentment, and divine knowledge are obtained.
Hearing the Name is equal to bathing at the sixty-eight places of pilgrimage.
By hearing the Name and reading it man obtaineth honour. 5 1 Surs are spiritual heroes.

2 The bull which the Hindus believe supports the earth. This is not believed in by the Sikhs. See below, pauri xvi.

3 Man shall not die again, but obtain deliverance.

4 Also translatedâ By hearing the Name one is praised by high and low.

5 Also translatedâ On hearing the Name man obtaineth honour by the knowledge acquired.

By hearing the Name the mind is composed and fixed on God. 1
Nanak, the saints are ever happy.
By hearing the Name sorrow and sin are no more.
By hearing the Name, the depth of the sea of virtue is sounded. 2
By hearing the Name men become Shaikhs, Pirs, and Emperors.
By hearing the Name a blind man findeth his way
By hearing the Name the unfathomable becometh fathom able.
Nanak, the saints are ever happy.
By hearing the Name sorrow and sin are no more.
The condition of him who obeyeth God cannot be described. Whoever trieth to describe it, shall afterward repent. There is no paper, or pen, or writer To describe the condition of him who obeyeth God. So pure is His nameâ
Whoever obeyeth God knoweth the pleasure of it in his own heart. 3

XIII

By obeying Him wisdom and understanding enter the mind;
By obeying Him man knoweth all worlds;
By obeying Him man suffereth not punishment;
By obeying Him man shall not depart with Jam 4 â
So pure is God's nameâ
Whoever obeyeth God knoweth the pleasure of it in his own heart.

1 Orâ by hearing the Name man easily meditateth upon God.

2 Also translatedâ man acquireth the best virtues.

3 Literallyâ he knows it in his own mind, that is, he obtains a pleasure which is incommunicable.

4 The god of death, previously called Dharmraj. This verse means that man shall not die again, but be absorbed in God.

By obeying Him man's path is not obstructed;
By obeying Him man departeth with honour and distinc tion;
By obeying Him man proceedeth in ecstasy 1 on his way;
By obeying Him man formeth an alliance with virtueâ
So pure is God's nameâ
Whoever obeyeth God knoweth the pleasure of it in his own heart.
By obeying Him man attaineth the gate of salvation;
By obeying Him man is saved with his family;
By obeying Him the Guru is saved, and saveth his disciples;
By obeying Him, O Nanak, man wandereth not in quest of alms 2 â
So pure is God's nameâ
Whoever obeyeth God knoweth the pleasure of it in his own heart.
The elect 3 are acceptable, the elect are distinguished;
The elect obtain honour in God's court;
The elect shed lustre 4 on the courts of kings.
The attention of the elect is bestowed on the one Guru. 5

If any one say he can form an idea of God, he may say so, 1 Magun. This word is understood to be for magan. Those who read magu na translateâ (a) By obeying Him man proceedeth not by the path of destruction. (l) Man proceedeth by the broad, not the narrow way.

2 This is explained to meanâ does not wander in transmigration.

3 Panch, literally five. The number conveys the idea of selection. There is a Hindustani proverb, Panchon men Parameshwar hat, Where five are assembled, God is in the midst of them. Others say that panch refers to the five classes of persons previously mentionedâ those who walk according to God's will, who know Him to be true, who praise Him, who hear His name, and who obey Him.

1 This is the interpretation of sohahi given by Bhai Chanda Singh in his commentary on the Granth Sahib.

5 The elect have one God as their Guru or spiritual guide, and meditate on Him.

But the Creator's works cannot be numbered.
The bull that is spoken of is righteousness, the offspring of mercy,
Which supported by patience maintaineth the order of nature. 1
Whoever understandeth this is a true man.
What a load there is upon the bull! 2
Beyond this earth there are more worlds, more and more.
What power can support their weight?
The names of living things, their species, and colours
Have all been written with a flowing pen.
Doth any one know how to write an account of them?
If the account were written, how great it would be!
What power and beautiful form are Thine, O God!
Who hath power 3 to know how great Thy gifts are?
By one word 4 Thou didst effect the expansion of the world,
Whereby hundreds of thousands of rivers were produced.
What power have I to describe Thee?

So powerless am 7, that I cannot even once be a sacrifice unto Thee.
Whatever pleaseth Thee is good.
Thou, 0 Formless One, art ever secure.

XVII

Numberless thy worshippers, 5 and numberless Thy lovers; Numberless Thine adorers, and numberless they who perform austerities for Thee; Numberless the reciters of sacred books and Veds; 1 Sim, the thread on which the world is strung. The Guru means by patience the adjusted balance of the world, everything being in equipoise.

2 Here Guru Nanak obviously rejects the Hindu story that the earth is supported by a bull.

3 We understand kut as the Arabic kmvwat. (kut be held to mean food, a meaning which the word so pronounced also bears in Arabic, the verse will be translated â Who knoweth the extent of Thy gifts of sustenance?

4 The Hindus believe this is Eko aharn, bahu sj-iim, I am one, let Me become many.

5 Literallyâ repetitions of God's name. Here the word is used by metonymy for those who repeat God's name.

Numberless Thy Jogis whose hearts are indifferent to the world;
Numberless the saints who ponder on Thine attributes and divine knowledge;
Numberless Thy true men; numberless Thine almsgivers;
Numberless Thy heroes who face the steel of their enemies;
Numberless Thy silent worshippers who lovingly fix their thoughts upon Thee.
What power have I to describe Thee?
So lowly am I, that I cannot even once be a sacrifice unto Thee.
Whatever pleaseth Thee is good.
O Formless One, Thou art ever secure.

XVIII

Numberless are the fools appallingly blind;
Numberless are the thieves and devourers of others' property;
Numberless those who establish their sovereignty by force; l
Numberless the cut-throats and murderers;
Numberless the sinners who pride themselves on committing sin;
Numberless the liars who roam about lying;
Numberless the filthy 2 who enj oy filthy gain;
Numberless the slanderers who carry loads of calumny on their heads;
Nanak thus describeth the degraded.
59 lowly am I, I cannot even once be a sacrifice unto Thee.
Whatever pleaseth Thee is good.
0 Formless One, Thou art ever secure.

1 Also translatedâ Numberless are those who issue oppressive orders.

2 Malechh. Whose desires are filthy, and who are deemed the lowest of the low, complete outcasts. In the Guru's time the word malechh was applied by Hindus as a term of opprobrium to Muham-madans. The Hindus still apply it to all who are not of their own persuasion.

Numberless Thy names, and numberless Thy places.

Completely beyond reach are Thy numberless worlds.
Numberless they who repeat Thy name with all the strength of their intellects. 1
By letters 2 we repeat Thy name, by letters we praise Thee;
By letters we acquire divine knowledge, and sing Thy praises and Thine attributes;
By letters we write and utter the word 3 of God;
By the letters recorded on man's head his destiny is declared.
He who inscribeth them on others, beareth them not on His own head.
As He ordaineth, so shall man obtain.
As great Thy creation, O God, so great is Thy fame
There is no place without Thy name.
What power have I to describe Thee?
So lowly am , that I cannot even once be a sacrifice unto Thee
Whatever pleaseth Thee is good.
0 Formless One, Thou art ever secure.
When the hands, feet, and other members of the body are covered with filth,
It is removed by washing with water.
When thy clothes are polluted,
Apply soap, and the impurity shall be washed away.
So when the mind is defiled by sin,
It is cleansed by the love 4 of the Name.
Men do not become saints or sinners by merely calling themselves so.

1 Also translatedâ (a) With their bodies reversed, that is, standing on their heads, a form of religious austerity practised in India.

(If) They who try to describe Thee shall have to carry loads of sin on their heads.

2 Letters here appear to mean sacred literature.

3 Ban generally means custom. Here it is understood to be used for bani, a word.

4 Water in which the dye of the Name has been dissolved.

The recording angels take with them a record of man's acts.
It is he himself soweth, and he himself eateth. Nanak, man suffereth transmigration by God's order.

Pilgrimage, austerities, mercy, and almsgiving on general and special occasions
Whosoever performeth, may obtain some little honour;
But he who heareth and obeyeth and loveth God in his heart,
Shall wash off his impurity in the place of pilgrimage within him.
All virtues are Thine, O Lord; none are mine.
There is no devotion without virtue.
From the Self-existent proceeded Maya (athi), whence issued a word which produced Brahma and the rest 1 â ' Thou art true, Thou art beautiful, there is ever pleasure in Thy heart! '
What the time, what the epoch, what the lunar day, and what the week-day,
What the season, and what the month when the world was created,
The Pandits did not discover; had they done so, they would have recorded it in the Purans.
Nor did the Qazis 2 discover it; had they done so, they would have recorded it in the Quran:

Neither the Jogi nor any other mortal knows the lunar day, or the week-day, or the season, or the month.

Only the Creator who fashioned the world knoweth when He did so.

How shall I address Thee, O God? how shall I praise Thee? how shall I describe Thee? and how shall I know Thee?

1 The verse is also translatedâ ' Blessing on Thee!" is said to have been the first salutation that Brahma addressed Thee.

2 Guru Nanak means the scribes who reduced the Quran to writing.

Saith Nanak, everybody speaketh of Thee, one wiser than another.

Great is the Lord, great is His name; what He doeth cometh to pass.

Nanak, he who is proud shall not be honoured on his arrival in the next world.

XXII

There are hundreds of thousands of nether and upper regions.

Men have grown weary at last of searching for God's limits; the Veds say one thing, thai God has no limit. 1

The thousands of Purans 2 and Muhammadan books tell that in reality there is but one principle. 3

If God can be described by writing, then describe Him; but such description is impossible.

0 Nanak, call Him great; only He Himself knoweth how great He is.

XXIII

Praisers praise God, but have not acquired a knowledge of Him,

As rivers and streams fall into the sea, but know not its extent.

Kings and emperors who possess oceans and mountains of property and wealth, 4

Are not equal to the worm which forgetteth not God in its heart.

1 The verse is also translatedâ The Veds have at last grown weary of searching for God's limits, but they cannot give the slightest description of Him.

2 There being only eighteen Purans, the expression in the text means a thousand times eighteen or an indefinite number. The word sahans is also understood by the gyanis to refer to rikhis and learned men in indefinite numbers.

3 That is, that God is the root or principle of all things.

4 Also translatedâ As the sea is the king of streams, so is God the monarch of all. They who possess mountainous wealth, c.

XXIV

There is no limit to God's praises; l to those who repeat them there is no limit.

There is no limit to His mercy, and to His gifts there is no limit.

There is no limit to what God seeth, no limit to what He heareth.

The limit of the secret of His heart cannot be known.

The limit of His creation cannot be known; neither His near nor His far. side can be discovered. 2

To know His limits how many vex their hearts. 3

His limits cannot be ascertained;

Nobody knoweth His limits.

The more we say, the more there remains to be said.

Great is the Lord, and exalted is His seat.

His exalted name is higher than the most exalted.
Were any one else ever so exalted,
Then he would know that exalted Being:
How great He is He knoweth Himself.
Nanak, God bestoweth gifts on whom He looketh with favour and mercy.
His many bounties 4 cannot be recorded,
He is a great giver and hath not a particle of covetousness.
How many, yea countless heroes beg of Him!
How many others whose number cannot be conceived!
How many pine away in sin! 5
How many persons receive yet deny God's gifts!
How many fools there are who merely eat!
How many are ever dying in distress and hunger!
0 Giver, these are also Thy gifts.

1 Also translated â There is no limit to the Praised One.
2 A metaphor taken from the banks of a river.
3 Billah, literally, cry in pain.
4 Kami, in Sanskrit, is work; in Persian, kindness, favour, or bounty. The context seems to show that the latter is intended.
5 Compare Man vekdn'n vena, the mind is encompassed with sin. Guru Amar Das.

Rebirth 1 and deliverance depend on Thy will:
Nobody can interfere with it.
If any fool 2 try to interfere with it
He shall himself know the punishment he shall suffer,
God himself knoweth to whom He may give, and He Him self giveth:
Very few acknowledge this.
He to whom God hath given the boon of praising and lauding Him, 0 Nanak, is the King of kings. 3

XXVI

Priceless are Thine attributes, O God, and priceless Thy dealings; 4
Priceless Thy dealers, priceless Thy storehouses;
Priceless what cometh from Thee, and priceless what is taken away;
Priceless Thy rate and priceless the time for dealing; 5
Priceless Thy justice and priceless Thy court;
Priceless Thy weights and priceless Thy measures; 6
Priceless Thy gifts and priceless Thy marks;
Priceless Thy mercy and priceless Thine ordinances.
How beyond all price Thou art cannot be stated.
Ever speaking of Thee men continue to fix their thoughts on Thee. 7

1 Band, to be enclosed in a womb.
2 Khdik. This word is also found in the Sri Rag ki War, Slok 2-thdo ndh'in khdika, there is no place for the fool.
3 Also translated â
To those few, O Nanak, the King of kings Giveth the boon of praising and lauding Him.

4 In the true Name.

5 Also translated â Priceless is Thy love, and priceless they who are absorbed in it.

8 We ivz. pramdn for parwdn. If the latter be read, the translation will be â Priceless Thy weights and priceless Thine acceptance of mortals. A third translation is â Priceless Thy scale and priceless Thy weights.

7 Also translated â Repeating that Thou art priceless, men continue to fix their attention on Thee.

They who read the Veds and Purans speak of Thee;
Learned men speak of Thee and deliver discourses on Thee;
Brahmas speak of Thee, and Indars speak of Thee;
The milkmaids and Krishan speak of Thee
Shivs speak of Thee, the Sidhs speak of Thee;
All the Budhas Thou hast created speak of Thee;
The demons speak of Thee, the gods speak of Thee;
Thy demigods, men, munis, 1 and servants speak of Thee;
How many speak of Thee or attempt to speak of Thee!
How many depart while speaking of Thee!
If Thou wert to create as many more as Thou hast created,
Even then few of them would be able to speak adequately of Thee.
Thou mayest be as great as Thou pleasest.
Nanak, only the True One Himself knoweth how great He is.
If any one were to speak improperly of God,
Write him down as the most ignorant of men.

XXVII

What is that gate, what is that mansion where Thou, 0 God, sittest and watchest over all things?
How many various and countless instruments are played! How many musicians,
How many musical measures with their consorts, and how many singers sing Thee!
Wind, water, and fire sing Thee; Dharmraj sings at Thy gate.
The recording angels, 2 who know how to write, and on whose record Dharmraj judgeth sing Thee.
Ishar, 3 Brahma, and Devi, ever beautiful as adorned by Thee, sing Thee.

1 Inspired saints who are popularly supposed to have attained divine nature.

2 Chitr and Gupt. Chitr means visible, Gupt invisible. According to the Sikhs, Chitr records man's overt acts, Gupt the designs of his heart. Both then report to Dharmraj. In Sanskrit literature Chitrgupt is one person, the recorder of Yama.

3 A title of Shiv.

Indar seated on his throne with the gods at Thy gate sing Thee.
Sidhs in meditation sing Thee; holy men in contempla tion sing Thee.
The continent, the true, and the patient sing Thee; un yielding heroes sing Thee.
The pandits and the supreme Rikhis, 1 reading their Veds, sing Thee in every age.
The lovely celestial maids who beguile the heart in the upper, middle, and nether regions sing Thee. 2
The jewels created by Thee with the sixty-eight places of Hindu pilgrimage sing Thee.

Mighty warriors and divine heroes sing Thee; the four sources of life sing Thee.

The continents, the worlds, and the universe made and supported by Thy hands sing Thee.

The saints who please Thee, and who are imbued with Thy love 3 sing Thee.

The many others who sing Thee I cannot remember; how could Nanak recount them? 4 1 There are said to be seven supreme Rikhis. The Veds were written by Rikhis.

2 Also translatedâ The lovely celestial maids who beguile the heart sing Thee in the upper, and the fish in the lower regions.

3 Rasdle is, literally, an abode of pleasure.

4 The following is offered as a free blank verse paraphrase of this pauri:â

What is that gate, that mansion what, where Thou Dost sit and watch o'er all Thy wondrous works? Many the harps and songs which tune Thy praise, Yea countless; Thy musicians who can tell? How many measures sung wilh high delight, And voices which exalt Thy peerless name! To Thee sing water, wind, and breathing fire; To Thee sings Dharamraj in regions drear; To Thee sing th' angels who men's deeds record For judgement final by that king of death. To Thee sing Shiva, Brahma, and the Queen Of Heav'n with radiant beauty ever crown'd. To Thee sing Indar and th' attendant gods Around Thy throne and seraphs at Thy gate. To Thee sing Sidhs in meditation deep, And holy men who ponder but on Thee. P 2

THE SIKH RELIGION tat God is ever true, He is the true Lord, and the true iame.

He who made this world is and shall be; He shall neither depart, nor be made to depart. 1

He who created things of different colours, descriptions, and species,

Beholdeth His handiwork which attesteth His greatness.

He will do what pleaseth Himself; no order may be issued to Him.

He is King, the King of kings, O Nanak; all remain subject to His will.

XXVIII 2

Make contentment and modesty thine earrings, self-respect thy wallet, meditation the ashes to smear on thy body;

Make thy body, which is only a morsel for death, thy beggar's coat, and faith thy rule of life and thy staff. 3

Make association with men thine Ai Panth, 4 and the conquest of thy heart the conquest of the world.

To Thee sing chaste and patient of mankind, Unyielding heroes of true faith approved. To Thee sing pandits and the chiefs of saints; The ages four and Veds to them assigned. To Thee sing maidens who delight the sense, This world of ours, high heaven, and hell below. To Thee sing gems from Vishnu's sea that rose, And eight and sixty spots of pilgrims' haunt. To Thee sing heroes and the men of might; The sources four from which all life doth spring. To Thee sing regions, orbs, and universe, Created, cherish'd, and upheld by Thee! To Thee sing those whose deeds delight Thine eye, The hosts who wear the colours of Thy faith. All things beside which sing Thy glorious name, Could ne'er be told by Nanak's lowly song.

1 Also translatedâ Creation shall depart, but not He who made it.

2 This and the following three pauris were composed by Guru Nanak after the Jogis had pressed him to adopt their dress and their religion.

3 This verse is also translatedâ Make the chastening of thy body not yet wedded to death thy patched coat, and faith thy beggar's staff.

HAIL! 1 HAIL TO HIM,
The primal, the pure, 2 without beginning, the indestruc tible, the same in every age!

XXIX

Make divine knowledge thy food, compassion thy store keeper, and the voice which is in every heart the pipe to call to repast.

Make Him who hath strung the whole world on His string thy spiritual Lord; let wealth and supernatural power be relishes for others.

Union and separation is the law which regulateth the world. 3 By destiny we receive our portion.

HAIL! HAIL TO HIM,
The primal, the pure, without beginning, the indestruc tible, the same in every age!
One Maya in union with God gave birth to three acceptable children. 4

One of them is the creator, the second the provider, the third performeth the function of destroyer. 5

As it pleaseth God, He directeth them by His orders.

He beholdeth them, but is not seen by them. This is very marvellous.

HAIL! HAIL TO HIM,
The primal, the pure, without beginning, the inde structible, the same in every age!

1 Adesh, the ordinary salutation of Jogis. This word is derived from ddi primal and Ish or Ishwar, God. Guru Nanak means that this salutation should only be offered to God.

2 Anil â literally, not of a blue colour, as Krishan is represented.

3 Also translatedâ favourable and unfavourable destinies shape men's actions. 4 Chele, literally, disciples.

5 Lai may either mean absorption or reaper (lave). Both meanings convey the idea of destruction.

XXXI

His seat and His storehouses 1 are in every world. What was to be put into them was put in at one time. 2 The Creator beholdeth His creation. Nanak, true is the work of the True One.

HAIL! HAIL TO HIM,
The primal, the pure, without beginning, the indestructible, the same in every age!

XXXII

Were one tongue to become a hundred thousand, and a hundred thousand to become twentyfold more,

I would utter the name of the one Lord of the world hundreds of thousands of times with all my tongues.

In this way I should ascend the stairs of the Lord, and become one with Him.

On hearing of the exaltation of the religious the vile become jealous. 3

Nanak, the former have found the Kind One, while false is the boasting of the false.

XXXIII

I have no strength to speak and no strength to be silent. 4
I have no strength to ask and no strength to give;
I have no strength to live, and no strength to die;
I have no strength to acquire empire or wealth which produce a commotion in the heart.
I have no strength to meditate on Thee or ponder on divine knowledge;
I have no strength to find the way to escape from the world.
He in whose arm there is strength, may see what he can do.
Nanak, no one is of superior or inferior strength before God.

1 To supply human necessities.
2 That is, before man is born, his portion is fully allotted him.
3 Literallyâ on hearing matters connected with heaven worms grow jealous.
4 This hyperbole means that man has no strength to do anything without God's assistance.

XXXIV

God created nights, seasons, lunar days, and week days,
Wind, water, fire, and the nether regions.
In the midst of these He established the earth as a temple.
In it He placed living beings of different habits and kinds.
Their names are various and endless,
And they are judged according to their acts.
True is God, and true is His court.
There the elect are accepted and honoured.
The Merciful One marketh them according to their acts.
The bad and the good shall there be distinguished.
Nanak, on arrival there, this shall be seen.

XXXV

Such is the practice in the realm of righteousness.
I now describe the condition of the realm of knowledge.
How many winds, waters, and fires! how many Krishans and Shivs!
How many Brahmas 1 who fashioned worlds! how many forms, colours, and garbs!
How many lands of grace like this 2 how many mountains! how many Dhrus and instructors 3 such as his.
How many Indars, how many moons and suns, how many regions and countries!
How many Sidhs, Budhs, how many Naths! how many goddesses and representations of them
How many demigods and demons! how many saints, how many jewels and seas!
How many sources of life! how many languages! and how many lines of kings!
How many possessors of divine knowledge! how many worshippers! Nanak, there is no end of them.

1 The Hindus believe it was through the agency of Brahma God created the world.
2 Where men reap the results of their acts.
3 Narad, who instructed Dhru to obtain his exalted dignity. Narad is said to have been a son of Brahma. His father advised him to marry, but he rejected his advice

saying it was only proper to love Krishan. Father and son then began to curse each other with immoral and disastrous results for both. One of Narad's epithets is Strife-maker.

XXXVI

In the realm of knowledge the light of divine knowledge is resplendent.
There are heard songs from which millions of joys and pleasures proceed.
Beauty is the attribute of the realm of happiness. 1
There things are fashioned in an incomparable manner.
What is done there cannot be described.
Whoever endeavoureth to describe it shall afterwards repent.
There are fashioned knowledge, wisdom, intellect, and understanding;
And there too is fashioned the skill of demigods and men of supernatural power.

XXXVII

Force is the attribute of the realm of action. 2 Incomparable are they who dwell therein. There are very powerful warriors and heroes They are filled with the might of Ram.â There are many Sitas 3 in the midst of greatness, Their beauty cannot be describedâ They die not, neither are they led astray 4 In whose hearts God dwelleth. There dwell congregations of saints; They rejoice; the True One is in their hearts. God dwelleth in the true realm. 5

He looketh on its denizens with an eye of favour, and rendereth them happy.
There are continents, worlds, and universes.
Whoever trieth to describe them shall never arrive at an end.

1 Sharm khand. Sharm is here not the Persian sharm y shame, nor the Sanskrit shram, toil. It is the Sanskrit sharman, happiness. The verse is also translatedâ Beautiful are the words of those who have attained the realm of the happy.

2 That is, the world.

3 SIta's name is apparently introduced here as she was the wife of Ram mentioned in the preceding line.

4 Na thage jah, literallyâ are not deceived.

5 Sach Khand.

There are worlds upon worlds and forms upon forms. They fulfil their functions according to God's orders: God beholding and contemplating them is pleased. Nanak, to describe them would be impossible. 1

XXXVIII

Make continence thy furnace, resignation thy goldsmith, Understanding thine anvil, divine knowledge thy tools, The fear of God thy bellows, austerities thy fire, Divine love thy crucible, and melt God's name therein. In such a true mint the Word shall be coined. This is the practice of those on whom God looketh with an eye of favour.

Nanak, the Kind One by a glance maketh them happy.

SLOK

The air is the guru, water our father, and the great earth our mother;
Day and night are our two nurses, male and female, who set the whole world a-playing. 2
Merits and demerits shall be read out in the presence of the Judge.
According to men's acts, some shall be near, and others distant from God.

They who have pondered on the Name and departed after the completion of their toil, 3

Shall have their countenances made bright, O Nanak; how many shall be emancipated in company with them! 4 1 Literallyâ would be as hard as iron.

2 Here the denizens of the world are likened to children. Their father is said to be water, the human sperm; the earth like a mother affords them nutriment; day supplies them with occupation; the night lulls them to rest; and the breath of the Guru imparts divine instruction.

In the East it is usual for the rich to have two nurses for a childâ a female nurse by night, and a male nurse to accompany and play with it by day.

3 The worship of God and the necessity of labour for one's liveli hood are eminently Sikh principles.

4 This slok is generally believed to be the composition of Guru Angad.

THERE is but one God whose name is true, the Creator, devoid of fear and enmity, immortal, unborn, self-existent, great and beneficent.

GURU HAR GOBIND

This War includes sloks. The sloks also were written by the first Guru, and should be sung to the air of ' Tunda As Raja '. 2

SLOK I Guru Nanak

I am a sacrifice to my Guru a hundred times a day, Who without any delay made demigods out of men.

Guru Angad

Were a hundred moons to rise, and a thousand suns to mount the sky;

Even with such light there would be appalling darkness without the Guru.

Guru Nanak

Nanak, they who very clever in their own estimation think not of the Guru,

Shall be left like spurious sesames in a reaped field.

1 The word War originally meant a dirge for the brave slain in battle, then it meant any song of praise, and in this collection it means God's praises generally. Wars were composed in stanzas called paun's, literally ladders, which were sung or chanted by professional minstrels.

The Asa ki War is repeated by religious Sikhs after the Japji as a morning divine service.

2 As, son of Chitrbir, was a holy prince against whom a false charge had been preferred by his lascivious stepmother, which led to his hands and feet being cut off as punishment. One of the many Oriental versions of the story of Potiphar's wife.

They shall be left in the field, saith Nanak, without an owner:

The wretches may even bear fruit and flower, but they shall be as ashes within their bodies.

PAURI I 1

God Himself created the world and Himself gave names to things.

He made Maya 2 by His power; seated He beheld His work with delight.

O Creator, Thou art the Giver; being pleased Thou bestowest and practisest kindness.

Thou knowest all things; Thou givest and takest life with a word. 3

Seated Thou didst behold Thy work with delight.

SLOK II Guru Nanak
True are Thy regions and true Thy universes;
True Thy worlds and true Thy creation;
True Thine acts and all Thy thoughts;
True Thine order and true Thy court;
True Thy command and true Thy behest;
True Thy favour and true Thy signs.
Hundreds of thousands and millions declare Thee true;
True is all Thy power, true all Thy strength;
True Thy praises, true Thy eulogies;
True Thy might, O true King.
Nanak, true are they who meditate on the True One.
They who are born and die are the falsest of the false. 4 1 The pauris in this collection are all by Guru Nanak, so in the original his name is omitted at their head.

2 In Sanskrit literature, Maya is styled anadi, without a beginning, hence uncreated, but this is not the doctrine of the Gurus. To believe that God did not create Maya would be to believe in a limitation of His power.

3 Also translated â Thou givest and takest life from the body.

4 Kach is here used as the correlative of sack, true.

Guru Nanak l
Great is His glory whose name is great; Great is His glory whose justice is true; Great is His glory whose seat is immovable; Great is His glory who understandeth our utterances; Great is His greatness who knoweth all our feelings; Great is His glory who giveth without consulting others; Great is His glory who is all in all Himself. Nanak, His acts cannot be described. All that He did and hath to do dependeth on His own will.

Guru Angad
This world is the True One's chamber; the True One's dwelling is therein.
Some by His order He absorbeth in Himself; others by His order He destroyeth. 2
Some at His pleasure He withdraweth from mammon; others He causeth to abide therein.
It cannot be even told whom He will regenerate.
Nanak, he to whom God revealeth Himself, is known as holy.

PAURI II
Nanak, God having created animals recorded their names, and appointed Dharmraj to judge their acts.
At His own court the real truth is adjudged; He separateth and removeth those who are attached to mammon.
There the false find no place: they go to hell with blackened faces.
They who are imbued with Thy name win; the de ceivers lose.
God recorded names and appointed Dharmraj to record acts.

1 In the original, Mahala I. It is so written to mark the distinction between the preceding verses, which are sloks, and the following verses, which are in a different measure.

2 By separating from Himself.

SLOK III Guru Nanak

Wonderful Thy word, wonderful Thy knowledge; Wonderful Thy creatures, wonderful their species; Wonderful their forms, wonderful their colours; Wonderful the animals which wander naked; Wonderful Thy wind; wonderful Thy water; Wonderful Thy fire which sporteth wondrously; Wonderful the earth, wonderful the sources of production; Wonderful the pleasures to which mortals are attached; Wonderful is meeting, wonderful parting from Thee; Wonderful is hunger, wonderful repletion; Wonderful Thy praises, wonderful Thy eulogies; Wonderful the desert, wonderful the road; Wonderful Thy nearness, wonderful Thy remoteness; Wonderful to behold Thee present. Beholding these wonderful things I remain wondering. Nanak, they who understand them are supremely fortunate.

Guru Nanak

By Thy power we see, by Thy power we hear, by Thy power we fear, or enjoy the highest happiness;

By Thy power were made the nether regions and the heavens; by Thy power all creation;

By Thy power were produced the Veds, the Purans, the Muhammadan books, and by Thy power all compositions;

By Thy power we eat, drink, and clothe ourselves; by Thy power springeth all affection;

By Thy power are the species, genera, and colours of creatures; by Thy power are the animals of the world. 1

By Thy power are virtues; by Thy power are vices: by Thy power, honour and dishonour; 2 1 Also translated â By Thy power vas created animate and inani mate nature.

2 Man abhman. The latter word is for apman, as so often in the Granth Sahib. Compare man abhiman madhe so sewak tijitn, He who hath regard for honour or dishonour is not a holy man.

By Thy power are wind, water, and fire; by Thy power is the earth.

Everything existeth by Thy power; Thou art the omni potent Creator; Thy name is the holiest of the holy.

Saith Nanak, Thou beholdest and pervadest all things subject to Thy command: Thou art altogether unrivalled.

PAURI III

Man having enjoyed himself becometh ashes, and the soul passeth away.

However great and wealthy a man may be, the ministers of Death throw a chain on his neck and take him away.

There an account of his acts is read; the Judge on his seat taketh the account and passeth sentence.

Such a man shall find no place of shelter; when he is beaten, who will hear his cries?

Man, blind that thou art, thou hast wasted thy life.

SLOK IV Guru Nanak

In fear 1 the winds and breezes ever blow;

In fear flow hundreds of thousands of rivers;

In fear fire performeth its forced labour;
In fear the earth is pressed by its burden;
In fear Indar moveth headlong: in fear sitteth Dharmraj at God's gate;
In fear is the sun, in fear the moon; they travel millions of miles without end;
In fear are the Sidhs, the Budhas, the demigods, and the Naths; in fear are the stars 2 and the firmament;
In fear are wrestlers, very mighty men and divine heroes;
In fear cargoes of men come and go.
God hath destined fear for every one; 3 Nanak, the Form less One, the True, is alone without fear.

1 The fear of God is, of course, meant.
2 Addne, from the Sanskrit udugan. The phrase is also translatedâ In fear is the firmament extended.
3 Literallyâ God hath written the destiny of fear on the heads of all.

Guru Nanak

Nanak, the Formless One is without fear; all the Rams were dust.
How many stories there are of Krishan! how many Veds and religious compositions! 1
How many beggars dance, and fall, and again beat time!
Actors enter the market-place and draw forth their appliances; 2
Kings and queens sing and utter nonsense; 3
They wear earrings worth hundreds of thousands, and necklaces worth hundreds of thousands. 4
The body on which they are worn, O Nanak, shall become ashes.
Divine knowledge is not sought in mere words; to speak concerning it were as hard as iron;
By God's grace man obtaineth it; skill and orders are useless therefor.

PAURI IV

If the Kind One look with kindness, then is the true Guru obtained.
The soul hath wandered through many births, and now the true Guru hath communicated the Word.
There is no benefactor so great as the true Guru; hear this, all ye people.
By meeting the true Guru who hath removed pride from his heart, and who preacheth the Truest of the true,
The True One is obtained.

SLOK V

Let all the gharis be your milkmaids, and the pahars your Krishans and Gopals 5:
Let wind, water, and fire be your jewels; and the moon and sun your avatars; 1 Also translated â How many expound the Veds!
2 Also translated â draw a crowd around them. This hymn pur ports to give a brief description of the miracle-plays of Ram and Krishan. 3 Literally â speak of the upper and lower regions.
4 Lakh takian. Takd is really a double pice, or about a halfpenny of English money, but in the plural it means money in general.
5 Gopals are herdsmen among whom Krishan used to sport.

The whole earth your stage properties and vessels, which are all entanglements.
Nanak, they who are devoid of divine knowledge are robbed; the minister of death hath devoured them.

Guru Nanak
The disciples play, the gurus dance,
Shake their feet, and roll their heads.
Dust flieth and falleth on their hair; 1
The audience beholding laugh and go home.
For the sake of food the performers beat time,
And dash themselves on the ground.
The milkmaids sing, Krishans sing,
Sitas and royal Rams sing.
Fearless is the Formless One, whose name is true,
And whose creation is the whole world.
The worshippers on whom God bestoweth kindness worship Him;
Pleasant 2 is the night for those who long for Him in their hearts.
By the Guru's instruction to his disciples this knowledge is obtained,
That the Kind One saveth those on whom He looketh with favour.
Oil-presses, spinning-wheels, hand-mills, potters' wheels,
Plates, whirlwinds, many and endless,
Tops, churning-staves, threshing-frames turn round;
Birds tumble and take no breath.
Men put animals on stakes and whirl them.
0 Nanak, the tumblers are innumerable and endless.
In the same way those bound in entanglements are swung round;
Every one danceth according to his own actsâ

They who dance and laugh shall weep on their departure; 1 Jhaia is a woman's head of hair. The actors, who in India are generally all men, wear female wigs.

2 Bhini. Literallyâ dewy; when the atmosphere is calm and the heat not excessive.

They cannot fly or obtain supernatural power. Leaping and dancing are human recreations; Nanak, they who have the fear of God in their hearts have also love.

PAURI V
Thy name is the Formless: by repeating it man goeth not to hell.
The soul and body are all Thine: what Thou givest man eateth: to say aught else were waste of words.

O man, if thou desire thine advantage, do good acts and be lowly.
Even though thou stave off old age, it shall come to thee in the disguise of death.
None may remain when his measure is full.

SLOK VI
The Musalmans praise the Shariat, read it, and reflect on it;
But God's servants are they who employ themselves in His service in order to behold Him.

The Hindus praise the Praised One whose appearance and form are incomparable;
They bathe in holy streams, perform idol-worship and adoration, use x copious incense of sandal.

The Jogis meditate on God the Creator, whom they call the Unseen,
Whose form is minute, whose name is the Bright One, and who is the image of their bodies. 2

In the minds of the generous contentment is produced in their desire to give.
Others give, but ask a thousandfold more, and still want the world to honour them.
Why mention thieves, adulterers, perjurers, evil and sinful men?

1 Some suppose kdr to be a noun meaning the lines Hindus draw on the ground to enclose cooking-places, within which others are not admitted.

! The Jogis, when in intensely deep meditation, close their eyes. On opening them and looking upward they suppose that they behold God in their own image in the firmament.

SIKH. I Q

Many depart from here after eating what they had amassed in previous births; 1 shall they have any business whatever in the next world? 2

The animals which live in the water, dry land, the four teen worlds, and all creationâ
What they say Thou alone knowest; for them too Thou carest.

Saith Nanak, the saints hunger to praise Thee; the true Name is their support.

In everlasting joy they abide day and night: may I obtain the dust of the feet of such virtuous men!

Guru Nanak and Shaikh Brahm discussed the question of the disposal of the dead. The Shaik maintained that a man who was burned would either go to hell or not rise at the day of judgement.

Guru Nanak

The ashes of the Musalman fall into the potter's clod;
Vessels and bricks are fashioned from them; they cry out as they burn.
The poor ashes burn and weep, and sparks fly from them.
Nanak, the Creator who made the world, knoweth whether it is better to be burned or buried.

PAURI VI

Without the true Guru none hath found God: without the true Guru none hath found God.

God hath put Himself into the true Guru; He hath made manifest and proclaimed this.

Salvation is ever obtained by meeting the true Guru who hath banished worldly love from within him.

Best are the meditations of him who hath fixed his mind on the True One:
He hath found the Giver of life to the world.

1 And have done nothing meritorious in this birth.

2 This verse is also translatedâ Many depart from here after spending what they possessed; had they any other business in this world?

SLOK VII

In pride man cometh, in pride he departeth; In pride is man born, in pride he dieth; In pride he giveth, in pride he taketh; In pride he earneth, in pride he spendeth; In pride man becometh true or false; In pride man meditateth evil or good; In pride he goeth to hell or heaven; In pride he rejoiceth, in pride he mourneth; In pride he becometh

filthy, in pride he is cleansed; In pride man loseth his caste and race; In pride are the ignorant, in pride the clever; In pride one knoweth not the value of deliverance or salvation;
In pride is mammon and in pride its effect on the heart;
In pride are animals created.
When pride is removed, God's gate is seen.
Without divine knowledge manworrieth himself by talking.
Nanak, the Commander hath thus ordained it;
As man regardeth God, so God regardeth him. 1
Guru Angad
It is the nature of pride that it produceth pride.
This pride is a trammel which subjecteth man to repeated transmigration.
What is the origin of pride, and by what device shall it depart?
For pride it is ordained that man wander according to his previous acts.
Pride is a chronic disease, but there is also a medicine for it in the heart.
If God bestow His grace, man shall avail himself of the Guru's instruction;
Saith Nanak, hear, O ye men, in this way trouble shall depart.

1 Also translatedâ (a) Treat men according to their acts. (Â) Treat others as thou wouldst be treated thyself. Q 2

PAURI VII

They who have meditated on God as the truest of the true, have done real worship and are contented;
They have refrained from evil, 1 done good deeds, and practised honesty;
They have lived on a little corn and water, and burst the entanglements of the world.
Thou art the great Bestower; ever Thou givest gifts which increase a quarterfold.
They who have magnified the great God have found Him.

SLOK VIII

Men, trees, the banks of sacred streams, clouds, fields,
Islands, peoples, countries, continents, the universe,
The sources of production from eggs, wombs, the earth, and perspiration,
Lakes, mountains, animalsâ O Nanak, God knoweth their condition.
Nanak, God having created animals taketh care of them all.
The Creator who created the world hath to take thought for it also.
It is the same Creator who made the world who taketh thought for it.
To Him be obeisance; blessings be on Him! His court is imperishable.
Nanak, without the true Name what is a sacrificial mark? what a sacrificial thread?
Guru Nanak

Man may perform hundreds of thousands of good acts and deeds, hundreds of thousands of approved charities,

Hundreds of thousands of penances at sacred places, sahaj jog 2 in the wilderness,

1 Literallyâ Have not put their feet into evil.
2 There are two forms of Jog or exercise for the union of the soul with God. Sahaj jog or raj jog is the repetition of God's name with fixed attention and association with the holy, as contradistinguished from the hath jog of Patanjali, the severest and most painful form of a Jogi's austerities.

Hundreds of thousands of braveries, and part with his life in the conflict of battle;
He may study hundreds of thousands of Veds and works of divine knowledge and meditation, and read the Puransâ
Nanak, these devices would be of no avail; true is the mark of grace.
The Creator who made the world hath decreed trans migration.

PAURI VIII

Thou alone art the true Lord who hath diffused the real truth.
He to whom Thou givest obtaineth truth, and he then practiseth it.
Man obtaineth truth on meeting the true Guru in whose heart the truth dwelleth.
The fool knoweth not truth, and hath wasted his life by obstinacy;
Why hath he come into the world?

SLOK IX Guru Nanak

A man may load carts with books; he may load men with books to take with him;
Books may be put on boats; pits may be filled with them.
A man may read books for months; he may read them for years;
He may read them for life; he may read them while he hath breathâ
Nanak, only one word, God's name, would be of account; all else would be the senseless discussion of pride.

Guru Nanak

The more one readeth and writeth, the more is one tor mented;
The more one wandereth on pilgrimages, the more one babbleth;
The more religious garbs man weareth, the more dis comfort he causeth his body.
Bear, O my soul, the result of thine own acts.
He who eateth not corn 1 hath lost the relish of life.
Men suffer much pain through their attachment to mammon.
They who wear not clothes suffer terribly day and night.
Man ruineth himself by perpetual silence; how can he who sleepeth in ignorance be awakened without a guru.
Even though man go barefooted, he must still suffer for his own acts. 2
If a man eat filth, and put ashes on his head,
The blind fool loseth respect; without the Name he obtaineth no abiding place.
The ignorant man who dwelleth in the wilderness and at burial and cremation- grounds, knoweth not God and shall afterwards regret.
He who meeteth the true Guru and fixeth God's name in his heart, obtaineth comfort.
Nanak, he on whom God looketh with favour obtaineth Him.
He becometh free from hopes and fears, and destroyeth his pride by means of the Word.

PAURI IX

The saints, O Lord, please Thy heart, adorn Thy gate, and hymn Thy praises.
Nanak, they who are outside Thy favour, find no entrance and wander in many births.
Some know not their origin, and have an excessive opinion of themselves.
I am a singer of low caste; others call themselves of high caste.
I only beg of those who meditate on Thee 3 1 Several faqirs do not eat corn, some go naked, some practise perpetual silence, some go barefooted, some eat filth, Â c.

2 The gyanis generally translateâ If a man go barefooted, he is merely suffering for his folly.

3 Also translatedâ I beg for a sight of those who meditate on Thee.

SLOK X Guru Nanak

False are kings, false their subjects, false the whole world;
False are mansions, false palaces, false those who dwell therein;
False is gold; false silver; false he who weareth them;
False the body; false raiment; false peerless beauty;
False husbands; false wives; they waste away and become dust.
Man who is false loveth what is false, and forgetteth the Creator.
With whom contract friendship? The whole world passeth away.
False is sweetness; false honey; in falsehood shiploads are drowned.
Nanak humbly assertethâ except Thee, O God, everything is thoroughly false.

Guru Nanak

Man is known as true when truth is in his heart; When the filth of falsehood departeth, man washeth his body clean.

Man is known as true when he beareth love to the True One;

When the mind is enraptured on hearing the Name, man attaineth the door of salvation.

Man shall be known as true when he knoweth the true way;

Having prepared the field of the body, put into it the seed of the Creator.

Man shall be known as true when he receiveth true instruction;

Let man show mercy to living things and perform some works of charity.

Man shall be known as true, when he dwelleth in the pilgrimage of his heart;

Let man after inquiry from the true Guru rest and abide in his own heart;

Truth is the medicine for all; it removeth and washeth away sin.

Nanak maketh supplication to those who are in possession of truth.

PAURI X

Be mine the gift of the dust of the saints' feet: if I obtain it, I shall apply it to my forehead.

Forsake false covetousness; concentrate thy mind and meditate on the Unseen One.

Thou shalt obtain a reward in proportion to what thou hast done.

If it have been so allotted from the beginning, man shall obtain the dust of the saints' feet.

Ruin not thyself with scant service.

SLOK XI Guru Nanak

There is a dearth of truth; falsehood prevaileth; the blackness of this age maketh men demons.

They who have sown the seed of the Name have departed with honour; how can half-seed germinate?

If the seed be whole, it will germinate in the proper season.

Nanak, unbleached cloth cannot be dyed without a base.

If the body be put into the vat of fear, modesty be made its base,

And it be dyed with devotion, O Nanak, there will not be a trace of falsehood in it.

Guru Nanak

Greed and sin are ruler and village accountant; falsehood is master of the mint.

Lust, his minister, summoneth and examineth men, and sitteth in judgement on them.

The subjects are blind and without divine knowledge, and satisfy the judge's greed with bribes.

Priests dance, play musical instruments, disguise, and decorate themselves;

They shout aloud, sing of battles, and heroes' praises.

Fools call themselves pandits and with tricks and cavilling love to amass wealth.

Pretended religious men spoil their religious acts, and yet want the door of salvation;

They call themselves continent, and leave their houses and homes, yet they know not the way.

Every one is perfect to himself: no one admitteth himself wanting.

If the weight of honour be put into the scale, then, Nanak, man shall appear properly weighed.

Guru Nanak

Man's evil becometh known, O Nanak; the True One seeth all.

Every one maketh endeavours, but it is only what the Creator doeth that taketh place.

Caste hath no power in the next world: there is a new order of beings.

They whose accounts are honoured are the good.

PAURI XI

They whom Thou didst so destine from the beginning meditate on Thee, O Lord.

There is nothing in the power of creatures; 0 God, it is Thou who hast created the different worlds.

Some Thou blendest with Thyself; others Thou leadest astray from Thee.

Thou art known by the favour of the Guru, through whom Thou revealest Thyself.

They who know Thee are easily absorbed in the True One.

SLOK XII Guru Nanak

Pain is medicine, worldly pleasure a disease; where there is such pleasure, there is no desire for God.

Thou art the Doer, I do nothing; if I try to do anything, it cometh to nothing.

I am a sacrifice unto Thee; Thou abides! in Thine omni potence:

Thine end cannot be seen.

Thy light pervadeth creatures; creatures are contained in Thy light; Thou fillest inanimate and animate creation. 1

Thou art the true Lord; beautiful is Thy praise; he who uttereth it is saved.

Nanak uttereth the words of the Creator; what is to be done God continueth to do.

Guru Angad

The Jogis deem it their duty to acquire divine knowledge, the Brahmans to read the Veds,

The Khatris to exercise bravery, the Sudars to work for others;

But the highest duty of all is to repeat the name of the one God. 2

He who knoweth the secret of this

Is a bright God himself, and Nanak is his slave.

Guru Angad

There is one God, the God of all gods, the Supreme God of souls.

He who knoweth the secrets of the soul and of God, Is a bright God himself, and Nanak is his slave.

Guru Nanak

Water remaineth if confined in a vessel; but it cannot remain without a vessel.

The mind controlled by divine knowledge is restrained; but without a guru there can be no divine knowledge.

1 Also translatedâ Thy power (kala) is inconceivable (a, not, and kalna, to know).

2 Also translatedâ

The Jogis speak of divine knowledge, the Brahmans of the Veds; The Khatris of bravery, the Sudars of working for others. All that they speak is concerning the one God.

PAURI XII

When the literate man is sinful he descrveth punishment; but punish not the illiterate saint.

As man acteth so shall he be described.

Play not such a game as shall bring thee defeat on arriving at God's court.

The literate and the illiterate shall be judged hereafter;

The headstrong shall be punished in the next world.

SLOK XIII Guru Nanak

Nanak, this body of ours 1 hath one carriage and one driver.

They are both changed in every age: the holy man knoweth this.

In the Sat age contentment was the carriage, piety the driver in front;

In the Treta age continence was the carriage, strength the driver in front;

In the Dwapar age penance was the carriage, truth the driver in front;

In the Kal age passion 2 is the carriage, falsehood the driver in front.

Guru Nanak

The Sam Ved saith that the Lord is white-robed, 3 that men desired truth, abode in truth, and that all were absorbed in truth.

The Rig saith that God's name is everywhere contained, that it is as the sun in heaven;

That by repeating it sins depart, 1 Meru is the large bead in which the two ends of a rosary are joined, without which it is believed that prayers repeated on the rosary are of no avail. Mer sharir here means man's body, which is superior to that of other animals.

2 Agan. Literally â fire. This word is often used for wrath, but Guru Nanak has more often inveighed against avarice or covetousness than against wrath, and perhaps it is the former that is taken as a special attribute of this degenerate age.

3 Sctambar. The Hans or Swan avatar.

And that then, Nanak, man obtaineth salvation.

The Yajur stateth that Kan Krishan, who was a Yadav, seduced Chandrawal;

That he brought the tree of life for a milkmaid, and amused himself in Bindraban.

The Atharv belongeth to the Kal age, when God's name was called Allah.

Men then wore blue clothes, and the Turks and Pathans exercised sway.

The four Veds are true according to the Hindus; but if they are read and studied there are found therein four different doctrines;

When man hath love and devotion and is himself lowly, it is then, O Nanak, he obtaineth salvation.

PAURI XIII

I am a sacrifice to the true Guru by meeting whom the Lord is remembered,

Who gave me the salve of divine instruction; with these eyes I then beheld God in the world.

The dealers who leave the Lord and attach themselves to mammon are wrecked.

The true Guru is a boat; few there are who consider this,

And those who do he mercifully saveth.

SLOK XIV Guru Nanak

The simmal-tree of the desert is very tall and very thick.

Why should the birds which go to it with hopes depart disappointed?

Because its fruit is insipid, its flowers unwholesome, and its leaves useless.

The tree which yieldeth sweet fruit is lowly, O Nanak, but its qualities and virtues are exquisite.

Every one boweth to himself; no one boweth to another.

If anything be put into a scale and weighed, the side which descendeth is the heavier. 1

J The man who is lowly is the most worthy.

The wicked man like a deer-stalker boweth twice more than any one else;

But what availeth bowing the head, if the heart be impure?

The following hymn was composed by Guru Nanak at Banaras on the occasion of a discussion with the local pandits who pressed him to dress in the style of the Hindus:â

Guru Nanak

You read books, perform your twilight devotions, argue, worship stones, and sit like cranes;

You utter falsehoods as excellent jewels; you meditate on the Gayatri three times a day;

You wear necklaces, put sacrificial marks on your fore heads, carry two dhotis, and put towels on your heads.

If you knew God's designs, you would know that yours is verily a vain religion.

Saith Nanak, verily reflect that without the true Guru you shall not find the way.

Some suppose that the following was addressed to Sultan Ibrahim Khan Lodi who it is believed at one time sought to persecute the Guru:â

PAURI XIV

Raiment and pleasing beauty man must leave on earth and depart.

Man shall obtain the fruit of the bad or good deeds he hath done:

He may have exercised sovereignty to his heart's content, yet must he proceed by the narrow road.

He shall be sent naked to hell, which will then appear very formidable to him;

And he shall regret the sins he committed.

The following slok, addressed by Guru Nanak to pandit Hardial, his family priest, when he came to invest him with a janeu, the sacrificial thread of the upper classes of

Hindus, has already been given:â 1 Traipal is understood to be for tripada, the gayatri or spell of the Hindus.

SLOK XV

Make mercy thy cotton, contentment thy thread, con tinence its knot, truth its twist.

That would make a janeu for the soul; if thou have it, O Brahman, then put it on me.

It will not break, or become soiled, or be burned, or lost.

Blest the man, O Nanak, who goeth with such a thread on his neck.

Thou purchasest a janeu for four damris, and seated in a square puttest it on;

Thou whisperest instruction that the Brahman is the guru of the Hindusâ

Man dieth, the janeu falleth, and the soul departeth with out it.

Guru Nanak

Though men commit countless thefts, countless adulteries, utter countless falsehoods and countless words of abuse;

Though they commit countless robberies and villanies night and day against their fellow creatures;

Yet the cotton thread is spun, and the Brahman cometh to twist it.

For the ceremony they kill a goat and cook and eat it, and everybody then saith ' Put on the janeu '.

When it becometh old, it is thrown away and another is put on.

Nanak, the string breaketh not if it be strong.

Guru Nanak

By adoring and praising the Name honour and a true thread are obtained.

In this way a sacred thread shall be put on, which will not break, and which will be fit for entrance into God's court.

Guru Nanak

There is no string for the sexual organs, there is no string for women;

There is no string for the impure acts which cause your beards to be daily spat upon.

There is no string for the feet, there is no string for the hands,

There is no string for the tongue, there is no string for the eyes.

Without such strings the Brahman wandereth astray,

Twisteth strings for the neck, and putteth them on others.

He taketh hire for marrying;

He pulleth out a paper, and showeth the fate of the wedded pair. 1

Hear and see, ye people, it is strange

That, while mentally blind, man is named wise.

PAURI XV

He to whom the Lord is compassionate and merciful will do the Master's work.

That worshipper whom God causeth to abide by His order, will worship Him.

By obeying His order man is acceptable, and shall then reach his Master's court.

He shall act as pleaseth his Master, and obtain the fruit his heart desireth;

And he shall be clothed with a robe of honour in God's court.

A man at Lahore presented a cow to a Brahman. The Brahman took her with him, but had not wherewithal to pay toll at the Sultanpur ferry. He was stopped by the

Khatri toll-keeper. The latter collected the cow's dung, and at once set about plastering his cooking-place therewith. Mardana went towards him, but was ordered off, lest he should defile the toll-keeper's cooking-place. Upon this Guru Nanak uttered the following:â

SLOK XVI

Thou takest toll for a cow and a Brahman, the cow-dung will not save thee.

Thou wearest a dhoti 2 and a frontal mark, and earnest a rosary, yet thou eatest the bread of malechhas.

1 That is, he draws a horoscope.

- Dhoti is a cloth tied round the loins, the Latin sulligacuhim.

Thou performest the Hindu worship at home, thou readest the Quran in public, and associatest with Muhammadans, 1 O my brother.

Lay aside hypocrisy, repeat God's name, and thou shalt be saved.

Guru Nanak

They who have strings on their necks eat men, recite the Muhammadan prayers,
And use knives to cut men's throats. 2
Although the Brahmans sound shells in their houses,
And enjoy their viands as they do themselves; 3
Yet false is their capital and false their dealings.
By uttering falsehood they maintain themselves.
Far from them is the abode of bashfulness and honesty:
Nanak, falsehood everywhere prevaileth.
On their foreheads are sacrificial marks; on their waists reddish 4 dhotis;
And in their hands knives; they are the world's butchers.
Putting on blue clothes, they are acceptable in the Muhammadans' court,
And, while taking bread from the malechhas, worship the Purans.
They eat he-goats killed with unspeakable words, 5
And allow no one to enter their cooking squares.
Having smeared a space they draw lines around it,
And sit within, false that they are,
Saying, ' Touch not! O touch not!
Â Or this food of ours will be defiled."

But their bodies are defiled; what they do is defiled; 1 Also translatedâ Thou actest like Muhammadans.

2 Also translatedâ They who read prayers devour men, and they who wear strings on their necks ply knives.

3 According to the holy books of the Hindus, Brahmans should not eat in the houses of men who recite Muhammadan prayers.

4 Kdkhdi, reddish, or partially soiled from frequent washing. The word is also applied to the tucking in of a dhoti in a particular way.

5 The Muhammadan expression Bismillah (in the name of God), used when slaughtering animals as well as on other occasions. It is, of course, unacceptable to Hindus.

Their hearts are false while they perform ablutions after their meals.
Saith Nanak, meditate on the True One;
If thou art pure, thou shalt obtain Him. PAURI XVI

All are within Thy ken, O Lord; Thou seest all, and Thou movest them beneath Thy glance.

God himself bestoweth greatness; He Himself causeth men to do good works.

He is the greatest of the great; great is His world; He appointeth all men to their respective duties.

If He cast a backward glance, He maketh monarchs as grass; 1
They may beg from door to door and receive no alms.

Guru Nanak composed the following slok on being invited by a dishonest shopkeeper to attend a shradh, or religious service, for his deceased father:â

SLOK XVII

If a robber break a house and sacrifice the fruits of that robbery to his ancestors,
The sacrifice shall be known in the next world, and make out the ancestors to be thieves.

The hand of the Brahman go-between shall be cut off; thus will God do justice.

Nanak, it is only the fruit of what man giveth from his earnings and toil that shall be obtained in the next world.

Guru Nanak

As a woman hath her recurring courses, so falsehood dwell-eth in the mouth of the false one, and he is ever despised.

He should not be called pure who sitteth and washeth his body;
Rather is he pure, Nanak, in whose heart God dwelleth.

1 Ghdh. Generally translated ' grass-cutters ' by the gyanis: a third interpretation too is current. In former times men of position appeared before conquerors with grass in their mouths, implying that they were the conquerors' cows whose lives should be saved. Accordingly, the phrase is also translated â and He would cause kings to put grass in their mouths.

SIKH. I R
PAURI XVII

Caparisoned horses fleet as the wind and women adorned with every aid to beauty 1 â

Men fix their hearts on them, dwell in mansions, pavilions and palaces, and make display;

They enjoy pleasures to their hearts' content; but they know not God and therefore fail.

They live by their authority, and, beholding their women's chambers, forget death;
But old age shall come and youth fail them.

A rich man gave a feast to which Guru Nanak and several Brahmans were invited. During the feast a child was born in the house, whereupon the Brahmans refused food and departed, deeming the house impure. Guru Nanak remonstrated with the following:â

SLOK XVIII

If the idea of impurity be admitted, there is impurity in everything.

There are worms in cow-dung 2 and in wood;
There is no grain of corn without life.

In the first place, there is life in water by which everything is made green.

How shall we avoid impurity? It falleth on our kitchens.

Saith Nanak, impurity is not thus washed away: it is washed away by divine knowledge. 3

Guru Nanak

Impurity of the heart is greed, impurity of the tongue is falsehood;

Impurity of the eyes is gazing on another's wealth, his wife, and her beauty;

Impurity of the ears is listening to slander.

1 Har rangi. Literally â with every colour.

2 In India cow-dung, besides being used for religious purposes, is ordinarily used as fuel by poor people.

3 In the current Janamsakhis it is stated that this slok was composed on the proposed purification of the Guru's house after the birth of his son, Sri Chand.

Nanak, even the pretended saint who practiseth such things, shall go bound to hell.

All impurity consisteth in superstition and attachment to worldly things.

Birth and death are ordained; as it pleaseth God, we come and go.

The eating and drinking which God sent as sustenance are pure.

Nanak, the pious persons who know God have no impurity.

PAURI XVIII

Magnify and praise the True Guru in whom there is all greatness.

If the Guru cause us to meet God, we shall behold His greatness.

If it please the Guru, he will cause God's praises to dwell in the heart.

He putteth his hand on our foreheads; and when he giveth the order, removeth evil from within us.

When God is pleased the nine treasures are obtained.

SLOK XIX

The Brahman having first purified himself sitteth in a purified square.

The purified food is placed before him; no one may touch it.

Being thus purified, he beginneth to eat and read Sanskrit verses.

If it is thrown into a filthy place; whose fault is that?

The corn was holy, the water was holy, the fire and salt were holy; when the fifth ingredient, ghi, 1 was added,

Then the food became holy.

When the food entereth a sinful body, it becometh impure as if spat upon.

The mouth which uttereth not the Name, and eateth even delicacies without the Name,

Consider, O Nanak, as if spat upon.

1 Clarified butter, always deemed pure by Hindus and kindred sects.

The following was Guru Nanak's remonstrance to a man who reviled the female sex:â

Guru Nanak

In a vessel 1 man is conceived, from a vessel he is born, with a vessel he is betrothed and married.

With a vessel he contracteth friendship; with a vessel he goeth through the world.

When one vessel dieth, another is sought for; to a vessel he is bound.

Why call her bad from whom are born kings?

From a vessel a vessel is born; none may exist without a vessel.
Nanak, only the one True God is independent of a vessel.
The mouth which ever praiseth Him 2 is fortunate and beautiful.
Nanak, that face shall be bright in the court of the True One.

PAURI XIX

Every one calleth Thee his own, O Lord; those who do not so call Thee Thou puttest away.

Every one must bear the result of his own acts, and adjust his own account.

Since ye are not to remain in this world, why practise ye pride?

Call no one bad; know this by reading these words.

Dispute not with a fool.

SLOK XX

Nanak, the mind and body of him who talketh evil are evil:

He is most evil, and most evil is his reputation.

The evil person is rejected in God's court; his face is spat upon.

The evil person is a fool, and receiveth shoe-beatings as punishment.

1 Woman is meant. The Greeks sometimes used the word O-KCUOS in the same sense.

2 Some suppose that woman is the missing word here, as the pre ceding part of the slok is a defence of women, not a eulogy of God.

Guru Nanak

If a man, foul within and fair without, puff himself up in the world,

His filth will not depart even though he bathe at the sixty-eight places of pilgrimage.

They who wear silk within and rags without, are good in this world.

They have conceived love for God and contemplate beholding Him.

In God's love they weep, in God's love they laugh, or are even silent.

They care not for anything except the true Master.

They beg for food at God's door, and only eat when He giveth it to them.

For them there is but one court as there is but one pen; 1 we and you shall meet for justice.

The accounts of the wicked shall be examined in God's court, and they shall be pressed, O Nanak, like oil in a mill. 2

PAURI XX

Thou Thyself didst create the world, and Thou Thyself didst infuse power into it.

Thou beholdest Thine own work, the losing and winning dice 3 upon earth.

Whatever hath come shall depart; his turn shall come to every one.

Why forget that Lord who owneth life and soul

With thine own hands arrange thine own affairs.

1 That is, there is no mediator between God and man. It is God Himself who decides man's fate.

2 This with half the last line is also translatedâ They who confound meum and tuum shall have their accounts examined in God's court, and shall be pressed, O Nanak, like oil in a mill.

3 That is, the sinners and the virtuous. The game of chausar or chaupar is played with sixteen pieces, called saris, and three dice, called pasa. The saris while being

moved round the board, like creatures in transmigration, are called kachi, unripe; when they reach their goal, they are called pakki or ripe.

SLOK XXI Guru Angad

What love is that which attacheth itself to worldly things?
Nanak, call him a lover who is ever absorbed in God.
He who deemeth what is good good, and what is bad bad,
Shall not be called a true lover if he proceed in this manner. 1

Guru Angad

He who offereth salutation and at the same time criticizeth God's works, hath made a mistake from the beginning.

Both his salutation and criticism are in vain; Nanak, such a person shall not obtain a place in God's court.

PAURI XXI

Ever remember that Lord by worshipping whom thou shalt find happiness.
Why hast thou done such evil deeds as thou shalt suffer for?
Do absolutely nothing evil, look well before thee;
So throw the dice that thou mayest not lose with the Lord,
Nay, that thou mayest gain some profit.

SLOK XXII Guru Angad

When a servant while performing service is proud and quarrelsome besides,
And talketh too much, he pleaseth not his master.
If he efface himself and perform service, he shall obtain some honour.
Nanak, he who longeth for God shall meet Him, and his longing shall be acceptable.
1 He shall not be called a lover, if he rail at God in adversity. This idea often occurs in Oriental poetry.

Guru Angad

What a man hath in his heart cometh forth; lip-worship is of no avail.
Man soweth poison and expecteth ambrosia; behold that for justice!

Guru Angad

Contracting friendship with a fool would never be pro fitable.
He acteth according to his understanding: let any one see and inquire into this.
One thing can be put into a vessel if another be first removed. 1
Commands will not succeed with God; supplications must be addressed to Him.
By practising falsehood falsehood is obtained: Nanak, there is pleasure in praising God.

Guru Angad

Friendship for a fool and love for a great man Are like lines drawn on water, which leave neither trace nor mark.

Guru Angad

If a man be a fool and do anything, he cannot do it well; Even though he do one or two things well, he will spoil the rest.

PAURI XXII

If the servant who is employed in service act according to his master's wishes,
His honour is all the more, and he receiveth double wages.
If he vie with his master, he will excite his jealousy,

Lose his large salary, and receive shoe-beating on the mouth.
Thank Him by whose gifts thou liveth
Nanak, commands will not succeed with Him; the Master must be implored.
1 The love of God will enter man's heart if he first expel worldly love.
SLOK XXIII Guru Angad
What sort of gift is that which we obtain by our own asking?
Nanak, wonderful is the gift we obtain when the Lord is pleased.
Guru Angad
What sort of service is that in which the fear of the master departeth not? 1
Nanak, he is called a servant who is absorbed in the love of his master.
PAURI XXIII
Nanak, God's end is not seen, nor hath He a thither or a hither side.
He Himself createth, and He Himself again destroyeth.
Some have chains on their necks, and some ride on many horses.
It is God who causeth to act and who acteth Himself; to whom else shall we complain?
Nanak, it is for Him who made the world to take care of it.
SLOK XXIV Guru Nanak
It is God Himself who made vessels 2 and He Himself who filleth them.
In some is contained milk; 3 others are put over the fire.
Some sleep on mattresses, and others stand and watch over them.
Nanak, God regenerateth those on whom He looketh with favour.
That is, when perfect understanding does not exist between master and servant, and the service is performed without love.
Here the word bhande means human beings generally. s That is, God's love, milk being deemed pure.
Guru Angad
God Himself arrangeth, He Himself putteth what He hath made into its proper place;
Having in this world created animals, He Himself be-holdeth their birth and death.
Whom shall we address, O Nanak, since God doeth every thing Himself?
PAURI XXIV
The greatness of the great God cannot be expressed;
He is the Creator, the Omnipotent, the Bounteous; He provideth His creatures with sustenance.
Man must do the work which God destined for him from the beginning.
Nanak, except in the one God alone there is no abiding place.
He doeth what He pleaseth.
SODAR 2
GURU NANAK, RAG ASA
WHAT is that gate, what is that mansion where Thou, O God, sittest and watchest over all things?
How many various and countless instruments of Thine are played! How many Thy musicians,

How many Thy musical measures with their consorts, and how many singers sing Thee!

Wind, water, fire sing Thee; Dharmraj singeth at Thy gate;

The recording angels, who know how to write, and on whose record Dharmraj judgeth, sing Thee;

Ishar, Brahma, and Devi, ever beautiful as adorned by Thee, sing Thee;

Indar seated on his throne and the gods at Thy gate sing Thee;

Sidhs in meditation sing Thee; holy men in contemplation sing Thee;

The continent, the true, and the patient sing Thee; unyielding heroes sing Thee.

The Pandits and the supreme Rikhis, reading their Veds, sing Thee in every age.

The lovely celestial maids who beguile the heart in the upper, middle, and nether regions sing Thee.

1 The Rahiras is a collection of hymns by Guru Nanak, Guru Amar Das, Guru Ram Das, and Guru Arjan. It is recited by the Sikhs as divine service at sunset.

2 The following hymn is so called because in the original it thus begins.

The jewels created by Thee with the sixty-eight places of Hindu pilgrimage sing Thee.

Mighty warriors and heroes sing Thee; the four sources of life sing Thee.

The continents, the worlds, and the universe made and supported by Thy hands sing Thee.

0 God, the saints who please Thee and who are imbued with Thy love sing Thee.

The many others who sing Thee I cannot remember; how could Nanak recount them?

That God is ever true, He is the true Lord, and the true Name.

He who made this world is, was, and shall be; he shall neither be born nor die.

He who created things of different colours, descriptions, and species,

Beholdeth His handiwork which attesteth His greatness.

He will do what pleaseth Himself; no order may be issued to Him to the contrary.

He is King, the King of kings, O Nanak; all remain subject to His will.

GURU NANAK, RAG ASA

As men have heard so all call Thee great;

But hath any one ever seen how great Thou art?

Thy worth cannot be estimated or described;

They who seek to describe it are absorbed in Thee

O my great Lord, deep and profound, brimful of excellences,

None knoweth the extent of Thine outline.

Though all meditative men were to meet and meditate upon Thee,

Though all appraisers were to meet and appraise Theeâ

They who possess divine and spiritual wisdom, priests and high priestsâ

Yet they could not describe even a small portion of Thy greatness.

All truth, all fervour, all goodness,

The excellences of perfect men,

Cannot be obtained in their perfection without Thee.

If Thy grace be obtained none can be excluded;

Of what account is the helpless speaker?

Thy storerooms are filled with Thy praises.
Who can prevail against him to whom Thou givest?
Nanak, the True One arrangeth all.
GURU NANAK, RAG ASA
If I repeat the Name, I live; if I forget it, I die;
It is difficult to repeat the true Name.
If man hunger after the true Name,
His pain shall depart when he satisfieth himself with it.
Then how could I forget it, O my mother?
True is the Lord, true is His name.
Men have grown weary of uttering
Even an iota of His greatness; His worth they have not discovered.
If all men joined and tried to describe Him,
That would not add to or detract from His greatness.
God dieth not, neither is there any mourning for Him;
He continueth to give us our daily bread which never faileth.
His praise isâ that there neither is,
Nor was, nor shall be any one like unto Him.
As great as Thou art Thyself, O God, so great are Thy gifts.
Thou who madest the day madest also the night
They who forget their Spouse are evil persons:
Nanak, without His name they are naught.
GURU RAM DAS, RAG GUJARI

O servants of God and the true Guru, the true Being, offer this supplication unto Him.

We insects and worms seek thy protection, O true Guru; mercifully enlighten us with the Name;

My friend and divine Guru, enlighten me with God's name.

Under the Guru's instruction, the Name is the helper of my soul; singing God's praises is my occupation.

Exceedingly fortunate are the men of God who have faith in Him and thirst for Him:

On obtaining the name of God, they are satisfied; when men meet the company of the saints, God's attributes are known.

They who obtain not the relish of God's name are unfor tunate, and shall go to the god of death.

Curses on the lives, curses on the hopes of living, of those who enter not the true Guru's protection and society! 1

The saints who have obtained the society of the true Guru are those on whose foreheads it was so written from the beginning.

Blest is that true society, Nanak, by meeting which the relish of God is obtained, and the Name manifested.

GURU ARJAN, RAG GujaRi 2

O my soul, why proposest thou exertion 3 when God Himself is engaged in effort for thee?

He even putteth their food before the insects which He created in rocks and stones.

1 Also translated â They who enter not the true Guru's protection and society have lived and shall live accursed.

2 It is said that on one occasion there was scarcity in Guru Arjan's langar khdna, or supply depot for holy men and mendicants. When the Guru's servants were making excessive efforts to collect provisions, he composed the followingbr the special occasion. It should not be understood from this hymn that the Guru discountenanced labour or exertion. The Guru himself was most active in his ministrations, in his poetical work, and in his compilation in one great volume of the compositions of his predecessors and of the most famous mediaeval Indian saints. He wrote â

O man, by striving and earning enjoy happiness; Nanak, by meditating on God, meet Him and thine anxieties shall vanish.

So also Guru Nanakâ

They who eat the fruit of their labour and bestow some portion,

O Nanak, recognize the right way.

3 Also translated- O man, why feelest thou anxiety?

O my God, they who meet the society of the saints are saved.

Through the favour of the Guru they obtain the highest rank; though they be as dry wood, they are made green.

No one can rely on mother, father, friends, children, or wives.

God provideth every one with his daily food; why, O man, art thou afraid?

The kulang flieth away hundreds of miles, leaving her young behind her.

Who feedeth them? Who giveth them morsels to peck at? Have you not considered this?

God holdeth in the palm of His hand all treasures and the eighteen supernatural powers.

Nanak is ever a sacrifice unto Thee; O God, Thou hast no end or bounds.

SO PURUKH 1

GURU RAM DAS, RAG ASA

That Being is pure, God is the pure Being, God is alto gether inaccessible and illimitable.

All meditate on Thee; all meditate on Thee; O God, Thou art the true Creator.

All creatures are Thine; Thou providest for them all.

0 saints, meditate on God who causeth all misery to be forgotten.

God Himself is the Lord, God Himself is the worshipper; 2 Nanak, what a helpless creature is man!

Thou, O God, the one Supreme Being, art fully contained in every heart and pervadest everything.

Some men are givers, some beggars; all are Thy wondrous sport.

Thou Thyself art the Giver; Thou art the Enjoyer; I know none beside Thee.

1 The following hymn is so known as these are its first words.

2 On the principle that God is everywhere and in every creature.

Thou art the totally infinite Supreme Being; what attri butes of Thine shall I recount?

The slave Nanak is a sacrifice unto those who serve Thee, unto those who serve Thee.

They who meditate on Thee, who meditate on Thee, O God, abide in happiness in this age.

They who meditate on God are emancipated, are emancipated, my friend; for them Death's noose is broken.

All fear hath departed from those who have meditated on the fearless, the fearless God.

They who have worshipped, who have worshipped my God, are absorbed in Him.

Blest, blest are they who have meditated on God; the slave Nanak will become a sacrifice unto them.

O Infinite One, Thine infinite storehouses are filled with Thy worship, Thy worship.

O Infinite One, many are Thy saints, many are Thy saints who praise Thee.

They offer various, various worship to Thee, O God; they practise austerities and repeat Thy name, O endless One.

Various, various saints of Thine read many Simritis and Shastars, perform their daily duties and the six acts prescribed for Brahmans; 1

But only they are saints, good saints, saith Nanak, who please God, the Omnipotent.

Thou art the primal Being, the illimitable Creator; there is none so great as Thou.

Thou art the same in every age; Thou art ever and ever the same; Thou art the eternal Creator.

What pleaseth Thee prevaileth; what Thou doest cometh to pass.

Thou Thyself didst fashion the whole creation, yet, being created, it shall disappear. 2

Nanak singeth the praises of the Creator who knoweth all things.

1 Reading the Veds, expounding them, making sacrifice, assisting others in doing the same, receiving alms and giving them to other Brahmans. 2 Only God Himself is permanent.

GURU RAM DAS, RAG ASA

Thou art the true Creator, my Lord.

What pleaseth Thee shall come to pass; what Thou givest I shall receive.

Everything is Thine: all meditate on Thee.

They to whom Thou showest kindness, obtain the jewel of Thy name.

The pious 1 have gained, and the perverse have lost it.

Thou Thyself hast separated these and blended those with Thee.

Thou art an ocean: all are contained in Thee.

There is none beside Thee.

All living creatures are Thy play.

When Thou didst desire separation, they who had met Thee were separated from Thee; when Thou didst desire union, Thou didst blend them with Thyself. 2

That saint whom Thou causest to know Thee shall know Thee.

And ever dwell on Thy praises.

They who have served God have found happiness,

And have become easily absorbed in His name.

Thou Thyself art the Creator; everything that is made is Thine;

There is none beside Thee;

Thou beholdest and knowest Thy handiwork.

The slave Nanak saith, under the Guru's instruction Thou becomest manifest.
GURU NANAK, RAG ASA
Man hath obtained a dwelling in that tank 3 whose water God hath made as hot as fire.

Man's feet cannot move in the mire of worldly love; we have seen him drowning therein.

1 Gurumukh, literally—they who follow the Guru's instruction.
2 Also translated—Those separated from the saints Thou didst separate from Thee; those united with them Thou didst blend with Thyself. 3 That is, the world.

O foolish man, thou hast not thought of the one God in thy heart;

Through forgetfulness of Him thy virtues have melted away.

1 am not continent, or true, or learned; I was born a stupid fool.

Nanak representeth, he hath sought the shelter of those who forget Thee not, O God.
GURU AKJAN, RAG ASA
Since thou hast now obtained a human body O man,

It is time for thee to meet God;

All else that thou doest is of no avail;

Join the company of the saints and only repeat God's name;

Apply thyself to preparation for crossing the terrible ocean.

Thy life is vainly passing in worldly love;

Thou hast not repeated God's name, performed penance, austerities, or other religious works;

Thou hast not served holy men or known God.

Nanak saith, base have been mine acts;

Preserve mine honour who have taken shelter in Thee.
GURU NANAK, RAG GAURI DIPAKI
IN the house in which God's praise is sung and He is meditated on,

Sing the Sohila and remember the Creator.

Sing the Sohila of my Fearless Lord; I am a sacrifice to that song of joy by which everlasting comfort is obtained.

Ever and ever living things are watched over; the Giver regardeth their wants.

When even Thy gifts cannot be appraised, who can ap praise the Giver?

The year and the auspicious time for marriage are re corded; relations meet and pour oil on me the bride.

O my friends, pray for me that I may meet my Lord.

This message is ever sent to every house: such invitations are ever issued.

Remember the Caller; Nanak, the day is approaching.
GURU NANAK, RAG ASA
There are six schools of philosophy, six teachers, and six doctrines.

The Guru of gurus is but one, though He hath various forms.

O father, preserve the system

In which the Creator is praised; 2 that will redound to thy glory.

As there is one sun and many seasons,

In which there are wisas, chasas, gharis, pahars, lunar and week days, and months;

1 The collection of hymns called Sohila is repeated at bedtime by pious Sikhs. It

consists of three hymns of Guru Nanak, one of Guru Ram Das, and one of Guru Arjan. The word Sohila is derived from sowan wela meaning in the Panjabi language the time for sleep.

2 The meaning is that Guru Nanak rejects the Hindu systems.

So O Nanak, there is but one God, although His forms are many.

GURU NANAK, RAG DHANASARI

The sun and moon, 0 Lord, are Thy lamps; the firmament Thy salver; the orbs of the stars the pearls enchased in it.

The perfume of the sandal is Thine incense, the wind is Thy fan, all the forests are Thy flowers, O Lord of light.

What worship is this, O Thou Destroyer of birth? Unbeaten strains of ecstasy are the trumpets of Thy worship.

Thou hast a thousand eyes and yet not one eye; Thou hast a thousand forms and yet not one form;

Thou hast a thousand stainless feet and yet not one foot; Thou hast a thousand organs of smell and yet not one organ. I am fascinated by this play of Thine.

The light which is in everything is Thine, O Lord of light.

From its brilliancy everything is brilliant;

By the Guru's teaching the light becometh manifest.

What pleaseth Thee is the real worship.

O God, my mind is fascinated with Thy lotus feet as the bumble-bee with the flower: night and day I thirst for them.

Give the water of Thy favour to the sarang Nanak, so that he may dwell in Thy name.

GURU RAM DAS, RAG GAURI PURBI

The city is greatly filled with lust and wrath; but these are destroyed on meeting the saints.

By predestination the Guru is found, and the soul is ab sorbed in the region of God's love.

Salute the saint with clasped handsâ this is a greatly meritorious act.

Prostrate thyself before himâ this is a greatly religious act.

The infidel knoweth not the taste of God's essence; he beareth the thorn of pride in his heart.

The more he moveth, the more it pricketh him, and the more pain he feeleth: his head shall feel death's mace.

1 The body. S 2

The saints of God are absorbed in God's name, and have destroyed the pain and fear of transmigration.

They have found God the imperishable Being, and great honour is theirs in the earth's continents and the universe.

0 God, we poor, and wretched, are Thine; preserve us, preserve us, Thou greatest of the great!

The Name is Nanak's support and prop; I have obtained happiness through being absorbed only in God's name.

GURU ARJAN, RAG GAURI PURBI I pray you hear me, my friends, it is time to serve the saints.

Earn here the profit of God's name, and in the next world ye shall abide in happiness.

Human life groweth shorter every day and night;

O man, meet the Guru and arrange thine affairs.

This world is involved in wickedness and superstition; they who know God are saved.

He whom God awakeneth and causeth to drink the essence of His word, knoweth the story of the Ineffable. 1

Purchase that 2 for which thou hast come into the world, and God by the Guru's favour will dwell in thy heart.

Thou shalt find a home with comfort and peace in God's own palace, and not return again to this world.

0 God, Searcher of hearts, Arranger, 3 fulfil the desires of my heart.

The slave Nanak craveth the happiness of being made the dust, of the saints' feet.

1 This and the concluding portion of the preceding line are also translatedâ

He whom the saint who knoweth God awakeneth, shall be saved, And shall quaff the essence of God's name: it is he who knoweth the story of the Ineffable.

2 God's name.

3 The gyanis often translate Bidhataâ He who gives man the fruit of his acts. The third Guru uses the expression in the same sense.

HYMNS OF GURU NANAK

THE following was addressed to a man addicted to intoxicants:â

The Giver gave man a pill of the intoxicant illusion.

In his intoxication he forgot death and enjoyed pleasure for four days.

The abstainers 1 obtained truth to keep them in God's court.

Nanak, know the True One alone as true.

By serving Him man obtaineth happiness and proceedeth with honour to His court.

The true wine is that which containeth the true Name; it is prepared without molasses.

I am a sacrifice unto those who hear and explain this.

Man is known as properly intoxicated when he obtaineth a place in God's court.

Bathe in the water of virtues; apply the perfume of truth to thy body;

Then shall thy face become bright, and the One Giver bestow hundreds of thousands of gifts on ihee.

Inform God, with whom resteth happiness, of thine unhappiness.

Why forget Him who owneth thy soul and life?

All clothing and food are impure without Him.

All else is false; what pleaseth Thee, O God, is acceptable.

A Sikh called Prema asked the Guru where God resided, in what state He dwelt, and how He 1 Sofiiin. These must not be confounded with the Sufis of Persia whose predilections are in the opposite direction. By abstainers are here meant the truthful.

could be found. The following was the Guru's reply:â

The virtues of the virtuous woman are blazoned abroad; she who is not virtuous regretteth it.

O woman, if thou desire thy Spouse, practise truth. He cannot be obtained by falsehood.
No boat or raft will take thee to the distant Beloved.
My Lord is perfect; His throne is secure.
He whom the perfect Guru maketh holy, shall obtain the True and unrivalled One.
God's palace is beautiful; it is adorned with bright gems, rubies,
Pearls, and diamonds; it is surrounded by a golden fortress, and is an abode of pleasure.
How shall I scale the fortress without a ladder? By meditating on God through the Guru I shall behold Him.
The Guru giving me God's name is my ladder, my boat, and my raft;
The Guru is the lake, the sea, and the boat; the Guru is the sacred stream.
If it please God, I shall go to bathe in the true tank x and become pure.
He is called the most perfect; He reposeth on a perfect throne.
His seat is perfectly beautiful; He fulfilleth the hopes of the hopeless.
Nanak, if man obtain the Perfect One how can his virtues decrease?
A man can only find favour with God by devotion:â
Accursed is her life who is separated from her Spouse; she is ruined by mammon.
Like a wall impregnated with kallar she crumbleth down day and night.
She obtaineth no rest without the Word; without her Beloved her grief departeth not.
O woman, what are thine adornments without thy Spouse? 1 The Guru is meant.
Thou shalt not obtain entrance into God's court; being false thou shalt be despised.
The Lord is wise and forgetteth not: He is true and a great husbandman.
He first prepareth the ground, 1 then soweth the seed of the true Name.
From the name of the one God the nine treasures are produced, and man obtaineth the marks 2 of His favour.
What shall be the condition of him who accepteth not the Guru's doctrine?
The blind 3 man hath forgotten the Name; the perverse is stone-blind.
His transmigration shall cease not; he shall be ruined by death and birth.
Woman may buy sandal, kungu, 4 and red lead for the partings of her hair,
Distilled aloe wood, sandal, betel, and camphor in great quantities;
Yet, if she please not her Spouse, all her preparations are vain:
All her enjoyments are vain, and all her adornments are useless.
Until she is permeated by the Word, how shall she obtain honour at God's court?
Nanak, blest is the woman who loveth her Spouse.
The Guru's idea of creation:â
From the True One proceedeth air, from air water.
And from water the three worlds; light was infused into every heart.
The Pure One becometh not impure: he who is imbued with the Word obtaineth honour.
Guru Nanak composed the following after a con- 1 That is, man's heart.
2 A reference to the thappds, or marks, put on crops before being divided among the partners of the land.
3 That is, spiritually blind.

4 A red composition, principally of saffron, used by women to ornament their foreheads.

versation with Samangir, a Sanyasi, at Talwandi. The Guru maintained the excellence of his own system and the advantage of repeating God's name obtained from the Gurü:â

If I turn myself into a woman, the Enjoyer will enjoy me.

Love not that which appeareth transient.

The Spouse enjoyeth on His couch the pious virtuous wife.

Having under the Guru's instruction obtained God's name as the water, quench the four fires. 1

The lotus of the heart shall then bloom, and thou shalt be completely satiated with nectar.

Nanak, make the true Guru thy friend, and thou shalt obtain happiness 2 in God's court.

The following is a homily addressed to a trader called Ramu whom the Guru met at Kartarpur:â

Trade, O trader, and take care of thy merchandise. Buy such goods as shall depart with thee. In the next world is a wise Merchant who will be careful in selecting the real article.

0 my brother, utter God's name with attention.

Take with thee God's praise as thy merchandise, so that, when the Merchant seeth it, He shall be satisfied.

How shall they whose wares are not genuine, be happy?

By trading in counterfeit goods the soul and body become counterfeit.

Like a deer snared in a noose, such a trader shall suffer great misery and ever lament.

The counterfeit shall not be received in the great God's treasury, and they shall not behold Him.

The counterfeit have neither caste nor honour; the counterfeit are none of them acceptable.

The counterfeit who do counterfeit work, shall lose their honour in transmigration.

1 The four fires areâ hinsa, cruelty; moh, worldly love; krodh, anger; and lobh, avarice.

2 Sack, literally truth, but in the compositions of the Gurus the word often means happiness.

Nanak, instruct thy heart by the Guru's word and advice.

They who are imbued with the love of God's name have no load of sin and no superstition.

They in whose hearts God dwelleth are without fear, and great shall be their gain by repeating His name.

The omnipresence of God:â

He Himself is the Relisher; He Himself is the relish; He Himself is the Enjoyer;

He Himself is the robe; He Himself the couch and the Spouseâ

My Lord, who is dyed with love, pervadeth everythingâ

He Himself is the fisherman and the fish; He Himself is the water and the net.

He Himself is the lead of the net; He Himself is the bait within it.
0 my friends, my Darling is in every way playful.
He ever enjoyeth the virtuous wife; see what a state is mine! 1
Nanak representeth, Thou art the lake, and Thou art the swan;
Thou art the lotus and the water lily, Thou art pleased on beholding them. 2

The following was a remonstrance to a Mulla and a Qazi who had entered on a discussion with the Guru:â

He is the Lord who hath caused the garden of the world to flourish 3 and grow green,

And who restraineth sea and land; hail to the Creator! Thou must die, O Mulla, thou must die. By all means fear the Creator.

1 Who, not being virtuous, am divorced from God.

2 The lotus opens its leaves by day and the water-lily by night. God is the sun and moon which behold them by day and night alternately.

3 Maula, a name of God in Arabic. The Hindi verb maulna means to bloom or blossom. There is in the original a pun on the word.

Thou art a Mulla or a Qazi only when thou really knowest God's name.

Even if thou be very learned thou must depart; none may remain when his measure of life is full.

He is a Qazi who hath renounced pride, and made the name of God alone his support.

He is, was, and shall be: He was not born, neither shall He die; True is the Creator. 1

Thou prayest five times a day, and readest thy Quran and holy books.

Nanak saith, when the grave calleth, man shall cease to drink and eat.

ASHTAPADI

The following was composed in a devotional paroxysm. Some suppose that it was uttered at Makka in reply to Qazis who had asked the Guru to tell them of the God he adored:â

Persuade thy heart to sing God's name with every breath thou drawest. 2

How great is He to whom one playeth and singeth, and where doth He dwell?

All Thy eulogists continue to praise Thee with affection.

Father, God is inaccessible and endless.

Pure is the Name; pure is the place of the true Cherisher.

How great Thy sovereignty is cannot be known; no one knoweth how to describe it.

If a hundred poets were to be found, they could not describe a particle of it, though they sang their utmost. 3

Nobody hath found Thy worth; every one as he hath heard describeth Thy glory.

Priests, prophets, saints, faithful men, martyrs,

Shaikhs, Strivers, Qazis, Mullas, Darweshes who have arrived at God's gate,

L True here apparently means abiding, eternal.

2 Also translatedâ As far as it can fix its attention.

3 Literallyâ even though they cried over it.

Obtain further blessings if they continue to recite God's praises.

He consulteth no one when He createth; He consulteth no one when He destroyeth; He consulteth no one when He giveth or taketh.

He knoweth His own might; He acteth and causeth others to act.

He beholdeth all men with favour, and bestoweth on those who please Him.

Neither His place nor His name is known, nor how great His name is among other names.

How great is that place where my Sovereign dwelleth!

None can reach it; of whom shall I inquire the way?

High or low caste influenceth not God when He maketh any one great.

Greatness is in the hands of the Great One; He giveth to whom He pleaseth.

He regenerateth man by His order without any delay.

Everybody crieth ' Give me much, much ', in the hope of getting it.

How great shall the Giver be called who giveth countless gifts!

Nanak saith, O God, Thy storehouses are full in every age, and never is there a deficiency.

It is said that a Qazi and a pandit asked the Guru how man could find God and be blended with Him. The following was the reply:â

All are wives of the Spouse and adorn themselves for Him.

In trumpery red dresses have they come for His in spection. 1

Love is not obtained by hypocrisy; counterfeit gilding degradeth.

In this way God the Spouse shall enjoy the wife.

The good wife is pleasing to Thee, O Lord; of Thy favour Thou decoratest her.

1 Literallyâ to be counted by Him.

She is decorated with the Guru's word; her body and soul are with her Beloved.

With hands clasped she standeth waiting on Him, and offereth Him true supplication.

She is imbued with the love of her Darling; she dwelleth in fear of the True One; and, when dyed with His love, her colour is the true one.

She is called the handmaiden of the Beloved, and an-swereth to the name of Lali. 1

Her true affection is not sundered; the True One blendeth her with Himself.

Her soul is imbued and saturated with the Word; I am ever a sacrifice unto her.

She who is absorbed in the True Guru, shall not sit down a widow.

Her Beloved is an abode of pleasure ever young and true; He neither dieth nor is born.

He ever enjoyeth His virtuous wife, and casteth true glances on her as she obey eth Him.

She maketh truth the parting of her hair, and love her dress and ornaments.

She maketh the indwelling 2 of God her sandal, and the tenth gate her chamber.

She lighteth the lamp of the Word, and weareth God's name as her necklet.

She weareth on her forehead the jewel of love, and she is beautiful among women.

Her beauty and wisdom are charming, and true is her infinite love.

She knoweth no man but her Beloved; it is only for the True Guru she feeleth love and affection.

But thou who art reckless on a dark night, 3 how shalt thou pass it without the Beloved?

Thy bosom shall burn, thy body shall burn, and thy mind shall burn, O woman.

L The jewel or precious one.

2 Chit wasaia; also translatedâ mental restraint.

3 In spiritual ignorance.

When woman enjoyeth not her Husband, her youth passct li in vain.

Her Husband is on the couch; his wife sleepeth and knoweth not His presence.

While I sleep, the Beloved awaketh; whom shall I go to consult? 1

Nanak, the true Guru, having taught me love, hath caused me to meet God, and 1 abide in His fear.

The mind is impure until it receives instruction from a true religious teacher:â

When the mind is impure the body is impure, and the tongue impure.

The mouth is impure by uttering impurity; how shall it be made pure?

The heart cannot be cleansed without the Word; from the True One truth is obtained.

O girl, what happiness is there without virtue?

Brahmans read books aloud, but understand not their meaning.

They give instruction to others as a business matter.

They wander about the world preaching falsehood; while they who abide by the Word are the best.

How many pandits and astrologers study the Veds!

They glorify battles and enmities, 2 but from quarrels rcsulteth transmigration.

However much they tell and preach what they have heard, man shall not be freed from his sins without the Guru.

All call themselves virtuous, but I possess no virtue.

Beautiful is the woman who hath God for her Spouse; that God pleaseth me.

Nanak, she who is united with God by the Word shall not be separated from Him.

The following was addressed to Hindu devotees whom the Guru met in his wanderings in the Hima layas:â 1 That is, there is no remedy for my negligence now.

2 The epic poems Ramayan and Mahabharat.

Though man perform lip-devotion, penance, and austeri ties, dwell at places of pilgrimage,

Bestow alms and perform acts of devotion, what are these without the True One?

As he soweth so shall he reap; human life is lost without virtue.

O silly one, happiness is obtained by being a slave to virtue.

She who under the Guru's instruction abandoneth evil, shall be absorbed in the Perfect One.

The following is a brief lecture against hypocrisy, with a few precepts to obtain future happiness:â

God carefully draweth the touchstone over men in order to assay them.

The counterfeit shall not be accepted; the genuine shall be put into His treasury.

Dispel hopes and fears, so shall thy filth be washed away.

Everybody asketh for happiness; nobody asketh for misery.

Great misery attendeth on happiness, but the perverse understand it not.

They who consider happiness and misery the same, and know the secret of the Word shall be happy.

Man may escape from the dangers of this world by accepting the Guru and hearkening to his instructions:—

The fearful ocean of the world is dangerous and formidable; it hath no shore or limit,

No boat, no raft, no pole, and no boatman;

But the true Guru hath a vessel for the terrible ocean, and ferrieth over him on whom he looketh with favour.

Love for God is inculcated by familiar Indian examples:—

O man, entertain such love for God as the lotus hath for the water.

Such love doth it bear it, that it bloometh even when dashed down by the waves.

The creatures which God created in water die without it, and therefore love it.

O man, how shalt thou be delivered without love?

God pervadeth the hearts of the pious, and bestoweth on them a store of devotion.

O man, entertain such love for God as the fish for the water.

The more it hath, the happier it becometh, and the greater its peace of mind and body.

Without water it could not live for a moment; God alone knoweth the sufferings of its heart.

O man, entertain such love for God as the chatrik for rain:

Though the tanks be full and the earth drenched, it will not drink from either.

If so fated, it shall obtain the rain-drops, otherwise it is fated to die.

O man, entertain such love for God as water for milk.

The water alone is consumed in boiling and alloweth not the milk to be consumed.

God uniteth the separated, and conferreth true greatness.

O man, entertain such love for God as the chakwi 1 for the sun.

She sleepeth not for a moment, for she knoweth that her mate is absent from her.

The perverse see not; to the pious God is ever present.

The perverse make calculations, but it is only what the Creator doeth that cometh to pass.

His worth cannot be ascertained, even though all men desire it;

But it can be ascertained under the Guru's instruction; by meeting the True One happiness is obtained.

1 The ruddy sheldrake, called by Anglo-Indians the Brahmani duck. Should the male and female birds be separated at night, for instance at different sides of a river, they are believed to call to each other unul they behold the morning sun when they renew their conjugal acquaintance.

If the True Guru be met, true love shall not sunder,

And the wealth of divine knowledge of the three worlds shall be obtained.

If any one acquire virtue, he will not forget the Pure Name.

The birds which peck on sea and land have played and gone away.

Man must depart in a ghari or two; his enjoyment is only for to-day or to-morrow.

He whom Thou blendest with Thyself shall be blended with Thee, and shall take his place in the true arena.

Without the Guru love is not produced, and the filth of pride departeth not.

He who recognizeth God in himself, and knoweth the secret of the Word, shall be satisfied:

But when man recognizeth himself through the Guru's instruction, what more remaineth for him to do?

Why speak of meeting God? Man hath met Him already,1 but it is only on receiving the Word he is satisfied.

The perverse obtain not understanding; separated from God they suffer punishment.

For Nanak there is but the gate of the one God; there is no other refuge.

It is said the following was addressed by the Guru, during his pilgrimage to the east, to a Raja called Harbans:â

Man is led astray by the reading of words; ritualists are very proud.

What availeth it to bathe at a place of pilgrimage, if the filth of pride be in the heart?

Who but the Guru can explain that the King and Emperor dwelleth in the heart?

All men err; it is only the great Creator who erreth not.

He who admonisheth his heart under the Guru's instruction shall love the Lord.

1 Because the soul has emanated from God.

Nanak, he whom the incomparable Word hath caused to meet God, shall not forget the True One.

God cannot be deceived and His merits cannot be described:â

By taking the protection of the Guru man shall be saved; counterfeit is the capital of the perverse.

The eight metals of the King are coined agreeably to His orders. 1

The Assayer Himself assayeth the coins, and putteth the genuine into His treasury.

Thy merits, O Lord, cannot be ascertained; I have seen and tested everything.

Thy merits cannot be expressed by words; if man remain true, he shall obtain honour.

Under the Guru's instruction Thou, O Lord, art praised; otherwise Thy worth cannot be described.

The Guru prefers the repetition of God's name to all other forms of devotion:â

My heart is penetrated by God's name; what else shall I reflect upon?

Happiness cometh to him who meditateth on the Word; perfect happiness to him who is imbued with God.

Preserve me as it pleaseth Thee, O God; Thy name is my support.

0 man, just is the will of the Master.

Love Him who made and adorned thy body and mind.

Were my body to be cut into pieces and burnt in the fire;

Were I to turn my body and soul into firewood, and burn them night and day;

Were I to perform hundreds of thousands and millions of religious ceremonies, all would not be equal to God's name.

1 Man is composed, according to Indian ideas, of hair, blood, nerves, skin, bone, seed, flesh, and fat. These correspond to ilu-eight simple or compound metals differently stated by Indian historians. Bhai Gur Das understands the eight metals to be the four castes of Hindus and the four great sects of Muhammadans.

Were a saw to be applied to my head and my body to be cut in twain; 1

Were my body to be frozen in the Himalayas, even then my mind would not be free from diseaseâ â

It would all not be equal to God's nameâ I have seen and examined everythingâ

Were I to make offerings of millions of gold, many ex cellent horses and excellent elephants;

Were I to make large presents of lands and cows, even then pride would remain in my heart.

The Guru hath given me the true gift that my mind is penetrated by God's name.

How many opinions, and how many interpretations of the Veds through obstinacy!

How many entanglements there are for the soul! the gate of deliverance is only obtained through the Guru's instruction.

Everything is inferior to truth; the practice of truth is superior to all else.

Call every one exalted; let no one appear to thee low.

The one God fashioned the vessels, and it is His light that filleth the three worlds.

By His favour man obtaineth the truth; what He granteth in the beginning none can efface.

The holy meet the holy; by love for the Guru man obtaineth consolation.

He who is absorbed in the True Guru pondereth on the Word of the Ineffable.

He who drinketh the nectar of the Name shall be satisfied, and go to God's court with a dress of honour.

The strain of ecstasy 2 resoundeth night and day in the hearts of those who bear great love to the Word.

1 Saws were kept at Banaras and Priyag for the immolation of Hindu devotees. The operator applied the saw first to the head and cut through the body to the middle thus dividing it into halves. Devotees believed that all their sins should thus be forgiven, and they should immediately enter a state of bliss.

2 Kinguri is a musical instrument, originally composed of two gourds or calabashes connected by a frame on which there were four strings. It is now generally made of one calabash, a frame and one j

Few there are who obtain understanding by admonishing their hearts through their guru.

Nanak, they who forget not the Name, and who act according to the Word shall be delivered.

The following principally inculcates the inutility of worldly possessions and the superiority of devotion:â

We see mansions painted and whitewashed with orna mented doors.

They were constructed to give pleasure to the heart, and through love and regard for worldly things, but they shall fall to ruin.

So the body which is empty within and possesseth no love, shall fall and become a heap of dust.

O my brethren, your bodies and wealth shall not accompany you.

God's name is the pure wealth; God giveth it through the Guru.

If the Giver give the true wealth of God's name,

The great Creator shall become man's friend, and no inquiry shall be made of him in the next world.

If God deliver man, he shall be delivered; God alone is the Pardoner.
The perverse man deemeth that daughters, sons, and relations are his.
He is pleased on beholding woman, but, as she bringeth joy, so she bringeth sorrow.
Holy men are imbued with the Word, and day and night enjoy divine happiness.
The mind of the wavering infidel wandereth in quest of transitory wealth.
Men ruin themselves by their search abroad while the Real Thing is in their homes.
The pious obtain It, the perverse miss It through pride.
O vicious infidel, know thine own origin.
string. The Jogis apply the word to the music heard in the brain by the practice of Jog.
Thy body made from blood and semen shall be brought to the fire at last.
The body is in the power of the breath according to the true mark on the forehead.
Men pray for a long life; no one desireth to die.
He is said to lead a happy life in whose heart God dwelleth through the Guru's instruction.
Of what account are they who are without the Name, and who therefore obtain not a sight of the great God?
As a man goeth astray at night in his sleep,
So doth he in whose heart there is pride and worldly love, and who is in the power of mammon.
To him who reflecteth under the Guru's instruction the world appeareth a dream.
As thirst is quenched when one findeth water; as the child is sustained by its mother's milk;
As the lotus cannot exist without water, and the fish would die without it,
So, Nanak, may I obtain divine happiness through the Guru's instruction and live singing God's praises!
Without the spiritual condition which is obtained by a repetition of the Name there is no salvation:â
I have become alarmed on seeing a terrible mountain in my Father's house. 1
Steep is the mountain and difficult to ascend; there is no ladder which will reach it;
But under the Guru's instruction I have found the secret; 2 the Guru hath caused me to meet God and I am saved.
O my brethren, the ocean of the world is difficult and formidable.
If I have a satisfactory interview with the perfect true Guru, he will deliver me by granting me God's name.
If I say I am perishable, it will not avail me; but if I really know that I am perishable, it will.
Everything that came into this world shall depart; the Creator alone is immortal.
1 Seeing the difficulties of this world.
2 That there is no mountain.
Be sure to praise the True One and love His abode.
Beautiful houses and palaces and thousands of strong holds,
Elephants, horses with their housings, and hundreds of thousands, yea, countless armed men

Will not depart with any one: Their masters pine away and die without gaining any advantage from them.

Thou mayest amass gold and silver, but wealth is an entangling net.

Man's authority may be proclaimed throughout the whole world, but without the Name death standeth over his head.

When the body falleth, the soul fleeth away; what shall be the condition of the evil doers?

The husband is delighted on beholding his sons and his wife on her couch;

He applieth distilled aloe wood and sandal; he weareth fine clothes and decorateth himself;

Yet shall he leave his family and depart; dust shall return to dust.

He may be styled a chief, an emperor, a king, a governor, or a lord;

He may be called the headman of a town or a governor; he may burn with pride;

Yet by perversely forgetting the Name he shall be as a reed burnt in the fire.

Having come into the world, he shall depart however proud he be.

The whole world is a chamber of lampblack; the body and soul which enter it shall be tarnished. 1

They who are preserved by the Guru are pure; the fire of their desires is extinguished by the Word.

Nanak, man obtaineth deliverance by the true name of the King of kings.

May I not forget God's name! may I purchase it as a jewel!

The perverse man perisheth in the terrible ocean of the 1 Literallyâ shall become ashes.

world; the holy man crosseth it, unfathomable though it be.

GHAR III 1

Definitions:â

How is Sat Sangat, the Society of the holy, known?

The name of the one God is mentioned there.

How are Duhaginsâ women separated from their husbands â known?

They are those who forgetful of their Spouse wander unhonoured.

They who are pleased with God's will,

Remove superstition from their minds.

Nanak, the true Guru, is known by his association with every one.

SRI RAG KI WAR Some virtues which contribute to perfection:â

Faith and resignation are the characteristics of the holy; patience is the viaticum of angels.

The perfect shall obtain a sight of God; the fool shall find no place with Him.

Caste is vain and contributes not to goodness or holiness:â

Castes are folly, names are folly: All creatures have one shelter, that of God. If a man call himself good,

The truth shall be known, O Nanak, when his account is accepted.

Man, no matter what his caste or social position may be, is exalted by devotion:â

What difference is there between a swan and a crane, if God look kindly on the latter?

Nanak, if it please Him, He can change a raven into a swan.

1 This is understood to mark time â three beats to a bar.

MAJH KI WAR

God as the Guru:â

The Guru is the Giver, the Guru is the house of snow, 1 the Guru is the lamp of the three worlds.

Nanak, the Guru possesseth the immortal wealth; by putting faith in Him happiness is obtained.

The ten stages of man:â

In man's first stage he loveth the milk of his mother's breast;
In his second he recognizeth his father and mother;
In his third his brother, his brother's wife, and his own sister;
In the fourth a love of play ariseth in him;
In the fifth he runneth after food and drink;
In the sixth he inquireth not a woman's caste in his lust;
In the seventh he collecteth things for a house to live in;
In the eighth his body is wasted by wrath;
In the ninth he groweth grey and his breathing is diffi cult;
In the tenth he is burnt and becometh ashes.
His companions accompany him to his pyre with loud lamentations.
The soul flieth away, showing the road of departure to others.
He came, he died, and departedâ leaving only a name.
After his death his relations offer food on leaves, and call the crows. 2
Nanak, the perverse love mental darkness.
Without a guru the world is lost.

Other divisions of human life:â At ten a child, at twenty a rake, at thirty man calleth himself handsome; 1 That is, he cools the fire of desires. Some suppose that hiwai ghar is for the Sanskrit himkar, the moon.

2 Portions (bait) of such offerings are set aside for cows, portions for dogs, and portions for crows.

At forty he is in his prime, at fifty his feet halt, at sixty old age cometh on;
At seventy he loseth his intellect, at eighty he cannot perform his duties;
At ninety he reclineth on his couch, and feeleth no strength whatever in himself.
I, Nanak, have sought and searched, and seen that the world is a mansion of smoke.

The following is said to have been addressed to a holy man called Thakur Das at Priyag:â

Were I to dwell in the cavern of a golden mountain or in a pit of water;
Were I to stand on my head on earth or in the heavens;
Were I to cover all my body with clothes, 1 and did I nothing but bathe;
Were I to shout aloud the white, the red, the yellow, and the black Veds; 2
Were I to remain dirty and filthy, 3 all this would be foolish and sinful.
Nanak, since I have pondered on the Word, I am not, I was not, and I shall not be. 4

Guru Nanak declares the folly of external puri fications:â
Man washeth his clothes and his body, and mortifieth himself.

Knowing not of the filth attaching to his heart, he rubbeth and cleanseth himself externally.

Being blind he is led astray, and falleth into Death's noose

He deemeth the property of others as his own, and suffereth for his pride.

Nanak, when pride is dispelled under the Guru's instructions, man meditateth on God's name,

Repeateth the Name, adoreth the Name, and through the Name is absorbed in happiness.

1 This is done by a sect called the Kaprias, who cover even their faces.

2 As the Brahmans do. 3 The reference is to the Jains. 4 That is, I am totally absorbed in God.

Some important subjects are briefly treated as follows:â

God hath caused the union of body and soul;

He who created them can separate them.

A fool while enjoying pleasure hath all pain:

Disease proceedeth from sinful pleasure.

From worldly rejoicing proceedeth mourning, separation from God, birth, and death.

The fool while boasting becometh involved in disputes:

The decision resteth with the True Guru; He putteth an end to disputes.

That which the Creator doeth cometh to pass; what man hath set in motion must stop.

The following was addressed by the Guru to a Qazi at Sultanpur:â

Thou utterest falsehood, eatest carrion, 1

Yet thou goest to admonish others.

Cheated thyself thou now cheatest thy companions.

Nanak saith, that is the sort of guide thou appearest!

As a Qazi beheaded a goat, some drops of blood fell on his garments, which he at once wiped off. He said that he could not join in prayer until the pollution had been removed. The following was uttered by the Guru on the occasion:â

If clothes become denied by blood falling on them,

How can the hearts of those who drink human blood 2 be pure?

Nanak, utter God's name with a pure heart regardless of thy dress.

All else is but worldly ostentation; thou, O Qazi, practisest falsehood.

The Qazi asked Guru Nanak who he was. The latter replied as follows:â

Since I am nobody, what shall I say: since I am nothing, what can I be?

1 Food obtained by peculation and bribery.

2 That is, who practise extortion or tyranny.

As God made me, I act; as He told me, I speak; I am thoroughly defiled with sin, and desire to wash it away.

Though I know nothing myself, yet I teach others; such a guide am I.

Nanak, he who being blind showeth the road to others and misleadeth all his companions,

Shall be shoe-beaten in the next world, and it will be seen what sort of guide he was.

Everything shall vanish except God:â
Of kings, subjects, and rulers none shall remain:
Shops, cities, bazars shall be destroyed by God's order.
Solid and beautiful mansions a fool deemeth his own;
Storehouses filled with wealth in a moment become empty.
Steeds, chariots, camels, elephants and their housings,
Gardens, properties, houses, and homes,
Tents, comfort able beds, and ornamental pavilionsâ where shall they be recognized?

The following was delivered to Sikhs who asked the Guru what pleasure God's praises afforded him:â

Were rivers to become kine, and springs to become milk and clarified butter;
Were the whole earth to become sugar so that the heart might ever rejoice;
Were the mountains to become gold and silver, and be studded with diamonds and rubies;
I would even then magnify Thee, and the desire to do so would not cease as I spoke.
Were the eighteen loads of vegetables of the earth 1 to become fruit, and grass to become rice;
Could I arrest the moon and sun in their courses, and were my seat to become immovable, 1 This is the sum total of the earth's flora according to ancient
Sanskrit writers. The idea was that if a leaf w r ere taken off every tree and plant, there would be formed eighteen loads, each of which an ordinary strong man could lift.
I would even then magnify Thee, and the desire to do so would not cease as I spoke.
Could I inflict pain by means of the two sinful beings Rahu and Ketu; l
Could I obtain authority over bloodthirsty kings and my glory thus shine forth,
I would even then magnify Thee, and the desire to do so would not cease as I spoke.
Were fire and frost to become my raiment, and the wind my food;
Were all the fascinating women of heaven to become my wivesâ all perishable 2 â
I would even then magnify Thee, and the desire to do so would not cease as I spoke.
Caste becomes deadly if exclusive reliance be placed on it for salvation:â
What power hath caste? It is the reality that is tested.
Poison may be held in the hand, but man dieth if he eat it.
The sovereignty of the True One is known in every age.
He who obeyeth God's order shall become a noble in His court.

The following allegory of mounted cavalry refers to the different stages of asceticism:â

The Master sent obedience to His orders as a steed into the world;
Reflection on the instruction which the Guru imparteth is its kettle-drums.
Some have mounted their steeds, others have them ready caparisoned; 1 Owing to the exigencies of prosody, only Rahu is mentioned in the original text. R t ahu and Ketu are two demons, who, according to Indian astrologers, inflict pain on mortals as they do on the sun and moon on occasions of eclipse.

2 Some understoodÂ Â to be the Sanskritay, wife. The gyanis translate-All the fascinating women of heaven may go, as far as I am concerned.

Some have loaded their baggage for the march, and others have set out.

In the following allegory the mill is the world, the corn is the soul, the husk the body, refuge in God the axle:â

When the field is ripe, it is cut; only the chaff and the hedge remain.
The corn is threshed with the husk, and the chaff is winnowed away.
Men then put together the two mill-stones and sit down to grind corn.
That which attacheth to the axle escapeth. Nanak hath seen a wonderful thing. 1
Good men, like sugar-cane, are subject to torture:â
See how sugar-cane is cut down and made into sheaves after the stalks are cleaned.
The labourers put it into a press and squeeze it.
Having expressed the juice, they put it into a pan, and it groaneth as it burneth.
The residue is collected and put into the fire beneath the pan.
Nanak, sweet things are thus ill-treated; come and see, O people.
It is useless to endeavour to instruct a fool:â
What can deep water do to a fish? What can the sky do to a bird?
What can cold do to a stone? What can married life do to a eunuch?
Even though thou apply sandal to a dog, he will still preserve his canine nature:
Even though thou instruct a deaf man, and read for him the Simritis;
Even though thou place a light before a blind man, and burn fifty lamps for him, all would be of no avail.

1 That the corn attached to the axle is not ground, that is, the soul which is attached to God is not tortured by Death.

Even though thou put gold before a herd of cattle, they would still pick out the grass to eat.
If a flux be put into iron it will melt, but not become cotton. 1
Nanak, the peculiarity of a fool is that what is said to him is ever lost.
When his Sikhs inquired how an alliance could be formed with God the Guru composed the fol lowing:â
When bronze, gold, and iron break,
The blacksmith weldeth them by means of fire.
When a husband falleth out with his spouse,
A reconciliation is effected in this world through children.
When the king asketh and his subjects give, a bond is established between them.
When a hungry man eateth, he establish3th an alliance with the world.
Drought formeth an alliance with rivers when they are flooded with rain.
There is an affinity between love and sweet words.
If any one speak the truth, he formeth a bond with know ledge.
By goodness and truth the dead establish a bond with the living.
Such are the affinities that are established in the world.
The only way to establish friendship with a fool is to smite him on the mouth. 2
By praising God man establisheth an alliance with God's court.
Nanak saith this deliberately.

The following seven sloks form part of the Guru's instruction to Shaikh Brahm, or Farid the second, of Pak Pat tan:â

The priests, the shaikhs, and the potentates of the world are all beneath the earth.

1 Its nature will not be altered.
2 Munh mar. Also translatedâ to remain silent.

Emperors pass away, but God ever flourisheth. There is only Thou, there is only Thou, O God!
Neither demigods, nor demons, nor men,
Nor Sidhs, nor Strivers, nor this earth shall abide.
There is One; is there any other?
There is only Thou, there is only Thou, 0 God!
Neither the just nor the generous,
Nor the seven regions beneath the earth shall remain.
There is One: is there any other?
There is only Thou, there is only Thou, O God!
Not the regions of the sun and the moon, Nor the seven continents,, nor the seven seas, Nor corn, nor wind shall abide. There is only Thou, there is only Thou, 0 God!
Our maintenance is in nobody's power but God's:
To all of us but one hope abidethâ
There is one: is there any other?
There is only Thou, there is only Thou, 0 God!
Birds have no money in their possession:
They only depend on trees and water.
God is their Giver.
There is only Thou, there is only Thou, O God!
Nanak, no one can erase
What is written on the forehead.
God it is who giveth man power and again taketh it away.
There is only Thou, there is only Thou, O God!

Guru Nanak thus discoursed to Prem Chand of Sarhind on the best way of occupying time:â

They who in the early morning praise God and meditate on Him with single heart,
Are perfect kings, and die fighting when occasion ariseth. 1 In the second watch there are many ways in which the attention of the mind is distracted.

1 This is understood to mean that they fight to the death with their deadly sins.

Many persons fall into the fathomless water, and cannot emerge however much they struggle.

In the third watch when hunger and thirst are both barking, food is put into the mouth.

What is eaten becometh filth, yet man again desireth food.

In the fourth watch drowsiness cometh, man closeth his eyes and goeth into dreamland. 1

Again rising in the morning he engageth in turmoil, and yet maketh preparations to live a hundred years.

If man feel love for God every moment during the eight watches of the day,
O Nanak, God will dwell in his heart and true shall be his ablution.
Man's continual thought should be devotion to his Maker:â
When Thou art near, what more do I desire? I speak verily.

He who is deceived by false worldly occupations reacheth not God's palace:
His heart is hard and he loseth his service.
The house which containeth not the True One, should be destroyed and rebuilt.
When its owner is weighed, how shall he be found of full weight?
If he lose his pride, no one will say he is of short weight.
The genuine shall be assayed, and selected at the gate of the All-seeing.
The true goods are only in one shop; they are obtained from the perfect Guru.
The advantages conferred on men by the True One:â
Without the True One all are false and practise falsehood.
Without the True One the false shall be bound and led away; 1 Pawar properly means trance, or suspended animation.
Without the True One the body is dust and shall be rolled in the dust;
Without the True One dress and food are all hunger;
Without the True One the false shall not attain God's court.
The false attached to avarice miss God's palace.
The whole world is deceived, and cometh and goeth in deception.
In the heart is the fire of greed which is quenched by the Guru's instruction.
The advantages of the Guru, who is likened to a life-giving tree:â
Nanak, the Guru is the tree of contentment, whose blossom is religion and whose fruit is divine knowledge.
It aboundeth in succulence and is ever green; it ripeneth by good works and meditation.
Honour is obtained by partaking of its relish; it is the greatest of gifts.
There is a tree of gold; its leaves are corals; its blossoms, jewels and rubies.
It beareth gems for fruit, and the heart of him who eateth it rejoiceth.
Nanak, it is obtained by him on whose forehead such destiny hath been recorded.
The sixty-eight places of pilgrimage are at the Guru's feet, and ever specially worship them.
Cruelty, worldly love, avarice, and wrath are four streams of fire:
They who fall into them are burnt, O Nanak, but de liverance is obtained by cleaving to good works.
The evil of forgetting God:â
In the heart and mouth of the perverse who never re member Thee,
Abide the bitterness of the gourd, the colocynth, and the nim, and the poison of the akk 1 and dhatura.

1 Calotropis procera.

Nanak, to whom shall I tell it? Whoso forget Thee wander bereft of Thy favour, O God.
The unequal conditions of men: â
The bird, man, by his ideas and his acts sometimes flieth high and sometimes low, 1
He sometimes percheth on a sandal-tree, sometimes on the branch of the akk-shrub, and sometimes again he loveth high flight.
Nanak saith, it is the custom of the Lord to lead all beings by His order.
Women's duty:â

If women adorn themselves with love and affection for their Spouse,
They shall not be restrained from their devotion to Him day or night.
They shall abide in His chambers, and the Word shall regenerate them;
They shall humbly supplicate the True One;
And they shall appear beautiful near their Spouse, walking according to His order.
They shall make hearty supplication to the Beloved.
Accursed the homes, wretched the lives of those who possess not the Word.
They whose hopes are fulfilled by the Word quaff nectar.
The Guru was requested to state the extent of his love of devotion:â
The desert is not satisfied with rain, and the hunger of fire is not appeased;
Kings are not satisfied with dominion; who hath ever filled the ocean?
How much hath Nanak inquired after the True Name and not been satisfied
Bhai Rama of Sultanpur inquired how God was known. The Guru replied:â

He to whom God giveth understanding understandeth; 1 Literallyâ is sometimes exalted and sometimes debased.

He to whom He giveth knowledge knoweth everything. Man merely worrieth himself when he preacheth for the sake of mammon.

The Commander, who created all things, Himself possesseth all knowledge. He Himself, Nanak, spoke the Word-Doubt shall depart from him to whom He gave it.

The Guru's reward for singing God's praises:â
Me, a minstrel out of work, God applieth to His work;
He ordered me in the beginning to sing His praises nigl t and day.
The Master summoned the minstrel to His true court,
And put on him a robe of true praise and eulogy:
He then obtained the ambrosial food of the true Name.
They who have eaten under the Guru's instruction are satisfied, and have obtained comfort.
The minstrel uttereth praise and singeth the Word.
Nanak, he who uttereth true praise obtaineth the Perfect One

RAG GAURI

The advantages resulting from the fear of God:â
The fear of God is very great and very heavy.
Man's wisdom is of little account, and so is his chatter
Walk with the load of fear on thy head;
Meditate on the Guru who is kind and merciful.
No one shall be saved without the fear of God:
His fear hath adorned man's love.
The fire of the fear of transmigration is burned away by the fear of God.
By fear the Word is fashioned and decorated.
What is fashioned without fear is altogether worthless:
Useless is the mould and useless the stroke thereon.
In the minds of many there is a desire to fashion the Word without fear;
But even though they perform a thousand artifices they shall not succeed.
Nanak, the speech of the perverse is nonsense;
What they write is worthless absurdity.

The following was addressed by the Guru to one who had remonstrated with him for having left his relations to lead a wandering life:â

Make wisdom thy mother, contentment thy father,
Truth thy brother â this is best.
People talk, but talking is of no avail.
The measure of Thy might, O God, cannot be obtained.
Modesty and attention are my two parents-in-law;
Good works I have accepted as my spouse;
Union with saints hath been my auspicious time for marriage, and separation from the world my wedding.
Saith Nanak, from such a union hath sprung truth as my offspring.

The composition of man's body and the inutility of pilgrimages; the body dies, but not the soul:â

The body is a mixture of wind, water, and fire;
Within it is the changeful play of the intellect.
The body hath nine gates and a tenth door;
O wise man, understand and reflect on this.
God speaketh, preacheth, and listeneth;
He who reflecteth on himself is a wise man.
The body is earth, the wind speaketh therein.
Consider, O wise man, what it is that diethâ
It is the quarrelsome and proud understanding.
The conscious soul dieth not.
The precious jewel, for which men go on pilgrimages,
Dwelleth within the heart.
Pandits read and argue,
But know not that which is within themselves.
When my spiritual ignorance dieth, I die not myself.
He who is everywhere contained dieth not.
Saith Nanak, when the Guru showed me God,
No one seemed to me to die or to be born.

One Sant Das propounded six questions to Guru Nanak:â

Is it known whence man hath come, Whence he hath sprung, in what he shall be absorbed,
How he is bound, how he obtaineth emancipation,
And how he shall be easily absorbed in the Imperishable?

The Guru replied:â

The Name is nectar in the heart as well as in the mouth:
Through it man is freed from worldly desires.
Man cometh in the course of nature and goeth in the course of nature.
Man is born according to the desires of his heart, and he is absorbed in the same way.
The pious man is emancipated and falleth into no en tanglements:
He is delivered by meditation on the Word and by God's name.
Many birds roost by night on a treeâ

Some happy, others unhappy—they whose minds have worldly love perish.
When night hath passed away, they gaze upon the sky: 1
They fly in every direction according to the destiny recorded for them.
They who are associated with the Name deem the world like a meeting-place of cowherds:
The poisonous vessels of lust and wrath have burst for them.
To those without the capital of the Name houses and shops are empty;
But by meeting the Guru the adamant doors of their understanding are opened.
A holy man is met by primal destiny.
God's perfect people are rendered happy by truth:
They barter their souls and bodies for divine knowledge and God's love.
Nanak toucheth their feet.
The following is a conversation between soul and body:—

The Soul: ' O body, thou thinkest thyself immortal, and that thou shalt be always happy—know that this world is a play.
1 When life ceases, their souls take flight.

Thou practisest avarice, covetousness, and excessive falsehood, and bearest many burdens.

I have seen thee, O body, trodden as ashes on the ground."

The Body: ' Hearken, hearken to mine instruction.

If thou have done good works, they shall abide with thee; O my soul, thou shalt not again find such opportunity.

The Soul: ' I address thee, O my body, hearken to my instruction.

Thou slanderest 1 and bearest false witness against others."

The Body: ' Thou covetest another's vine, 2 O soul; thou committest theft and evil deeds."

The Soul: ' When the soul departeth, thou shalt remain behind like an abandoned woman.

Thou, O body, shalt remain but as a dream—what good deeds hast thou done? '

The Body: ' Whatever I took by stealth was pleasing to thee.

Thou hast no honour in this world, and thou shalt be rejected in the next; thou hast lost thy human dwelling in vain."

I am very unhappy, O father, saith Nanak, no one careth for me.
Arabian and Turkish steeds, gold, silver, and loads of raiment
No one taketh with him; they leave him in this world, O fool.
Sugar, fruit, all have I tasted; it is only Thine ambrosial Name which is sweet.
Man diggeth deep foundations and constructeth edifices on them, but they shall become at last heaps of dust.
He hoardeth, and hoardeth, and giveth to no one; the fool thinketh that all is his own.
Rawan nominally possessed a golden Lanka and a golden palace, but they were no one's property.
Hear, O foolish and ignorant soul:
What pleaseth God shall be done.
My Lord is a great Merchant, we are His retail-dealers.

1 Ninda chinda is an alliteration.
2 This is understood to be meant for neighbour's wife.

Our souls and bodies are all His capital; He it is who killeth and re-animateth.
The Guru reflects on the power of the deadly sins which lead men to destruction:â
The others 1 are five, I am but one; how shall I protect my house?
They ever assail and plunder me; to whom shall I complain?
Utter God's holy name, O my soul;
Before thee is Death's army fierce and numerous.
God erected a palace, 2 put doors to it, and the woman 3 sitteth within.
Deeming the world sweet, she ever sporteth, but these five men rob her.
When Death destroyeth the palace, her chamber is sacked, and she being alone is captured.
She is beaten by Death's mace, and his chains are riveted on her neck; the five men have taken flight.
The housewife wanteth gold and silver; friends want banquets.
Nanak, they who commit sin for these things shall go bound to Death's city.

Kinganath Jogi pressed Guru Nanak to become his disciple; the Guru replied that he had already learned the science of Jog. He composed the following hymn on the occasion:â

Make restraint of thine inmost heart thine earrings, thy body the patched coat;
Reduce thy five senses to subjection, O Jogi, and make a pure heart thy staff.
In this way shalt thou obtain the way of jog.
Make the fact that there is but one Word and none other thy devotion to tubers and roots.
If God could be obtained by merely shaving the head, we should make a god of the Ganges. 4 1 The deadly sins which rob the body. 2 The body.
3 The soul. 4 Where pilgrims shave their heads.
It is the one Lord who saveth the three worlds; thou thinkest not of Him, O fool.
If thou apply thy mind to words through hypocrisy, thy doubts shall never leave thee.
If thou turn thy thoughts to the feet of the one God, why pursue avarice and greed?
If thou repeat the Name of the Bright One, thy soul shall be absorbed in Him.
O Jogi, why utterest thou so much deceit?
Thy body is mad, 1 thy mind is silly, thou passest thy life talking of thy property.
Nanak representeth, it is after the naked body is burnt the soul regretteth lost opportunities.

Man's precious life should not be wasted, but should be devoted to God's service and not to the acquisition of wealth:â
Man loseth his nights in sleeping and his days in eating:
His human life, valuable as a diamond, he parteth with for a kauri.
Thou knowest not God's name; O fool, thou shalt here after regret.
Thou buriest endless wealth in the earth, yet thy desire for it departeth not. 2
They who departed desiring endless wealth lost the Endless One.
If all were to obtain according to their desires, they would be happy.
Whatever all may desire, a man's fate is decided by his acts.

Nanak, He who fashioned creation taketh care of it.
It is not known on whom God's order will confer greatness.
The fervour of the Guru's devotion:-
Were I to become a fawn, live in the forest, and gather and eat tubers and roots,
I should ever and ever be a sacrifice to my Lord, who is obtained through the favour of the Guru.
I am a retail-dealer of Thine, O God; 1 Because smeared with ashes.
2 Also translatedâ Thou desirest not the Endless One.
Thy Name is my stock-in-trade and my merchandise.
Were I to become a koil and live in a mango-tree, I should still tranquilly meditate on the Word.
Through my love my Lord, whose form appeareth un equalled, would naturally meet me.
Were I to become a fish and dwell in the water, I should still remember Him who watcheth over all animals.
My Spouse dwelleth on this side and on that; I shall stretch forth mine arm to touch Him.
Were I to become a serpent and dwell in the ground, I should still abide in the Word and my fears would depart.
Nanak, they are ever the happy married wives whom God hath absorbed in His light.

GAURI ASHTAPADI

Without a religious guide man would run riot in evil and haste to perdition:â
The heart is an elephant, the body a forest,
The Guru the goad; when the mark of the true Word is made on the elephant,
He shall obtain honour in the King's court.
God cannot be known by cleverness.
Without chastening the mind how can God be appraised?
In the house is nectar which the thieves are taking away: 1
No one tried to restrain them.
If any one guard the nectar, God Himself will confer greatness on him.
Worldly wealth, comforts, and pleasures would never satisfy the Guru without devotion to God.
I may apply distilled aloe wood and sandal to my body,
I may wear silks and satins,
But without God's name how shall I obtain happiness?
What shall I wear? in what dress shall I show myself?
How shall I obtain happiness without the Lord of the world?
I may have rings in mine ears and a necklace of pearls on my neck, 1 The name of God is in the heart. The evil passions plunder it.
A red coverlet, flowers, and red powder; 1
But where should I search for happiness except with the Lord of the world?
A beautiful woman with expressive eyes
May make the sixteen decorations and render herself very lovely,
Yet without worshipping the Lord of the world she would ever be despised.

One may have in his house or palace a comfortable couch;
A flower-girl may scatter flowers on it day and night,
Yet without God's name its owner would be unhappy.
Excellent horses, elephants, lances, musical instruments,
Armies, mace-bearers, and attendants are worthless
And vain shows without the Lord of the world.
I may be called a Sidh, and I may summon wealth and supernatural power to me;
I may make for my head a crown, a regal hat, and an umbrella,
Yet how should I obtain real happiness without the Lord of the world?
I may be styled a lord, an emperor, or a king,
I may say ' Now then ' 2 to inferiors; all this would be false display.
Without the Guru's instruction my business could not be adjusted.
Egotism and selfishness are forgotten under the Guru's instruction.
Through the Guru's instruction it is known that God is in the heart.
Nanak supplicateth, seek Thy shelter, O God.
The Guru describes the condition of the holy and the means of salvation:â
He who serveth the one God knoweth not others:
He layeth aside the bitter things deceit and evil.
By love and truth shalt thou meet the Truest of the True.

1 For frontal marks and the parting of the hair.
2 Abe labe in Panjabi is a much more contemptuous expression than ' now then '.

If there be any such saint of God,
His filth shall be washed away, and he shall meet God by singing His praises.
Reversed are the lotuses of all men's hearts:
The fire of evil inclinations burneth away the world,
While those who meditate on the word of the Guru are saved.
The bumble-bee, the moth, the elephant, the fish,
And the deer 1 suffer the consequences of their acts and die.
Absorbed in worldly desires man knoweth not the Real Thing;
He thinketh of lust and love for woman.
Which with wrath ruin all sinners.
He who forgetteth the Name, loseth his honour and his senses.
The perverse being who alloweth his mind to covet another's house,
Hath a halter round his neck, and is entangled in diffi culties;
While the pious shall be delivered by singing God's praises.
As a widow, who giveth her body to a stranger,
And through lust or money falleth into another's power,
Is never satisfied without a lover;
So man readeth books and reciteth the Simritis;
He also readeth, heareth, and expoundeth the Veds and the Purans;
But without being dyed with God's essence his mind is very unstable.
As the chatrik loveth and thirsteth for the rain-drops,
As the fish is delighted with the water,
So Nanak is satisfied quaffing God's essence.

There was a hill king called Amar Singh who 1 The animals mentioned suffer for the gratification of their senses. The bee scents the lotus and is entangled; the moth looks on the lamp and is burnt; the elephant, to gratify his lust, rushes into a trap; the fish is hungry and takes the bait; and the deer is lured to his death by the hunter's bell.
was dethroned by his brother. On being expelled he went to Guru Nanak for advice. The following was given him:â

They who wear religious garbs are full of pride and know not God.
Few are they whose minds are reconciled to devotion under the Guru's instruction.
The True One is not obtained by the practice of egotism.
When pride departeth, the supreme dignity is obtained.
Kings under the influence of pride make many expedi tions:
They are ruined by pride and remain subject to trans migration.
He who meditateth on the Guru's word shall lose his pride;
He shall dismiss his wandering thoughts, and destroy his deadly sins.
He in whose heart is the truth shall easily arrive at God's court,
And, knowing God, shall obtain the supreme state.
The Guru dispelleth the doubts of those whose works are true;
And they shall obtain a fixed seat in the court of the Fearless.
What do they retain who die talking of their possessions?
He who meeteth a perfect Guru putteth an end to his contentions.â
What there is, is nothing in realityâ
The pious who are saturated with divine knowledge sing God's praises.
The fetters of pride cause man to wander in trans migration.
Nanak, it is the saint of God who obtaineth happiness.
Death impends over all, but cannot harm the holy:-
Even Brahma was subject to death from the beginning.
1 Literallyâ Brahma entered the house of death.
He found not the end of Vishnu's lotus in the nether regions; 1
He accepted not God's order, and was led astray in error.
Whatever is created Death destroyeth.
God hath preserved us by our meditating on the word of the Guru.
Maya deludeth all the gods and goddesses.
Death looseth not his hold on him who serveth not the Guru.
God is imperishable, invisible, and inscrutable.
Emperors, rulers, and kings shall not abide.
Having forgotten the Name they shall undergo death's torture.
The Name is my support; I shall abide as Thou keepest me, O Lord.
Chiefs and kings have no abiding-place.
Bankers die after accumulating wealth and money.
0 God, grant me Thine ambrosial name as my wealth. Subjects, lords, headmen, sovereignsâ

None is found permanent in this world.
Irresistible death striketh false mortals on the head.
One alone, the Truest of the true, is immovable.
All those whom He created He will again destroy. 2

Man obtaineth honour when he knoweth God under the Guru's instruction.
Qazis, shaikhs, and faqirs in religious garbs
Call themselves great, but through pride their bodies are in pain.
Death will not release them without receiving the true Guru's consolation.

1 According to many Hindus Vishnu was the creator of the world. From Vishnu's navel there grew a lotus from which the god Brahma was produced. Brahma on attaining intelligence began to consider the source of his birth. It could not be from such an insignificant thing as a lotus. He rejected the idea and kicked the lotus at the same time, whereupon he descended into it and remained long wandering in its stem until he repented of his error. He then rose to the top where he sat enthroned as before.

2 Literally â draw within Himself. Creation is God's extension; destruction, His contraction.

The net of Death is over man's tongue and eyes;
It is over his ears when he listeneth to unchaste language.
He is robbed day and night without the Word.
Death cannot espy him in whose heart
God's true name dwelleth, and who singeth God's praisesâ
Nanak, the pious shall be absorbed in the Word.
A prayer to God for protection:â
As a herdsman guardeth and keepeth watch over his cattle,
So God day and night cherisheth and guardeth man and keepeth him in happiness.
O Thou compassionate to the poor, I seek Thy protection; look on me with favour.
Preserve me in this world and the next.
Wherever I look there art Thou contained; guard me, O Guardian.
Thou art the Giver, Thou art the Enjoyer, Thou art the support of the soul.
Man must supplement his prayers by good acts:â
Without meditating on divine knowledge man ascendeth or descendeth according to his acts.
Without praising the Lord of the world the darkness of ignorance shall not be dispelled.
We see that the world is perishing through covetousness and pride.
By serving the Guru, God and the true gate of salvation are attained.
What hath man brought into the world? What shall he take away when he is entangled in Death's noose?
Like a well-bucket firmly attached to a rope, he is now in heaven, now in hell.
A spiritual guide is necessary for salvation:-
His account is settled who through the Guru's favour knoweth God.
God, called the Pure One, who is in every heart, is my Lord.
Man shall not be emancipated without the Guru's instruction; see and ponder upon this.
Even though man performed hundreds of thousands of ceremonies, all would still be darkness without the Guru.
What shall we say to those who are blind and devoid of wisdom?
Without the Guru the way cannot be seen; how shall we reach the goal?
Man calleth the counterfeit genuine; but he knoweth not what the genuine is.

A blind man he calleth an assayer; wonderful is this age.
Man saith, the sleeper is awake, and he who is awake sleepeth;
He saith, they who are alive are dead, and he weepeth not for those who are really dead;
He saith, that he who is coming hath gone, and that he who hath gone is coming;
He calleth another's property his own, and with his own he is not satisfied;
He calleth what is sweet bitter, and what is bitter sweet;
He slandereth those who love Godâ such is what I have seen in this age.
Man serveth a handmaiden, 1 but the Master he seeth not.
He churneth tank water, and no butter is produced.
He who can explain this is the Guru for me.
Nanak, he who knoweth himself is unequalled and un rivalled.

GAURI CHHANT

The longing of the pious for God is compared to the longing of the young bride for her spouse:â
Painful is the night for the young bride; without her
Beloved she sleepeth not.
She pineth away through grief at His absence:
The woman pineth away through grief at His absence, saying ' How shall I look upon Him? ' 1 Mammon.
Ornaments, dainty food, sensuous enjoyments are all vain and of no account for her.
Intoxicated with the wine of youth and melting with pride milk cometh not to her breast.
Nanak, she meeteth her Spouse when He causeth her to meet Him; without Him no sleep cometh to her.
The bride is unhonoured without her beloved Lord.
How shall she be happy without embracing Him?
Without a spouse there is no domestic happiness; ask thy friends and companions.
Without the Name there is no love or affection; but, with the True One, woman abideth in happiness.
They in whose hearts there is truth and contentment, meet the Friend; under the Guru's instruction the Bride groom is recognized.
Nanak, the woman who abandoneth not the Name shall be easily absorbed in God through it.
Come, friends and companions, let us enjoy our Beloved.
I will ask my Guru and write His words of love.
The Guru hath communicated to me the true Word; the perverse shall regret they have not received it.
When I recognized the True One, my roaming mind became fixed.
The wisdom of the True One is ever new, so is the love of His Word.
Nanak, true peace of mind is obtained from His look of favour; meet Him, my friends and companions.
My desires have been fulfilled; the Friend hath come home to me.
A song of rejoicing was sung at the union of Husband and wife.

His praises and a song of joy were sung; the bride is happy in His love and her heart is in raptures.

Her friends are also happy, her enemies unhappy; true profit is obtained by repeating the name of the True One.

With clasped hands the woman prayeth that she may night and day be steeped in God's love.

Nanak, the Beloved and His spouse unite in dalliance; my desires have been fulfilled.

RAG ASA The Creator bestows good gifts:â

If a beggar at God's gate cry aloud, God heareth him in His palace.

God may give him consolation or repulse him; He alone bestoweth greatness.

God knoweth man's virtues and inquireth not his caste; in the next world there is no caste.

God acteth Himself and causeth to act.

Thou, O Creator, payest heed to man's complaints.

Since it is Thou alone who actest,

Why should we be dependent on any but Thee? What is the world to us?

Thou Thyself didst create; Thou Thyself dost bestow;

Thou forbiddest evil inclinations.

If Thou by the Guru's favour dwell in the heart,

Suffering and the darkness of ignorance shall depart therefrom.

Thou givest truth to those whom Thou lovest;

Thou givest truth to none besides.

If Thou give truth to any one, saith Nanak, there shall be no inquiry made of him hereafter.

The following was addressed to a votary of Krishan, who was worshipping his god with music and dancing:â

Make understanding thy fife, the love of God thy drum; By these joy and earnest desire are ever produced in the heart.

This is devotion; this is austerityâ

In this wise dance beating time with thy feet.

Deem knowing how to praise God as beating time: Other dances are sensuous pleasures. Play truth and contentment as thy pair of cymbals; Make the perpetual vision of God the bells for thy feet; Make love for none but God thy measures and songsâ In this wise dance beating time with thy feet.

Ever make the fear of God in thy heart and soul, Whether sitting or standing, thy gyrations. Make the knowledge that thy body is ashes thy recum bent posture 1 â

In this wise dance beating time with thy feet.

Thine audience shall be the disciples who love instruction,

Who hear the true Name from the Guru's lips,

And repeat it again and againâ

Nanak, in this wise dance beating time with thy feet.

The following was intended to show God's supe riority to His creatures Ram and Krishan, who are now adored as gods by the Hindus:â

God having created the atmosphere supported the whole earth and set bounds to water and fire.

The fatuous Rawan 2 had his ten heads cut off; what greatness was obtained by slaying him?

What praise of Thine, O God, shall be uttered?

Thou pervadest everything; Thou lovest all Thy creatures.

Having created living beings, Thou holdest their ways in Thy hand. What greatness was obtained by putting a nose-ring on the black serpent of the Jamna? 3

Whose husband art Thou? Who is Thy wife? Thou pervadest all things.

Brahma, the granter of favours, with his progeny went to ascertain God's greatness, But could not find His limits; what greatness was obtained by slaying Kans? 4

When the sea of milk was churned and its gems brought 1 A part of an Oriental dance.

2 Rawan, king of Ceylon, abducted Sita, Ram's wife, and was killed by him.

3 This was one of the feats of Krishan, who, in some ways, resembles the Hercules of Greece.

4 Kans, king of Mathura, is called Krishan's maternal uncle. It was foretold that the offspring of Krishan's mother, Devaki, should kill Kans, so he employed all his efforts to destroy her children. Krishan, however, was not destroyed, but succeeded in fulfilling the terms of the prophecy.

SIKH. I X forth, the demigods and demons each claimed the merit thereof.

What greatness was obtained by the distribution of the gems to each? Saith Nanak, if men try to conceal Thy greatness, O God how can it be concealed?

The Guru in his anxiety to meet God compares himself to a bride who rejoices in her approaching marriage:â

When the Bridegroom kindly came to my house,

My female companions met me and arranged for the marriage.

My heart was glad as I gazed upon the play; the Bride groom came to wed me.

Sing, sing, O ladies, the bridal song with wisdom and reflection.

The Life of the world hath come to my house as my Bridegroom.

My marriage having been brought about through my Guru, when I met him I recognized my Spouse

Whose Word filleth the three worlds; when my pride departed my heart was glad.

God arrangeth His own affairs; they are not arranged by others:

They consist in bestowing truth, contentment, mercy, and faithâ a few pious persons know this.

Saith Nanak, God alone is the Spouse of all.

She on whom He looketh with favour is the happy wife.

In the opinion of the Guru human life is worthless without holiness:â

A cow without milk, a bird without wings, and tillage without water are of no avail.

What is an emperor to whom no obeisance is made? Dark is the chamber in which Thy name, O God, is not.

Why shouldest Thou forget me when I am in great affliction?

When affliction befalleth me, forget me not.

Man's eyes grow blind, his tongue loseth its taste, his ears hear not;

He can only move by being supported—these are the fruits of non-service.

Make the Word the garden tree, plant it in good soil,1 and irrigate with love.

The one Name is the fruit of all such trees; how shall men obtain it without good works?

All creatures are Thine, O Lord; none obtaineth his reward without devotion to Thee.

Woe and weal are distributed according to Thy will; without Thy name real life remaineth not.

How may man live except by dying by the Guru's teaching? If one live otherwise, he shall not know the way.

Saith Nanak, Thou, O Lord, restorest life; Thou pre-servest man as Thou pleasest.

The following was addressed by way of admoni tion to a Brahman:—

Making my body the loin-cloth, my heart the Brahman,

Divine knowledge my sacrificial thread, meditation my grass 2 and leaves,

I shall beg for God's name and praises instead of the alms of the Brahmans;

And by the favour of the Guru be absorbed in God.

0 Brahman, so meditate on God

That His name may become thy purification, His name thy learning, and His name thy wisdom and good acts.

The sacrificial thread is only on thy body as long as thou hast life.

Make the remembrance of the Name thy loin-cloth and frontal mark,

And it shall abide with thee in this world and the next.

Search for nothing but the true Name;

Make God's love thy worship, the burning of the love of wealth thine incense.

Look only on the one God, search for none other.

1 The heart.
2 The kusha (Poa cynosuroides used by the Brahmans in worship.

He who repeateth God's name with his mouth and pon-dereth on it,

Beholdeth Him at the tenth door of the firmament. 1

His doubt and fear who liveth upon the love of God flee away.

If the sentry be on the alert, thieves will not break in.

Deem the knowledge of the one God thy frontal mark,

And the consciousness that God is within thee thy dis crimination. 2

God cannot be overcome by other ceremonial acts.

He who merely readeth religious books hath not found His worth.

His secret is not known from the eighteen Purans or the four Veds.

Nanak, the true Guru hath shown me God.

The following was addressed to a pandit who inquired how salvation could be obtained:—

The body like a frail earthen vessel is miserable; in birth and death it suffereth further pain.

How shall the dangerous ocean of this world be crossed? It cannot without the divine Guru.

There is none but Thee, O my Beloved; there is none but Thee, O God.

In all colours and forms art Thou; Thou pardonest him on whom Thou lookest with favour. â

My mother-in-law 3 is perverse; she will neither let me dwell at home, nor meet my Beloved.

Since I have worshipped the feet of my companions and friends, 4 my Beloved through the kindness of the Guru hath looked on me with favour.

Reflecting on myself and chastening my heart I see that there is no friend like Thee.
As Thou keepest me so I live; I endure woe and weal as Thou bestowest them.

1 In the brain in a state of ecstasy.
2 In the matter of eating, drinking, wearing, living, and worshipping.
3 Mammon. 4 The saints.

I have dispelled hopes and desires, and I no more long for mammon.

The holy man who hath found shelter in the society of the saints, obtaineth the fourth state. 1

He in whose heart the invisible and inscrutable God dwelleth, possesseth all divine knowledge, meditation, devotion, and penance.

Nanak, he whose heart is dyed with God's name shall readily obtain devotion under the Guru's instruction.

The following is supposed to have been composed by the Guru on the death of his father:â

Abandon love of family and love of everything.
Abandon worldly love; it is all sinful.
Abandon worldly love and superstition, O my friends.
Repeat the true Name with your tongues and your hearts.
His children weep not and his mother afflicteth not herself for him 2
Who possesseth the nine treasures of the true Name.
The world is ruined by such love as the worldly feel;
Only some rare pious man may be saved.
Through such love as that one is born again
He who feeleth such love goeth to the city of Death.
Practise acceptance of the Guru's instruction as thy devotion and penance.
He who breaketh not with worldly love shall not be accepted.

If God look on man with favour such love shall depart, O Nanak, and he shall be absorbed in God.

When Guru Nanak went to Gorakhmataâ the present Nanakmataâ he found religious men of 1 Ancient Indian writers enumerate four states of lifeâ-jdgrat, waking; swapan, dreaming; sukhnpati, deep sleepâ evcisav ns Kaotvw xt8' ovap xrjsev opa. (Plato, Apology); and uriya, mental absorption in God, in which state man is said to have obtained salva tion during life. He then forgets the troubles of the world and is immersed in happiness.

2 The gyanis also translateâ His heart crieth not or longeth for mammon.

several sects assembled there. The following was composed after a discussion with them:â

He who meditateth on knowledge conferreth favour on others;
When he correcteth his evil passions he dwelleth at a place of pilgrimage;

The tinkling bells of ecstasy resound for him when he turneth his heart to God.
What can Death do to me in the next world?
When man hath abandoned desires he is a Sanyasi.
If a Jogi be continent, he enjoyeth his body. 1
He who in his heart meditateth mercy, is a Digambar: 2
He tortureth himself, but not others.
Thou, O Lord, art one, but many are Thy manifestations.
Nanak knoweth not Thy wonderful play.

As a wife fears that she is forgotten by her spouse, so the holy man fears that he is neglected by God:-
I am not possessed of one virtue to cleanse my polluted body.
My Lord awaketh; I sleep the livelong night.
How shall I thus become dear to my Spouse?
My Lord awaketh; I sleep the livelong night.
Even though I approach His couch smitten with desire, know not if I shall then please Him or please Him not.
How know I what shall occur, O mother?
Without beholding God I cannot abide.
I have not tasted love; my thirst is not quenched;
My youth hath fled, and I mourn for what is lost.
Even now I awake smitten with desire:
I have become sad, and remain without hope.
If woman adorn herself with the rejection of pride,
Her Spouse will enjoy her on the couch.
Then, Nanak, shall she please her Spouse's heart;
She will abandon pride and be absorbed in Him.

1 The ecstasy he feels from the practice of Jog is sufficient for him.
2 Who wanders naked.

It is necessary to fear as well as love God so as to keep His commandments:â In this world woman is very silly. I know not the worth of my Spouse; He is one, there is none other.

If He cast a glance of favour on me, I shall meet Him. In the next world woman shall know the truth, And easily recognize her Beloved. If she obtain such wisdom by the Guru's favour, She shall please her Spouse's heart. Saith Nanak, if she adorn herself with fear and love, Her Spouse will ever enjoy her on the couch.

When man has parted with all worldly love, he has prepared himself for deliverance:â No one hath a son, no one hath a mother. 1 Through deceitful worldly love man wandereth in doubt.

0 my Lord, I am Thy creation; 1 utter Thy name when Thou givest it me.

Man may wail aloud for his many transgressions, But he shall only be pardoned if it be God's will. By the Guru's favour evil inclinations depart-Wherever I gaze there is only one Godâ Saith Nanak, if man attain such wisdom, The True One will absorb that true one in Himself.

The following was addressed to a worldly-minded Raja:â

Thou mayest have lakhs of armies, lakhs of musical instruments and lances; lakhs of men may rise to do thee homage;

Thy dominion may extend over lakhs of miles; lakhs men may rise to do thee honour-All that would be fruitless, wert thou not credited in God's account.

Without God's name the world is only trouble.

If the fool be never so much admonished, he remaineth the blindest of the blind.

1 Everything is illusion.

Thou mayest earn lakhs of rupees; thou mayest amass and spend lakhs; lakhs may come and lakhs may go;

But, if thy soul obtain not credit in God's account, where else shall it obtain it?

Lakhs of Shastars may be explained to thee; lakhs of pandits may read the Purans for theeâ

All would be unacceptable didst thou not obtain credit in God's account.

From the true Nameâ the kind Creator's nameâ honour is obtained.

If it dwell day and night in the heart, O Nanak, man shall be delivered by God's favouring glance.

The temptations to which man is exposed by his senses:â

The five evil passions dwell concealed within the heart;

Wherefore it remaineth not fixed, but wandereth like a pilgrim.

My mind remaineth not fixed on the Merciful One:

Avaricious, deceitful, sinful, and hypocritical, it is excesively attached to worldly love.

When I meet my Beloved I will adorn myself,

And put on necklaces of flowers.

I have five companions and one husband. 1

It is ordained from the beginning that the soul depart.

The five senses shall weep in unison,

Saith Nanak, when the soul is arrested to give its account.

ASA ASHTAPADI

Guru Nanak expatiates on the advantage of the Guru's instruction and the repetition of God's name:â

Man may perform all devotion, all penance, and resort to every expedient; , Yet he is as if he wandered in a wilderness, and could not find the way.

Without knowing God, no one is acceptable.

1 This is the relation of the soul to the five senses or organs of perception.

Without the Name man is despised. 1

The Lord is permanent; the world cometh and goeth.

Mortals shall be emancipated by being the holy man's slaves.

The world is bound by worldly love and many desires;

Yet some reject it under the Guru's instruction.

The lotuses of the hearts of those who have the Name within them bloom,

And they fear not Death,

The world which loveth women is overcome by them.

Men attached to sons and wives forget God's name.

They waste in vain their human lives and lose their game.
To serve the true Guru is the best thing.
They who utter words of pride in public,
Never apply the unction of salvation to their hearts
They who burn worldly love under the Guru's instruction,
And ever meditate on the pure Name in their hearts,
Hold and restrain their wandering minds.
By God's favour the Guru associateth such persons with the congregation of the Sikhs.
Without a guru man forgetteth God and suffereth trans migration.
Him whom God regardeth favourably He blendeth with Himself.
If I speak of the beautiful One, I cannot describe Him.
If I discourse of the Ineffable, I cannot find His worth.
All pain and pleasure depend on Thy will, O God.
All pain shall be erased by the True Name,
And men shall hear instruments played without hands and anklets without feet.
If man understand the Word, he shall behold the True One.
When the True One is in the heart, all happiness is there also.
The Preserver preserveth men by His favouring glance.
He who effaceth himself knoweth the three worlds.
He who understandeth the Word, shall be absorbed in the True One.
1 Literallyâ has ashes thrown on his head.
Nanak, the Creator will congratulate him Who without respite meditateth on the Word.
How deliverance may be obtained:â
He who burneth his hopes and desires by the Word,
Who uttereth and causeth others to utter God's name,
Shall by means of the Guru find the way to God's own abode.
His body shall become gold by God's incomparable light,
And he shall behold God's form in the whole three worlds.
I possess God's true name as wealth which shall never fail.
God pervadeth the five elements, the three worlds, the nine regions, and the four quarters of the universe.
The Almighty supporteth the earth and the heavens.
The wandering mind He bringeth back.
Whoever is a fool seeth not with his eyes;
His language giveth not pleasure, and he understandeth not what is told him.
Intoxicated with evil passions, he quarrelleth with the world;
While on the other hand a man becometh good by association with the good,
Pursueth virtue and purifieth himself from vice.
Without serving the Guru peace is not obtained.
The Name is diamonds, jewels, and rubies;
It is the pearl of the heart, God's own wealth.
Nanak, God assayeth man, and maketh him happy with a glance.
The following was addressed to a hypocritic;

JÂ gi:-
Men sing songs while meditating evil;
They intone measures and style themselves knowing.
Without the Name the heart is filthy and meditateth evil.
Whither goest thou? O man, remain at home.
The pious are satiated with God's name, and by searching easily find Him.
The bodily sins of lust, wrath, and worldly love are in the mind:
So are painful greed, avarice, and pride. How can the mind be satisfied without God's name? They who lave their hearts know the True One. The holy man knoweth the condition of his heart.

The mind obtains composure by devotion:â
The apostate's mind is a furious elephant
Which wandereth distracted in the forest of worldly love.
Impelled by Death it rusheth here and there,
While the pious search and find God in their hearts.
Without the Guru's word the mind is not at rest.
Remember God's very pure name and relinquish bitter pride.
Say how shall this stupid mind be happy:
Without understanding, it shall suffer the torture of Death.
God will cause man to meet the true Guru, and will pardon him.
The True One will thrust aside the tortures of Death.
Wealth is perishable; devotion to God an abiding gain:-
When the body perisheth, whose shall be its wealth?
Without the Guru how shall God's name be obtained?
God's name is wealth which accompanieth and assisteth us.
Day and night he is pure who fixeth his attention on God.
What have we but God's name?
Treating pleasure and pain as the same I forsake not the Name: God will pardon and blend me with Himself.
The fool loveth gold and woman;
Attached to mammon he forgetteth the Name.
Him whom Thou, O God, pardonest Thou causest to repeat Thy name.
Death's myrmidons cannot overtake him who singeth Thy praises.
O Hari, who art God, the great Giver,
Mercifully preserve us as Thou pleasest.
Under the Guru's instruction God is pleasing to my mind;
Disease is removed and pain averted.
There is no other medicine, charm, or spell. By remembering God, sin is destroyed. As I behold creation I am amazed and astonished God is contained in the hearts of demigods and men. God who filleth every place, I hold in my heart. There is none equal to Thee, O Lord. He who loveth worship hath God's name in his mouth. In the company of such saints and worshippers Man breaketh his shackles and meditateth on God. Pious men are emancipated by a knowledge of God through the Guru.

Death's myrmidons cannot inflict pain on him Who awaketh in the love of God's name. God to whom His saints are dear, abideth with them. Nanak, salvation is obtained by bearing love to God.

The following on the disregard of worldly things was addressed to a selfish Brahman:â

He who serveth the Guru knoweth the Lord;
His pain is erased who recognizeth the True Word.
Repeat God's name, my friends and companions.
On serving the true Guru ye shall behold God with your eyes.
Entanglements are mother, father, and the whole world;
Entanglements are sons, daughters, and women;
Entanglements are religious ceremonies performed through ostentation;
Entanglements are sons, wives, and worldly love in the mind;
An entanglement is the tillage done by the tillerâ
He suffereth for his selfishness when the King demandeth revenueâ
An entanglement is traffic without meditating on God.
Man is never satisfied; worldly love is everywhere diffused. 1
An entanglement is the perishable wealth which merchants amass.
1 Also translatedâ Man is not satisfied with the extension of his wealth.
Without devotion to God man findeth no place.
Entanglements are Veds, religious discussions, and pride.
By the entanglements of worldly love and sin man perishethâ
Nanak taketh shelter in God's nameâ
He whom the true Guru preserveth is freed from his entanglements.

The following was addressed to a mixed assembly of professedly religious men:â

I have searched in every direction, but found no friend.
If it please Thee, O Lord, Thou art mine and I am Thine.
I have no other gate than Thine; whom shall I salute?
I possess Thee alone, O Lord; Thy true name is in my mouth.
The Sidhs strive for supernatural power; Pirs also desire wealth and supernatural power.
May I not forget the one Name under the true Guru's instruction!
Why do the Jogis, the Bhogis, 1 and the Kaprias wander in foreign lands?
They heed not the Guru's instruction or the Real Thing that is within them.
Pandits, preceptors, and astrologers ever read the Purans,
But know not the Thing within themâ God who is con cealed within the heart.
Some anchorets perform austerities in forests, others ever dwell at places of pilgrimages.
Those benighted people know not themselves; why have they become ascetics?
Some who are called Jatis try to restrain their seed:
Without the word of the Guru they shall not be saved, but shall wander in transmigration.
Different persons are family men, worshippers, penitents; but it is only they who are attached to the Guru's instruc tions,
Who hold fast the Name, charity, and ablutions, and who awake in God's service.

1 A sect of Indian Sybarites.

Through the Guru the gate of Thy house, O Lord, is known; when men go there they recognize it.

Saith Nanak, may I not forget Thy name, and may my heart be reconciled with the True One!

Precepts for salvation:â

By restraining his mental desires man shall assuredly cross the terrible ocean.

Thou, O Lord, wast in the beginning and in the primal age; Thou art the Merciful; I have entered Thine asylum.

Thou art the Giver; we are Thy beggars; O God, grant us a sight of Thee.

0 man, meditate on the Name under the Guru's instruc tion, and thou shalt be happy in the temple of thy heart.

Renounce falsehood and avarice; and then shalt thou recognize the True One.

Be absorbed in the Guru's instruction, and thou shalt know what is best for thee.

This mind is a grasping tyrant enamoured of greed:

Under the Guru's instruction greed is removed, and man arriveth at an understanding with God.

If man sow a barren field, how shall he obtain profit?

The obstinate man is not pleased with the truth; he is buried in falsehood.

Renounce avarice, ye blind; it bringeth great unhappi-ness.

If the true Lord dwell in the heart, the poison of pride shall be removed.

Forsake the evil way of mammon, my brethren, or ye shall be plundered.

Day and night praise the Name under the protection of the true Guru.

The mind of the perverse is a stone or a rock; accursed and vain is his life.

However much a stone be put into the water, it is dry at the core.

God's name is wealth, the true Guru hath given it.

Nanak, he who forgetteth not God's name drinketh distilled nectar.

The advantage of domestic devotion:â

Why should I go searching in the wood? My heart is a verdant forest.

The true Word hath come quickly to my heart and abideth there.

Wherever I look there is God; no one else is seen.

Whosoever doeth the Guru's work shall find God's court.

The True One blendeth with Himself him who is pleasing to His mind;

He blendeth with Himself him who ever walketh accord ing to His will.

If the true Lord dwell in the heart, it becometh fixed.

God then granteth greatness in which naught is wanting.

How shall one reach God's court by occasional service?

He who embarketh in a boat of stone shall be drowned with his cargo. 1

An inculcation of devotion regardless of worldly opinion:â

He whose mind is imbued with God's name discourseth of the True One.

What care I for men if I please Thee?

As long as there are life and soul, meditate on the True One.

The profit of singing God's praises is that man obtaineth happiness.

True is Thy work; grant it me, Thou Merciful One.

I live by praising Thee; Thou art my prop and my support.

I am the servant and the porter at Thy gate; Thou knowest my pain.

I am astounded at Thy service which hath removed my pain.

Holy men through Thy name shall reach Thy court and Thy presence. 2 1 Also translatedâ in the ocean.

2 Also translatedâ They who know the Name under the Guru's instruction shall reach God's court,

That time is auspicious when man recognizeth the true Word.

Practise truth, contentment, and love; and then the worship of God's name shall be thy viaticum.

Banish sin from thy mind, and the True One will bestow truth:

The True One bestoweth true love on the true.

What pleaseth Thee, O God, is the real justice.

True are the gifts which the true and merciful One granteth.

Serve Him day and night whose Name is priceless.

Thou, O God, art the most high; I who am Thy servant am low.

Saith Nanak, O True One, look on me with favour that I who am separated from Thee may meet Thee.

ASA CHHANT

It is said that Bhai Budha and Mula, a Sikh, went to the Guru and asked him what afforded the highest gratification. His reply was the following:â

O woman in the prime of youth, my Beloved is playful.

When a wife entertaineth great love for her Spouse, He mercifully taketh delight in her and enjoyeth her.

The wife shall meet her Spouse if the Lord God Himself show her favour.

Her bed is pleasant in the company of her Beloved; her seven tanks 1 are filled with nectar.

Show me compassion and kindness, O Compassionate One, that I may obtain the true Word and sing Thy praises.

Nanak, the young woman, having seen God her Spouse, is delighted and her heart is enraptured.

O young woman, beautiful without art, pray only for the love of the one God.

God is pleasing to my soul and body, and I am charmed with His companionship.

She who is dyed with God's love and prayeth to Him, shall abide in happiness through His name.

1 The five organs of perception, with intellect and understanding.

When thou embracest virtue thou shall know God; virtue shall abide with thee and vice be put to flight.

Without Thee I cannot abide for a moment; I derive no satisfaction from merely conversing of Thee.

Nanak, she whose tongue and heart are moistened with God's essence, calleth for her Beloved.

O my friends and companions, my beloved is a merchant.

I have purchased from him God's name whose sweetness and value are infinite.

If woman's house be pleasing to the inestimable, true, and beloved God, she shall be happy.

Other women enjoy dalliance with God; I cry aloud standing at His door.

Thou, Cause of causes, Omnipotent, Harbinger of pros perity, arranges! man's affairs.

Nanak, she on whom God looketh with favour is a happy wife; she treasureth up the Word in her heart.

In my house is a true song of rejoicing; God my lover hath visited me.

Imbued with love He enjoyed me; I have exchanged hearts with Him.

I gave God my heart and took Him as my Spouse; He enjoyeth me as He pleaseth.

She who offereth her soul and body to the Beloved is supremely happy through the Word, and obtaineth the ambrosial fruit in her own home.

It is not obtained by intellect, or study, or by great cleverness; what the heart desireth is obtained by love.

Nanak, God is my Beloved; I belong to none besides. 1

As the deer is snared, the bumble-bee caught by the lotus, and the fish falleth into the net, so man's soul becomes the prey of Death.

Hear, O black deer, 2 why art thou enamoured of the garden? 3

The fruit of sin is sweet, but only for four days; it then groweth bitter.

1 Also translatedâ I conceal not the fact.
2 Man. 3 The world.

SIKH. I Y

The fruit for which thou greatly cravest, shall become very bitter without the Name.

That fruit is as a wave of the ocean, or as a flash of lightning. 1

There is no protector but God; yet He hath been for gotten by thee.

Verily, saith Nanak, think of it, thou shalt die, O black deer.

0 bumble-bee, 2 thou wanderest among the flowers, and very great shall be thy suffering, when the lotus closeth on thee.

1 have inquired of my Guru regarding the true knowledge of God.

I have inquired of the true Guru regarding the knowledge of God; O bumble-bee, thou art enamoured of the flowers.

When the sun riseth, 3 the body falleth, and the soul shall be boiled in hot oil.

0 demon, without the Word thou shalt be bound and punished on the road of death.

Verily, saith Nanak, think of it, thou shalt die, O black bee.

My soul from a strange land, 4 why fallest thou into entanglements?

When the true Lord dwelleth in thee, why shouldst thou be entangled in Death's net?

When the fisherman casteth his net, the fish leaveth the water with tears in its eyes.

The love of mammon is dear to the world; all doubts on the subject shall at last be set aside. 5

Serve God heartily, and dispel thy mental anxieties.

Verily, saith Nanak, think of it, O my soul from a strange land,

Rivers which separate in their course can only meet again by chance.

In every age what is sweet is full of poison; some rare holy man knoweth this.

1 That is, such fruit is very transitory.
2 The soul in another aspect. 3 When death comes.
4 Which has migrated from another body.

5 Also translated—But at last it shall be delivered from its error.

Some rare person who thinketh of the true Guru knoweth divine knowledge and recognizeth God.

Without God's name the fools and the heedless wander in superstition and are ruined.

They whose hearts contain not God's true name and service, at last groan and weep.

Verily, saith Nanak, they who have been long separated meet by the True Word.

RAG GUJARI

Guru Nanak orders man to repeat God's name and engage not in idol worship:—

If the heart be made the scraper, 1 the Name the sandal,

And good acts be mixed with it as kungu, that shall be the real worship of God in the heart.

Worship God by meditating on His name, for without the Name there is no worship.

If any one were to wash his heart as the surface of the idol is washed,

His impurity should be removed, his soul should become pure, and he should depart to deliverance.

Even beasts have their merits; for the oil-cake they eat they give milk, but the Brahmans make no return for the offerings made them.

Without the Name accursed is man's life and the acts he performeth.

God is near, think Him not distant; He ever careth for and remembereth us.

Eat what He giveth, said Nanak verily.

The Guru's God is superior to the demigods of the Hindus:—

Brahma sprang from the lotus of Vishnu's navel, and having attuned his throat began to recite the Veds;

Yet he could not see God's limits, and remained in the darkness of transmigration.

Why should I forget the Beloved who is the support of my soul, 1 Ursa. A stone on which sandal for worship is scraped. Y 2

Whom the perfect worship, whom munis serve, on whom gurus meditate,

Whose lamps are the sun and moon, and whose one light pervadeth the three worlds?

The pious have light day and night, but for the perverse there is only sable darkness.

The Sidh sitteth in meditative posture and ever argueth, but can he see God even with both his eyes?

They in whose hearts there is light are awakened by the sound of the Word; the true Guru decideth their arguments.

O Lord of demigods and men, infinite, unborn, Thy true palace is unrivalled.

Saith Nanak, O Life of the world, grant me peace and save me by Thy favouring glance.

GUJARI ASHTAPADI

The Guru's heart is ever filled with devotion:— I ask Thee, O God, for nothing at any time I but the love of Thy pure name; grant it to me, O Bright One.

The chatrik Nanak prayeth for the nectareous water of Thy name; mercifully grant him to sing Thy praises.

There is no happiness without true devotion:—

O Sire, how many people wear religious garbs to beg and fill their bellies!

O mortal, there is no happiness without God's service; without the Guru pride departeth not.

O Sire, what shall I ask? Nothing appeareth per manent; in this world are the ebb and flow of life.

Saith Nanak, grant me the Name as my wealth, that I may wear it as a necklace on my heart.

The Guru only claims to be a religious instructor from the ranks of the people:â 0 Sire, I am not high, or low, or middling; I am of God's people, and I seek His protection.

1 Ab tab. Also translatedâ I only look for Thy Pure name, not the worthless things of this world.

It is only they who are dyed with the Name who are free from worldly love and forget mourning, separation, and disease.

My brethren, by the favour of the Guru God's service is obtained.

He in whose heart is the Word of the true Guru, ob-taineth the Pure God, heedeth not Death and oweth him nothing.

The following instruction was addressed to Pandit Ram Chand at Banaras:â

The saints worship God with love; they thirst for the truth, and hear it with excessive love.

They who cry aloud in trouble obtain rest by prayer and heartily loving God.

O man, repeat God's name and seek His protection.

Repeat God's name and do good works; thus shalt thou cross over the ocean of the world.

O mortal man, to repeat God's name under the Guru's instruction is a happy thought.

By mentally repeating God's name one's mind obtaineth a treasure of real divine knowledge and peace.

In this world man's fickle mind pursueth wealth and becometh intoxicated with worldly love;

But, on being imbued with the Guru's word and teach ing, God's name and service become firmly implanted in the heart.

Doubts which ruin the world by the disease of trans migration, cease not by wandering to places of pilgrimage.

The place of God is the abode of unmixed happiness; he who is truly wise repeateth God's name as his penance.

Every one is saturated with worldly love, and therefore endureth the great pain of birth and death.

Man shall be saved by hastening to the asylum of the true Guru and repeating God's name in his heart.

Man's mind becometh stable, and he practiseth divine meditation under the Guru's instruction.

Pure is the heart which containeth truth and the excellent jewel of divine knowledge.

O man, by fear, love, and service, and by fixing thine attention on God's feet shalt thou cross the terrible ocean.

O God, put into my heart Thy name which is the purest of the pure; my body is in Thy sanctuary.

Extricate me, O God, from the waves of avarice and covetousness, and put Thy name as capital into my heart.

Chasten my mind. Thou spotless One, saith Nanak, I seek Thy protection.

BIHAGRE KI WAR

Reflections on the Hindu idol-worshippers:â

The Hindus have forgotten God, and are going the wrong way.

They worship according to the instruction of Narad. 1

They are blind and dumb, the blindest of the blind.

The ignorant fools take stones and worship them.

0 Hindus, how shall the stone which itself sinketh carry you across?

RAG WADHANS

The Guru enjoyed a vision of God in his dreams, and on awaking felt the pain of separation from Him:-

The peacocks are crying with joy; O sisters, the rainy season hath come.

The fervent woman, O God, is enamoured of Thy glances which bind her like a rope.

1 am a sacrifice to a sight of Thee, O God; to Thy name I am a sacrifice.

Since Thou art my Master I am proud; without Thee what pride should I have?

0 woman, break thy couch with its frame and thine arm with their bracelets, 2

Since, notwithstanding thy decorations, the Lord is enamoured of others.

Thou needest not a bracelet-dealer, or silver, or glass bracelets: 1 Narad's Panchardlrd inculcates idolatry.

2 Literallyâ break thy bracelets on thy couch and along with them its frame and thine arms.

Burn the arm which embraceth not the Bridegroom. All my companions went to enjoy the Bridegroom; whose door shall I, wretched that I am, approach?

0 Lord, I think myself well behaved and very clever, yet I have no charm to please Thee.

1 plaited my tresses with cosmetic and filled the parting of my hair with vermilion;

Yet when I went before Thee I was not accepted; I shall die of excessive grief.

I am weeping; the whole world weepeth; yea, even the birds of the forests weep for me.

One thing weepeth not for me, the separation which parted me from my Beloved.

He came to me in my dreams and again vanished, upon which I wept my fill.

I cannot go to Thee, O Beloved, or send any one to Thee.

Return, O happy sleep, perhaps I may again behold my Lord.

What shall I give him, saith Nanak, who telleth me of Thee, O God?

I will cut off my head and give it to him to sit on; without my head I will perform his service.

Why do I not die and give up my life since my Lord hath chosen another?

WADHANS CHHANT

The following was addressed to the Hindus, who set the highest religious value on ablutions:â

Why wash the body defiled by falsehood?

The practice of truth is the acceptable ablution.

When there is truth in the heart, then man becometh true and obtaineth the True One.

Understanding is not obtained without favourable destiny; man ruineth himself by vain babbling.

Wherever thou sittest speak civilly, and fix thine attention on God's word.

Why wash the body defiled by falsehood?

When Thou, 0 Lord, didst cause me to speak, I spoke.

Thine ambrosial name is pleasing to my soul.

Thy name is sweet to my soul; a load of sorrow hath fallen from off me.

When Thou gavest the order, happiness came and took its seat in my heart.

I pray to Thee, who didst create the world, for Thy favour,

When Thou didst cause me to speak, I spoke.

The Master granteth man his term of human life according to his past acts.

Fall not into a quarrel by calling any one evil.

Enter not into a quarrel with the Lord; thou shalt only ruin thyself.

Why be jealous and vex him with whom thou associatest?

Bear what God giveth thee; it is forbidden to remon strate; speak not nonsense regarding it.

The Master granteth man his term of life according to past acts.

God created all things and looketh on them with favour.

Nobody desireth what is bitter; every one desireth what is sweet.

Everybody may ask for what is sweet, but God will do as He pleaseth.

Alms-offerings and various good works are not equal to the Name.

Nanak, they who are the objects of God's favour from the beginning, have obtained His name.

God created all things and looketh on them with favour.

WADHANS ALAHANIAN

Some one inquired why God, who is ever present, is never visible. The Guru replied:â

The Lord who created the world and again drew it within Himself, is known by His omnipotence.

Search not for the True One afar off; He is in every heart, and is known by the Guru's instruction.

By the Guru's instruction know the True One who made creation; think Him not distant.

Meditate on the Name and thou shalt obtain happiness: without the Name man is not victorious in the arena of the world.

He who established the world knoweth its ways; what shall any one say?

He who established the world spread the net of mammon; accept that Lord with thy heart.

WADHANS KI WAR

Guru Nanak as usual pays no attention to cere monial:â

Perish the ritual by which I forgot my Beloved!

Nanak, that is the true love which preserveth me in honour with the Lord.

RAG SORATH

The Guru's reflections on death and future punishment:â
Death must come to all and all must part company;
Go and ask the wise if men shall meet hereafter or not.
They who have forgotten my God shall suffer great pain.
Certainly praise that true Being,
From whose glance of favour happiness ever resulteth.
Praise Him, for He is Great. He is, was, and ever shall be.
Thou alone, O God, art the Benefactor of all; no gifts are obtained from man.
What pleaseth Thee taketh place; what avail womanly tears?
How many kings have departed having exercised sove reignty over millions of fortresses on earth?
They whom the world could not contain have had rings put on their noses. 1
If man thought of future torments why should he devote himself to enjoyment? 2
Nanak, man shall have to wear on his neck as many chains as he hath sins.
If he possess virtues, which are as brothers and friends, his chains shall be cut off.
They who have no Guru shall not be accepted hereafter; they shall be beaten and expelled.

1 Have been made slaves.
2 Literallyâ Why should he eat sweet things?

The following is in opposition to all except deistic forms of religion:â
There appeareth no partner of Thine; then whom shall I praise but Thee?
Nanak, the slave of slaves representeth, God is known by the Guru's teaching.
The Guru's conception of God:â
The Unseen, Infinite, Inaccessible, Inapprehensible God is not subject to death or destiny. 1
He is of no caste, unborn, self-existent, without fear or doubt.
I am a sacrifice to the Truest of the true.
He hath no form, or colour, or outline; He becometh manifest by the true Word.
He hath no mother, father, son, or kinsman; He feeleth not lust, and hath no wife
Or family; He is pure, endless, and infinite; all lighl is Thine, O Lord.
God is concealed in every heart; His light is in every heart.
He whose understanding's adamantine doors are opened by the Guru's instruction, fixeth his gaze on the Fearless One.
God having created animals made them subject to death, and retained all contrivances in his own power.
He who serveth the True Guru obtaineth the real boon, and is delivered by repeating the Word.
Truth is contained in pure vessels; few there are whose acts are pure.
By seeking Thy protection, saith Nanak, the soul blendeth with the Supreme Soul.
The condition of a man who has no Guru to com municate God's name:â
As a fish without water, so is the infidelâ dying of thirst.
If thy breath be drawn in vain, O man, thou shalt die without God.

1 Also translatedâ God is not bound by the influence of His acts.

O man, repeat God's name and praises;

But how shalt thou obtain this pleasure without the Guru? It is the Guru who uniteth man with God.

Meeting the society of holy men is as a pilgrimage for the holy.

The advantages of bathing at the sixty-eight places of pilgrimage are obtained by beholding the Guru:â

As a Jogi without continence, devotion, truth, or content ment,

So is the body without the Name; Death will punish it since it containeth sin in its heart.

God is not found by loving the infidel; He is found by loving the true Guru.

Saith Nanak, he who is absorbed in God's praises obtaineth the Guru who is the dispenser of weal and woe.

Man should cultivate true piety in his own home:â

The nectareous water of life, 1 for which thou earnest into the world, is with the Guru.

Abandon garbs, disguises, and cleverness; this water 2 is not obtained by devotion to mammon.

O man, remain at home; go nowhere, my friend.

By searching abroad thou shalt suffer much affliction; the water of life is in thy heart at home.

Forsake vice and pursue virtue; thy vice thou shalt regret.

Thou knowest not good from evil; thou shalt again and again wallow in the mire.

Inside thee is the great filth of covetousness and false hood; why washest thou thine outside?

Ever repeat the Pure Name under the Guru's instruction, then shall thy heart be pure.

Abandon covetousness and slander, forswear falsehood and thou shalt obtain the true fruit through the Guru's instruction.

O God, preserve me as Thou pleasest; Nanak praiseth Thy Word.

1 That is, God's name. 2 Literallyâ this fruit.

God is the invisible Benefactor and is pleased when men obey His behests:â

All creatures are subject to destiny from the beginning; there is none not subject to it.

God alone is not subject to destiny; He beholdeth the work of His own omnipotence; He causeth His order to be executed.

0 man, repeat God's name and thou shalt be happy; Day and night worship the feet of the Guru the Giver and the Enjoyer.

Behold Him without thee as He is within thee; there is none other.

Under the Guru's instruction regard all men as equal, since God's light is contained in the heart of each.

Restrain in its place thy wandering mind; thou shalt know how to do this on meeting the Guru.

On beholding the Invisible thou shalt be astounded; thou shalt forget thy misery and obtain happiness.

Quaff nectar and thou shalt obtain supreme happiness and abide in thine own home.

Sing His praises who destroyeth the fear of birth and death, and thou shalt not be born again.

God x the First Principle, the Pure One, is in all things; of this there is no doubt.

Nanak hath obtained God the Infinite Supreme Being as his Guru.

SORATH ASHTAPADI

The Guru deprecates idolatry and then gives his notion of an ideal Bairagi, or renouncer of the world:â

May I not fall under the power of mammon, worship any but God, or visit tombs and places of cremation!

May I not enter the strange house impelled by greed! 2 may the Name extinguish my greed!

The Guru showed me God in my own home; my heart became easily enamoured of Him, my brethren.

1 Soiam, I am He. Compare ' I am that I am'.

2 May I not go to worship in a heathen temple for the sake of mammon.

Thou art wise, Thou art far-seeing; it is only Thou, O Lord, who givest wisdom.

My heart hath no love for the world; it is tinctured with its hate; the Word hath penetrated my heart, O my mother.

He who loveth the true Lord and continually repeateth His hymns, beholdeth His light in his own heart.

Countless persons call themselves Bairagis, but only he who is pleasing to God is a Bairagi.

Such a Bairagi treasureth the Word in his heart; he is ever absorbed in the fear of God and serveth the Guru.

He thinketh on the one God, his mind wavereth not, and he restraineth its wanderings.

He is intoxicated with God's love, ever absorbed in divine pleasure, and he singeth the praises of the True One.

If the mind, which is like the wind, dwell even for a little on the name of Him who liveth at ease, happiness shall result, my brethren.

My tongue, eyes, and ears are tinctured by the True One; Thou, O Lord, hast extinguished the fire that con sumed me.

He is a Bairagi who abandoneth desires and assumeth an attitude of contemplation in his own home.

He who is filled with the alms of the Name is contented and quaffeth nectar at his ease.

As long as there is a particle of worldly love, there is no contempt of the world.

All the world is Thine, O Lord; Thou alone art the Giver; there is none other, my brethren.

Perverse creatures ever abide in misery; God conferreth greatness on the holy.

Infinite, endless, inaccessible, inapprehensible, Thy worth cannot be obtained by speaking.

Sun Samadh, 1 Mahaparamarath, 2 and Lord of the three worlds are names of Thine.

All animals born in the world have their destinies recorded on their foreheads, and must bear what is destined for them.

1 He who is in deep and silent meditation.

2 The great supreme Being.

It is God who causeth man to perform good acts and maketh them steadfast in His service.

When man feareth God, the filth of his soul and body departeth, and God Himself giveth him divine knowledge:

Only he who hath tasted it, knoweth its flavour, as a dumb man enjoyeth sweets. 1

How describe the Indescribable, my brethren? Ever walk according to His will.

If God cause man to meet the generous Guru, understand ing is produced; he who hath no Guru hath no under standing.

Walk as God causeth you to walk, my brethren; what other device can man adopt?

Some are led astray in error, others love God's service; Thy play, O Lord, is incomprehensible.

Men obtain the result of what Thou hast applied them to; Thou leadest them by Thine order.

We can serve Thee if we have anything of our own; our souls and bodies are Thine.

God is merciful to him who hath met the true Guru; the ambrosial Name is his support.

He to whom the attributes of God, who dwelleth in heaven, become manifest, shall obtain divine knowledge and medita-tion from them.

God's name is pleasing to him; he uttereth it himself and causeth others to utter it; and he only speaketh of the Real Thing.

The Deep and Profound is obtained by the instruction of the Guru and priest; without such instruction the world would go mad.

Nanak, he whose heart is pleased with the True One is a perfect Bairagi, and naturally fortunate.

The following was the Guru's instruction to a Brahman:â

Hopes and desires are entanglements, my brother; thy religious ceremonies are also entanglements.

1 The dumb man eating sweets enjoys a pleasure which is incom municable.

Man, my brother, is born in the world as the result of bad and good acts; 1 he perisheth when he forgetteth the Name.

Maya bewitcheth the world, my brother; all thy religious ceremonies are worthless.

Hear me, thou Pandit with the religious ceremonies-Meditation on the Supreme Being is the only religious ceremony, my brother, from which happiness is derived.

Thou standest chattering of the Shastars and Veds, my brother, and makest it a worldly affair.

The filth of sin which is within thee shall not be washed away by hypocrisy.

Like the hypocrite, the spider is ruined when her web is blown by the wind and she falleth headlong.

By evil inclinations many are ruined; by love of mammon they are lost.

Without the true Guru the Name is not obtained, and without the Name doubt depart eth not.

My brother, serve the true Guru and thou shalt be happy, and released from transmigration.

True peace is obtained from the Guru. When the mind is pure, man shall be absorbed in the True One.

He who serveth the Guru knoweth the way; without the Guru it cannot be found.

What religious acts can he perform who hath greed in his heart? He uttereth falsehood and eateth poison.

O Pandit, if thou churn coagulated milk, butter shall be produced;

If thou churn water, thou shalt obtain but water; this is the way of the world.

The unseen God dwelleth in every heart, yet without the Guru man is ruined by wandering.

Maya hath bound this world on all sides with her cable:

Without a guru its knot cannot be untied; man groweth weary in striving.

1 If a man's acts were totally bad, he could not obtain human birth. Human birth is only obtained when good and bad acts are in equipoise.

This world is led astray by superstition; words are of no avail.

By meeting the Guru, my brother, the fear of God entereth the heart. To die in the fear of God is man's true destiny.

In God's court the Name is superior to ablutions, alms, and similar religious acts.

He who, by the Guru's goad, hath driven the Name into his heart to abide there, shall become free from hypocrisy.

Man is a banker's shop, the unrivalled Name is his capital.

The merchant who meditateth on the Guru's instruction secureth the capital.

Nanak, blest are the merchants who on meeting the Guru engage in such traffic.

Deprecation of idolatry:â

My brethren, you worship goddesses and gods; what can you ask them? and what can they give you?

Even if a stone be washed with water, it will again sink in it.

RAG DHANASARI

The Guru reposes his hopes in God and confirms his devotion to Him:â

My soul is in fear; to whom shall I complain?

I have served Him who causeth us to forget our sorrows; He is ever and ever the Giver.

My Lord is ever young; He is ever and ever the Giver.

Night and day serve the Lord, and in the end He will deliver thee.

Hark, hark, my friend, 1 thus shalt thou cross over.

O Merciful One, by Thy name shall I cross over; I am ever a sacrifice unto Thee.

In the whole world there is only one True Being; there is no second.

He on whom God looketh with favour will serve Him.

How shall I, O Beloved, abide without Thee?

Grant me the favour to remain attached to Thy name.

1 Literallyâ woman.

There is none other, O my Beloved, to whom I may go to address myself.

I serve my Lord, I beg from no other:

Nanak is His slave and ever a sacrifice unto Him.

O Lord, I am ever a sacrifice to Thy name, for which I could bear to be cut to pieces.

Life is but brief, and man ought to make the best use of it:—

We men live but for a moment; we know not if we shall live the space of two gharis.

Nanak representeth, serve Him to whom belong our souls and lives.

O fool, consider how many days thy life shall last.

0 Lord, my breath, body, and soul are all Thine; Thou art very dear to me.

The poet Nanak thus speaketh; O True Cherisher,

If Thou give nothing to any one, what pledge can he give Thee?

Nanak representeth, he who is destined from the beginning to obtain something shall obtain it.

The deceitful person who, instead of thinking of God's name, practiseth deceit,

Shall be led captive to the gate of Death, and shall then as he is led along regret lost opportunities.

As long as we are in this world, Nanak, hear somewhat and speak somewhat of God.

I have searched and found no resting-place; wherefore in the midst of life be in death.

The Guru moralized as follows on seeing a thief arrested:—

If a thief praise the magistrate, the mind of the latter is not pleased thereby;

If he revile the magistrate, it cannot displease him in the least.

Nobody will be surety for a thief.

1 Man can obtain nothing from God except as the result of His favour. If man receive nothing from God, no surety is needed.

How can what a thief doeth be good?

Hear, O fool, dog, and liar,

The True One knoweth thee, O thief, without thy speaking.

A thief may be well dressed, a thief may be ingenious,

Yet he is only worth a double paisa, the price of a bad rupee.

If thou put a bad coin with others,

It will be found counterfeit on being assayed.

As man acteth, so shall be his reward:

He himself soweth and he himself eateth the fruit.

Even though man praise himself,

Yet will he act according to his understanding.

If he tell hundreds of lies to conceal the truth,

He shall still be false even though the whole world call him good.

If it please Thee, even a fool is acceptable. Nanak, God is clever to know man's secret.

A Brahman, a Qazi, and a Jogi entered into discussion with the Guru, and he gave them the following instruction:—

The body is the paper, the mind the order written thereon. Silly man readeth not the lines of destiny on his forehead. In God's court three destinies 1 are engraved. Lo! what is counterfeit is there of no avail. Nanak, if there be sterling silver within us, Everybody will say that it is real. The Qazi telleth lies and eateth filth. The Brahman taketh life and then batheth. The ignorant Jogi knoweth not the way of union with God,â The whole three ruin the world. 2 He is a Jogi who knoweth the way to God, And who by the Guru's favour only recognizeth the One.

He is a Qazi who turneth away men from the world, And who by the Guru's favour while alive is dead.

1 Superior, medium, and inferior destinies.

2 Literallyâ the three form the boundary of the wilderness, that is, preach the whole of what ruins mortals.

He is a Brahman who reflecteth upon God: He shall be saved himself, and shall save all his relations. Wise is he who cleanseth his heart: A Musalman is he who cleanseth his impurity. He who readeth and acteth on what he readeth, is accept able.

He shall bear on his forehead the stamp of God's court.

DHANASARI ASHTAPADI

God is pleased with love and service, not with idolatry or pilgrimages:â
God maketh Himself manifest and beholdeth men.
He is not pleased by obstinate penance nor by many religious garbs.
He who fashioned the vessel of the body and poured into it His ambrosial gifts,
Will only be satisfied with man's love and service.
They who, though ever reading, forget God's name shall suffer punishment,
And notwithstanding their great cleverness undergo trans migration.
He who repeateth the Name and thus eateth the food of fear,
Shall become a pious worshipper and be absorbed in God.
He who worshippeth stones, visiteth places of pilgrimage, dwelleth in forests,
And renounceth the world, wandereth and wavereth.
How can his filthy mind become pure?
He who meeteth the True One shall obtain honour.

DHANASARI CHHANT

They who utter falsehood are unhappy:â If a woman please her Spouse, she shall be honoured in
His house:
If she utter falsehood it is of no avail:
If she utter falsehood it is of no avail; her Spouse will not look at her.
Without merits, forgotten by her Spouse, and false, painful are her nights.
RAG SUHI Man ought to practise devotion at home:â
Man dwelleth not at home, but wandereth abroad.
Why doth he forsake ambrosia and eat poison?
Embrace such knowledge, O my soul,
As may make thee a servant of the True One.
Although every one speaketh of divine knowledge and meditation,
Yet the whole world wandereth bound by its own entangle ments.
He who performeth service is a servant of Him
Who pervadeth the water, the dry land, the nether regions, and the firmament.
I am not good; there is nobody bad.
The representation of Nanak isâ he who thinketh so is saved.

SUHI ASHTAPADI

The Guru depreciates himself, and utters a prayer to the Almighty:â
In me are all demerits; I have not one merit:
How shall I meet my Spouse?
No beauty or lustrous eyes are mine,
No family, no manners, or sweet speech.
The woman who cometh adorned with divine knowledge,
Shall be a happy wife if she please her Spouse.

0 God, mercifully attach her to Thy feet Who hath neither beauty nor good features, Who remembereth not God at the last moment, Who hath no wisdom, understanding, or cleverness.

The woman, who though very wise pleaseth not her Spouse, Who attached to mammon is lost in superstition, Shall, if she dismiss her pride, be absorbed in her Beloved, And obtain Him who is her nine treasures.

1 suffered through being separated from God in many births.
O Beloved Sovereign, take my hand.
Saith Nanak, the Lord is, was, and shall be.
The Beloved will enjoy her who is pleasing to Him.
Miscellaneous instruction of the Guru:â
False and fleeting is the dye of the safflower, lasting for only four days.

Without the Name man wandereth in error; the evil passions x rob him, false that he is.

He who is tinctured with the True One shall not be born again.

How canst thou who art dyed with the love of God, be otherwise dyed?

Serve the Guru who giveth God's dye, and apply thy heart to the True One.

Even though man wander in every direction, he shall not obtain spiritual wealth without good fortune.

If robbed by vice thou wander in the forest like a huntsman, thou shalt not find shelter.

They whom the Guru protecteth are saved; their hearts are dyed with his instruction.

They who wear white clothes, but whose hearts are filthy and hard,
Never utter the Name, but like thieves become absorbed in mammon.
They who know not their own humble origin are beasts and cattle.

Man though ever and ever engaged in pleasures, ever and ever desireth more enjoyment.

He thinketh not of the Creator, so misery attacheth to him again and again.

How shall he in whose heart the Dispenser ot weal and woe I dwelleth, want for anything?

They whose accounts are not adjusted shall be summoned; j the executioner shall smite them on their heads.

When the account is called for it must be given; it will be i examined and considered.
Man shall be saved by his love for the True One; the Pardoner will pardon him.

If he make any one else than God his friend, he shall die and be blended with the dust.

1 Literallyâ thags.

Man beholding various phases of life is led astray, and going astray suffereth transmigration;

But he shall be emancipated by a favouring glance from God, and God will blend him with Himself.

O listless man who possessest not divine knowledge, search not for it without the Guru.

Man is ruined by allowing himself to be drawn in different directions; the effects of both evil and good acts remain with him.

The god of death spieth every one who is without the Word, and who feeleth not the fear of God.

He who made and sustained the world giveth support to all.

Why forget Him who is ever and ever the Benefactor?

May Nanak not forget the Name which is the support of the supportless!

Sum CHHANT

The following is now sung by Sikhs at marriages and other festivities:â

Friends I have come to my house:

The True One hath caused me to meet them.

When it pleased God He caused me to meet them without mine own effort; by meeting the elect happiness is found.

I have obtained what I set my heart on.

When I meet the saints my soul is happy; night and day my hearth and home look bright.

The unbeaten sound of the five musical instruments playeth since saints have come to my house.

Come, beloved friends,

Sing a song of rejoicing, O women.

Sing a true song of rejoicing; then shall you be pleasing to God and rejoice through the four ages. 2

The Spouse hath come to my house, the place is adorned by Him. His instruction hath adjusted mine affairs.

I applied the great salve of divine knowledge to mine eyes, and saw God's form which filleth the three worlds.

1 Saints are meant.

2 Also translatedâ Then shall you be pleasing to God to whom songs of rejoicing are sung through the four ages.

HYMNS OF GURU NANAK 343

Meet me, O companions, sing with zest a song of rejoicing, since my Spouse hath come home to me.

My soul and body are bedewed with nectar,

And in my heart is the jewel of love:

In my heart is the precious jewel, and I ponder on the Primal Essence.

To animals Thou art the opulent Giver 1; Thou givest to every individual.

Thou art wise; Thou possessest divine knowledge; Thou art the searcher of hearts; Thou Thyself didst create the world.

Listen, my friends, the charming Bridegroom hath fasci nated me, and my soul and body are bedewed with nectar.
O Supreme Spirit of the world,
True is Thy play:
True is Thy play, O Incomprehensible and Infinite One; who can cause us to understand but Thee?
Without Thee how many can call themselves Sidhs, Strivers, or wise?
The Guru hath stayed the soul which was maddened with the misery of death.
Nanak, he who removeth his demerits by the Word, obtaineth God through his aggregate of merits.
The Guru is waiting for God as a fond wife for her husband:â
Come, my Friend, that I may behold Thee.
Standing at my door I am watching for Thee; in my heart is excessive longing;
In my heart is excessive longing; hear me, my Lord, I have reliance on Thee.
On beholding Thee I have become free from desire; the pain of birth and death is at an end.
In all things is Thy light; from it art Thou known, but Thou art found by love.
Nanak, I am a sacrifice to the Friend; the True One is found when my mind cometh home.
SUHI KI WAR God will assay man's qualities:â
Nanak when a man bringeth and putteth money in his house he examineth it;
So in the Lord's court the counterfeit and the genuine shall be tested.
Bathing at places of pilgrimage only renders men more impure:â
Men of evil minds and thievish bodies go to bathe at places of pilgrimage.
One part of their filth departeth by bathing, but they con tract double more. 1
A gourd may be externally washed, but it containeth undiluted poison within.
Holy men are good without bathing; a thief is always a thief whether he bathe or not.
Men should traffic in God's name from their earliest years:â
There are two lamps for fourteen shops, 2 And as many shopkeepers as souls: When the shops are opened, the traffic beginneth. Every one who cometh into the world is transient. Religion is the broker who putteth a mark on the goods. Nanak, they who profit by the Name are acceptable. For those who obtain the greatness of the true Name Gratulations resound on their arrival at their own homes.
In evil association there is no hope of amendment:â
It is the habit of thieves, adulterers, prostitutes, and pimps
To contract friendship with the irreligious and dine with them.
They take no thought for God's praises; the devil ever dwelleth in their hearts.
1 Their bodily filth departs, but their mental filth and hypocrisy increase.
2 There are the sun and the moon for the fourteen worlds.
HYMNS OF GURU NANAK 345
If sandal be rubbed on a donkey, he will still roll in the dust.
Nanak, by spinning falsehood the web of falsehood is woven.
False is the cloth therefrom and its measurement; false the raiment and the pride thereof.

The repetition of God's name is superior to the call of the Muazzin l or the horn of the Jogi,

Whether the Muazzin repeateth the call to prayer or the Jogi bloweth horns, and the bards join the chorus,

Some are givers, others are beggars; to me Thy name alone is acceptable.

Nanak, I am a sacrifice to those who have heard and accepted it.

The following sloks in the Suhi ki War contain miscellaneous instruction and reflections of the Guru:â

I am a sacrifice to those whose words consist of God's praises.

Every night is for the married woman; let me who am separated from Thee, O God, obtain even one night.

They who have not obtained the sweets of love or the delights of the Bridegroom,

Are like the guest of an empty house who goeth as he cometh.

A curse on the lives of those who eat to distend their bellies

Nanak, without the true Name all love is turned into hate.

You say, O Panditsâ l As darkness is dispelled when a lamp is lighted, 4 So by reading the Veds sinful inclinations are destroyed."

say, l When the sun riseth, the moon is not seen.

4 Where divine knowledge appeareth mental ignorance is dispelled.

4 You, O Pandits, read the Veds and study them, 4 But the reading of the Veds is a secular occupation.

Without understanding this every one shall be disgraced, l Who calls to prayer from the top of a mosque.

' Nanak, the man who listeneth to the Guru's instruction shall be saved.

' They who delight not in the Word and who love not God's name, ' Speak offensively with their tongues, and shall ever be disgraced.

' Nanak, they act according to their destiny which none can erase."

RAG BILAWAL

It would not redound to God's glory to call Him by the names of the Hindu incarnations.

Thou art an emperor; if I call Thee lord, how will that be to Thy greatness?

If Thou inspire me, I will praise Thee, O Lord; I am foolish myself and can say nothing.

Give me understanding to sing Thy praises,

That I may abide in truth according to Thy will.

All that there is cometh from Thee; Thou lovest all.

I know not Thy limit, O my Lord; what skill have I, a blind man?

What shall I say? while talking I see that I cannot describe the Indescribable.

I speak as it pleaseth Thee; and this is only in the smallest degree for Thy greatness.

Among so many dogs I, a strange dog, bark for my belly's sake.

Even though Nanak perform no service, he will still bear his Master's name

The Guru's faith in God.

My body I have clothed with a Qalandar's dress, I have turned my heart into a temple, and I bathe in that place of pilgrimage.

The one Word dwelleth in my heart, and I shall not be born again.

My soul is pierced by the Compassionate One; O my mother,
HYMNS OF GURU NANAK 347
Who knoweth another's pain? I think of no one but God.
0 inaccessible, imperceptible, unseen, and boundless God, take thought for me.
Thou fillest sea and land, the upper and lower regions; Thy light is in every heart.
My faculty of learning and my understanding are all Thine; I have built my heart as a temple to Thee.
1 know none but Thee, O my Lord; I ever sing Thy praises.
Men and lower animals all seek Thy protection; all anxiety for them resteth with Thee.
What pleaseth Thee is good; this is Nanak's sole repre sentation.

LUNAR DAYS

The Guru counsels disregard of mammon:â
What name shall I repeat except that of the Lord of the world?
Under the Guru's instruction God's court is seen in one's own home.
They who are attached to mammon shall regret it;
They shall go in fetters to Death's gate and suffer trans migration.
What have they brought, and what shall they take away?
They shall receive blows from the god of death on the head.
No one can be emancipated without the Guru's instruction.
No one can be saved by the practice of hypocrisy.
Heartfelt devotion is superior to all offerings and ablutions:â
On the tenth day of the lunar month repeat the Name as your offerings and ablutions.
Night and day lave yourselves in the attributes and knowledge of the True One.
When doubts and fears have fled, impurity shall not cling toj: he true heart.
A frail cord will soon snap:
Know that the world is as the cord.
Fix thy mind firmly on the True One and thou shalt be happy.

RAMKALI

In his devotional enthusiasm the Guru indulges in self-depreciation:â
Some read the Veds, 1 some the Purans:
Some repeat names 2 on their rosaries and meditate on them.
I know not and never knew anything; I recognize only Thy name.
I know not, O God, what my lot shall be.
I am ignorant and devoid of divine knowledge; O Lord, I seek Thy protection, mercifully preserve my self-respect and honour.
The mind sometimes riseth and sometimes falleth to the nether regions. 3
The greedy mind remaineth not still; it searcheth for mammon in all directions.
Man entered the world doomed to die; yet he amasseth wealth for long life.
While others depart, O Lord, we see the burning fire approaching us also.
No one hath a friend, no one hath a brother, no one hath a father or mother.
Nanak representeth, if Thou give Thy name, it will assist me at the last hour.
After the death of a Hindu a lamp is kept burning for several days to light the soul of the departed to the next world. It is then floated on water. Guru Nanak indites the following homily on the custom:â 1 Literallyâ Sanskrit.

2 Some invoke gods and goddesses.

3 Sometimes man is elated and sometimes depressed.

Adore God 1 in the following way—Make thy body into a raft 2 by which thou mayest cross over.

Put on it the fire of thy heart,
And the lamp shall burn untiringly day and night.
Float such a lamp on the water
As shall procure thee all knowledge.
The knowledge of God is a good material;
God will accept a lamp made out of it.
Make good deeds thy wheel, and mould thy lamp on it;
It will accompany thee in this world and the next.
When God looketh on him with an eye of favour,
Some rare pious man knoweth how to make this lamp.
This lamp shall be permanent in his heart,
And shall not be extinguished when he dieth.
Float such a lamp on the water
As shall not be shaken or put out by the wind,
And by whose light God's throne may be seen.
Khatris, Brahmans, Sudars, and Vaisyas
Find not such a lamp by thousands of researches and calculations;
But if any of them light such a lamp as I have described,
He shall, O Nanak, obtain deliverance.

The following was addressed to a Jogi:â

The Jogi runneth about begging for clothes and food;

He burneth with the pangs of hunger, and he shall also have misery hereafter.

He who hath not received the Guru's instruction, loseth his honour by his own stupidity.

Some rare man obtaineth God's service by the Guru's teaching.

The Jogi who knoweth the way dwelleth in a peaceful home.

He who is satisfied with the alms of love and the Word beholdeth all men with an equal eye.

1 Literallyâ fix thine attention on God.
2 The little raft on which the lamp is placed.

The five oxen 1 draw the carriage of the body:
The whole goeth well by the contrivance of God.
When the axle breaketh, the carriage turneth over;
Its timber is scattered and it is burnt in the fire.
Meditate, O Jogi, on the Guru's instruction.
Consider weal and woe, union and separation of friends as the same.
Let the Name and meditation on the Guru's instruction be thy dainties. 2
The wall of thy body shall remain permanent 3 by repeat ing God's name.
By the practice of sahaj jog thou shalt be freed from entanglements,
And shalt repress lust and wrath under the Guru's ad monition.
Make the protection of God and the Guru earrings for thy heart.

Nanak, it is by devotion to God man shall be saved.
ASHTAPADI
God is in man's heart and ought not to be sought for elsewhere:â
O Nanak, may I obtain the greatness of the Name! there is no religious work superior to it.
If man go elsewhere to ask for what he hath at home, he shall be received with reproaches.

It is said that Guru Nanak on his excursion to the Himalayas met a Jogi called Chetnath, who reproached him with not being a Jogi, a Sanyasi, or a saint, but only a pretended guru. The following was Guru Nanak's reply:â 0 Jogi, thou buildest a hut and preachest to the world: If, abandoning thy devotional attitudes, thou beg from door to door, how shalt thou obtain the True One?

1 The five organs of action.
2 Sweets are given to Jogis at the time of their reception into a monastery.
3 There is a belief that the Jogis live for hundreds of years as the result of their austerities.

Thou lovest mammon and woman,
And art neither an anchoret nor a worldly man.
0 Jogi, keep thy seat, 1 and the pain of thy worldly love shall depart.
Thou art not ashamed to beg from door to door;
Thou singest songs, but knowest not thyself.
How shall the great fire which burneth thee be ex tinguished?
If the love of God attach to thy heart under the Guru's instruction,
Thou shalt easily enjoy the alms of contemplation.
Thou hypocritically appliest ashes to thy body,
And shalt be punished for thy worldliness by Death's mace.
The impure vessel 2 of thy heart cannot hold the alms of love.
Thou art bound by bonds and shalt suffer transmigration.
Thou dost not restrain thy seed, and yet thou callest thyself continent.
While saying ' Mother ', thou beggest and fallest in love with woman.
Thou art without compassion and God's light shineth not in thee.
Thou art immersed in every species of entanglement.
With a patched coat and a bag thou assumest many guises.
Likeaconjurer thouperformest manytricks to deceive men.
The fire of anxiety burneth thy heart-How shalt thou be saved without good works?
Thou makest rings of crystal for thine ears.
Without the highest divine knowledge there is no emanci pation.
Thou art beguiled by the pleasures of the tongue and sensual organs.
Thou hast become a beast, and the mark of it shall not be erased.

1 That is, go not a-begging.
2 Khapar. A wooden vessel shaped like a skull. It is carried by Jogis for the alms they receive.

There are three classes of people and three classes of Jog. 1 He who meditateth on the Word shall need no mourning. He who meditateth on the way of jog is a Jogi: By the true Word he shall become bright.

The Guru in an address to a pandit rejects astrology:—
Thou calculatest auspicious moments, but reflectest not
That God is beyond auspicious moments.
He who meeteth the Guru knoweth them.
When there is the Guru's instruction man recognizeth God's will.
Speak not falsehood; O Pandit, tell the truth,
If pride depart by means of the Word, God's abode shall be attained.
The astrologer after calculating draweth out a horoscope;
He readeth it to himself and others, but knoweth not the reality.
Deem the Guru's word the highest of all;
Utter no other discourse; it were all in vain.
Thou bathest, and washest, and worshippest stones,
But without being imbued with God thou art the filthiest of the filthy.
Abandon pride, and thou shalt meet God the real wealth.
Repeat God's name, and thou shalt succeed in obtaining emancipation.
Thou readest not thine epic poems nor reflectest on the Veds:
Drowned thyself, how canst thou save thine ancestors?
Few understand that God is in every heart.
When man meeteth the true Guru, he obtaineth under standing.
By making calculations such as thine doubt and sorrow enter the mind;
But, when the Guru's protection is sought, happiness result eth.
Having sinned we come to him for protection.
1 People and jog are subdivided according to the three qualities.
According to man's acts in a former state the Guru causeth him to meet God.
God cannot be obtained unless man enter the Guru's protection;
Otherwise he is led astray in superstition and suffereth transmigration.
He who hath not God in his heart and whose conduct is not according to the Word,
Shall be bound at Death's gate and punished for his sins.
Men call themselves Teachers, Pandits, and Missars; 1
But they who are tinctured with mammon shall not reach God's mansion.
He who by the Guru's favour hath the support of the Name,
Is unequalled amongst millions.
One man appeareth evil and another good; but they are both contained in the True One:
The learned man understandeth this by the aid of the true Guru.
A few holy men who know the one God,
Have ended their transmigration, and become absorbed in Him.
They in whose hearts is the one God,
Possess all excellences and meditate on the truth.
They who act as pleaseth the Guru
Are true, O Nanak, and shall be absorbed in the True One.
The following was addressed to a rich sinner who visited the Guru:—
O silly man, as thou earnest so shall thou depart; as thou wert born so shalt thou die;

As thy enjoyment so shall be thy suffering; through forgetfulness of the Name thou shalt fall into the terrible ocean.

Thou art proud on beholding thy beauty and wealth.

Thou hast extended thy love to gold and woman; why hast thou forgotten the Name and gone astray?

1 A title applied to Brahmans by Hindus.

SIKH, i A a

Not having practised continence, truth, self-restraint, or virtue, thou shalt suffer in the skeleton of a ghost.

Alms-gifts, ablutions, and austerities are of no avail; without association with the saints, thou hast been born in vain.

Through the covetousness that attacheth to thee thou hast forgotten the Name; thy life hath been wasted in transmigration.

Death will hasten to seize thee by the hair and punish thee; and, when he eateth thee, thou shalt have no con sciousness for repentance.

Day and night thou revilest others and art jealous of them; the Name is not in thy heart, and thou hast not universal benevolence.

Without the Guru's instruction thou shalt not obtain salvation or honour; without God's name thou shalt go to hell.

Thou practisest disguise for a brief period like a conjurer, while thou art steeped in worldly love and sin.

Seeing the extension of thy wealth here and there, thou hast become intoxicated with worldly love.

Thou commit test sin on a large scale, and without remembering the Word hast fallen into error.

Thou hast suffered great pain from the disease of pride; but it shall depart when thou receivest the Guru's in struction.

The infidel seeing happiness and wealth coming to him becometh proud in his heart.

He who owneth this body and wealth will take them back; he who feeleth anxiety regarding them shall have sorrow.

At the last moment nothing shall depart with thee; whatever is seen is the result of God's kindness.

God is the primal and infinite Being; by treasuring His name in the heart man shall be saved.

Thou weepest for the dead; who heareth thy weeping? He whom thou weepest for might have fallen to the dragon in the sea of terror.

The infidel beholding his family, wealth, houses, and mansions falleth into needless entanglements.

Man cometh when God sendeth him, and he goeth away when God calleth him.

God continueth to do what is proper; the Pardoner pardoneth.

0 brethren, search for the society of those who have tasted God's elixir.

When man taketh the Guru's protection, then wealth, supernatural power, wisdom, divine knowledge, and the boon of emancipation are obtained.

The pious consider woe and weal as the same, and are free from joy or sorrow.

Nanak, he who chasteneth himself under the Guru's instruction obtaineth God, and God absorbeth him in Himself.

DAKHANI OAMKAR L

Men who are generally impure cannot obtain emancipation until their hearts are thoroughly purified:â

As borax melteth gold,
So lust and wrath melt the body.
The gold is drawn over the touchstone, and must, until thoroughly pure, endure the fire.
When it assumeth a high colour 2 the Assayer is satisfied.
The world is a beast, and pride is its butcher. 3
As thou actest with thine own hand, so shall be thy recompense.
He who made the world knoweth its worth.
What else is to be said? Talking availeth not.

RAMKALI KI WAR I

The following is a satire on the professedly religious men of the time:â

They who call themselves virtuous, commit sin and pretend that they are doing good.

1 This is a composition of Guru Nanak made in the south of India in praise of God.
1 The body must be purified as gold is by melting. God the Assayer is satisfied with it when it assumes a bright colour. 3 Pride is killing the world.

Gurus go to private houses to impart instruction.
A woman loveth man for the money he earneth for her;
Otherwise he may come or go as he pleaseth.
Nobody obeyeth the Shastars or the Veds;
Everybody worshippeth himself.
The Qazi sitteth to administer justice;
He turneth over his beads and invoketh God,
But he taketh bribes and doeth injustice.
If any one call him to account, he will read and cite texts.
The Muhammadan creed nlleth the ears and hearts of the Hindus.
They carry tales to the judge and plunder the populace: j
They make squares for cooking so as to appear pure.
See what the Hindus are like.
Jogis with long hair and ashes on their bodies keep wives.
Children scream before and behind them.
They miss the right road and obtain not union with God.
Why do they put ashes on their heads?
Nanak, this is the state of this degenerate age,
That men only speak of themselves and think themselves the best.
The following is also a satire on Brahmans, Muhammadan priests, and Jogis:â
A Brahman goeth to the house of a Hindu,
Readeth texts, and putteth the sacrificial thread on a boy's neck.
If the boy commit sin after putting on the thread,
He shall not be accepted for all his ablutions and washings.

The Musalman may praise himself,
But without a guru or a priest he shall not be accepted.
Even when the road is pointed out, few travel by it.
Without good works heaven is not obtained.
Men seek the way in a Jogi's monastery;
And on that account put rings in their ears and become his disciples.
With earrings on they wander about the world,
While the Creator they pretend to search for is everywhere.
All souls are travellers:
When the death-warrant cometh for them there must be no delay.
He who knoweth God in this world, shall recognize Him in the next.
All others, whether Hindus or Musalmans, are chatterers.
All men's accounts shall be taken in God's court;
And no one shall be saved without good works.
He who repeateth the name of the Truest of the true,
Shall not, O Nanak, be examined hereafter.
Only the good shall be saved when the final reckoning is called for:â

Nanak saith, O man, hear true instruction-God seated in judgement will produce His book and call on thee for thine account.

The stiff-necked who owe anything shall be summoned;
And the angel Azrail placed over them.
They shall see no way of escape; they shall be entangled in the narrow streets.
Falsehood is at an end, O Nanak, and truth shall at last prevail.
The following was addressed to a proud Muham-madan governor:â
At thy waist is a handsome sword, thou art mounted on a handsome steed:
Be not proud, saith Nanak, lest thou fall on thy head.
Only good men can remain in the society of the saints:â

Between the lake and the swan there is affinity from the beginning; so it pleased the Lord.

In the lake there are diamonds and pearls which form the swan's food.

Cranes and ravens, however cunning they may be, cannot remain in lake Mansarowar.
1
They cannot subsist there; their food is different.

1 It is said that Lake Mansarowar in the Himalayas contains pearls, which are food for swans, but not for cranes and ravens.

By the practice of truth, truth is obtained; O false ones, false is your pride.
Nanak, they for whom it was so ordered from the beginning meet the True Guru.
My Lord is effulgent, if any one reflect on it.
Nanak, serve Him who giveth ever and ever;
Nanak serve Him by whose service sorrow departeth,
Sins are erased, merits take their place, and peace abideth in the heart.

RAG MARU ASHTAPADI

A hypocritical Sanyasi called Brahmpuri was mentioned to the Guru as a very worthy man. The Guru, knowing his real condition, composed the following:â

The perverse having through avarice abandoned their own homes, ruin themselves by casting covetous eyes on the houses of others.

They have ruined their state as householders; they have not met the True Guru, and through their stupidity are involved in a whirlpool.

Of wandering in foreign countries and reading texts they grow weary, and their covetousness increaseth.

Of weak intellect, they know not the Word; they fill their bellies like cattle.

0 Sir, the way of the Sanyasi should be this:â

He should under the Guru's instruction only think of the one God, love His name, and be satisfied with it.

But the hypocrite mixeth ochre, dyeth his dress with it, and weareth the garb of a beggar;

He teareth his clothes to make a patched coat, and putteth money into his wallet;

Blind that he is and bereft of shame, he beggeth from house to house and preacheth to the world;

Led astray by superstition he knoweth not the Word and loseth the game.

The fire which is within him is not extinguished without the Guru, yet he heateth himself with external fires 1 also.

1 The penance of five fires is frequently spoken of and resorted to

HYMNS OF GURU NANAK

There is no worship without serving the Gam; how man of himself recognize God?

He who slandereth others shall abide in hell, and be separated from the Supreme Spirit.

He who wandereth to the sixty-eight places of pilgrimage is ruined thereby; how can he wash away the filth of his sins?

He sifteth dust, applieth it to his body, and looketh for the way of mammon.

He knoweth not the one God who is with him whether he be at home or abroad; if any one tell him the truth, he groweth angry.

While reading texts his mouth uttereth falsehoods; that is all the wisdom a man without a guru possesseth.

How can man obtain happiness without repeating the Name? How shall he be honoured without the Name?

Some shave their heads, some twist long hair round them or wear a top-knot; others through pride remain silent;

But without the love of divine knowledge their minds waver and hasten in every direction.

Maddened by worldly love they reject nectar and drink deadly poison.

They obey not God's order; their evil deeds shall not be effaced, and they shall enter the bodies of beasts.

The Kapari with a bowl in his hand and excessive greed in his heart

Abandoneth his own wife, and filled with lust coveteth his neighbour's.

While preaching he knoweth not God's word, and attacheth himself to a prostitute.

With poison in his heart he pretendeth that he hath no doubts, but Death will disgrace him.

He who serveth the True Guru and removeth pride from his heart, is a true Sanyasi;

He desireth not clothes or food, but taketh what is freely offered him; by Hindu devotees during the sultriest time of an Indian summer. They light fires around them in the four directions; the sun over them is the fifth.

He chattereth not; he amasseth the wealth of patience; and his passions he subdueth with God's name.

Blessings on that man, who whether householder, Sanyasi, or Jogi, fixeth his attention on God's feet.

He who in the midst of desires is without desires, and who loveth the one God is a Sanyasi.

He who drinketh God's essence and preserveth a religious attitude in his own home shall obtain peace.

The mind of the pious man who knoweth God wavereth not, but restraineth its wanderings.

He who under the Guru's instruction searcheth the house of the body, shall obtain the boon of the Name.

Brahma, Vishnu, and Shiv are most exalted when they are imbued with the contemplation of the Name.

Thy light, O Lord, is in the sources of production, in com positions, in the firmament, in the lower regions, and in all creatures.

By repeating hymns containing God's true name and clasping it to the heart, all happiness and final deliverance shall be obtained.

No one can be saved without the Name; Nanak, that is the true way to swim across.

The following was delivered in a fit of extreme religious fervour to Mihan and Sihan:â

Woman, however many friends she may make, wan-dereth like an itinerant minstrel in transmigration.

She who is separated from God obtaineth no access to Him; how shall she be patient?

My soul is imbued with the love of the Beloved.

I am a sacrifice; I would cut myself in pieces for Thee; look at me even for an instant with a glance of favour.

Separated as I am from my Beloved in my father's house, how shall I meet him in my father-in-law's?

I wear demerits round my neck; I am ruined without the Beloved; I am pining to death.

If in my father's house I remember the Beloved, I shall find a dwelling in His.

The wife who hath found her Beloved, the Lord of excel lences, sleepeth in peace.

She maketh a silken coverlet and mattress for her couch, and arrayeth herself in a costly robe.

The wife whom her husband abandoneth passeth the night in grief.

Whatever dainties she tasteth and whatever dresses she weareth,

Her youth passeth in vain without her Beloved; she pineth away through separation from Him.

Hear the song of the True One under the Guru's instruction.

True is the throne of the True One; she on whom He looketh with favour loveth Him.

The possessor of divine knowledge applieth the salve of truth to her eyes, and then beholdeth Him who seeth all things.

He who under the Guru's instruction dispelleth his pride and arrogance, shall understand and know God.

They who please Thee, O God, are like Thee; how many unhappy wives there are like me:

Nanak, their Spouse parteth not from those who are imbued with the love of the True One.

God is the only true friend and relation:â

Nor sisters, nor brothers, nor mothers-in-law remain with one:

But, O companions, the true relationship with the Beloved, when found through the Guru, shall never be sundered.

I am a sacrifice to my Guru, I am ever a sacrifice unto him.

I have grown weary of wandering so far without a guru; now the Guru hath united me with my Beloved.

Paternal and maternal aunts, grandmothers, and wives of husbands' younger and elder brothers

Come and go; they tarry not but depart like relays of passengers.

Maternal uncles and their wives, brothers, fathers, and mothers abide not.

Assembled in great crowds at the river they depart with their baggage like travellers.

0 my companions, my Husband is dyed with the true colour.

The true Husband never forsaketh; He enjoyeth one with delight.

All seasons are good for those who love the True One.

The woman who knoweth her husband enjoyeth happi ness day 1 and night.

The ferryman calleth out at the ferry, ' Come on, make haste; you delay."

1 have seen at the other side those whom the Guru put into the boat.

Some have loaded their baggage, some have set out with it, and others are weighed down by their loads.

They who have made true traffic are with the true God.

I am not good, nor do I find any one bad.

Nanak, he who effaceth his pride is as the True One.

MARU SOLHE God has no incarnations:â

God's secret is not found in the Veds or the books of the Musalmans;

He hath not father or mother or son or brother.

There is no friend like God, who is to be obtained through the Guru by those who lead a holy life:â

I have no friend like God

Who gave me soul and body, and infused into me under standing.

He cherisheth and watcheth over all creatures; He is wise and knoweth the secrets of hearts.

The Guru is like a lake; we are his beloved swans:

In the water are many jewels and rubies.

God's praises are pearls, gems, and diamonds; singing them maketh soul and body happy.

1 Deh in the original, pronounced exactly like its English equivalent.

God is inaccessible, unfathomable, altogether distinct from His creation.

The great Sustainer of the earth hath no end.

God saveth man through the true Guru's instruction; He blendeth with Himself those who are absorbed in His love.

How can there be emancipation without the true Guru?

He loveth the primal God who was before all time,

Who mercifully granteth emancipation in His court, and pardoneth the sins which man committeth.

The true Guru is the giver and procurer of emancipation.

He prescribeth nectareous essence and cureth all diseases.

He whose avarice is extinguished and whose mind is cool, shall owe no tax to Death the tax-gatherer.

The body greatly loveth the soul;

The latter is a male Jogi, the former a beautiful woman.

He enjoyeth her in dalliance day and night, but goeth away without taking leave.

God having created the world arrangeth it;

He speaketh in the wind, water, and fire.

The mind of him who associateth with evil passions wavereth; he suffereth the consequences of his acts.

They who forget the Name shall have to endure pain and misery.

How can they tarry when they receive the order to depart?

They shall plunge into the pit of hell and suffer like fishes out of water.

The apostate shall undergo the pain of transmigration in eighty-four lakhs of species.

Man shall suffer according to his acts.

There is no salvation without the true Guru; man shall be seized and bound according to his acts.

Very narrow is the way like the edge of a sword.

Man's account shall be taken, and he shall be pressed like sesame.

There no mother, father, wife, or son will befriend thee,â without love for God there is no emancipation.

However numerous one's friends and companions may be in the world,

There are no real friends but the Guru and God.

Salvation dependeth upon serving the Guru, and night and day singing God's praises.

Abandon falsehood, pursue truth,

And thou shalt obtain the fruit thy heart desireth.

Few are they who traffic in true merchandise; they who do so obtain profit.

Depart with the merchandise of God's name,

And thou shalt easily obtain a sight of God's court.

A perfect man under the Guru's instruction searcheth for God, and thus beholdeth Him who looketh on all alike.

God is infinite, but under the Guru's instruction is found by a few

Who teach their hearts the Guru's word.
Accept the true Guru's word as true; thus shalt thou be absorbed in God.
Narad and Saraswati are Thy servants, O Lord.
The greatest of the great in the three worlds are Thy servants.
In all things is Thy might; Thou bestowest on all; everything is Thy creation.
Some worship at Thy gate, and thus dispel their sufferings.
They who are emancipated by the true Guru, receive a robe of honour in Thy court.
The true Guru breaketh the entanglements of pride, ant hindereth the mind from wandering.
Meet the true Guru, look for the way
To reach God, and thus have no account against thee.
Efface pride and serve the Guru, O Nanak, and thou shalt be dyed with God's love.
Miscellaneous instruction of the Guru:â The Creator is the true Lord Who carefully supporteth the globe of the earth. The Creator beholdeth the work of His hands; true and independent,
He created the different species of animals.
Two travellers 1 have struck out two roads.
There is no emancipation without the perfect Guru; it is profitable to repeat the true Name.
The perverse man readeth, but knoweth not the way:
Led astray by error he knoweth not the Name.
The false evidence the evil man giveth for a bribe becometh like a halter round his neck.
Brahmans read the Simritis, the Shastars, and the Purans:
They engage in disputations, but know not the Real Thing:
Without the true Guru they find not the Real Thing.
They who are purified by the True One walk in the true way.
Everybody praiseth God and speaketh of Him as he hath heard.
God is wise and assayeth the true.
They on whom God looketh with favour are holy and praise His word.
How many speak of God according to what they have heard!
They speak of Him according to what they have heard, but know not His limit.
He to whom the Unseen hath manifested Himself knoweth the story of the Ineffable.
When one is born gratulations resound;
The ignorant sing songs of rejoicing;
But he who is born shall assuredly die, and undergo the destiny allotted him.
It is my God who effecteth union and separation of the soul and body.
He who created the world assigned His creatures woe or weal;
But the holy who wear the armour of mildness are un affected by them.
Good are they who deal in the truth;
By the Guru's wisdom they obtain the true merchandise.
He who possesseth the wealth of the true merchandise, is enraptured with the true Word.

1 The founders of the Hindu and Muhammadan religions.
Loss accrueth from false dealings.

The pious carry on their dealings according to God's will.

Their capital remaineth intact, their stock-in-trade safe, and they escape from Death's noose.

Every one speaketh of God according to his own pleasure.

The perverse who are attached to mammon, know not how to speak of God.

The understanding and utterance of the blind man are blind; he shall suffer the pain of transmigration.

In pain he is born, in pain he dieth.

His pain cannot be removed except by seeking the Guru's protection.

In pain he is created, in pain he perisheth. What hath he brought with him? what shall he take away?

True are the acts of those who are subject to the Guru;

They shall not suffer transmigration or feel the edge of Death's sword.

He who abandoneth the branches of the tree of the world, 1 and only knoweth God the essential root of all things, enjoy eth true delight in his heart.

Death shall not punish godly people,

Nor shall they experience the pain of the difficult road.

They worship God's name in their hearts and mention no other.

They who repeat not God's praises shall be punished at last;

While they who please Thee, O God, shall abide according to Thy will:

They shall go with a robe of honour to Thy court and be happy by the True King's order.

Many describe Thine attributes, O Lord; what availeth my speaking?

The greatest of the great find not Thy limit.

Nanak, may I obtain the truth! preserve mine honour, O Lord; Thou art the Monarch of monarchs! 1 Worldly entanglements.

The following is said to be instruction given to Taru and Bharu during the Baisakhi fair at Kar-tarpur:â

Put away from you lust, wrath, and slander;

Abandon avarice, and covetousness, and you shall be free from care.

He who breaketh the chain of superstition shall be free, and feel divine pleasure in his heart.

The happy and incomparable perfect Guru showeth man

Day and night the light within him, and he beholdeth it

Like a bright flash of lightning at night.

Meet the true Guru, and God Himself

Who placed the lamps of the moon and sun in the firma ment of heaven will save you.

Continue to love God, and you shall behold the Unseen One pervading all three worlds.

He who obtaineth the ambrosial essence loseth his avarice and his fear.

He who effaceth himself obtaineth the fearless position.

He who acteth according to the pure Word shall attain a lofty degree, the loftiest of the lofty.

The Name of the Unseen and Inapprehensible is un equalled;

The juice of the beloved Name is exceeding sweet.

God's praises be given to Nanak, and in every age repeat ye His name whose end is not known.

The heart which hath obtained the diamond of the Name

Shall obtain patience by repeating and reverencing it.

Put the Destroyer of fear into thy stubborn heart, and thou shalt not be born again.

Man is saved by love of devotion and the Guru's word.

I crave the boon of the praise of God's name.

If God be pleased, He will cause us to meet the true Guru and save the whole world.

Death's myrmidons and Death himself worship the feet of those

Who repeat God's name under the Guru's teaching and directions.

Man's state and condition become exalted by exalted company, and he crosseth over the terrible ocean of the world.

This world which is a terrible ocean, is crossed over by the Guru's instruction â

And by dispelling the heart's doubts.

Let man take the five arrows, 1 put them on the bow of his brain and kill Death.

How shall the apostate obtain knowledge of the Word?

Without a knowledge of the Word man undergoeth transmigration.

Nanak, salvation dependeth upon the instruction of the Guru whom God by perfect good fortune hath caused us to meet.

The Fearless One, the true Guru is our protector.

The great God is obtained by devotion.

For him who obtaineth the Bright One under the Guru's instruction, the unbeaten strain of joy resoundeth.

The Fearless One is He on whose forehead no destiny is recorded.

He is in visible, but we behold Him through His omnipotence.

He transcendeth the world â, He is unborn and self-existent, O Nanak, and is obtained by the Guru's instruction.

Only the True Guru knoweth the state of man's heart.

He is fearless who recognizeth the Guru's instructions,

Beholdeth God within him, knoweth that He pervadeth creation, and alloweth not his mind to wander elsewhere.

He in whose heart God dwelleth is fearless,

And day and night delighted with the bright Name.

Nanak, God's praises are obtained from the society of the saints, and man is thus easily blended with Him.

He who knoweth that God is with him whether at home or abroad,

Who remaineth attached to the world and bringeth home his wandering mind,

Shall obtain, O Nanak, the ambrosial essence of the True One who dwelleth in the three worlds, and who was before all things.

1 The five virtues.

MARU KI WAR I Man shall certainly be responsible for his acts:â

Creation was by God's order; in His court the truth is accepted.

The Lord will call for man's account; 0 man, stray not on beholding the world.

Nanak, God will keep an account of the love and affection of him

Who watcheth over his heart, and is a pure-minded darwesh.
The condition of really holy men:â
For those who dwell apart and live on the bread of alms God is everywhere:
The diamonds of their hearts are pierced with God's diamond, O Nanak, and their necks are gorgeous with jewels.
True devotion and repetition of the Name secure salvation:â
Recognize God's primal love, 1 and worship the great God. Shall Death then, O Nanak, strike thee on the head? Nay; the Name shall cause thee to meet God.
Many sects appeal to the Veds, but it is heartfelt devotion which secures salvation:â
The drum of the Veds loudly resoundeth for many a faction.
Remember God's name, Nanak; there is none but Him.
Where man is proud there art Thou not; where Thou art, there no pride is.
0 men of divine knowledge, understand this riddleâ the story of the Ineffable One is in the heart,
But without the Guru the Real Thing cannot be found: it is concealed though it dwelleth in every heart.
1 Explained to be the love of God which disposes Him to protect the child in the womb.
God is known by meeting the true Guru and implanting his instruction in the heart.
When pride departeth, doubt, fear, and the pain of trans migration depart.
By the wisdom of the Guru the Unseen is seen, Man's intellect becometh exalted, and he is saved.
Nanak, repeat the spell of God in whom the three worlds are contained.

BHAIRO

To engage in ritualistic practices is of no avail:â
To give a feast, make a burnt offering, offer alms, perform penance and worship, and endure bodily pain for ever are all of no avail.
Without God's name salvation is not obtained; the holy man obtaineth it by the Name.
Without God's name it is useless to be born in the world.
To eat poison, to speak for the sake of poison (mammon) without the Name is to die an unprofitable death and wander in transmigration.
To read books, discuss grammar, and pray three times a day are all of no avail.
Without the Guru's instruction, O mortal, where is salvation? without God's name man is entangled and dieth.
Even though man take up the beggar's staff and pot, and adopt the hair-tuft, the sacrificial thread, and the dhoti of the Hindus, go to places of pilgrimage, and wander far and wide,
Yet shall he not find comfort without God's name; he who repeateth it shall be saved.
Even though man weave his hair into a crown, apply ashes to his body, doff his clothes, and wander naked,
Yet shall he be not satisfied without God's name; it is under the stress of prenatal acts man assumeth a devotional garb.

Thou, O God, art in all creatures that are in the water, the dry land, the nether regions, and the firmament.

By the favour of the Guru preserve Thy servant; Nanak stirring God's elixir hath drunk it.

RAG BASANT

The following was written with buoyant feeling after the departure of a cold winter in the north of India:â

All hail to the great month 1 in which spring ever beginneth. Ever and ever remember the Sustainer of the earth, and thy heart shall rejoice.

0 silly man, forget thy pride,

Subdue thy pride and meditate on God in thy heart; adopt the most excellent virtues.

Good acts are the tree, God's name its branches, religion its flowers, divine knowledge its fruit,

Attainment of God its leaves, and the dispelling of mental pride its dense shade.

They who behold God's power with their eyes, hear it with their ears, and repeat the true Name with their tongues,

Obtain the full wealth of honour and tranquilly meditate on God.

The great season hath come, be careful and do good works.

Nanak, the pious who continue absorbed in God shall be perennial and never wither.

SARANG KI WAR

The following is a refutation of the general Indian ideas on the subject of impurity:â

There is no impurity in songs, 2 there is no impurity in knowledge; 3

There is no impurity in the moon's or sun's different phases; 1 Basant, the Indian spring, is generally considered to begin between the i2th and i4th of March.

2 As supposed by the Musalmans.

3 The Brahmans assert that the Veds should not be communu to women and Sudars. During the period of Brahmanical ascemleru y in India the Sudais were forbidden under pain of death to read the Vedsâ they might only repeat God's name Among the Sudars are included all women.

There is no impurity in corn, there is no impurity in ablution; 1

There is no impurity in rain which falleth everywhere;

There is no impurity in earth, there is no impurity in water;

There is no impurity contained in air.

There are no virtues, Nanak, in the man who is without a guru.

It is he who turneth away from God whose mouth is impure.

The Guru mentions things which confer purity on men of different classes:â

Nanak, the following handfuls 2 of water are pure if any one know how to fill themâ

Divine knowledge for the Pandit, continence for the Jogi

Contentment for the Brahman, alms out of what he hath himself earned for the family man, 3

Justice for the king, meditation on the True One for the learned.

Although water when drunk will quench thirst, the heart cannot be washed with it.

Water is the generator of the world, and shall finally destroy everything.

The futility of idolatry:â

Thou in thy house keepest an idol with its attendant gods: Thou washest it and worshippest it; Thou offerest it kungu, sandal, and flowers; Thou fallest at its feet and propitiatest it to the utmost Yet it is by continually begging of men thou clothest and upportest thyself.

1 As supposed by the Jains, who avoid water.

2 Chuli, as much water as can be taken in one hand. Water is taken in handfuls by Hindus and drunk as grace before and some times after meals accompanied by sacred texts. Hindus also use water in the same way when taking solemn oaths.

3 As contradistinguished from the almsgiving of thieves out o! their plunder. 4 Such as Lakhshmi, Garur, Ganesh, c.

For such foolish acts shalt thou receive the punishment of the foolish.
The idol giveth thee not when hungry, nor presenvth thee from death.
It is like a foolish quarrel among the blind.
God has no partner, wherefore supplication should be made to Him direct:â
If Thou have any partner, 0 God, I will speak of Thee in his presence.
But Thou hast no partner, therefore will I praise Thee to Thy face. Thy name giveth sight to the blind.
One of the Guru's reflections on this degenerate age:â
In the Kal age men have faces like dogs, and eat carrion.
They bark as they utter falsehood, and have no regard for honesty.
They who have no honour while alive, shall have an evil reputation after death.
What is destined taketh place, Nanak; what the Creator doeth cometh to pass.
They who deceive men by selling them charms and amulets shall not find salvation:-
Accursed the lives of those who write God's name to sell it.
They whose crop is spoiled require no place for a har v-t-heap.
They who are devoid of truth and modesty will recvivr no assistance hereafter.
The ways of wisdom:â
Call not by the name of wisdom the wisdom which is spent in wrangling.
By wisdom the Lord is worshipped; by wisdom honour is obtained.
It is by wisdom what is read is understood, it is by wisdom alms are properly bestowed.
Nanak saith, these are the ways of wisdom, all iÂ lsr are ways of wickedness.
The virtues and practices which are most potent to secure deliverance:â
They who make truth their fasting, contentment their place of pilgrimage, divine knowledge and meditation their ablutions,
Mercy their idol, and forgiveness their rosary, are fore most in God's favour.
Nanak, few there are who make the right way their loin cloths, meditation on God their cooking squares,
Good deeds their frontal marks, and God's love their food.
Better to live by honest labour than by beg ging:â
Men without divine knowledge sing hymns.
The hungry Mulla maketh a home of his mosque. 1
One man who earneth nothing slitteth his ears; 2
Another becometh a beggar and loseth his caste.
Touch not at all the feet of those

Who call themselves gurus and pirs, and go begging.
They who eat the fruit of their labour and bestow some thing, O Nanak, recognize the right way.

RAG MALAR

Some moral commandments:—

Cease to covet another's wife and another's goods; shun the deadly sins of pride,
Evil inclinations, slander, and lust and wrath the executioners.
The inaccessible and illimitable God dwelleth in man's heart.
He shall obtain nectar in his own heart, whose conduct is according to the Guru's precious instruction;
And who considereth woe and weal and the blame and praise of the world as the same.
1 He spends all his time in his mosque, so as to receive the more alms. 2 The Jogi.
Wisdom, knowledge, and understanding are obtained from God's name; the love of God is obtained by association with the saints.
Day and night profit is obtained from God's name given by the beneficent Guru.
He on whom the Creator looketh with favour obtaineth instruction from the Guru's words.
The body is the palace, the temple, and the house of God; into it He putteth His eternal light.
Nanak, the pious are invited to God's palace; He will blend them with Himself.

MALAR ASHTAPADI

The Guru by familiar Indian examples expresses his love for God:—

The chakwi will not sleep at night in the absence of her mate.
When the sun riseth she gazeth on her beloved, and boweth, and toucheth his feet.
O my Beloved, dear to me is Thy love, which shall be my companion.
I cannot live for a moment in this world without Him; so much do I thirst for Him.
The lotus on the lake on beholding the sunbeams of heaven naturally rejoiceth:
O my Beloved, such is the longing I feel in my heart that my light may be blended with Thine.
The chatrik without water crieth ' Prio, prio!" and scream-eth aloud.
There is terrible thunder, it raineth on every side, but without its special raindrops the chatrik's thirst departeth not.
The fish which is born and liveth in water, obtaineth weal and woe according to its previous acts.
It cannot live for an instant without water; its death or life dependeth on it.
Woman is separated from her Beloved who liveth abroad: she sendeth Him a message through the true Guru.
All cry out ' Prio, prio! ', but they can only obtain their Beloved if it please the Guru.
The Beloved is with us; He ever associateth with the true; He blendeth with Himself those on whom He looketh with favour.
God is the life within all lives; He pervadeth every heart.
Through the Guru's favour He is manifest at home, and men become easily absorbed in Him.

Arrange thine own affairs, O man; the Lord of the earth is the Giver of happiness.
When by the Guru's favour man findeth God in his heart, then, O Nanak, his burning is extinguished.

MALAR KI WAR

Prayers ought not to be offered for worldly advan tages:â
They who offer prayers shall die, and so shall they who are prayed for.
Nanak, it is not known where they shall be placed by God's order.
The punishments that await the impenitent wicked:â
Some have chains on their necks and are being led off to prison;
But by recognizing Him who is the truest of the true, they shall be freed from their bonds.
He who obtaineth favourable destiny knoweth the True One.
Man's fate is decided by God's order; when man goeth before Him he shall know this.
Recognize the Word which will cause thee to cross the terrible ocean.
Thieves, adulterers, and gamblers shall be pressed like sesame;
Slanderers and backbiters shall be carried away by the flood.
The pious who are absorbed in the True One shall be known in God's court.
Worldly advantages distract men's minds from devotion:â
Empire, wealth, beauty, nobility, and youth. in ii robbers;
These robbers have robbed the world without respect lm any one.
They who fall at the Guru's feet, however, rob them. 1
The Guru's humility, the transitory character of human life, and the efficacy of the Name:â
The world is very transient like a flash of lightning;
Yet, foolish heart of mine, thou thinkest not of the grave.
I am low and wretched; Thou, O God, art an ocean of generosity.
Grant me only one thingâ Thy name; the poisonous things of the world please me not.
By the skill of God even a fragile vessel holdeth water. 2
Thou art omnipotent; I have come into the world by Thy power.
Nanak, the dog of Thy court, is growing madder every day for Thy love.
The world is fire, God's name is what cooleth it.
The bliss of divine composition:â
Blest the paper, blest the pen, blest the ink-bottle, blest the ink,
Blest the writer, Nanak, who writeth the True Name.
He who batheth in the immortal water of divine know ledge taketh with him the sixty-eight places of pilgrima-.

RAG PRABHATI

A satire on Hindu sects and ritualists:-Jogis go to ruin in twelve sects, Sanyasis in tm. The Jogis, the Kaprias, and the plucked-headed Sara without the Word have halters round their necks.

1 That is, deprive them of the power of robbing.
2 A frail mortal may be possessed of divine knowledge.

They who are tinctured by the Word are perfect Bairagis,

Who beg to obtain alms in the wallet of their hearts that their love may be fixed God alone.

The Brahmans read the epic poems before devotional acts, and cause others to perform them;

But without knowing God they know nothing; the perverse are separated from God and miserable.

They who obtain the Guru's instruction are pure, and shall be honoured at the true court.

Night and day they love the jewel of the Name, and are blended with the True One in every age.

All religious acts, purifications, austerities, devotion, penance, and pilgrimages abide in the Word.

Nanak, if the true Guru be found, he will unite man with God, when sorrow and sin and death shall be no more.

PRABHATI ASHTAPADI

The feats of the Jogis and the tenets of the six religious systems of the Hindus are ineffectual to secure salvation:â

The niwali feat, 1 the suspension of breath in the dorsal chamber; 2 the turning the brain into a still, making expiration and inspiration like the Jogis, and suspending the breath are of no avail.

Without the true Guru man knoweth nothing; he is led astray in error, sinketh, and dieth.

The fool is defiled, and the more he washeth, the more is he defiled; the filth of his heart shall never depart.

All religious acts are vain except the repetition of the Name; they are like conjuror's tricks which deceive the spectators.

The six religious duties are contained in the name of the Bright One.

1 This consists in passing a tape through the body to cleanse the stomach and intestinesâ a feat of the Jogis.

2 The Jogis assert that they can draw breath from the lower vertebral column to the brain, and suspend it when they please in its passage. We shall further on find that the passage is called the serpent's way. When the breath finally reaches the brain, it is said to distil nectar which produces a state of exaltation.

Thou art, O God, an ocean of merits; in inr arc demerit.

The pursuit of worldly things is a foolish and sinful at i.

The blockhead thinketh too highly of himself, and can-not understand his duty.

The perverse desire fascinating wealth, and their speech is evil.

According to the Hindus foul is the ablution of the Chandal, and vain are his religious ceremonies and decorations.

False is the wisdom of the perverse; their acts produce strife.

In the impure man is pride; he obtaineth not the flavour of the Lord.

Insipid the pleasure of doing other than the repetition of God's name.

ADDITIONAL SLOKS

When Guru Nanak visited Ceylon he gave the following advice to its queen, who was proud of her beauty and her state:â

Hear, young woman with the gazelle eyes, hear my serious and weighty words.
First examine thy goods and make thy traffic.
Dismiss I the evil and welcome the good.
Consider, O young woman, what proclamation to give by which thou mayest find friends.
Give thy soul and body to thy friends, and thou shalt thus enjoy the utmost hilarity.
Love not that which is transitory;
Nanak, I am a sacrifice to those who understand this.
In spiritual matters consult the holy:-If thou art to cross the water, consult those who have the skill to cross:
They are very wise and will keep clear of the whirlpool.
The dangers of the world:-
There are continual showers, squalls, and tonvnts hundreds of thousands of waves succeed one another. 1 Dohidichai. Literallyâ make a proclamation to depart.
Address the True Guru, and there shall be no fear that thy bark will founder.
Another of the Guru's reflections on the sinful-ness of his age:â
Nanak, to what hath the world come?
No companion or friend remaineth.
Love hath ceased among brethren and kinsmen;
Faith is lost on account of mammon.
The following was composed by Guru Nanak on seeing women mourning:â
They are saying ' Hai hai! ' and ' Oh Oh! ';
They beat their cheeks and pluck out the hairs of their heads;
They utter God's name 1 without meaning it: if they were absorbed in it,
Then would Nanak be a sacrifice unto them.
The Guru went to visit a man of reputed sanctity, but on finding him a hypocrite composed the following:â
The raven washeth and rubbeth itself in a small pool in the desert;
Its mind and body are full of demerits and its beak of filth.
The swan of the lake, not knowing that the raven was an evil bird, associated with him.
Such is affection for the infidel; O man of divine know ledge, understand the allusion.
Congratulate the congregation of the saints, and act like a holy man.
Pure is the ablution, O Nanak, when the Guru is deemed the river of pilgrimage.
The really holy are few:â
The saints are few, not many; deceit and wrangling prevail in the world. 2 1 Oh hai. He is.
2 Also translatedâ They who act as become faqlrs are few in the world.
HYMNS OF GURU NANAK; M
The following has reference to the concremation of widows:â
Nanak, the widow followeth her husband and dieth:-hath no power to live.
But she who dieth struck by the news of her husband's death is acceptable.
When the Allwise hath struck her with the arrow of love, it cannot be extracted.
She whom God hath struck with it is struck, and being struck is acceptable.

The body is frail and cannot be saved without God's grace:â
Who can wash a vessel which is fragile in its construction?
The body is a compound of five elements; it hath a false gilding.
If it please God, the vessel shall be acceptable;
The supreme light shall shine and God's praises resound in it.
Pride without merit:-
Nanak, those men are the real donkeys who are proud without merit.
A definition of a Brahman:-
He is a Brahman who knoweth God, Who performeth works of devotion, penance, and self restraint;
And who observeth the religion of mildness and
Such a Brahman shall burst his bonds, obtain salvation,
And be worthy of worship.
A definition of a Khatri:-He is a Khatri who is brave in good deeds And who employeth his body in charity. 1 The Khatri who inspecteth his ground before 5 gifts,
Shall be acceptable in God's court.
The Khatri who practiseth greed, covetousness, and falsehood,
Shall suffer for his misdeeds.
The Guru required complete self-sacrifice from his disciples:â
If thou desire to play at love with me,
Come my way with thy head in the palm of thy hand.
Put thy feet on this road;
Give thy head and regard not human opinion.
The Guru, faith, truth, and the capital of God's name are necessary for salvation:â
Without the Guru there is no divine knowledge, without faith no meditation;
Without truth there is no credit, and without capital no balance.
If Ram had been God he would not have lost his queen Sita, and he would himself have healed his half-brother Lachhman instead of calling on Hanuman to do so:â
Ram Chandar mourned in his soul for Sita and Lachhman:
He remembered Hanuman, 1 and he came to meet him.
The misguided demon Raw an did not know it was not Ram but God who did this.
Nanak, God is independent: Ram could not erase his destiny.
A purse-proud person addressed improper language to the Guru. When the Guru's disciples took this amiss, the Guru uttered the following:â
Impute not blame to the Rai; 2 his intellect is forsaking him in his old age.
1 See the story of Hanuman going for a plant to heal Lachhman, in Dowson's Dictionary of Hindu Mythology.
2 This word means a nobleman.
HYMNS OF GURU NANAK 383
The blind man talketh much and falleth into the pit. Whatever the Perfect One hath done is perfect; there is no deficiency or excess in it.
Nanak, the pious who know this, shall be absorbed in the Perfect One.
END OF VOL. I
OXFORD PRINTED AT THE CLARENDON PRESS
BY HORACE HART, M. A. PRINTER TO THE UNIVERSITY

PLEASE DO NOT REMOVE CARDS OR SLIPS FROM THIS POCKET
UNIVERSITY OF TORONTO LIBRARY
m UrnÂ